W9-DEW-520

THE MAX WILLSKY HISTORY COLLECTION

The Joint Free
Public Library
of
Morristown
& Morris Township

FEUDING ALLIES

FEUDING ALLIES

The Private Wars of
the High Command

William B. Breuer

John Wiley & Sons, Inc.

New York • Chichester • Brisbane • Toronto • Singapore

Copyright © 1995 by William B. Breuer
Published by John Wiley & Sons, Inc.

Library of Congress Cataloging-in-Publication Data:

Breuer, William B.
    Feuding allies : the private wars of the high command / William B.
Breuer.
        p. cm.
    Includes bibliographical references and index.
    ISBN 0-471-12252-1 (acid-free)
    1. World War, 1939–1945. 2. Allied Forces. 3. Command of troops.
    4. Military psychology. 5. Jealousy.   I. Title.
D744.B69 1995
940.53—dc20   95-11638

Printed in the United States of America

10 9 8 7 6 5 4 3 2 1

Dedicated to
BRIGADIER GENERAL PAUL W. TIBBETS, JR.,
United States Air Force (Ret.),
a valiant American patriot
and peacemaker
who is greatly admired
by millions of veterans
and their families

The only thing worse than having allies is not having allies.

— *Winston S. Churchill*

CONTENTS

PART THREE   Road to Victory

PART ONE

A Time of Peril

CHAPTER 1

Washington: Hotbed of Rivalries

A THICK BLANKET of glistening snow caressed bleak wartime Washington, D.C., a city gripped by an acute case of jitters and foreboding. For the first time since the War of 1812, when a British army captured Washington and burned the Capitol and other government buildings, there was a threat of enemy attack—either by subversive forces or by aircraft. It was late December 1941, less than three weeks since a woefully unprepared America had been bombed into global conflict by the Japanese at Pearl Harbor, after which German dictator Adolf Hitler declared war on the United States.

Washington had been turned into an armed camp. Several American soldiers and marines, wearing old pie-plate helmets, were manning a World War I machine gun on the front lawn of the White House. On the roof of the mansion were other relics: Two 90-millimeter antiaircraft guns along with shells that had been sitting in crates for thirty years.

On the frozen ground around the majestic Capitol, a mile up Constitution Avenue from the White House, other GIs were bundled up against the icy gales blowing off the Potomac River but standing alert with bayonet-tipped rifles, ready to lunge at any Nazi or Japanese who might try to get past them.

Wild rumors were rampant. One report held that German intelligence, months or years earlier, had planted scores of fanatic Nazi agents in and around Washington. On a given signal from Berlin, it was said, these moles would don German army uniforms, dig out hidden weapons, and murder President Franklin D. Roosevelt, Secretary of War Henry L. Stimson, and other top officials. If captured, the secret agents would claim that they were soldiers in uniform and therefore immune from execution.

As a security precaution, friendly aircraft were prohibited from flying over Washington. So when three nervous soldiers manning an ancient antiaircraft gun atop a downtown building thought they saw the dim contours of a plane swooping in low in the darkness, they fired a shell in the direction of the perceived threat. The projectile hissed across the city and exploded against the front of the revered Lincoln Memorial, gouging out a huge chunk. Fortunately, only a very frightened night watchman, who no doubt thought he had been

3

singled out for enemy attack, was in the structure at the time. He was unin-
jured.

Washington was also afflicted with spy mania. German or Japanese saboteurs were thought by many to be lurking behind every tree or riding streetcars
in search of targets marked for extinction. Consequently, metropolitan police
were given strict orders to be alert for and arrest anyone whom they judged to
look "suspicious."

Shortly after Christmas in 1941, Field Marshal John Dill arrived in Washington to take up his new duties as senior British liaison officer to the U.S. War
Department. A few weeks earlier, Dill had been removed by Prime Minister
Winston S. Churchill as chief of the Imperial General Staff, Britain's top army
post.

Dill, Churchill had stated, was worn out from eighteen months of carrying
the heavy burden of his duties in the face of continuous threat of invasion by the
Germans. Actually, it was rumored in London that the courteous and reserved
field marshal, who had no taste for argument, was not sufficiently aggressive in
the eyes of the Prime Minister.

Soon after his arrival as Churchill's man in Washington, Dill was asked
about the specific nature of his job. The dryly humored field marshal confessed
he did not know, but presumed he would be a handy target at which American
leaders could aim their wrath against the British.

Accustomed to months of wartime austerity in England, Dill was shocked
by the prosperous lifestyle of Americans and by their belief that the Japanese
and Germans could be quickly polished off without undue disruption of normal
conditions on the home front. "This country is the most highly organized for
peace you can imagine," he wrote to his successor, Field Marshal Alan Brooke,
in London. "I have never seen so many motor cars, but not a military vehicle.
. . . At present this country has not—repeat not—the slightest conception of
what war means, and their armed forces are more unready for war than it is
possible to imagine. Eventually they will do great things, but [now] the whole
organisation belongs to the days of George Washington."[1]

A few days before Christmas, America's capital was "invaded" by the
British for the first time since the redcoats sacked the city 130 years earlier. This
time, the English came as allies, arriving on the new battleship *Duke of York*.
Headed by sixty-seven-year-old Winston Churchill, the large delegation had
come to meet with President Roosevelt and other top American leaders to
integrate Britain's war interests and operations with those of the United States.

Known as the British Bulldog, Churchill for months had been a beacon of
hope in an otherwise dark free world. Back on May 10, 1940, after Great Britain
had been at war with Nazi Germany for eight months, Neville Chamberlain
resigned as Prime Minister at the age of seventy. The mild-mannered Chamberlain had spent two years prior to the outbreak of hostilities trying to appease
Adolf Hitler. That afternoon, King George VI summoned Churchill, First Lord

of the Admiralty, to Buckingham Palace and asked him to replace Chamberlain. Churchill eagerly accepted.

On that same day, the German Führer (leader) unleashed his war machine, the most powerful history had known, on the western front. In only six weeks it would overrun France, Belgium, and the Netherlands in a blitzkrieg (lightning war).

It was England's blackest hour. She stood alone, an island under siege. Plans had been developed to evacuate the government to Canada to continue the war from there. Across the Channel, the German Wehrmacht (armed forces) was ready to leap to England and conquer the virtually defenseless nation.

Unbeknown to British intelligence, the German Military Government of England, the branch created to administer the nation after its capture, had compiled a secret *die Sonderfahndungsliste, G.B.* (Special Search List, Great Britain). It contained the names, occupations, and addresses of twenty-three hundred British government officials, military leaders, clergymen, educators, and other "undesirables" who would be seized at once and turned over to the Gestapo (secret police) for "processing." Names were in alphabetical order. Number 49 on the list was "Churchill, Winston Spencer, Ministerpresident, Westerham/ Kent, Chartwell Manor."

As Great Britain teetered on the brink of extinction, Providence came to her aid. Before dawn on June 22, 1941, Hitler launched Operation Barbarossa. Three million German troops, paced by swarms of Stuka dive-bombers, swept across the borders of the Soviet Union on a two-thousand-mile front. Although initially taken by surprise, the Red Army fought back. By the time Churchill arrived in Washington, much of the Wehrmacht was engaged deep inside Russia.

On learning that Hitler had declared war on the United States only two days after the Pearl Harbor attack, Churchill's joy was boundless. This was the answer to his prayers. He regarded the United States as "a gigantic boiler—once the fire is lighted under it there is no limit to the power it can generate."[2]

Now, as the guest of President Roosevelt, Churchill and his bustling entourage turned White House routines topsy-turvy. The Prime, as he was called by the Americans, habitually worked into the wee hours of the morning, then slept until noon in his second-floor room in the East Wing.

Roosevelt and Churchill hit it off well during the Prime Minister's two-week stay. Both were outgoing, expansive men who enjoyed hearing an occasional risqué joke and imbibing during cocktail hour—and at other times.

One afternoon Roosevelt, who was confined to a wheelchair, twelve-pound braces on each leg, because of polio contracted in his late thirties, wheeled into The Prime's bedroom. The rotund Churchill was pacing the floor, totally naked, puffing on a big black cigar and dictating to a male secretary. Slightly embarrassed, the President spun around to leave. Churchill called him back, declaring, "The prime minister of Great Britain has nothing to conceal from the president of the United States."[3]

At the first session of the two leaders and their military chiefs in the White House on December 26, Churchill made an impassioned sales pitch. Knowing that the American people were furious at Japan over the Pearl Harbor treachery, The Prime would have to sway Roosevelt and U.S. military leaders into adopting a Germany-first policy. After Adolf Hitler and Nazi Germany were crushed, the full power of the United States and Great Britain then would be hurled at the Japanese.

The Germany-first strategy was adopted after minimal wrangling. However, the concept did not sit too well with one of the American conferees, Major General Joseph Stilwell, who had been brought to Washington by Army Chief of Staff George C. Marshall to lead the first American assault overseas. Known in the army as Vinegar Joe because of his acidic tongue, Stilwell complained that "the Limeys have sold Roosevelt a bill of goods. . . . [Churchill] and his staff officers have the President's ear, while we have the hind tit."[4]

As the sessions droned on day after day, thinly veiled animosity between the Americans and the British grew thicker. The British were insufferable in their arrogance, the Americans felt. Neither side could mask its irritation and dislike for the other.

Among the few who were able to rise above the squabbling was a relatively obscure, newly minted American brigadier general, Dwight D. Eisenhower. Only seventeen months earlier, Ike, as he had been known since childhood, had been a lieutenant colonel. Now he was engaged in high-level discussions that could decide future world history.

While subtle barbs were being flung back and forth across the conference table, Eisenhower tried time and again to bring the focus back to the true topic: Global strategy. His ability to remain calm and reasonable was remarkable considering that he shared some of his colleagues' anti-British prejudices. "The conversations with the British grow wearisome," Eisenhower wrote in his diary. "They're difficult to talk to, apparently afraid someone is trying to tell them what to do and how to do it."[5]

When the conference topic shifted to aid to China a few days later, Eisenhower again chose to vent his feelings in his diary: "The British, as usual, are scared someone will take advantage of them, even when we furnish everything [arms, supplies, and equipment]. . . . The British are certainly stiff-necked."[6]

Although the leaders of both nations had agreed on the Germany-first concept, a dispute arose when General Marshall put forth a revolutionary proposal at a conference of American and British military chiefs in the four-story Munitions Building. Connected by a second-floor overpass to the identical Navy Building, the stucco structure had been built as temporary quarters in World War I and was still in use.

"I am convinced that there must be one man in command of an entire theater of operations," Marshall told the two groups. Unprepared for the far-reaching proposal, the British were leery. Marshall, a "newcomer to war," seemed to be making a pitch to seize control of all Anglo-American forces and operations.[7]

Marshall knew he was butting his head against a stone wall; the British remained adamantly opposed to the concept of a sole commander. So that night, he had Eisenhower draw up a draft of model instructions for a theater commander. He deliberately chose the Far East, the only region where armed forces of both nations were currently fighting. Marshall and Eisenhower called the theater ABDA, an acronym for Australian, British, Dutch, and American. They were careful to list the Americans last.

When the draft was presented to the British chiefs the next day, Marshall instituted a ploy he thought might win them over: He suggested that British General Archibald Wavell be named supreme commander of ABDA. Wavell was battle tested, having been commander in the North African desert against the brilliant young German general Erwin Rommel, known as the Desert Fox. In July 1941, Churchill, who disliked and had little confidence in Wavell, had transferred him to the post of commander in chief in India, halfway around the world.

Now, George Marshall spoke glowingly of Wavell's attributes—which only heightened British suspicions. Throughout the Far East at this time, the Allies were facing defeat after defeat at the hands of rampaging Japanese armies. Wavell, the British suspected, would be a convenient scapegoat for major reversals yet to come.

Undaunted, Marshall, who had ongoing access to Franklin Roosevelt, hurried to call on the President. These two Americans functioned in a climate of mutual respect, but they would never reach an informal relationship. Professionally proficient, the chief of staff was aloof in his dealings with others. Roosevelt was always "Mr. President." Once when the convivial Roosevelt had placed his hand on the general's shoulder and called him "George," the other had glared at the President in disapproval and said, "It's *General* Marshall, sir." After that, Roosevelt would never again try to call the army chief by his first name, as he did most of his other generals and admirals.

Roosevelt, who had enormous faith in Marshall's views, readily agreed to the concept of a single commander for each global theater. That same day, Marshall hurried to a meeting in the Navy Building and won over the American admirals to his command concept.

With a unified American front, Marshall again approached the British chiefs the next afternoon. He met stiff resistance from Britain's senior service—the Royal Navy. British admirals, steeped in long tradition, took no orders from generals. Marshall continued to bore in, pointing out that the Japanese, including their powerful navy with its own traditions, had a single commander, General Hideki Tojo, who was known in his homeland as The Razor because of his sharp mind.

As the debate rambled on into the hours of darkness, the British were finally worn down. With the understanding that the directive draft be a subject of future compromise, they capitulated and agreed to the single-commander concept. When the meeting broke up minutes later, Field Marshal Jack Dill rushed up to General Marshall and threw his arm around the startled American's shoulder—but received no rebuke. The usually standoffish Marshall merely beamed, euphoric in the wake of his hard-earned victory.

Now Marshall needed Winston Churchill's approval. He arranged a meeting with the Prime Minister for late in the morning of the next day. When Marshall arrived, Churchill was still in his pajamas in bed, eyeglasses perched on the end of his nose, poring over a sheaf of dispatches that had arrived overnight from several corners of the world. While The Prime remained in bed and smoked a cigar, Marshall made his pitch. Churchill listened, scowling. He clearly disliked the single-commander scheme.

"What on earth would an army officer like Archibald Wavell know about naval warfare?" Churchill grunted. "What in the hell does an admiral know about handling a tank?" Marshall barked back.[8]

Despite the crucial decision to be reached, Churchill interrupted the general in midsentence to take one of his twice-daily baths. Minutes later he emerged from the bathroom, wearing only a towel on his head and a scowl on his face. For nearly an hour, the tenacious Prime Minister continued to resist. Then, suddenly, he concurred with the single-commander concept. He said he was impressed by its "broad-mindedness." Translation: Roosevelt liked the plan and Churchill knew he would try to draw concessions on other matters from the President in the future.

Despite the two weeks of bickering, the Washington conferences did manage to organize and coordinate the Anglo-American war effort. In the beginning of the partnership, the United States would be almost wholly dependent on Britain for intelligence. Even as ominous war clouds had drifted toward the United States from both Europe and the Far East in early 1941, America had remained the only major power without a global intelligence agency. In a hostile and volatile world, Uncle Sam had been staggering around without eyes or ears.

Sensing the frightening deficiency in national defense, President Roosevelt, on July 11, 1941, had signed an executive order designating William J. "Wild Bill" Donovan, a New York Wall Street lawyer and a highly decorated hero of World War I, to head the office of Coordinator of Information (COI). It was an intentionally vague title (later to become the Office of Strategic Services, or OSS). Privately, so as not to touch off an uproar from American isolationists, the President instructed Donovan to launch "political warfare" against the nation's enemies.[9]

Almost at once, Donovan, a stocky, gray-haired extrovert, became a mystery man in Washington. Harpoons were hurled at him and his fledgling COI from all corners. Charles A. Lindbergh, the famed Lone Eagle who had been the first person to fly solo across the Atlantic, declared that the COI was "full of politics, ballyhoo, and controversy." Lindbergh was a leading light in America First, an organization bent on keeping the United States out of war.[10]

The creation of the COI stirred up the fussing-and-feuding pot in Washington. At the War Department, hidebound generals snorted that the new cloak-and-dagger agency was "a fly-by-night civilian outfit headed up by a wild man who was trying to horn in on the war." Others disparagingly labeled the COI staff "Donovan's Dragoons."

Bill Donovan held the rank of colonel in the reserves, a status that brought him into conflict with career generals. The army's G-2 (intelligence officer) refused to speak to a "reserve" colonel and communicated with Donovan through an intermediary only when absolutely necessary. J. Edgar Hoover, the strong-willed director of the spy-busting Federal Bureau of Investigation (FBI), was embroiled in a squabble with the chief of navy intelligence. Yet each man managed to find time to take potshots at Bill Donovan and the COI.

Part of the reason for the steaming controversy raging in Washington between intelligence services was that the army and navy were grossly unprepared for the new type of world war that had suddenly been thrust upon them. Lieutenant General Henry H. "Hap" Arnold, head of the army air corps, offered this diagnosis: "The G-2 men cannot see over the hill to the necessity of establishing an agency for securing the new kind of information needed to fight [a world conflict]."[11]

Wild Bill Donovan's task was mind-boggling. Within months, he was expected to create a global apparatus that would engage in espionage, sabotage, "black" propaganda, and related subversive antics. He would have to catch up with the secret service operations of Germany, the Soviet Union, Japan, Great Britain, and other major powers whose covert organizations had been steeped in the nefarious trade for centuries.

For his field agents, Donovan sought out and recruited "hell-raisers who are calculatingly reckless, of disciplined daring, and eager for aggressive action." This rare breed—he called them "cowboys"—flocked to Donovan's call.

One night in mid-January 1942, while Roosevelt and Churchill were in conference a short distance away, Bill Donovan's cowboys penetrated the Spanish Embassy in Washington. There they photographed top-secret codebooks and assorted documents of Generalissimo Francisco Franco's pro-German government. When J. Edgar Hoover learned of the nocturnal caper he was furious, for he believed Donovan had poached on an FBI preserve. However, Hoover made no formal protest and bided his time.

Shortly thereafter, Donovan's agents paid another nighttime visit to the Spanish Embassy. They were tailed by FBI men in two unmarked cars. After the intruders forced their way inside the embassy, the FBI vehicles slipped in front of the building and parked. A few minutes later, the strident blasts of their sirens pierced the stillness for blocks around. Then the cars sped away, just before Donovan's "burglars" scurried out of the building.

Meanwhile, a feud had erupted between diplomats of the U.S. State Department and Bill Donovan and his footloose operatives. "Donovan has been a pain in the ass to a number of the regular agencies of the government—including the

State Department," Assistant Secretary of State Breckenridge Long wrote in his diary. "He is into everybody's business—knows no bounds or jurisdiction—tries to fill the shoes of each agency charged with responsibility for a war activity. He has agents all over the world."[12]

In the early weeks of January 1942, President Roosevelt continued to be confronted by a thorny question: What should be done with Admiral Harold R. Stark, the chief of naval operations? Known to friends by the nickname Betty, the mild, professorial Stark found himself on the hot seat after the Pearl Harbor tragedy (although he was hardly to blame for it). Roosevelt knew it would deflate public morale should the top navy officer be sacked as an incompetent.

The President solved his dilemma by naming hard-nosed Admiral Ernest J. King as commander in chief, U.S. Fleet (COMINCH). King, it was said, secretly took pride in knowing that countless subordinates looked upon him as "the toughest son of a bitch in the entire navy." Although Stark would retain the hollow title of chief of naval operations, King would be in charge of the fleets. More significantly, he would report not to Stark, but directly to the President.

Shortly after Ernest King assumed his new duties, Roosevelt dropped him a handwritten note. Half in jest, the President said that he understood King shaved with a blowtorch and trimmed his nails with torpedo-net cutters. King was just the man Roosevelt was seeking: A rough and tough type to shake up a navy gripped by inertia in the wake of the horrendous blow it had received at Pearl Harbor.

One of the sixty-two-year-old King's periodic visitors was Admiral Andrew B. Cunningham, senior British naval representative in Washington. Called "ABC" after his initials, Cunningham projected dignity and grace; he was cool, competent, and the embodiment of the proud Royal Navy. When circumstances warranted, however, Cunningham could also be tough. General Eisenhower, who would come to admire the admiral more than he did any other Briton, described him as "a real sea dog."[13]

Cunningham's one-on-one sessions with King were usually stormy, and their relationship turned into a powder keg. The inevitable explosion was not long in coming. At a press conference in Washington, Admiral Cunningham charged that American participation in the crucial Battle of the Atlantic was entirely inadequate. Since March 1941, when England was on the brink of invasion by Germany, the "neutral" United States had been shipping airplanes, guns, tanks, trucks, and ammunition in a steady flow across the North Atlantic and Mediterranean sea routes to the hard-pressed British armed forces. To cut off Britain from her source of supply and strangle the besieged nation into submission, Hitler launched his U-boat (submarine) wolf packs onto the trade routes, exacting a horrendous toll on British shipping. Churchill had given the name Battle of the Atlantic to that oceanic death struggle.

Ernest King, who considered Admiral Cunningham's press conference remarks a personal slap, was enraged. A few days later, when Cunningham came calling, a trifling matter erupted into a major verbal maelstrom that echoed throughout the halls of the Navy Building. Cunningham had merely asked that four American submarines be utilized to patrol the European side of the Atlantic.[14]

Although suave and customarily affable, Cunningham could shout and pound the table with the best of them if the occasion demanded. This confrontation in the Navy Building was one of those instances. Finally, King leaped to his feet, face flushed with anger, and yelled, "Britannia may have ruled the waves for three hundred years, but she doesn't anymore!" Pointing a long, bony finger, the American declared: "There's the door!"[15]

Strident clashes with Admiral King were not the sole domain of the British. General Eisenhower, although three ranks below the chief of naval operations, tangled frequently with King. In December 1941, shortly after the Pearl Harbor debacle, the fifty-one-year-old Eisenhower had been brought to Washington by Army Chief of Staff George Marshall to become second in command at the War Plans Division (WPD).

Dwight Eisenhower, who had an extremely colorful vocabulary, repeatedly crossed swords with the navy, which, he felt, was determined to fight its own war in the Pacific. Impossible to do, Ike told his staff. He was especially furious over what he considered to be the navy's refusal to cooperate with the army in long-term war planning. In his frustration, Eisenhower wrote disparagingly of the navy: "What a gang to work with!"[16]

Eisenhower was also upset with the sea service over its apparent haste to build warships to replace those destroyed at Pearl Harbor. The navy, in his opinion, should have been constructing "aircraft carriers and more aircraft carriers" to fight a modern war in the Pacific. Unkind remarks were made privately about the navy's "World War I battleship mentality."

Eisenhower dreaded having to call on King to discuss mutual business. He thought the admiral was "the antithesis of cooperation, a deliberately rude person, which means he's a mental bully." The general wrote in his diary, "One thing that might help win this war is for someone to shoot King!"[17] A few days later, he penned, "King is an arbitrary, stubborn type, without too much brains."

In Ernest King's presence, understandably, Eisenhower suppressed his true feelings and was a portrait of military correctness when dealing with a ranking officer. Once, at the specific direction of General Marshall, Eisenhower called on King to discuss a crucial matter that had arisen. The War Plans chief tersely made his request. Scarcely looking up from the papers he was reading on his desk, the admiral replied with one sharp word: "No!"

Eisenhower controlled his temper. Then, in a firm but polite tone, the new general scolded the admiral, who was eleven years his senior. King was not giving Marshall's request proper consideration, Eisenhower said, and, in what must have been a blow to the admiral's rank-conscious outlook, he added that King's attitude was not good for needed cooperation between navy and army.

King was stunned. He glared at the younger man in silence. No one—not even President Roosevelt—spoke to the admiral in that manner. Then in a soft voice, King said, "Now, Eisenhower, just state your problem again." When the general did so, King replied that he thought Marshall's request could be achieved.[18]

While a war of words raged in Washington, halfway around the globe in the Philippines, General Douglas MacArthur's ragtag, ill-equipped, and partly trained force of twenty-five thousand American and forty-five thousand Filipino soldiers was battling for its life against a Japanese army that had landed on the main island of Luzon. MacArthur was not unduly concerned. He expected large reinforcements of personnel, airplanes, guns, ammunition, and supplies to be rushed to the Philippines, after which he would launch counterattacks to drive the Japanese from Luzon.

MacArthur had been kept in the dark about Washington's Germany-first policy, so he had no way of knowing that large-scale help would never be sent. The general and his men had been written off as expendable, to be sacrificed on the altar of strategic expediency.

CHAPTER 2

Howls along Constitution Avenue

IN HIS WAR DEPARTMENT OFFICE in the Munitions Building early in 1942, Dwight Eisenhower was toiling through fourteen-hour workdays, seven days a week, struggling with an awesome array of problems. As chief of the Far East section of the War Plans Division, his primary task was a gut-wrenching one: Presiding over the agonizing destruction of Douglas MacArthur's American-Filipino force, which included numerous close friends. Because of Uncle Sam's unreadiness for war, there was not much to send MacArthur, whose men were now trapped on the Bataan peninsula in southern Luzon.

It was Eisenhower's painful duty to stretch out ultimate defeat in the Philippines in order to buy time to collect troops and airplanes and build a base in Australia, twenty-five hundred miles to the south. He ordered two transport ships to carry supplies from San Francisco to Brisbane and dispatched two Pan American clippers to fly to Australia with ammunition. Now that the United States was at war, there was plenty of money, so Eisenhower sent $10 million to Australia to hire blockade runners with private boats to make supply runs to MacArthur. "Pirates," Ike called them. Indeed, they were. Once their craft were loaded with supplies and they had been paid hefty sums, most of the pirates sailed from Brisbane to neutral ports in the Far East. There they sold the supplies intended for MacArthur's men on the black market and splurged with their newfound wealth.

Back in 1933, MacArthur, then the four-star army chief of staff, had appointed Major Eisenhower as his personal assistant. Those were difficult times for the two men and for the army in general. Congress was ladling out minuscule funds to the armed forces. Most career officers disapproved of President Franklin Roosevelt's foreign policy, especially his recognition of the communistic Soviet Union. As if the situation for the army in Washington was not bad enough, Roosevelt had recruited a legion of brash, left-leaning young New Dealers who scorned professional military officers.[1]

Roosevelt described his New Deal as "use of the authority of government as an organized form of self-help for all classes and groups and sections of our country." The New Deal's main thrust was in hiring hundreds of thousands of unemployed men and women and paying them with taxpayer money. Mac-Arthur and Eisenhower privately lambasted the President and his liberal programs, but concentrated primarily on their military careers.

Eisenhower, who, much to his chagrin, had seen no combat in World War I, was anxious to get in the field as a line officer. But MacArthur, impressed by his aide's skills, foresight, and aggressiveness, refused to let him go.

In 1935, MacArthur's tour of duty as chief of staff came to an end. Now, Eisenhower was convinced, he could get out in the field with the troops. However, Congress voted commonwealth status for the Philippines. The new President, Manuel N. Quezon, pleaded for MacArthur to come to Manila as his military advisor.

It was an offer MacArthur could not turn down. In addition to his salary as a permanent major general on the active list, he would receive $33,000 a year in pay from the Philippine government, a hefty sum at the time. What's more, MacArthur would be provided a plush, six-room, air-conditioned penthouse (free of rent) in the luxurious Manila Hotel.

MacArthur took Dwight Eisenhower with him to the Philippines.

"I was dragooned," Eisenhower would later declare. After four years in the Philippines, he returned to the United States in late 1939. Soon the two officers were conducting long-distance sniping at each other.

"Eisenhower," MacArthur told confidants, "was the best clerk I ever had."

When asked by a woman if he had ever met the flamboyant MacArthur, Eisenhower replied, "Met him? Why, ma'am, I studied dramatics under him for five years in Washington and four years in the Philippines!"[2]

Now, in early 1942, Douglas MacArthur demanded in a cable that the navy sally forth from Hawaii and break through the Japanese blockade of the Philippines. Eisenhower replied that the Japanese had seized the Pacific islands of Guam, Wake, the Marshalls, and the Gilberts, which gave their land-based planes air superiority. Thus, the navy was helpless to rush to MacArthur's assistance.

In his cubbyhole office in Malinta Tunnel on Corregidor, a tiny island fortress perched two miles off Bataan in Manila Bay, MacArthur was furious after reading the cable from his former aide. His tired, filthy, hungry, and ill men on Bataan were battling for their lives with obsolete weapons and insufficient or faulty ammunition. The thought of immaculately tailored, well-fed, and comfortably housed staff officers in Washington was maddening to MacArthur and his commanders.

MacArthur ranted to aides that "faceless staff officers" in Washington (presumably meaning Marshall and Eisenhower) were deliberately deceiving him and his beleaguered troops. Were there more determination in the War Department, he declared, supplies and reinforcements could reach Bataan and Corregidor.[3]

For his part, Eisenhower filled his diary with scathing denouncements of his former boss: "In many ways, MacArthur is as big a baby as ever. But we've got to keep him fighting."[4]

A few days later, a message was received from MacArthur in which he recommended his chief of staff, Major General Richard K. Sutherland, as his successor "in the event of my death." Revealing his lack of appreciation for the perilous situation in the Philippines, Eisenhower scrawled in his diary, "Douglas likes his bootlickers."[5] After another MacArthur cable called again for the navy to break the Philippines blockade, Eisenhower's diary entry read, "MacArthur refuses to look facts in the face, an old trait of his."[6]

Then General Marshall began sending encouraging messages. He notified MacArthur that 125 P-40s and fifteen B-24 heavy bombers were aboard ships sailing westward. What the chief of staff did not say was that the convoy would be diverted to Australia, twenty-five hundred miles to the south of the Philippines.

"We are doing our utmost . . . to rush air support to you," Marshall said in another cable. "The President has seen all of your messages and directs Navy to give you every possible support in your splendid fight."[7]

At about the same time, Marshall cabled the following: "Looking toward the quick development of strength in the Far East so as to break the enemy's hold on the Philippines. Our great hope is that the development of overwhelming airpower in the Malay Barrier will cut the Japanese communications south of Borneo and permit an assault in the southern Philippines. . . . A stream of four-engine bombers is en route. . . . Another stream of similar bombers started today from Hawaii. Two groups of medium bombers leave next week. Pursuit planes are coming on every ship we can use."[8]

Douglas MacArthur and his commanders were elated. However, they apparently misinterpreted the precise intent of these cables. Had Marshall meant to convey that these bombers and fighter planes were bound for the Philippines, or that they were heading for Australia, where strength would be built up for an *eventual* return to the Philippines? Or had Marshall deliberately intended to mislead MacArthur so that the men who now called themselves the Battling Bastards of Bataan would fight on and thus buy precious time?

President Roosevelt, meanwhile, called in White House reporters and spoke glowingly of plans to relieve the embattled forces on Bataan. A consummate politician, Roosevelt was well aware of MacArthur's enormous popularity on the home front: The media had dubbed the general the Lion of Luzon. "The United States Navy," the President declared, "is following an intensive and well-planned campaign which will result in positive assistance to the defense of the Philippine Islands."[9]

Roosevelt's aides were horrified. There was no substantial help on the way to the Philippines. Realizing that he had made a monumental blunder, Roosevelt instructed his press secretary, Steve Early, to begin damage control promptly. Early told the press that Roosevelt's remarks should not be misinterpreted. Emphasis should be placed not on the immediate, but rather on the ultimate.

However, the President's upbeat message was plastered on newspaper front pages across the nation. Based on these heartening words from Roosevelt in the media and from George Marshall in cables, MacArthur composed an encouraging statement to his fighting men and ordered every company commander on Bataan to read it to his troops: "Help is on the way from the United States. Thousands of troops and hundreds of airplanes are being dispatched. . . . It is imperative that our troops hold until these reinforcements arrive."[10]

That exhortation to his ragged, dispirited soldiers would prove to be the most embarrassing episode of MacArthur's lengthy career. Never would he forgive President Roosevelt and General Marshall for what he told aides were "bald-faced lies."

Douglas MacArthur, a West Pointer, and George Marshall, a graduate of Virginia Military Institute, had taken a disliking to each other as far back as 1917, when they were both young colonels serving in France with the American Expeditionary Force (AEF) in World War I. There the antagonism between the two men grew. MacArthur quickly became known throughout the AEF as a dashing, bold combat leader with a flamboyant style. Marshall was regarded as the brightest young colonel on the staff of General John J. "Black Jack" Pershing at the AEF's Chaumont headquarters in France, an expert at planning operations and skilled in moving tens of thousands of troops into position.

A free spirit, Colonel MacArthur donned eccentric apparel to lead his men in battle: A smashed-down garrison cap instead of a steel helmet, a four-foot muffler, a turtleneck sweater, and, on occasion, a black sweater with an army "A" he had earned at West Point as a baseball player. From his mouth, a cigarette holder protruded at a jaunty angle. His only weapon was a riding crop.

The men in the 42nd "Rainbow" Division loved their thirty-seven-year-old colonel. They called him the Beau Brummell of the AEF and the Fighting Dude. He would emerge from the war wearing the Distinguished Service Cross and a chestful of other decorations for "conspicuous valor in the face of the enemy."

As MacArthur's fame and widespread publicity in the press back home continued to grow, a coterie of staff officers hostile to MacArthur began to emerge at Chaumont. George Marshall, low-keyed and reserved, was among them. When MacArthur's regiment was in reserve prior to launching an attack, the rakish leader received word that thirty-three of the 42nd Division's best and brightest officers were suddenly ordered transferred to other units. MacArthur was furious, smelling the proverbial rat among his enemies at Chaumont.

After rushing to the AEF headquarters, the colonel received a cool reception. He protested vigorously, but his pleas were ignored. No sooner had he returned to his unit than an even more shocking report arrived: The entire 42nd Division was to be split up as replacements for other formations.

Again MacArthur dashed to Chaumont. This time he bypassed his antagonists, George Marshall included, and buttonholed an old friend, Brigadier General James G. Harbord, Pershing's chief of staff. MacArthur pleaded with him to intervene. Harbord did, and Pershing designated another division to provide replacements.

Colonel MacArthur's victory did little to endear him to his antagonists in what he would call the "Chaumont crowd." MacArthur may have been afflicted with a touch of paranoia. He told an aide that the clique around General Pershing was out to get him.[11]

Shortly before the conclusion of the "war to end all wars" (as it was naively billed by Allied statesmen), MacArthur was elevated to brigadier general. After several tours of duty in the United States, he was appointed army chief of staff by Franklin Roosevelt a few weeks after Roosevelt's election to his first term as President in 1932.

As much as MacArthur abhorred Roosevelt's trumpeted New Deal, which was designed to "put America back to work," the general enrolled 275,000 young men into a Roosevelt brainstorm, the Civilian Conservation Corps (CCC). Perhaps there was reason for MacArthur's interest in this aspect of the New Deal: He suggested that the CCC youths be used as the nucleus of an army reserve. That trial balloon was quickly shot down.

Helping MacArthur establish these youths into U.S. Forest Service camps in forty-seven states was his old antagonist, Colonel George Marshall. Marshall's efforts did him no good, for MacArthur had never forgotten those whom he was still convinced had conspired against him at Chaumont fifteen years earlier. Aging General John Pershing, who had retired as America's only six-star General of the Armies, personally telephoned Chief of Staff MacArthur (whom he had once promoted to brigadier general) and said he would consider it a personal favor if George Marshall was elevated to one-star rank. Instead, Colonel Marshall was exiled to Chicago, where he was assigned a dead-end job: Instructor in the Illinois National Guard.

In 1935, when MacArthur's one-year extension as chief of staff was nearing an end, he subtly got word to President Roosevelt that he would like to see an old friend, Major General George S. Simonds, succeed him. With Simonds running the War Department, MacArthur would have a direct pipeline into doings in the executive branch of government and the army. This was especially important because numerous members of the old Chaumont crowd were now in high posts.

A few weeks later, MacArthur was on a westbound train with Eisenhower when he received a telegram from Washington. It announced that the President had selected Major General Malin Craig, a Chaumont insider, to be the new chief of staff. The message also said that MacArthur was being reduced to permanent two-star rank.

Dwight Eisenhower had never seen his boss so furious. He later wrote of MacArthur's reaction, "It was an explosive denunciation of politics, bad manners, bad judgment, broken promises, arrogance, unconstitutionality, insensitivity, and the way the country had gone to hell."[12]

Despite MacArthur's view that his enemies had again conspired against him, the old warrior went out in a blaze of glory after he returned to Washington. Knowing that MacArthur was leaving for the Philippines, Roosevelt told him, "Douglas, if war should suddenly come, don't wait for orders to come home. Grab the first transportation. I want you to command my armies!"[13]

Now, six years later, Douglas MacArthur, trapped with his steadily weakened force on Bataan and Corregidor, was buying time for America to rearm. In the United States, demands that MacArthur be extricated from the Philippines were being published daily in newspapers. He had become a folk hero, the one American general who was actually fighting an enemy. A Democratic congressman, Knute Hill, introduced a bill that would make MacArthur supreme commander of all U.S. military forces—ground, sea, and air.

George Marshall, understandably, did not take kindly to the proposed legislation. Not only would its passage put MacArthur over Marshall, but the chief of staff told Secretary of War Stimson that he envisioned endless squabbles between MacArthur and the navy.

In the days ahead, Roosevelt faced growing pressure over MacArthur's plight. At a press conference, a reporter asked the chief executive whether friction existed between MacArthur and Washington over the failure to reinforce the Philippines. Roosevelt hemmed and hawed to the point of incoherency: "I wouldn't do any—well, I wouldn't—I am trying to take a leaf out of my notebook. I—not knowing enough about it—I try not to speculate myself."[14]

At the same time Roosevelt was fending off reporters about the ultimate fate of Douglas MacArthur, the Lion of Luzon might have been left to die on Corregidor had not John Curtin, the Prime Minister of Australia, been engaged in a long-distance hassle with Winston Churchill. Early in the war, Australia, as part of the British Empire, had sent three divisions of "diggers" (as Aussie soldiers called themselves) to fight Erwin Rommel in the North African desert. Now, under threat of a Japanese invasion, Curtin bluntly told Churchill that he wanted the divisions back—right now.

Churchill rejected the request. If Rommel and his Afrika Korps were to be halted short of Cairo and the crucial Suez Canal, every empire soldier would be needed. Consequently, a strained relationship developed between Curtin and Churchill.

Curtin, a shrewd poker player, then put his best cards on the bargaining table. He would modify his demands to bring home the diggers immediately if an American general was named as supreme commander in the southwest Pacific, with a firm pledge from President Roosevelt that U.S. troops would be sent to Australia to help defend the country.

Churchill took up the proposal with Roosevelt, who weighed the matter in the lonely confines of his White House study. On a bleak February day, while the rest of the nation observed Washington's Birthday, the President reached a decision. MacArthur would have to be saved from death or capture. But Curtin, who had instigated Roosevelt's consideration of the matter, would not be told that an effort would be made to get MacArthur to Australia. Odds were enormous against the general's successful escape from Corregidor through the Japanese land, sea, and air blockade. The fewer people who knew of the President's decision, the better.

On February 23, one day after Roosevelt reached his decision, General MacArthur was poring over a cable that had just arrived on Corregidor. Signed by George Marshall, the communication alerted MacArthur that President Roosevelt might order him to leave Corregidor and go to Mindanao, the southernmost island of the Philippines, six hundred miles away. There he would remain for a week, the signal stated, after which he would continue on to Melbourne, Australia—twenty-six hundred miles below Mindanao.

To MacArthur's aides, the Marshall message meant that Washington wanted not only to save America's most famous general, but also to deny the Japanese an enormous propaganda bonanza if MacArthur remained on Corregidor and was captured. The idea was to bail him out of the Philippines trap while there was still time. In the capital of Dai Nippon (Greater Japan), an American turncoat who called herself Tokyo Rose was broadcasting that MacArthur would soon be apprehended and hanged in Tokyo as a war criminal.

When MacArthur made no reply to Marshall's cable, another coded signal reached Malinta Tunnel on February 28. This one was a direct order from President Roosevelt: The general was to "proceed to Australia and assume command of all U.S. troops [there]."

MacArthur and his staff painstakingly reviewed all the cables received from Washington since the general first set up his command post on Corregidor on Christmas Day of 1941. The study seemed to confirm the view of MacArthur and his aides: There was an army waiting for him in Australia.

MacArthur hesitated. If he disobeyed President Roosevelt, he could be court-martialed. However, if he followed the order, he would be accused of deserting his men.

MacArthur could not bring himself to leave. He dictated his resignation from the United States Army and planned to cross Manila Bay and fight to the end as a volunteer rifleman on Bataan. Alarmed, his staff prevailed on him to tear up the resignation, stressing that the best hope for salvaging the situation in the Japanese-dominated Philippines was to leave and take charge of the army waiting for him in Australia.

A week later, Roosevelt prodded the reluctant general: "Situation in Australia indicates desirability of your early arrival." Finally, after three more days, MacArthur agreed to depart. Until he returned, the U.S. and Philippines forces would be turned over to Major General Jonathan M. "Skinny" Wainwright, a gaunt old cavalryman.

"I'll be back with as much as I can as soon as I can," MacArthur assured Wainwright.

1942

At sundown on March 11, four patrol torpedo (PT) boats, their engines on the verge of breaking down from long use during attacks on Japanese ships, sneaked out of Manila Bay and set a course for Mindanao, six hundred miles to the south. On board were MacArthur and fifteen of his key officers, along with his wife, Jean, and their four-year-old son, Arthur IV. Commanded by Navy Lieutenant John D. Bulkeley, the plywood and mahogany PT boats roared at full speed, mainly at night, through uncharted waters. There was a constant threat that the boat hulls would be ripped open by coral and the occupants spilled into the shark-infested sea. Most of the navigating was done by using the equivalent of a Boy Scout compass and by dead reckoning. Violent storms nearly capsized the craft; Japanese warships were dodged.

As dawn broke on the third morning, a lookout spotted Cagayan Point on Mindanao. In a masterpiece of seamanship and evasive action, Lieutenant Bulkeley had hit the target right on the nose.[15]

A few days later, two B-17 Flying Fortresses sent from Australia picked up MacArthur and his entourage and flew to the Darwin region, along the northern coast. Reaching Melbourne after a two-thousand-mile trip by rail, MacArthur was greeted by thousands of cheering Australians.

"I have come through, and *I shall return!*" he told them.

The general and his family had just reached their quarters in the Menzies Hotel when a staff officer gave MacArthur the greatest shock of his career: The army that he thought was waiting for him to lead back to the Philippines did not exist. There was but a handful of serviceable airplanes in the entire land—and not a single tank.

Back in the United States, Operation Bolero, the buildup of American forces in England for eventual offensive action, promptly ran onto rough shoals. President Roosevelt, apparently without consulting his Joint Chiefs, responded to heavy pressure from General MacArthur and Australian Prime Minister John Curtin and authorized sending twenty-five thousand troops to the Land Down Under.

Curtin cabled Roosevelt, "Without any inhibitions of any kind, I make it quite clear that Australia looks to America, free of any pangs as to our traditional links with [Great Britain]."[16]

On learning that Curtin had bypassed him and gone directly to Roosevelt, Winston Churchill was furious. His chagrin and indignation mounted when he received word that Curtin and MacArthur had established direct contact.[17]

Within hours of Roosevelt's decision to dispatch troops to Australia, General George Marshall and Admiral Ernest King leaped headlong into the fray. Marshall rushed a memorandum to Roosevelt, pointing out that such an action would jeopardize Bolero. The chief of staff bluntly stated that the President would have to make a choice: Bolero or Australia.[18]

Ernest King held a directly opposite viewpoint. He dispatched the following message to the White House: "As important as the mounting of Bolero may be, the Pacific problem is no less so, and is certainly more urgent."

Roosevelt backtracked, insisting that he had not intended to send troops to Australia but had only wanted that possibility studied. This no doubt came as a surprise to the navy and army officers who had been directed by the President to ship the twenty-five thousand soldiers to Australia.

"I do not want Bolero slowed down," the President added.[19]

Bolero had been rescued, but Roosevelt's vacillation deeply frustrated Eisenhower, who had been promoted to head the War Plans Division. "Bolero is supposed to have the approval of [Roosevelt] and [Churchill]," he wrote in his diary. "But the struggle to get everyone behind it is never ending."[20]

Although the President had pledged his commitment to Bolero, of the 132,000 American soldiers shipping overseas in the early months of 1942, all but twenty-thousand sent to Iceland and to Ireland sailed for the Pacific. "The Navy wants to take all the islands in the Pacific, have them held by Army troops to become bases for Army pursuit [planes] and bombers," Eisenhower raged in his diary. "Then the Navy will have a safe place to sail its vessels."[21]

For his part, Admiral King was not happy with Eisenhower and his planners. He complained that the "War Department is just like the alimentary canal. You feed it at one end, and nothing comes out at the other but crap."[22]

In the meantime, George Marshall set about reorganizing the clanking machinery of the U.S. Army, the structure of which had been intact since 1903. Too many people had to approve too many documents before even minor action could be taken.

For decades, major generals in charge of infantry, field artillery, cavalry, armor, and coast artillery had ruled over and jealously guarded their own independent fiefdoms. Marshall was determined to create a unified army bent on fighting the Germans and the Japanese, rather than on waging internal wars.

What Marshall needed to get the reorganization job done was a hard-nosed, blunt-speaking hatchet man. Joseph T. McNarney, a newly appointed brigadier general, fit the description and went to work. Most of the generals torn kicking and howling from their private domains were bitter toward Marshall. They called McNarney and his aides the "Soviet Committee," referring to the ruthless tactics utilized by Josef Stalin and his cohorts.

When the reorganization had been completed and approved by Marshall, there were but three top commands: Army Air Forces, under Major General Henry H. "Hap" Arnold; Ground Forces, commanded by Major General Lesley McNair; and the Services of Supply, led by Major General Brehon Somervell. Marshall would keep at his headquarters only Eisenhower's War Plans Division, which had been streamlined and renamed Operations Division.

Finally, after four decades, the structure of the U.S. Army was prepared for global war.

CHAPTER 3

A "Sales Force" Goes to London

EARLY ON THE MORNING OF APRIL 1, 1942, Generals George Marshall and Dwight Eisenhower were ushered into the Oval Office of the White House. President Roosevelt, puffing on a cigarette in a long holder, greeted the officers warmly. Also in the room were the military and government advisors known as the President's war cabinet.

Roosevelt had convened the session to be briefed by Marshall on a plan to implement the Germany-first strategy. Drawn up by Eisenhower, now a major general, and his Operations staff, the plan was based on the continuation of Bolero, the buildup of U.S. forces in the British Isles. Two possible assaults, code-named Roundup and Sledgehammer, were envisioned.

Roundup called for an attack across the English Channel against France in the spring of 1943, at which time it was thought there would be thirty American and eighteen British divisions in England. This invasion would be supported by whatever aircraft the British could provide and by fifteen hundred American fighter planes and one thousand bombers—most of which had not yet been built.

Sledgehammer, a much smaller operation to invade Normandy, would be launched as early as September 1942—five months away—to draw off German troops from the Russian front if it appeared that the hard-pressed Red Army was about to collapse. Marshall estimated that a division and a half of American troops and three British divisions would be available for Sledgehammer.

For three hours, Roosevelt and the others discussed these strategies. Sledgehammer and Roundup were unanimously endorsed. Just before the session broke up, fifty-three-year-old Harry Hopkins, Roosevelt's closest civilian advisor, turned to Admiral Ernest King, who had recently been elevated to chief of naval operations. Knowing that King was a Pacific-first advocate, Hopkins said, "I want to make sure everyone is in accord on this strategy, Admiral King. Do you see any reason this cannot be carried out?"

King offered a lukewarm reply: "No, I do not."[1]

Roosevelt was delighted that offensive action was being planned. For nearly four months, the American people had been deluged with a torrent of bad

22

news from the Pacific, where the Japanese streamroller was running wild. The President ordered Marshall, King, Hopkins, and their entourage to rush to London and sell Winston Churchill and the Imperial General Staff on the Roundup/Sledgehammer strategy. This secret mission was code-named Modicum.

That night, Secretary of War Henry Stimson optimistically wrote in his diary, "Mark this day as a memorable one in the war."[2]

In England, Churchill and his advisors were stupefied by news from Field Marshal John Dill in Washington that the Americans were contemplating cross-Channel attacks at an early date.

"Sheer madness!" Alan Brooke warned the Prime Minister. "Any cross-Channel attack this year will meet with total disaster!"

There was ample reason for Brooke's pessimism. Dug in on the far side of the Channel were twenty-five combat-tested, fully equipped, and expertly led German infantry and panzer divisions, backed by a potent Luftwaffe. Although Bolero troops had been trickling into the British Isles since January, they were green and, in many cases, poorly led. The great bulk of the needed weapons, tanks, and equipment was yet to be built. Most of the required landing craft had not reached the blueprint stage.

Field Marshal Brooke was no amateur in the art of war. Born into a family with a long military tradition, he was decisive, yet a man of few words. While speaking, he conveyed an unfortunate air of disdain, whether slugging it out with American generals or conversing with subordinates. Brooke's avocation of bird-watching belied his combat experience. Tough and shrewd, he had served in World War I as an artillery commander, and he led a British corps in France against the Germans after the outbreak of war in September 1939.

On learning that the American delegation was on its way to London, Brooke wrote in his diary, "[George] Marshall is a pleasant man . . . rather over-filled with his own importance."[3] Brooke's view of his "pleasant" American counterpart would soon undergo a drastic revision.

On the beautiful morning of April 4, 1942, George Marshall, Ernest King, Harry Hopkins, and their party lifted off in a Boeing flying boat from Chesapeake Bay and headed for Bermuda, where there would be a two-day stopover. After the second leg of the flight to Northern Ireland, the Americans arrived in London on April 8. There was a secretive aura about the visit. General Marshall was wearing civilian clothes and had the nom de guerre Mr. C. G. Mell. Hopkins was Mr. A. H. Hones.

Twenty-four hours later, Marshall met with Churchill and Brooke in the Prime Minister's bombproof bunker forty feet below St. George Street. The two men listened without comment while Marshall briefed them on Sledgehammer/Roundup. When the American stressed that a direct assault across the Channel against France was the best strategy for bringing the war to an early close, Brooke snapped sarcastically, "Yes, but not the way we want it to end!"[4]

Brooke was convinced that the Americans had given no thought to strategy after a landing on the French coast. "Do we go west, south, or east?" the field marshal asked. Marshall made no direct reply.[5]

During another session in Churchill's bunker, Brooke spoke out strongly against the cross-Channel strategy in a tempestuous encounter with Marshall. That night the field marshal scrawled in his diary, "We [the Allies] are hanging on by [our] eyelids everywhere. . . . In the light of the existing situation, Marshall's plan for a cross-Channel attack in September 1942 is just fantastic." He added, "[Marshall] is a good general at raising armies, but his strategical ability does not impress me at all. In fact, in many respects, he is a dangerous man."[6]

After three days of discussions, Churchill gave Marshall cautious approval for offensive action "in 1942, perhaps, in 1943 for certain." Marshall took that declaration to mean that the British agreed to Sledgehammer or Roundup. However, General Hastings "Pug" Ismay, Churchill's personal military advisor, reflected the view of the Prime Minister and Brooke when he wrote in his diary, "I think we [the British] could have come much cleaner than we did. We were frankly horrified [over Sledgehammer] because of what we have seen in our lifetime—60,000 British casualties in one day, in July 1916 [in World War I]. We who survived have gotten into our minds: *Never again!*"[7]

Convinced that Sledgehammer or Roundup was nailed down, Marshall and his party left London for Northern Ireland to inspect American troops. A day later, at a Scottish village, "Mr. A. H. Hones" and "Mr. C. G. Mell," both wearing civilian clothes, tried to place a telephone call to the President of the United States from an inn. They were overheard by a startled employee, who called the constable. He was ready to arrest the two strangers as Nazi spies—or drunks. But first he placed a call to Scotland Yard in London. Fortunately, the officers there were aware of the civilian code names being used by the two Americans and kept them from being thrown into a Scottish jail.[8]

While Marshall was in Scotland, he received depressing—but not unexpected—news. A bloody curtain had been lowered on the drama in the Philippines. Weakened by malaria, dysentery, beriberi, and scurvy, the Battling Bastards of Bataan were finally crushed. On April 10, with his men starving and nearly out of ammunition for their ancient weapons, General Jonathan Wainwright surrendered. Three weeks later, after a stubborn, yet hopeless fight, Corregidor would fall.

The American home front was shocked and dismayed. But late in April, when Marshall, King, and Hopkins flew back to Washington, the entire nation was in the midst of a euphoric hangover. On April 18, a handful of American pilots, led by Lieutenant Colonel James H. "Jimmy" Doolittle, had bombed the Japanese homeland.

Lifting off from the carrier *Hornet* eight hundred miles from Japan, sixteen two-engine B-25 bombers swept low over the water and reached Tokyo, Yokohama, Nagoya, and Kobe undetected. Doolittle's men dropped their lethal cargoes, then most of the planes flew on to China.

In Japan, Doolittle's bold fliers had made an impact far greater than the actual bomb damage, which was minimal. They had scored an enormous psychological victory, skyrocketing American morale and causing Japanese warlords to lose great face. For months, General Hideki Tojo had been assuring the Japanese people that their homeland never would be bombed.

After his return to Washington, George Marshall immediately rushed to the White House to advise President Roosevelt that Churchill and Brooke had agreed to the Sledgehammer/Roundup concept. Based on this report, the President cabled Josef Stalin that the Western Allies would invade France either in September 1942 or in spring 1943.

In London, Winston Churchill and Alan Brooke were horrified after reading a copy of Roosevelt's cable to Stalin. The British had agreed only that planning should begin for Sledgehammer in the event the Soviet army appeared to be collapsing.

Churchill and Brooke apparently decided that some drastic action would have to be mounted, even if it met with disaster, to hammer into the heads of the inexperienced American leaders the folly of a frontal assault across the English Channel in September 1942. In the utmost secrecy, Operation Rutter was born.

Churchill apparently was prepared to sacrifice thousands of empire soldiers and scores of badly needed warplanes to shock the Americans out of pursuing an infinitely more dangerous course: A premature assault against the French coast that might cost the Anglo-Americans five hundred thousand men, their weapons, vehicles, guns, equipment, a large part of their navies and air forces—and the war against Nazi Germany.

Rutter would be a large-scale raid against Dieppe, a heavily defended French port that had once been a lair for pirates. Planning was launched under Lieutenant General Bernard L. Montgomery. Taking part in the raid would be 6,058 troops, mainly men of the Canadian 2nd Division, supported by 262 vessels and fifty-six squadrons of Royal Air Force (RAF) fighters, more planes than existed at the time of the Battle of Britain against the Luftwaffe in 1940.

Everything connected with Rutter was done in the climate of a plot. Churchill ordered steps taken which had few, if any, precedents. Nothing was put on paper about deliberations by the British Chiefs. Only a tiny clique of officers known for their discretion were made privy to the true reason for Rutter.

Even the First Lord of the Admiralty was not told why 262 ships were to be assembled in Channel ports. Troop commanders were not to be informed of their target, Dieppe, until they and their men were sealed into sea transports.

On May 13, troop training began. The date for the attack was set for July 4. There would be plenty of time for rehearsals, but none was held. In violation of standard doctrine, there would be no cover or deception plans to confuse the German defenders. This order was especially mystifying, for it indicated that Churchill and the British chiefs did not want the Wehrmacht to be distracted away from Dieppe.

All the while, the supersecret British XX-Committee (or Double-Cross Committee) was ordered to lie low on the Rutter operation. For two years, crafty members of the XX-Committee had been using captured Nazi agents to radio false information to the German Abwehr (secret service) in Hamburg to confound the Oberkommando der Wehrmacht (German high command) about British weaknesses and intentions. Now the XX-Committee was instructed *not* to have the double agents mislead the Germans about the purpose of the ships collected in England's Channel ports for Rutter.

Across the Atlantic, General Marshall had become disturbed by the lack of progress of Bolero, the American buildup in the British Isles. He also had begun to doubt whether Major General James E. Chaney, the senior U.S. Army officer in London, had the toughness and ability to command what would eventually be the largest American army base overseas.

Consequently, Marshall told Dwight Eisenhower to fly to London to be his eyes and ears with regard to the situation there. On May 25, Eisenhower's aircraft landed at Prestwick, Scotland. There he took a train to London, where he spent the next day in conference with General Chaney and his staff. Eisenhower was appalled. Chaney and his aides were "completely at a loss." Incredibly, they were still wearing civilian clothes as though it were peacetime and were putting in only eight-hour workdays, with weekends off. Equally shocking, Chaney and his staff knew none of the British military leaders and had no contact with the British government.

A day later, Eisenhower was driven to Kent, where he observed a field exercise conducted by General Bernard Montgomery, a diminutive man who was particularly condescending toward Americans. Later, Eisenhower attended a lecture at which Montgomery critiqued the exercise by his British troops. While Monty, as he was known to friends, talked, the chain-smoking Eisenhower lighted a cigarette. After three or four puffs, Montgomery suddenly stopped speaking and began sniffing the air.

"Who's smoking?" he demanded to know.

Taken aback, Eisenhower confessed that he was the culprit.

"I do not permit smoking in my presence," Montgomery snapped.

Sheepishly, Eisenhower extinguished his cigarette and the lecture resumed.[9]

Marshall's troubleshooter returned to Washington on June 3 and briefed the chief of staff on the dreadful situation in London. It was clear that General Chaney would have to be replaced, and Eisenhower recommended General Joseph McNarney for the post. Marshall turned down the suggestion on the grounds that McNarney, who had ruthlessly revamped the entire structure of the War Department, was too valuable in Washington. Marshall had another candidate in mind: Dwight Eisenhower.

In the meantime, the global situation for what Churchill had dubbed the Grand Alliance (Great Britain, the United States, the Soviet Union, and China) grew from bleak to horrendous. In May and June, the Russian army suffered more than 250,000 casualties in the Crimea, and powerful German forces had launched an offensive to seize Russia's rich Caucasian oil fields. Stalin rushed Foreign Minister Vyacheslav Molotov to London to demand that the Western Allies open a second front in France—and soon—to relieve the enormous pressure on the reeling Red Army.

Molotov told Churchill that without a second front in France, the Soviets were in danger of collapsing. He hinted that Stalin would make peace with Hitler. Churchill was unimpressed, convinced that the Soviet situation was not as drastic as Molotov portrayed. The Russian appeal was rejected: Great Britain was faced with its own military debacle in North Africa.

There, Lieutenant General Neil Ritchie's Eighth Army was fleeing eastward in disarray with Erwin Rommel's elite Afrika Korps close behind. Ritchie's routed army did not halt for several hundred miles until it reached a tiny Arab village, El Alamein. In two weeks, Eighth Army had lost nearly five hundred tanks and seventy-five thousand men.

In nearby Cairo, panic reigned at British Middle East headquarters. Such huge quantities of secret papers were hastily burned in anticipation of Rommel's imminent arrival that on Ash Wednesday the sky over the Egyptian metropolis was heavy with black smoke.

Bent on preventing an ultimate disaster, Churchill sacked Ritchie and rushed General Montgomery, who had supervised the planning of Operation Rutter, to replace him. Scrappy and wiry, the outspoken Montgomery at times infuriated both his superiors and his subordinates. But he had the trait Churchill was seeking—supreme self-confidence.

In the wake of Churchill's rebuff, Foreign Minister Molotov hurried on to Washington to renew his urgent plea for a second front. There, his reception was quite different. President Roosevelt and General Marshall were deeply alarmed by the threat of the Soviet Union, with its millions of soldiers, making a separate peace with Adolf Hitler. Consequently, Roosevelt told the Russian diplomat to inform Stalin that the Western Allies would launch a second front against German-held Europe in September 1942, barely two months away.

On the afternoon of July 3, Canadian troops boarded ships in southern England. Guns and tanks were loaded. Hundreds of aircraft were being checked out at fields behind the coast. Rutter would hit Dieppe at dawn. Quite suddenly, Mother Nature repudiated the predictions of British meteorologists and the weather turned violent in the Channel. As a result of this unforeseen storm, the troops disembarked.

Unaware of the true intention of Rutter, its commanders pointed out that the entire operation had been compromised, and they told the British Chiefs that it would be idiotic to remount it. Their urgent recommendation would go unheeded. Rutter still might be needed.

In the War Department and White House in Washington, tensions were growing over a cable received from Winston Churchill on July 8: "I am most anxious for you to know where I stand myself at the present time. I have found no one [in London] who regards Sledgehammer as possible. I should like you to do [Torch] as soon as possible, and that we in concert with the Russians should try Jupiter."

Torch was the code name for an invasion of French-held northwest Africa, and Jupiter called for landings in Norway.

George Marshall was furious. Three times the British had seemingly agreed to an invasion of France and three times they had reneged. Now, Marshall was convinced, Churchill was proposing strategies that would do little to shorten the war but much to preserve the British Empire.

On July 15, Roosevelt summoned Marshall, Admiral King, and Harry Hopkins. They were ordered to leave for London the next morning to thrash it out with the British.

"It is time to fish or cut bait," the President said. He wanted a final decision within a week.

In London, Field Marshal Brooke was notified of the forthcoming delegation. "It will be a queer party," he observed in his diary. "Harry Hopkins is for operating in [North] Africa, Marshall wants to operate in Europe, and King is determined to stick to the Pacific."[10]

Hearing of the forthcoming visit of the American delegation, Churchill resurrected Rutter. The order was given despite warnings by unit commanders that the operation against Dieppe had been compromised and thus might result in appalling casualties. There would be but one change: The code name for the raid became Jubilee. The new target date was August 18.

At 5:19 P.M. on July 17, the Stratoliner carrying President Roosevelt's "sales force" rolled to a stop at Scotland's bustling Prestwick Airport. There the Americans boarded a waiting private train sent by Prime Minister Churchill and soon were speeding southward through the Scottish Highlands.

George Marshall had rejected Churchill's invitation to stop briefly at Chequers, the Prime Minister's retreat in Buckinghamshire outside bomb-battered London. Orders were given for the train to pass Chequers and go directly to London. Before the confrontation with the British chiefs, Marshall wanted to talk with the newly named commander of European Theater of Operations, United States Army (ETOUSA), Dwight Eisenhower, who had recently been promoted to three-star rank.

Shortly after dawn on Saturday, July 18, the private train chugged into London's Euston Station. On hand to greet the American delegation was Eisenhower, who looked drawn and tired. For the past seventy-two hours, straight, he and his staff had been toiling to prepare reports for Marshall to use as ammunition in the strategy showdown with the British.

Marshall was unaware that his snub of Winston Churchill had ruffled the tail feathers of the Prime Minister, Alan Brooke, and other British brass. A deliberate slight, they were convinced. A cunning ploy to gain a psychological edge in what promised to be heated debates. When the Americans learned of their ire, Harry Hopkins was promptly dispatched to Chequers to pay proper homage to Churchill's ego.

At noon the next day, Hopkins, a tousle-haired man who habitually wore rumpled suits, arrived at Chequers. The Prime Minister had been pacing about like an angry bear. Not only was Churchill upset by Marshall's perceived snub, but he also was furious to learn that Marshall and Admiral King were already engaged in informal discussions with the British chiefs of staff. Churchill, friends often said, could stomach about anything except being locked on the outside looking in.

As Hopkins lounged in a plush armchair, Churchill strode about the room, hands clasped behind his back, puffing on a Havana cigar and lecturing his visitor on protocol. Speaking crisply, Churchill declared that *he* was the one the American party should have called on first, that *he* was the one the United States government would have to deal with, and that the British army, navy, and air force were under *his* command. Continuing to pace, Churchill pulled from his pocket a British book of war laws. As he finished reading each page aloud, he ripped it out, crumpled it, and hurled it into the blazing fireplace.

Hopkins listened to Churchill's temperamental outburst without comment, considering it to be merely another round in the ongoing slugfest between the American and British allies. Now it was Hopkins's turn. For an uninterrupted half hour, he harangued Churchill about Britain's shortcomings and lack of cooperation with the Americans.

After Hopkins's loud rebuttal lost its steam, both men felt better. A few more rounds of Scotch and soda were consumed, the two combatants shook hands warmly and wished each other well, and Hopkins left for London.

CHAPTER 4

A Showdown over Strategy

THAT SAME MORNING, JULY 18, 1942, George Marshall and Dwight Eisenhower were huddled in Marshall's sumptuous suite in Claridge's, London's most prestigious hotel. The entire fourth floor had been taken over by the American "sales force." A soldier stood guard at the door of each of fifteen suites, a marine at the sixteenth, Admiral King's. Those arranging the converted headquarters no doubt had wanted to make certain that the admiral would not be unduly offended by having an army sentry.

Marshall and Eisenhower were intently discussing the operational plan for Sledgehammer, which Ike had just drawn up. The cross-Channel invasion would hit at the major French port of Le Havre; a British general would be in command of the six divisions, two of them American. The target date was set for September 15, 1942.

Eisenhower made no effort to sugarcoat his plan. In his estimation, the chances of the first assault division getting ashore were one in two, while the chances of establishing a beachhead with all six divisions were about one in five. In other words, there was a projected 80 percent possibility that Sledgehammer would meet with disaster.

Despite these daunting odds, Eisenhower thought that the chance was worth taking if it meant keeping eight million Russian soldiers in the war. To sit by idly and watch the Red Army collapse, he emphasized, would result in the Anglo-Americans being "guilty of one of the grossest military blunders of all history."[1]

In his conclusion, Eisenhower said that the risk should be taken and Sledgehammer launched. Marshall concurred.

On the eve of the American-British strategy confrontation, Commander Harry Butcher, Eisenhower's aide, wrote in his diary, "Upon the discussions in the next few days may rest the future history of the world."[2]

At 10:00 A.M. on July 20, the showdown over future strategies convened at the War Office. The participants had barely settled into their chairs when heated arguments erupted. The principal gladiators were George Marshall and Field

Marshal Alan Brooke. Since their first meeting seven months earlier, animosity had been simmering between the two men. Marshall resented Brooke's patronizing attitude toward American generals—"newcomers to war from the colonies." Brooke, for his part, felt that Marshall, who had never led as much as a platoon in combat, was a "political general." Earlier, Brooke had confided to his diary that Douglas MacArthur, a World War I hero, not Marshall, should be the U.S. chief of staff.

The War Office sessions were exhausting, acrimonious, and prolonged. Brooke pounded away at Marshall, ridiculing Sledgehammer. A failure would not help the Russians, the field marshal declared scornfully, and even if six divisions were put ashore, German units would not be drawn away from the Eastern Front.

Marshall fired back that something had to be done to keep the Soviets in the war and that Sledgehammer was the only operation that could achieve that goal.

As the bitter dispute raged on, attacks became personal. Brooke accused Marshall of "trying to assume the powers of the [U.S.] commander in chief, which are President Roosevelt's prerogative."

Marshall, his face flushed, shot back: "How do you expect to win the war—by defensive actions?"

Brooke explained his grand design for victory: Bomb the German homeland day and night, establish a naval blockade of German ports, keep the enemy off balance with commando raids and clever deceptions that would force Hitler to garrison some two thousand miles of European coastline, strike at German morale with a propaganda blitz, encourage enemy rebellion from within, and conduct military operations on the fringes of the Führer's vast empire. When these combined pressures indicated a weakening of German strength and morale, then—and *only* then—should the Western Allies launch a frontal assault across the English Channel against France.

Brooke proposed implementing this strategy and establishing a second front to take the heat off the Russians with an invasion of Algeria and Morocco, two colonies in French Northwest Africa. Marshall scoffed. Why go chasing off a thousand miles from the south of England in search of an enemy to fight when there were plenty of Germans only twenty-five miles across the English Channel from Dover?

Back and forth the altercation continued, with charges and countercharges. Under the conference table, Harry Hopkins slipped a note to George Marshall: "I feel damned depressed!"

On July 22, the British conferees voted unanimously to reject Sledgehammer. Curiously, perhaps, Admiral Harold Stark, the former U.S. chief of naval operations who had been exiled to London as an advisor when Ernest King won the intramural power struggle in the Navy Building, joined the British in the voting.

Marshall, downcast and frustrated, cabled President Roosevelt that the two sides were hopelessly deadlocked. Back came a reply: The President wanted American ground troops in action in 1942. Hopkins, largely a political creature, convinced Roosevelt that an October 30 deadline for an offensive should be set. Not only would that early date help the hard-pressed Soviet army, but the timing would be just before the off-year congressional elections.

The bickering resumed at the War Office. Finally, the Americans surrendered if for no other reason than to break the deadlock. Sledgehammer was out; French Northwest Africa was in. However, Marshall declared that the "African venture" should not be allowed to slow down Bolero, the buildup of U.S. power in the British Isles in order to launch Roundup, the cross-Channel attack, in spring 1943.

Privately, Churchill, Brooke, and the British chiefs were delighted that their strategy had been accepted, but they were not yet ready to celebrate. President Roosevelt would have to give his stamp of approval to the North African operation, now code-named Torch.

Early the next morning, a glum Dwight Eisenhower was having breakfast at a converted apartment building at 20 Grosvenor Square in London, headquarters of ETOUSA. With him was his deputy, Major General Mark W. Clark. Due to his sharp nose and equally sharp mind, the tall, gangling, forty-six-year-old Clark had been dubbed the American Eagle by Churchill.

Since taking charge of American forces in Europe, Eisenhower had forbidden pessimistic talk or attitudes at his headquarters, but on this morning he was unable to live up to his own directive. Sipping a cup of coffee and dragging on a cigarette, Ike expressed his deep concern that Torch would cause wide dispersal of Anglo-American forces. But what disturbed him most was that the Western Allies would be fighting Frenchmen, not Germans.

"Hell's bells!" Eisenhower snapped, using a favorite expression. "The French are supposed to be our friends!"[3]

His nagging disappointment was shared by Clark. "July 22, 1942, will go down as the blackest day in history!" Eisenhower said.[4]

On the evening of Saturday, July 25, one week after the U.S. delegation had arrived in London, a lively party given by Harry Hopkins and Steve Early, Roosevelt's press secretary, was in full swing in a suite in Claridge's. Wine and champagne were flowing. Guests from the United States included eight or nine denizens of high society in New York and Washington who had found an excuse to be in London to soak up the "wartime excitement."

Heavily burdened Dwight Eisenhower, who had been conferring with General Marshall in another suite, dropped by briefly for a drink. Eisenhower had a distaste for such social functions but was beaming and vibrant. He was still largely an unknown. A New York society matron pleasantly inquired of the three-star general, "Tell me, Colonel, what brings you to London?"

In midafternoon, Hopkins talked by transocean telephone to Franklin Roosevelt in Washington and was shocked to learn that the President had not received the cable from Marshall and King that told of the tentative decision reached on Torch. That lapse was remedied when the cable was sent again. Should Roosevelt reject Torch, the delegation would remain in London for renewed wrangling with the British chiefs.

Just past 6:00 P.M., Hopkins dashed into a bedroom to take a call from Roosevelt. The President told his advisor that the Marshall-King cable had finally arrived, that he had convened his confidants, and that an invasion of French Northwest Africa had been approved.

George Marshall was anxious to get back to Washington, where a mountain of crucial matters had piled up and were waiting to be resolved. Yet pressing business remained to be done in London. Foremost was the appointment of a supreme commander for Torch. British sentiment favored Marshall. Roosevelt, however, would not release his chief of staff. "I would not sleep at night with George Marshall out of Washington," the President told confidants.

A day before departing London, Marshall summoned Eisenhower to his suite at Claridge's. When the general arrived, his mentor was in the toilet. Typically, Marshall wasted no time. Through the closed door, he yelled that Eisenhower was to be supreme commander of Torch.[5]

Eisenhower's appointment would have to be confirmed by Churchill and the British chiefs. Their agreement was certain, since the United States would be providing most of the troops for Torch.

Now there remained a thorny matter for Marshall and Admiral Ernest King: A confrontation with Charles André Joseph Marie de Gaulle, the contentious, self-appointed leader of the Free French. De Gaulle, through an emissary, had requested an audience with King and Marshall in what the Americans concluded was a bid for a political endorsement of the fifty-one-year-old Frenchman.

In the wake of the French army's humiliating defeat by the Wehrmacht in only six weeks in 1940, de Gaulle, an obscure major general, had escaped to Great Britain, established a London headquarters at Carlton Gardens, and called his resistance organization the Free French. Then, de Gaulle electrified millions of his countrymen with a ringing pronouncement: "France has lost a battle, but France has not lost the war!"

Now, two years after setting up his London command post, de Gaulle demanded that Marshall and King call on *him* as head of a foreign government. When the two Americans declined, the stiff-necked Frenchman relented and agreed to pay a visit to Marshall and King after it was pointed out to him that the two Americans had four-star rank while de Gaulle was entitled to wear only the equivalent of two stars.

With an aide and a translator at his heels, the six-foot, four-inch general strode regally into Marshall's suite at Claridge's. Instead of a private meeting with Marshall and King as equals, de Gaulle saw that there were at least ten

Americans in the room, including Dwight Eisenhower and Mark Clark. Purposely, the Frenchman was being received not as head of a government but only as a general with presumed authority over a handful of French soldiers.

The climate was frosty. Finally, an awkward silence was broken when de Gaulle began a recital of the French troops he claimed were loyal to him even though they were commanded by other French generals. These units were scattered across North Africa, in the Mediterranean, and on a few islands in the Pacific, de Gaulle said.

The Americans made no response. More strained silence. Then de Gaulle said that the Free French all over the world were anxious for the Western Allies to open a second front. Could he be briefed on the Anglo-American strategy? Marshall launched into a vague dissertation that resulted in the Frenchman learning no more than he could have gained by reading British and American newspapers.[6]

After thirty minutes, de Gaulle apparently realized that he could extract neither an endorsement nor information from the stonewalling American brass. Suddenly, he rose from his chair, saluted, shook hands, spun on his heel, and departed. A man of enormous ego and pride, he would never forgive the Americans for the humiliation they had inflicted on him, the leader of the Free French.

While the London debates were raging, Reichsführer Heinrich Himmler, head of the Gestapo and chief of the Schutzstaffel (SS), Adolf Hitler's elite private army, was seated at his desk in Berlin reading translated intercepts of transoceanic telephone conversations between Roosevelt and Churchill, and by General Mark Clark, Commander Harry Butcher, and other Americans.

An SS general who was feeding the intercepts to Himmler, a one-time chicken farmer, noted, "The [London] conference will probably determine where the second front is to be established and when."

For many months, Roosevelt, from a soundproof room in the basement of the White House, and Churchill, from his bunker in London, had been conferring freely over the transoceanic telephone hotline in full confidence that they were protected from German eavesdroppers by a "scrambler," which distorted the words going over the wire, then restored them when they reached the opposite end of the line. What the two leaders did not know was that the Deutsche Reichspost, the German postal organization, had perfected electronic means to unscramble the scrambler on the Allied hotline.

This technique was installed in a supersecret monitoring station built near Eindhoven in the Netherlands. So exclusive was this listening post that only Hitler, Himmler, and Foreign Minister Joachim von Ribbentrop received translated intercepts. German intelligence, in essence, had a direct pipeline into Anglo-American strategy discussions.

Each time the Führer was handed a sheaf of intercepts that disclosed the intense squabbling between the American and British leaders, he reminded confidants that Germany was fighting a coalition of nations. Historically, such a coalition was not a stable entity and could split open at any time.

Despite this German eavesdropping bonanza, the Oberkommando der Wehrmacht was unable to learn of the Allies' invasion locale or target date. The highest intelligence priority was set for unlocking these secrets.

On the night of August 9, the telephone rang in Dwight Eisenhower's apartment in the Dorchester Hotel, a short walk from 20 Grosvenor Square.

"Ike, I just got into this goddamned town," the voice on the other end squawked. "I'm holed up in Claridge's and don't know what in the hell to do with myself!"

"Georgie!" Eisenhower cried, recognizing the high-pitched voice of his old friend Major General George S. Patton, Jr. "God, am I glad to hear from you. Come right over!"

A week previously, Patton had rushed to Washington from the California desert, where he had been training armored units. George Marshall had summoned him to take command of a task force that would sail from the United States to take part in the North Africa invasion. Torch was still hardly more than a concept, so a concerned chief of staff had dispatched Patton to England to assess the situation there "personally and frankly."

George Patton was flamboyant in his personal lifestyle, profane yet devout, and independently wealthy.[7] He became one of the Army's best-known figures when he accompanied General John "Black Jack" Pershing's expedition into Mexico just prior to America's entry into World War I. There he gained renown by tracking down a notorious Mexican outlaw whose band had been raiding across the border into U.S. territory. He killed the bandit in a two-man shootout and brought the corpse back to camp strapped over the front fender of an automobile.

In World War I as a lieutenant colonel, Patton's army-wide reputation as an aggressive fighting man and military innovator gained further luster. He became America's leading expert on tank warfare and led a tank brigade in the fierce battles at Saint-Mihiel and in the Meuse-Argonne offensive, where he was wounded.

Now, twenty-four years later, George Patton had arrived in London, eager to take another crack at "the goddamned Hun."[8] Thirty minutes after he telephoned Eisenhower, the fifty-six-year-old general, ramrod straight and immaculately tailored, burst into the supreme commander's Dorchester apartment. Eisenhower was delighted to see his buoyant friend. Since July 24, when President Roosevelt anointed Torch, Ike had been surrounded by a thick pall of gloom. Even he had begun to have private doubts about Torch, and he looked forward to the spiritual fix that the ebullient Patton could provide.

Over a few drinks after dinner, Patton and Eisenhower held an intense discussion about Torch. Ike's hope for a morale boost from the fire-eating Patton soon vanished. The tank leader himself was gripped by qualms. He felt that the small number of troops—nearly all of them green and only partially trained—assigned to his task force by "those goddamned fools in Washington" would be insufficient to defeat the hostile units he expected to encounter.

In the days ahead, Patton dashed around London. Everywhere he encountered what he called "defeatism." Provoked by "the views of a bunch of weak-kneed sons of bitches," Patton was transfigured from a lukewarm advocate of Torch into a staunch salesman for the operation.

Three days after Patton arrived, Eisenhower convened a meeting of top U.S. Navy brass to convince the doubting service that Torch was the best operation the Western Allies could mount at that time. Patton was invited to attend. Among those present were Admiral Harold Stark, the navy representative in London, and Captain Frank P. Thomas, who was representing Vice Admiral Royal E. Ingersoll, commander of the Atlantic fleet.

The atmosphere was tense. The navy was unhappy over the decision reached by Roosevelt and Churchill to put all navy personnel and ships in the charge of Eisenhower, an army general. Ike, they said privately, did not know the difference between a cruiser and an aircraft carrier.

Captain Thomas, who did most of the talking for the navy, projected a bleak outcome for Torch, citing numerous obstacles to success, even hinting at disaster. George Patton, a long cigar clenched in his teeth, scowled at the navy spokesman. Aides noticed a surefire sign of Patton's deep anger: His neck had turned red.

After Thomas finished his morbid presentation, Patton stubbed out his cigar in an ashtray and rose to his feet to challenge, point by point, the navy officer's assertions. One angry word led to a hundred, and soon a shouting match erupted. Patton's voice could be heard yelling "weak-kneed bastards" and similar terms.

Eisenhower thumped vigorously on the table and called for order. "Torch is an order from the President of the United States and the Prime Minister of England," he said when calm had been restored. "Whether we like it or not, it has to be carried out, despite any obstacles. If there isn't a single protective warship, my orders call for moving into North Africa, and I am going to do it, warships or not—even if I have to go alone in a rowboat!"

Only a week after Franklin Roosevelt had stamped his approval on Torch, Winston Churchill was advised by his emissaries in Washington that "certain influential American leaders" were again hammering away at the President to convince him that Sledgehammer, the cross-Channel attack in the fall of 1942, was still the best course of action. These influential leaders were George Marshall and Secretary of War Henry Stimson.

Learning that Washington still might be trying to undermine Torch in favor of Sledgehammer, Churchill and his military leaders ordered that earlier plans for a reconnaissance in force against Dieppe be dusted off and the operation remounted under the code name Jubilee. Thousands of Canadian and British troops were unaware that they were about to be sacrificed.

CHAPTER 5

Skirmishes among the Admirals

ALTHOUGH MUCH OF Washington's focus had been on creating global strategy, the Navy Building was rocking with internal skirmishes during the first five months of 1942. Admiral Ernest King and his superior, Secretary of the Navy Frank Knox, were engaged in a power struggle to decide which man would have ultimate authority over the sea service. Knox, the hard-bitten King felt, was a meddler.

In Frank Knox, the token Republican in Roosevelt's cabinet, Ernie King had a worthy adversary. Knox, who had been a daily newspaper publisher before accepting Roosevelt's call to be navy secretary in 1940, had made it known promptly that he was the boss. His first action had been to visit the fleets and invite the admirals to call on him one by one. Each would be expected at a precise time.[1]

Now, early in June 1942, Admiral King completed a plan to drastically reorganize the navy's structure and, presumably, to grasp the reins of authority from Secretary Knox. Under the new setup, there would be only four administrative divisions. The primary authority would be in Operations, which was directly under King's control, and the function of the other three divisions was to support Operations.

King's plan was complicated, perhaps deliberately designed to blur who in the navy hierarchy had the ultimate authority over whom and what. When the navy chief presented his plan to Roosevelt, the President was dismayed. It was clear to him that Ernie King had launched a power grab. Roosevelt disapproved of an overhauling of the navy structure "in the middle of a war" and stated that "it would take the navy at least a year just to learn what is meant by all of this."

King was unimpressed by the views of the commander in chief of the armed forces. Returning to the Navy Building, he ordered his revamping plan implemented without informing either the President or Secretary Knox. Within hours, Roosevelt heard that King was ignoring his objections. Infuriated, the President ordered King and Knox to a showdown in the White House.

The Oval Office climate was chilly on the morning of June 9 when the discussion began. Asked by the President to justify his high-handed action,

King equivocated. He pleaded that he was merely obeying earlier Roosevelt orders for the armed forces to achieve maximum efficiency, that he was trying to do what General Marshall already had been permitted to do for the army. He had thought the President wanted him to act as he had done.

A few days later, Roosevelt was still steaming about King's defiance of his wishes, viewing him as a loose cannon on the navy's deck. The President sent word to King that he himself would reorganize the navy structure. Tactfully, he added that King's plan would be "held in abeyance"—that is, it was dead.[2]

Three days later, on June 12, Roosevelt directed Frank Knox to cancel every directive that Admiral King had created with regard to navy reorganization. Clearly, the President was still angry. As a safeguard that his order be carried out, Roosevelt instructed Knox to send him a copy of the cancellation notice.

"The more I think of [King's] orders, the more outrageous I think it is that [King] went ahead to do, without your approval or mine, what I had already disapproved," Roosevelt wrote to Knox. "I am very much inclined to send for the officers down the line and give them a good dressing down. They are old enough to know better—and old enough to know that you are the Secretary of the Navy and that I am commander-in-chief of the Navy."[3]

Convinced that King was bent on diluting civilian authority, Knox schemed to get the Big Bear (as Roosevelt privately called the admiral) out of Washington on the pretext that King should go to Honolulu and take command of the Pacific Fleet. That suggestion caught King off guard. Was not Admiral Chester W. Nimitz, the Pacific Fleet commander, doing a good job? he asked. Certainly, Knox replied, but the navy's top leader should be in Honolulu. King was astonished. As chief of naval operations, his function was to be an advisor to President Roosevelt. And as a member of the Joint Chiefs of Staff, he would have to be where the President was.

Soon King resumed his efforts to reorganize the command structure of the navy, with himself in almost total control. Word leaked to Roosevelt, who wrote a terse note to Frank Knox: "Tell Ernie once more: No reorganizing of the Navy setup during the war. Let's win it first."[4]

In Melbourne, General Douglas MacArthur was still seething at Franklin Roosevelt and George Marshall, who, he felt, had tricked him into leaving Corregidor by implying that an army was waiting in Australia. MacArthur's anger intensified as days passed, then weeks, and he heard absolutely nothing from Washington about the role he was to play in the Pacific war.

Ever alert to signs of treachery by old enemies within the services, MacArthur was irate when he learned from friends in Washington that an obscure brigadier general in the War Department had recommended that MacArthur be appointed U.S. ambassador to the Soviet Union. As absurd as the suggestion was, the Lion of Luzon was convinced that the "New Deal cabal" or the "navy cabal" or the "Chaumont crowd" was responsible for trying to shunt him off to a politician's role in Moscow in order to get him out of the way.[5]

MacArthur was partially correct. Led by Ernest King, the admirals and their staffs had a fetish of being hostile to the general. "The extraordinary brilliance of [MacArthur] is not always matched by his tact," Secretary of War Stimson noted in his diary, "but the Navy's astonishing bitterness against him seems childish."[6]

While MacArthur was stewing in Melbourne, in Washington the army and the navy were embroiled in an ongoing squabble over which of the two services would be the quarterback and carry the ball in the Pacific. Ernest King argued that since the conflict against Japan would be conducted largely at sea, it would be foolish to name an army officer as supreme commander in the Pacific. King had no intention of risking his aircraft carriers and other capital ships in the hands of a general.

King had his own candidate for supreme commander: White-haired, unassuming, capable Admiral Chester Nimitz, who had taken charge of the Pacific Fleet ten days after Pearl Harbor. However, Nimitz was junior in rank to the army candidate, Douglas MacArthur. For his part, George Marshall was dead set against entrusting large numbers of army troops to an admiral.

Nearly five months after the United States went to war against Japan, the bitter command dispute was resolved—by compromise. Violating military doctrine, the Joint Chiefs created two theaters of operations. MacArthur, based in Australia, would be supreme commander of the Southwest Pacific Area, and Nimitz, headquartered in Honolulu, five thousand miles east of the Philippines, would have the same title in the Pacific Ocean Area.

Now that MacArthur had received specific authority, all troops, ships, and airplanes in the Southwest Pacific were *his*. At times, however, he complained to aides that "they" (meaning the Washington hierarchy) were making him a victim of "shoestring logistics." That view had merit. Never would the Southwest Pacific be allocated as much as 15 percent of American manpower and the sinews of war.

At age sixty-two, Douglas MacArthur looked twenty years younger. His dark hair had receded and his piercing blue eyes either mesmerized those he was seeking to woo or scared the hell out of those who had gained his displeasure. He walked with a brisk step and carried his paunch, concealed by broad pleats on his trousers, like a military secret.

MacArthur's subtle air of aloofness and what some considered to be his stage props—a gold-encrusted cap, thirteen rows of "fruit salad" (ribbons representing decorations), and a walking cane—caused a few high-ranking U.S. officers to regard him as arrogant. Junior officers, however, idolized him, imitating his every move and gesture. The general never played cards or swapped jokes or barracks tales, and seldom drank. Every morning before climbing out of bed, he read passages from the Bible.

By the early summer of 1942, General Hideki Tojo's rampaging Japanese juggernaut had conquered the Philippines, Singapore, Hong Kong, the Dutch East

Indies, Malaya, Borneo, the Bismarcks, Siam, Sumatra, the Gilberts, the Celebes, Timor, Wake, Guam, and part of the Solomons. Japanese bombers were pounding Darwin in northern Australia, and the citizens of Brisbane, Canberra, Melbourne, and Sydney feared an imminent invasion.

The Japanese Empire now radiated for five thousand miles from Tokyo in nearly every direction. Emperor Hirohito, a diminutive, mild-mannered father of six, reigned over one-seventh of the globe.

In Washington, generals and admirals were astonished by the power, speed, and skill of the Japanese blitzkrieg, which dwarfed Adolf Hitler's vaunted campaigns in Europe. A grim conclusion was reached in the War Department and the Navy Building: With full mobilization of American manpower and resources, and at a frightful cost in lives, reconquering the Pacific would take at least ten years.

Japan's war of conquest had only begun. In Tokyo, the warlords were contemplating an invasion of California on the west coast of the United States. First, they would have to capture Midway Island as a base for the next leap to Hawaii, 1,150 miles to the southeast. Then it would be on to Los Angeles and San Francisco.

Admiral Isoroku Yamamoto, the Harvard-educated commander of the Combined Imperial Fleet and architect of the sneak attack on Pearl Harbor, sent a formidable naval task force to seize Midway. Yamamoto was unaware that the United States had cracked Japan's "unbreakable" navy code. Two American armadas, which included three aircraft carriers, intercepted the Japanese fleet near Midway on June 4.[7]

A violent clash ensued. By the time the battle was over, the Japanese navy had been dealt the worst defeat in its history. All four Japanese carriers and a heavy cruiser had been sunk by American carrier-based pilots, and 260 planes had been shot down or destroyed.

War is never totally one-sided. The U.S. carrier *Yorktown* and a destroyer were sunk and about 150 aircraft were lost. For the first time since Pearl Harbor, six months earlier, the Japanese warlords' dream of invading California had been turned into a nightmare, thanks to America's ingenious code-busters and the guts of her carrier pilots.

Shortly after the smashing American naval victory at Midway, intelligence reports disclosed that a large force of Japanese soldiers—along with bulldozers, steamrollers, and other heavy equipment—had gone ashore on Guadalcanal, a ninety-two-mile-long primitive island in the eastern Solomons, eight hundred miles northeast of Australia. When word reached Washington that the Japanese were constructing an airfield, Admiral Ernest King ordered Chester Nimitz in Honolulu to prepare to invade Guadalcanal and nearby Tulagi, a much smaller island. King's action was a brazen one: He had issued the order without the prior knowledge or approval of either President Roosevelt or the Joint Chiefs.

Hearing of King's order in Australia, Douglas MacArthur exploded in wrath. Guadalcanal, where King planned to land ten thousand men of the 1st Marine Division, lay within the boundaries of MacArthur's Southwest Pacific domain.

King, a shrewd veteran of high-level infighting, had anticipated the angry outcries that ensued. He explained to the Joint Chiefs that he had not actually ordered Nimitz to invade the Solomons, but rather had only directed him to *prepare* for the operation in the hopes that Roosevelt and the Joint Chiefs would give it the green light.

At a tempestuous meeting on June 25, King presented to the Joint Chiefs the navy plan to invade the Solomons, an area of stinking swamps, tropical diseases, rugged mountains, cannibals, poisonous snakes, and giant rats. George Marshall was angry. He pointed out that the invasion targets were in MacArthur's theater, but the fiery admiral indicated that he would go ahead with the operation—with or without army concurrence.

Over the next three days, Marshall pondered the Solomons situation. He was irate over King's high-handedness in laying on a major operation, then expecting the Joint Chiefs to rubber-stamp it. Marshall's dark mood intensified when he received a cable from a furious MacArthur, who complained heatedly that the navy was engaged in a conspiracy to take full control in the Pacific and turn the army into an occupation force for islands seized by the marines, which were under navy command.

Finally, King and Marshall reached a compromise. MacArthur would maintain his command independence, but the line between his Southwest Pacific and Nimitz's Pacific Ocean theaters—the 160th degree of east longitude—would be moved west to the 159th degree, placing the eastern Solomons in Nimitz's bailiwick.

Buoyed by his victory over the army, King set about to expand the navy's influence in the Pacific. On July 4, he huddled with Chester Nimitz in San Francisco and laid out a grandiose strategic plan. After the Solomons were captured, King declared, the navy's next objectives would be the heavily fortified islands of Guam, Saipan, and Truk, eight hundred to one thousand miles north of the Solomons.

No doubt Nimitz was startled to learn that this strategy was King's own idea and that the President and the Joint Chiefs were unaware of and had not agreed to these operations. Nor had the navy chief taken into consideration the need to coordinate strategy with MacArthur, who, as the entire world knew, had set his sights on an eventual return to the Philippines.

After arriving back in Washington from the conference with Nimitz, King ordered Vice Admiral Robert L. Ghormley to rush from London, where he was serving as an advisor, to Noumea, New Caledonia, east of the Solomons. The vice admiral was to take command of Operation Watchtower, the code name for the invasion of Guadalcanal and Tulagi.

Within hours of reaching New Caledonia, Ghormley, a former football star at the Naval Academy, flew to Australia to coordinate operations with General MacArthur. Although Watchtower would be a navy-marines affair, MacArthur was preparing his own offensive. Three weeks earlier, he had received approval from the Joint Chiefs to seize Rabaul, a Japanese bastion on New Britain, six hundred miles northwest of Guadalcanal, on the presumption that Washington would send him adequate troops and military hardware to conduct the operation. Now it became clear to MacArthur that he would not receive the means necessary to capture Rabaul.

Admiral Ghormley and MacArthur were convinced that their forces were inadequate for simultaneously invading the Solomons and launching an offensive against Rabaul. Together they fired off a cable to the Joint Chiefs, urging a delay in both operations until they received more troops, ships, landing craft, and airplanes.

When the message reached Washington, Ernest King was furious. He charged that MacArthur was fainthearted, a strange accusation against a man renowned for his courage and boldness. King either was unaware of, or refused to recognize, the stark reality of the situation in Australia. Although combat units and aircraft had been trickling into the Land Down Under, MacArthur's forces were still few in number.

King rushed to confer with George Marshall. "Three weeks ago MacArthur stated that if he could be furnished amphibious forces and two carriers, he could push right through to Rabaul," the navy chief fumed. "He now feels that he not only cannot undertake this extended operation but not even the Solomons operation."[8]

King felt that MacArthur was sulking, refusing to cooperate in the Guadalcanal mission because he had not been appointed supreme commander of the entire Pacific. "MacArthur could not understand that he was not to manage everything," he would later growl.[9]

As the days passed, King became increasingly disenchanted with Admiral Ghormley. In New Caledonia, the vice admiral learned through the navy grapevine that King was angry over what appeared to be Ghormley's foot-dragging and his connivance with MacArthur, as King discerned it, to postpone or scuttle Watchtower. Maneuvering to protect himself, Ghormley cabled King that he had sufficient forces to invade the Solomons if MacArthur would provide air support. As Ghormley must have known, MacArthur, himself trying desperately to pry additional men and equipment from Washington, had no airpower to spare.

In the meantime, General Marshall had grown weary of constantly bickering with the navy. "King never lets up," he told Secretary of War Stimson. "He has not receded one inch from his demands on us."[10]

Field Marshal John Dill, the senior British liaison officer in Washington, was astonished by the bloodletting in Washington during the summer of 1942.

Dill cabled Field Marshal Alan Brooke in London: "The violence of inter-service rivalry in the United States these days has to be seen to be believed and is an appreciable handicap to their war effort."[11]

Early in August, an American invasion fleet of eighty-two ships sailed from New Caledonia and set a course westward for the Solomons. Five days later, on August 7, men of the 1st Marine Division, under Major General Alexander "Archie" Vandegrift, hit the beaches on Guadalcanal and Tulagi. By sundown the next day, the marines, whose average age was nineteen, had seized Tulagi and secured their primary objective, the nearly completed Japanese airfield on Guadalcanal.

Thirty-six hours after the initial landings, seven Japanese cruisers and a destroyer, cloaked by darkness off Savo Island, surprised the Allied warships shielding the troop transports and supply ships lying to off the beaches. In less than an hour, the Japanese naval force sank the American cruisers *Astoria, Quincy,* and *Vincennes,* sent the Australian heavy cruiser *Canberra* to the bottom, and inflicted damage on a cruiser and two destroyers. It was one of the worst whippings that the U.S. Navy had ever been given.

Vice Admiral Mikawa Guninchi was on the verge of a monumental victory, since the American transports and supply ships lying off Guadalcanal were easy targets. Fearful of bombing attacks after dawn, however, he gave the order to pull back. Had he bored in on the thin-skinned ships, Guninchi would have stranded Archie Vandegrift's marines on Guadalcanal with only a three days' supply of ammunition and thirty-six hours' worth of food.

Thousands of miles from the Guadalcanal violence, tension gripped Admiral Nimitz's headquarters in Honolulu. After a terse report from General Vandegrift that his marines had stormed ashore with minimal opposition, nothing more was heard from the Solomons or from Admiral Ghormley on New Caledonia. As communications are prone to do during tense battle situations, the radios had gone haywire. Two days later, communications were restored.

In Washington, a delayed report from Admiral Nimitz reached Ernest King's quarters in the early morning hours. The duty officer awakened King, who turned on a bedside lamp and read the dispatch, which told of the horrible damage that had been inflicted on the navy off Savo Island. It was the greatest shock of King's long career.

Unconvinced, the admiral told the duty officer that the decoding must have been faulty. A check with Ghormley in New Caledonia confirmed the accuracy of the report.

King promptly ordered a blackout of news on the sinkings, ostensibly to prevent the Japanese from learning of the magnitude of the American naval setback. However, he may have had more than the enemy in mind, for the Japanese in the naval force must have seen the American ships go under. Watchtower was King's baby. Perhaps he was concerned about how official Washington would react to the depressing news.

Secrecy became the password in the Navy Building. King eventually informed President Roosevelt of the catastrophe, and Secretary Knox and General Marshall were advised—several days later. Although many on King's staff were aware of the sinkings, they remained closemouthed, even fearing to engage in cautious whisperings with one another about the calamity.

Incredibly, the Joint Staff Planners (JSP), a group of about thirty senior officers from all three services, was kept in the dark, even though JSP was responsible to the Joint Chiefs for global strategy. Long after the Savo Island debacle, *New York Times* correspondent Hanson W. Baldwin, who had been in the Southwest Pacific at the time of the Guadalcanal invasion, was invited by the JSP to give his impressions of the operation.

While in the middle of his presentation, Baldwin routinely ticked off the names of the warships that had been sunk off Savo Island. Suddenly, a navy planner, Captain Charles R. Brown, leaped to his feet and, in red-faced fury, shouted, "I object to that, I object to that! Admiral King has given the strictest orders that no one is to know about this!"[12]

Baldwin was flabbergasted by the outburst. He assumed that the JSP had known all along about the sinkings. As it turned out, until that moment no one in JSP, except for King's officers, had had an inkling about the disaster.

On July 20—only four months after his escape from Corregidor—Douglas MacArthur moved his headquarters from Melbourne northward to Brisbane, twelve hundred miles closer to the oncoming Japanese. Within hours of his arrival, he learned through Magic (the code name for intercepted enemy radio messages) that a large Japanese convoy was sailing from the stronghold of Rabaul.

A few days later, Major General Tomitaro Horii's fourteen thousand veteran soldiers disembarked from the convoy and went ashore at Buna and Gona, villages on the northeastern tail of New Guinea and 110 air miles above Port Moresby, the only Allied conclave north of Australia. MacArthur concluded that Horii's force intended to climb southward over the towering Owen Stanley Mountains and seize virtually undefended Port Moresby as a springboard to Australia.

MacArthur did not know it, but Washington already had written off Australia, a continent nearly the geographical size of the United States and home to ten million people, most of whom lived along the eastern seaboard. If Australia had to be abandoned to the Japanese, the lone American base for launching offensives toward Japan would be Hawaii, in the central Pacific.

Even had MacArthur been advised that the U.S. hierarchy was prepared to scuttle Australia, the supreme commander had no intention of losing it by default. At a staff conference forty-eight hours after he reached Brisbane,

MacArthur paced back and forth as his aides looked on in silence. Pacing signaled that the general was mulling over a major problem. Suddenly, he spun around and said in a voice trembling with emotion, "I'll defend Australia in New Guinea!"

New Guinea? MacArthur's aides were stunned. With a strong enemy force driving on Moresby, they were convinced that the 1,500-mile-long island was a lost cause.

MacArthur calmed their concerns. "If you didn't expect it," he stressed, "then neither will the Japs."

Now MacArthur was confronted by the ugly logistical facts. There were three infantry divisions in Australia to send to Port Moresby, but with the Japanese navy roaming the sea-lanes, he feared a disaster might ensue should his troops be sent in ships.

Then Major General George C. Kenney, who was attending his first staff conference as MacArthur's new air chief, leaped to his feet. Short, tough, and gregarious, the fifty-two-year-old Kenney blurted, "Hell, I can land twenty-six thousand soldiers on Moresby's five airfields, keep them supplied, and provide them with all the equipment they need to drive the Jap bastards back to Buna!"[13]

Amidst the pessimism engulfing his staff, MacArthur was delighted. He threw an affectionate arm around Kenney, saying, "This fellow has given me a new and powerful brandy! I like the stuff!"[14]

Within hours, Kenney's bombers, each loaded with twenty Australian or American soldiers, began a shuttle service to Port Moresby, where Tomitaro Horii's warriors eventually were halted only a few miles from the coastal town after nearly two months of bloody fighting. Ten thousand Japanese soldiers had been lost. Among the dead was General Horii.

Despite meager manpower and resources, MacArthur launched what he called a "hit-'em-where-they-ain't" campaign up the rugged spine of New Guinea on the first lap of the five-thousand-mile ocean-and-jungle road to Tokyo.[15] Instead of launching costly frontal assaults against enemy strongholds along the coast, he would leapfrog around them, leaving their garrisons to wither on the vine.

CHAPTER 6

A Visit with Uncle Joe

WHILE DOUGLAS MACARTHUR'S FORCES in New Guinea and Chester Nimitz's marines on Guadalcanal were battling tenacious Japanese soldiers, Winston Churchill, Alan Brooke, and their entourage flew from London to Moscow on an urgent mission. They would explain to Soviet dictator Josef Stalin why the Anglo-Americans could not invade France across the English Channel that fall, but would instead strike French Northwest Africa. It was August 12, 1942.

It would be the first meeting between Churchill and Stalin. For the British, it would be a delicate confrontation, even though Stalin was supposed to be an ally. Churchill, in particular, had a deep distrust of the Soviet leader and would have to choose his words carefully. Through secret sources, the Prime Minister knew that, although the Red Army and the German Heer (army) were slaughtering one another on the battlefields of Russia, there were clandestine contacts between members of the Soviet and Wehrmacht general staffs—a bizarre situation, indeed. If it served the inscrutable Stalin's interests, Churchill felt, Anglo-American plans for Torch would not be long in reaching the eyes and ears of Adolf Hitler.

Torch security officers were concerned that Stalin, through such an act of treachery, would hope to draw the British and Americans deeper into the fighting. So Churchill decided in advance that specific dates and landing locales for Torch would be withheld from the Soviets.

Stalin, on the other hand, was convinced that the United States and Great Britain were engaged in a diabolical conspiracy to let the Soviet and German armies bleed one another into impotence, while the Western Allies sat and watched from a distance. Then, in the Soviet dictator's view, the Anglo-Americans would land forces in France and take control of most of western Europe.

On the morning after Churchill and his party arrived in Moscow, a joint session was convened in a large conference room in the Kremlin, the seat of government of the Soviet Union. Surrounded by huge walls that had stood since 1492, the Kremlin was actually a fortress a mile and a half around. It contained a bewildering number of complex buildings dating from different periods in history.

These were strange allies: Winston Churchill, an aristocrat born to wealth and a staunch pillar of capitalism, and Josef Stalin, the son of a poor cobbler and

47

a fervent missionary for the global spread of communism. It had been a shotgun wedding, one entered into to bring about the downfall of a common deadly foe: Adolf Hitler and nazism.

Once, when asked by his secretary whether he had qualms about climbing into bed with the high priest of communism, Churchill replied, "If Adolf Hitler invaded Hell I would get up in the House of Commons and speak a few words of praise for the Devil!"

Now, in the Kremlin conference room, Churchill and the five-foot, six-inch Stalin, resplendent in a field marshal's uniform, came face to face for the first time. An eerie veil of tension seemed to hang in the large chamber. Although both leaders had hordes of military and government aides present, Churchill and Stalin did most of the talking.

Stalin, blunt and calculating, and Churchill, eloquent and equally calculating, clashed almost at once. Both leaders used interpreters, which slowed the proceedings to a frustrating crawl, although the British later would learn that Stalin spoke and understood English.

For more than an hour, Churchill briefed the Soviet leader as to why the Western Allies could not attack across the English Channel in 1942. As planned, he was deliberately vague about Torch.

Churchill was a great speaker, sure of himself, always convinced that his cause was right. When he became fixed on an idea (and Torch largely had been his plan), he would argue for it relentlessly until opponents of the idea were exhausted and ready to run up the white flag of surrender.

When Churchill concluded his presentation, the chamber was silent. Finally, Stalin, through his interpreter, demanded to know of what good an offensive on the periphery of Hitler's empire would be to the Soviets, considering that the triumphant Wehrmacht already was knocking on the door of Leningrad, at the gates of Stalingrad, and less than fifty miles from Moscow. For half an hour, the British Bulldog spoke on the "enormous advantages" that would accrue to all members of the Grand Alliance by the Anglo-American invasion of North Africa.[1]

Again, silence flooded the room. Then the Soviet chief asked Churchill, "Why is Great Britain afraid to fight the Germans?"

The Prime Minister bristled at the direct accusation of cowardice. Rising to his feet, he spoke for forty minutes on the "heroic British battlefield achievements" during the war and reminded Stalin that Great Britain had stood alone against the awesome power of Hitler's war juggernaut for an entire year before the Wehrmacht plunged into the Soviet Union in June 1941.

That night over drinks, Churchill told his aides that Uncle Joe (as he and Roosevelt privately called Stalin) had "all the charm of a cobra—and is just as deadly."

When the conference reconvened early the next morning, verbal brickbats soon were being hurled. In even stronger terms, Stalin again charged that the British were cowards. Churchill, his face flushed crimson, was furious. He unleashed a torrent of oratory in defense of the British armed forces, speaking so rapidly that his interpreter could not keep up. Stalin, expressionless, listened without comment.

Calling a truce to permit tempers to cool, the British and Soviet delegations spent the following day exchanging routine written memoranda. That night, Churchill called on Stalin to bid farewell and was greeted with what passed as warmth—which should have put the Prime Minister on guard. For six hours, far into the night, the talk and the vodka flowed in equal proportions. Churchill consumed somewhat more than his share of the heady Russian beverage.

In the warm glow of fellowship, Stalin spoke admiringly of the courage of the British leaders and armed forces—a complete reversal of earlier denunciations—and praised the Prime Minister for his vision and skill in conceiving Torch. In turn, Churchill impetuously promised a second front in France in the spring of 1943, an operation that he and Field Marshal Brooke had been vehemently opposing.

Grinning amiably and nodding, Stalin replied, "I'll hold you to that promise, Mr. Prime Minister!" It appeared that the wily Soviet leader had extracted with guile (and vodka) what he had failed to obtain through bombast at the conference table: Assurance that the Anglo-Americans would launch a cross-Channel invasion soon.

Shortly after dawn, Churchill, Brooke, and their party took off for Cairo to consult with British generals now charged with facing newly promoted Field Marshal Erwin Rommel and his Afrika Korps. They were eager to reach Cairo for another reason. Jubilee, the suicide assault against Dieppe, had hit on August 19, but lack of communications prevented Churchill and his party from learning the results of the raid while in Moscow.

No sooner had Churchill's plane touched down at the Cairo airport than the group was told that Jubilee had been a major catastrophe. Sixty percent of those in the assault—3,622 men—had been killed, wounded, or captured. The Royal Air Force, which could ill afford to lose aircraft, had suffered the destruction of 106 planes, and the Royal Navy lost 550 men along with a warship and thirty-three landing craft.

Churchill sent a cable to Clement Attlee, the Deputy Prime Minister, in London: "My personal impression of Jubilee is that the results fully justify the heavy costs."

"[Jubilee] is a lesson to the people who are clamoring for an invasion of France," Field Marshal Brooke wrote with disdain in his diary. He was referring, of course, to Franklin Roosevelt, George Marshall, Dwight Eisenhower, and Henry Stimson.

If the Dieppe raid was a British machination to dissuade the Americans from pushing for a cross-Channel invasion of France in the spring of 1943, it produced results. Marshall, Eisenhower, and Stimson were stunned by the Dieppe debacle. Now their gaze was riveted on Torch.

By fits and starts, the invasion of French Northwest Africa was beginning to take shape. Led by George Patton, the Western Task Force would sail directly from Hampton Roads, Virginia, and go ashore at Casablanca. Two other task forces would depart from the United Kingdom, sail through the narrow mouth of the Mediterranean Sea at Gibraltar, and storm ashore at Oran and Algiers. After defeating whatever hostile forces might be encountered at Casablanca, Patton would drive hundreds of miles eastward to link up with the Oran and Algiers forces.

Rocky shoals lay ahead, however. On August 25, General Mark Clark, whom Eisenhower had named to direct Torch planning, was rousted out of bed at 3:10 A.M. in his apartment at the Dorchester Hotel to read a copy of a cable sent by General Marshall to Eisenhower. Forty-eight hours earlier, D-day for Torch had been set for October 15. Now, Marshall's cable stated that the U.S. Joint Chiefs felt that Torch was on too large a scale and that Algiers should be dropped as an invasion site due to "the limited military forces available."[2]

"The hazard is too great," Marshall said, "especially considering the extreme seriousness of the effect on the peoples of occupied Europe, India, and China if the United States should fail in its first major operation."[3]

Eisenhower and Clark were shocked. This was the most depressing news yet. "The war's going to be over before we even get into it!" the supreme commander said with chagrin.[4]

Both men were still downcast when they arrived at 10 Downing Street that night to dine with Winston Churchill. The British Bulldog spoke glowingly of Torch as "one of the great opportunities of the war," then abruptly asked the Americans what was on their minds. Clark, the chief planner, spoke up. He was fed up with the confused situation and with the latest change in signals.

While most young, ambitious major generals would have kept their own counsel, such was not Mark Clark's style. He felt that the Anglo-American leadership had been floundering too long.

"Mr. Prime Minister, the greatest need is for someone with necessary power to make some decisions and stick to them," Clark said bluntly. Eisenhower shifted uncomfortably in his chair; two-star American generals simply didn't speak to the Prime Minister of Great Britain in that manner. An awkward silence filled the dining room.

Undaunted, Clark added, "We're in the middle of day-to-day changes. There have been so many changes, we are dizzy. We'd like to get one definite plan so we can go to work on it."[5]

Puffing on his ever-present cigar, Churchill stared for a time at Clark. However, the Prime Minister seemed to feel that the general had hit the nail directly on the head. "I'll get in touch with President Roosevelt at once," he said evenly.[6]

Conversation and drinks flowed until 2:00 A.M. As Clark was leaving, he renewed his personal offensive. "The planners [of Torch] are tired of piddling around. Every minute counts. What we need is a green light!"[7]

Mark Clark, by pointedly ripping the indecisiveness of the Anglo-American hierarchy, had put his promising career in jeopardy. Either the high-level brass would cease "piddling around" or Clark might be sacked and spend the remainder of the war in a paper-shuffling post in the bowels of the War Department in Washington.

Churchill was true to his word. He contacted Roosevelt the next morning, and, after considerable wrangling, the two Allied leaders reached agreement. As had been originally planned, there would be three, not two, landings: Casablanca, Oran, and Algiers. Closing out the conversation, Roosevelt exclaimed, "Hurrah!" Replied Churchill, "Okay, full blast!"[8]

Within hours, the piddling resumed. A hassle broke out over the precise date for D-day, which already had been moved twice. When George Marshall told Franklin Roosevelt that Eisenhower was trying to set a firm D-day, the President held his hands together in mock prayer and said, "Please [have him] make it before election day!" Midterm congressional elections would be held on November 3.[9]

At the same time, Churchill invited Eisenhower to spend a weekend at the Prime Minister's country retreat, Chequers. Ike, a great admirer of Churchill, was on his guard, aware that the sly, eloquent Prime Minister presumably wanted something. He did. Eisenhower was pressured to designate D-day "as soon as possible." The thrust was not lost on the general: He knew that the people of Great Britain had been taking a pounding from the Luftwaffe for more than two years and were demanding that the Western Allies strike back at Hitler.

As for Mark Clark, the general was just about at the end of his tether. He called together the thirty-seven American and British officers on his staff at Norfolk House. "Some of you are less confused than others about Torch," the outspoken general said. "So let's all get equally confused!"

Late in August, Eisenhower got a severe jolt. A colonel sent by General Marshall arrived with news that the U.S. Navy would not be able to provide sufficient warships to protect George Patton's convoy on its three-thousand-mile journey from Virginia to Casablanca through waters infested by German U-boats.

Furious, Eisenhower fired off a series of cables to Admiral Ernest King in Washington, demanding a greater effort by the navy. King responded brusquely: No! There were no ships to spare.

Eisenhower persisted. So many cables flew back and forth between London and Washington that the general exclaimed, "I feel like I'm involved in a transatlantic essay contest!"[10]

In the early morning hours of September 3, Commander Harry Butcher awakened Eisenhower and handed him a cable from George Marshall. Admiral King, who had presumably been under heavy pressure from President Roosevelt, had managed to scrape up enough warships to escort Patton's task force.

Elated, Eisenhower leaped out of bed. "Thank the Lord for little favors!" he said. It was one of his favorite expressions.

In Washington, George Patton, eager to get into action, was engaged in a long-distance war of words with the navy. Cavalryman Patton would shoot from the hip in the direction of Norfolk, Virginia, where Rear Admiral H. Kent Hewitt, commander of the Western Task Force naval operation, had his headquarters at the Nansemond Hotel. Hewitt in turn would unlimber his big guns and fire verbal volleys toward Washington, where Patton had an office in a musty third-floor loft in the Munitions Building.

Impetuous by nature, Patton was inclined to underestimate the true problems of the navy and air corps, often dismissing the concerns of those services as thinly veiled cowardice. Kent Hewitt, who had earned the Navy Cross for gallantry in World War I, gave an initial impression of being deliberate, even hesitant, because he carefully weighed the pros and cons of any proposal. The stage was set for a head-on collision, which would not be long in coming.

On August 24, Admiral Hewitt, a large, gray-haired man who at the age of fifty-five was known throughout the navy for his tact and insistence on giving credit to others, and a group of his key officers flew to Washington for their first face-to-face session with George Patton. The general took an immediate dislike to the admiral's seemingly casual approach to the task. His irritation turned to hostility when Hewitt's staff interjected what Patton considered to be "defeatist views." It was almost as though the navy was trying to sabotage Torch, he thought.[11]

Then came the explosion. Patton raked the navy brass with heavy barrages of profane abuse. Minutes later, Hewitt and his aides, convinced that they could not work with a madman, got up and left the room.

Kent Hewitt was enraged. He went directly to his boss, Ernest King. Unless the army removed the combustible Patton from the Western Task Force, Hewitt declared, the navy should pull out of the Torch venture—presumably leaving Patton and his troops to swim the Atlantic.

King rushed to see George Marshall and made a formal demand: Dump Patton from command of the Western Task Force.

Marshall had no intention of scuttling the bold soldier. Outlining Patton's virtues, he offered suggestions on handling the army's bad boy and hoped that Admiral Hewitt and other navy leaders would overlook Patton's tantrums for the good of Torch.

Despite Marshall's plea to his navy counterpart, it looked as though Patton might be sacked—an outcast from the war before he even got into it. A leery Kent Hewitt, however, finally agreed to continue to work with Patton, who remained unrepentant.

Shortly after the altercation in the Munitions Building, three British planning experts arrived in Washington at the request of General Marshall to share their know-how on amphibious operations with the Americans. Astonished that the respective headquarters of Patton and Hewitt were more than two hundred miles apart, they suggested that all army and navy personnel involved in such intricate operational planning, where hour-to-hour coordination was vital, move under one roof.

Hearing of this proposal, Patton roared, "Go anywhere near that bunch of rattlesnakes? Not me!"[12]

CHAPTER 7

"Like a Bulldog Meeting a Cat"

AMONG THE MANY UNKNOWN ELEMENTS related to Torch was Dwight Eisenhower, the supreme commander of Allied Force Headquarters (AFHQ). A year earlier, he had been an obscure staff colonel in Texas. Although he had never heard a shot fired in anger, commanded so much as a combat platoon, or even been in a war zone, Eisenhower had total control of all American and British armed forces committed to the North African invasion.

Now the affable three-star general faced the ultimate challenge: Overcoming petty jealousies, towering egos, and divergent national interests in order to weld a genuine allied coalition. Eisenhower's daunting task was to prove that, despite historical precedent to the contrary, the coalition command concept could work—even thrive.

Adding to his burdens, well-meaning old army friends presented the general with a litany of failures of allied coalitions going back to the days of the Greeks, five hundred years before Christ, and on down through the centuries to the savage disputes between French and British commanders in 1940, when Hitler's war machine conquered much of western Europe.

It was whispered in Ike's ear that if Torch met with disaster—a distinct possibility—a scapegoat would be required. Eisenhower, of course, would serve as that traditional symbol of incompetence and failure.

Against this foreboding background of potential strife, an outwardly buoyant Eisenhower assembled his AFHQ staff. He was determined to create an integrated group of British and American officers—land, sea, and air—who could work together harmoniously on a daily basis, with all lines of national interests erased. Ike had no illusions. His staff officers would have to comprehend one another's accents, slang, and ingrained administrative procedures.

"When they came together for the first time," Eisenhower would say, "it was like a bulldog meeting a cat."[1]

Eisenhower named General Mark Clark as his deputy, or number-two man. Long regarded as one of the U.S. Army's brightest young officers, Clark had been wounded as an infantry captain during World War I. Taking Clark's place as commander of the U.S. II Corps (which would sail from the British Isles) was

Major General Lloyd R. Fredendall, age fifty-eight. During World War I, Fredendall had been a staff assistant to General "Black Jack" Pershing. George Marshall had selected Fredendall for the job; Eisenhower knew of him only by name. Fredendall, like Eisenhower, never had seen combat, but Marshall assured Ike that the new corps commander was an outstanding leader.

Torch naval commander was British Admiral Andrew B. "ABC" Cunningham. A man of action, the fifty-eight-year-old officer had been the acting commander of the Royal Navy's Mediterranean Fleet when war broke out in 1939 and had distinguished himself in battles with the formidable Italian Fleet. Eisenhower would come to admire many of his British colleagues, none more so than ABC.

Heading the British First Army (also to sail from Britain) would be Lieutenant General Kenneth A. N. Anderson, who had been a divisional commander in the ill-fated campaign of 1940, when the British had to rapidly evacuate France at Dunkirk and return to England, leaving behind nearly all heavy artillery, tanks, and vehicles. Anderson would prove to be a poor choice for the post.

For his own chief of staff, Eisenhower badgered George Marshall to send him Major General Walter Bedell Smith, who was serving in Washington as secretary of the general staff. Marshall finally relented and Smith, known to army friends as Beetle, arrived in London.

No sooner had the square-jawed, stern-faced Smith warmed his chair at Grosvenor Square than he succeeded in antagonizing many of the officers, both American and British. However, at age forty-eight, he rapidly became the second most powerful man in the Anglo-American military coalition. Smith was AFHQ's "no" officer. It was he who decided who would and who would not get to see Eisenhower—a duty that earned him enemies far faster than friends.

Beetle Smith coordinated the avalanche of administrative details and frequently represented Eisenhower at meetings. It was soon apparent to other top officers in AFHQ that when Smith spoke, his views were those of the supreme commander. Eisenhower trusted his chief of staff totally and considered him to be a "godsend—a master of detail with clear comprehension of the main issues." Most other AFHQ bigwigs considered Smith to be, in the words of one Briton, "a son of a bitch, first class."

Eisenhower was delighted with his chief of staff and chose to overlook the turmoil created by Smith's bellicose actions. He tried to smooth the ruffled feathers of a British general by explaining, "Remember, Beetle is a Prussian and one must make allowances for it."[2]

Another member of Ike's staff was thirty-four-year-old Kay Summersby, who had been his personal driver since the previous June. She not only impressed her boss with her ability to guide his olive drab Buick through London's maze of narrow, winding streets during blackouts, but also occasionally boosted the morale of the overburdened general with her vivacious personality.

Born Kathleen McCarthy-Morrogh on the island of Inish Beg, off the coast of Ireland, Summersby had come to London ten years earlier. When war broke out in 1939, she joined the British Auxiliary Territorial Service (ATS) as a private and was assigned to Eisenhower as his driver in the spring of 1942.

No doubt because of her beauty and engaging demeanor, tongues in Eisenhower's headquarters soon were wagging over the true relationship between the Irish divorcée and the supreme commander. Gossip intensified as the weeks passed, and staffers began referring to Summersby as "Ike's chauffeuse," a word that had connotations beyond her ability to expertly steer an automobile. Many thought Eisenhower was carrying his desire to improve American relations with the British too far.

Some even claimed that the flirtatious Kay had begun to dominate Eisenhower. On one occasion, when Ike's naval aide, Harry Butcher, and Major General Everett S. Hughes were invited to lunch with Eisenhower, the two guests gazed at each other in amazement as the supreme commander suddenly jumped to his feet and left the room after being summoned by Private Summersby.

As an Irish citizen, Summersby was officially disqualified from being privy to any secrets of Torch. Yet, as was well known at AFHQ, generals and admirals discussed top-secret matters quite openly in her presence.

On the afternoon of September 14, Summersby was idling away the time in General Eisenhower's outer office at 20 Grosvenor Square. Suddenly a voice called out, "Kay, the Big Boss wants to see you—pronto!" Eisenhower told her to get his sedan ready. They had to rush to Telegraph Cottage, his pastoral hideaway thirty minutes outside London. As the car sped through rural Kensington, Eisenhower, seated in the back with an aide, seemed preoccupied and was uncharacteristically quiet. Only once did Summersby hear him mumble something about "big doings for a lieutenant colonel. . . ."

Summersby also remained silent, for she long had made it a policy never to ask questions or interrupt Eisenhower during periods of meditation. While driving her boss in recent weeks, she had heard much top-secret talk about Torch from the backseat of the Buick. She presumed this mad dash had something to do with the invasion.

Reaching the cozy Telegraph Cottage, mysteriously named decades earlier by its elderly owner and now being rented for $32.50 per week, Eisenhower strode briskly to the garden, where he shook hands with a slightly stooped American wearing an ill-fitting uniform. The visitor later would be introduced as Lieutenant Colonel McGowan.

Inside the cottage, Summersby and two GI orderlies eavesdropped shamelessly from the kitchen window as Eisenhower and McGowan spent the afternoon in the garden whispering to each other as though German spies were hiding in the nearby bushes.

At dusk, the two whisperers moved inside next to the crackling fireplace. Within minutes, one after the other, high-level Allied military officers arrived. Soon the group was joined by U.S. Ambassador to England John G. Winant and

W. Averell Harriman, President Roosevelt's chief troubleshooter. In the kitchen, Summersby and the two GIs had their ears cocked, trying to solve the unexplained mystery of the clandestine gathering. Why were these leaders paying so much attention to a lieutenant colonel with an unmilitary bearing?

Actually, McGowan was the code name for Robert D. Murphy, the American underground chief in French Northwest Africa. A dark, heavy-set man who exuded confidence, Murphy had long advocated that the Allies launch an offensive there. He had established numerous contacts with possible Allied collaborators in the French officer corps, had knowledge of French coastal defenses, and purported to be able to fathom the often complex French army mentality.

Unbeknown to Murphy himself or to Eisenhower, he already had made a staunch enemy: Charles de Gaulle. The leader of the Free French claimed that Murphy had an extremely narrow vision of the French in North Africa. Murphy, de Gaulle held, thought that the French nation consisted of the people who dined with the American in Algiers and Oran at night.

Now, beside the roaring fireplace in Telegraph Cottage, Murphy tried to describe the complexities of French politics and the views of French army leaders, who were still smarting from the shellacking they had received from the Wehrmacht in France more than two years earlier. Eisenhower sat mesmerized, listening with "horrified intentness."

Murphy explained that three major French factions were engaged in bitter strife with one another: De Gaulle's Free French, based in London; aged Marshal Henri Philippe Pétain's puppet French government, headquartered in southern France at Vichy, which many thought was actively collaborating with the Germans; and various splinter factions of the French colonial forces in North Africa.

Murphy recommended that the Allies appoint General Henri-Honoré Giraud, an "outsider," to command French forces after the invasion. Giraud had been a junior officer in World War I. Captured by the Germans in 1940, he was imprisoned in Königstein in Saxony for two years and then pulled off a daring escape to Switzerland. In recent months, Giraud had been holed up in a country house in unoccupied France.

What Murphy failed to recognize was that the fifty-seven-year-old general was out of touch with the political situation and did not have the power to halt French resistance in North Africa. Instead, Murphy told Eisenhower that he had been assured by General Charles Mast, chief of staff to the corps commander in Algiers, that all French officers and troops would rally behind Giraud if he was to enter Algiers. His appearance would result in the Allies coming ashore unopposed.

Incredibly, Eisenhower seemed to have bought the "Giraud solution"—as did Murphy before him. There was no solid evidence, except for General Mast's viewpoint, that professional French officers, who already had soundly rejected de Gaulle's call to rally to him, suddenly would disobey the orders of their superiors and Marshal Pétain (whose orders they had obeyed for more than two years) and follow General Giraud—especially while French territory was being invaded, with Giraud on the side of the "aggressors."

But, when Murphy asked for the date of the Torch invasion, Eisenhower refused to divulge it. "Tell the French we are coming sometime in February," he lied.

Soon it was past midnight. Before departing from Telegraph Cottage, Murphy made one more strenuous pitch for Giraud. When the underground leader suggested that Giraud should be put in charge of the entire Torch invasion force on the grounds that the Frenchman outranked the three-star Eisenhower, the supreme commander waved the idea aside as ridiculous.[3]

Since the birth of Torch, the Combined Chiefs of Staff had issued a strict order that General Charles de Gaulle be kept in the dark concerning all aspects of the operation. He was not even to know of the existence of Torch. In light of this strict security edict, a group of high-level American and British officials convened in London on September 15. Along with Dwight Eisenhower and Mark Clark, those present included Ambassador John Winant and W. Averell Harriman.

The group was shocked upon reading the draft of a letter that President Roosevelt intended to send immediately to Charles de Gaulle. "We're coming into North Africa at an early date," the President wrote.

It was an incredible situation, and it dramatized the confusion rampant in the Anglo-American alliance. On the one hand, AFHQ had security officers whose only function was to make sure that de Gaulle remained uninformed about Torch; on the other, Roosevelt was about to spill the beans to the Free French leader. To make matters worse, Roosevelt suggested in his draft that one of de Gaulle's arch-rivals for control of the French army after the invasion, General Henri-Honoré Giraud, be designated commander in chief of all troops—French, British, and American.

Eisenhower, Clark, and others in the conference realized that the Free French organization was, as one of them put it, "leaky as a sieve." If the Roosevelt letter was sent, it might well serve to tip off Adolf Hitler and the Oberkommando der Wehrmacht.

A discreetly worded cable explaining the security hazards involved in such a presidential letter was transmitted to the White House. Roosevelt's naive communication to "Mon Cher Generale" was never dispatched.

In the days ahead, other security lapses rocked AFHQ. Four days after the top-level conference squashed Roosevelt's letter, an aide entered Eisenhower's office and told him that a French colonel was in the reception room, loudly demanding to see the supreme commander—immediately. Ike winced, but directed that the colonel be shown into his office.

The colonel identified himself as de Gaulle's chief of staff. Offered a chair, the Frenchman declined. He stood stiffly at attention and spoke formally in fluent English. "I am directed by General de Gaulle to inform General Eisenhower that General de Gaulle understands that the British and Americans are going to invade *French* Northwest Africa," he said. "General de Gaulle wishes to say that he expects to be designated commander in chief. Any invasion of French territory that is not under French command is bound to fail."

A long silence followed. Then Eisenhower, without changing expression, replied, "Thank you." Saluting smartly, the French colonel strode briskly from the room. His forehead furrowed, Eisenhower turned to a staff officer. "Do you suppose there has been a breach of security somewhere?"

As Torch planning progressed, a top American officer, Brigadier General Lucien K. Truscott, Jr., attended a conference at the headquarters of Combined Operations, the panel charged with planning and conducting hit-and-run raids. Broad strategy for raids in connection with Torch was outlined by British Rear Admiral Louis Mountbatten, advisor to Combined Operations.

Returning to his own office late that afternoon, Truscott, who had gone on the ill-fated Dieppe raid as an observer (and was nearly killed), scribbled notes concerning the discussion on a scratch pad. Before leaving for the day, he locked up all the papers on his desk, including the conference notes—or so he thought. Then he locked the office door.

Early the next morning, a Torch security officer, the Marquis of Casa Maury, called on General Truscott. Invited to be seated, the grim-faced marquis said, "I prefer to conduct my business standing." Taking a piece of paper from his coat pocket, the British officer unfolded it and handed it to the general. "Did you write this?" he asked.

A puzzled Truscott confessed that he had; it was a memorandum he had jotted down the previous afternoon on the Combined Operations briefing by Mountbatten. He added that he could not understand how the security officer had gained possession of it. Truscott was shocked by the reply: The memorandum had been found in the courtyard in front of the building by a gardener.

The marquis proceeded to lecture the American general on the frightening consequences that could befall Torch should Truscott's memorandum fall into the hands of German agents. Mystified as to how the notes got into the courtyard, Truscott accepted in silence the rebuke given him by an officer he outranked.

Truscott felt that his security violation might result in his being sacked by General Marshall, sent back to the United States, and disciplined—possibly reduced in rank a notch or so. The security colonel assured him that, in this instance, no harm had been done, that Truscott would no doubt be less careless in the future, and that in the interest of Anglo-American harmony, the matter would be considered closed.

In the days ahead, Truscott pondered long and hard over how the top-secret notes he had written had made their way to the courtyard. He concluded that he had inadvertently failed to lock them in his desk. But he was certain that his office door had been locked securely. The mystery would never be solved.[4]

CHAPTER 8

The French Political Mess

PILED ON TOP OF Dwight Eisenhower's mountain of military and logistics problems related to Torch was a seemingly unsolvable tangle dubbed the "goddamned French political mess" by one exasperated American general. It included bitter squabbling between factions, national pride, towering egos, and conflicting definitions of honor. Mixed up in all of this confusion was incessant jockeying for power.

For more than two years, a dispute had raged over which of two French governments was the legally constituted one. In 1940, after the German blitzkrieg crushed the French army—reputedly the world's best—in only six weeks, Maréchal de France Henri Philippe Pétain, the revered World War I hero of Verdun, decided that France must be spared needless suffering at all costs. When asked to head the French government whose capital was Vichy, Pétain felt duty-bound to accept the post in order to gain the best lot he could from the Germans for the French people.

Adolf Hitler had no intention of allowing conquered France to actually govern itself, and thus permitted Pétain to become the puppet ruler. At the age of eighty-four, the bewildered marshal was never in control of the Vichy government and was helpless to halt the constant power struggles within it.

Vichy was a pleasant resort town of thirty-two thousand on the banks of the Allier River in south central France. In the Allied world, *Vichy* came to stand for collaboration with Hitler and the Nazis.

At the time of France's surrender, the professional officers of the army and navy had to reach anguishing decisions: Should they flee to England and continue the fight under the ad hoc French government set up in London by Charles de Gaulle, or abandon the struggle and accept orders from Marshal Pétain in Vichy? Most chose to pledge their loyalty to Pétain.

Although de Gaulle was being paid a hefty salary and his Free French organization was financed by the British treasury, the lanky general despised Winston Churchill and Franklin Roosevelt. Through a curious thought process, he blamed the American President for France's defeat. De Gaulle's contempt for

Churchill knew no limits, and the Frenchman had stated privately that the British, not the Germans, were hereditary enemies of France.

For his part, Churchill contemptuously labeled de Gaulle "Joan of Arc" and railed to confidants that the Frenchman "owes everything to us."

Churchill, a perceptive man, was fully aware of the extensive damage de Gaulle was inflicting on the Western Allies' harmony and war effort. British and American leaders were convinced that once France had been liberated from the Germans, de Gaulle would make an all-out effort to establish himself as dictator. The prudence of arranging "a little accident" for the pesky French general was suggested in British intelligence circles, but Churchill and Roosevelt refused to take action against de Gaulle for a cogent reason: Ninety percent of the French people regarded him as a visible symbol of their continued resistance against their German masters.

Within the officer corps of the French army and navy, however, de Gaulle was loathed as a "traitor." Most of the officers were posted in Algeria and Morocco, longtime colonies in French Northwest Africa. Under the terms of the 1940 armistice with Germany, 110,000 French troops were permitted to garrison the two colonies, and another ten thousand were posted in unoccupied (southern) France.

This complex loyalty situation presented one of the major imponderables of Torch: Would the French army and navy vigorously resist invasion of French territory by two other nations, or would the Americans and British be welcomed as liberators and comrades-in-arms against Nazi Germany?

As planning for Torch continued at a feverish pace, ugly rumors began to surface about strong-arm tactics being used by the Free French under Charles de Gaulle. It was whispered in London that after a Frenchman had been smuggled out of his homeland and reached England, he was taken in tow by henchmen and harshly interrogated about his political views. If his opinions differed from those of de Gaulle, or if the Frenchman did not envision the general as the eventual ruler of France, he was subjected to physical abuse until he "saw the light."

While German intelligence labored mightily to unlock the secret of Allied intentions, Torch security leaks began to multiply. The looming invasion of North Africa was being discussed openly in the hotels and bars of London.

One alarming incident occurred right in the headquarters of General Eisenhower at 20 Grosvenor Square. Page 117 of the daily diary kept for the supreme commander by his aide, Harry Butcher, came up missing. It had simply vanished. This page carried a top-secret directive from the Combined Chiefs of Staff outlining objectives for Torch. A frantic search by all ranks, from the supreme commander on down, failed to turn up a clue as to the whereabouts of the missing page.[1]

Meanwhile, the American and British high commands—including President Roosevelt and Prime Minister Churchill—were bedeviled by the specter of

Soviet dictator Josef Stalin revealing to the Germans plans about the invasion of North Africa. Then, in early October, a bombshell was dropped on the Allied leaders in London and in Washington. Ivan Maisky, the Soviet ambassador to England, leaked the outline of Torch to two British newspaper correspondents.

Eisenhower, Churchill, and British security authorities were dumbfounded. Was this a devious Soviet plot? Maisky, an experienced diplomat, must have realized that leaking such crucial secrets severely jeopardized Torch. Had he acted on instructions from Stalin? There was nothing the Anglo-Americans could do about the incredible breach of security; after all, Ambassador Maisky *was* an ally.

If jitters gripped London, pessimism and doom were hovering over the eastern United States. Outwardly, General George Patton was characteristically buoyant. But on October 20—three days before his Western Task Force was to shove off from Hampton Roads near Norfolk, Virginia—the pugnacious cavalryman wrote a letter to his wife, Beatrice, with instructions that it be opened "only when and if I am definitely reported dead."[2]

To his brother-in-law and confidant, Frederick Ayer, Patton poured out his true feelings in a note: "The job I am going on is about as desperate a venture as has ever been undertaken by any force in the world's history." The general asked Ayer to take care of his wife and children "should anything happen to me."[3]

On Sunday morning, October 18, Mark Clark, Eisenhower's deputy and the chief Torch planner, walked briskly into his office at Norfolk House at 9:55 A.M. "I've got a red-hot message for you from General Marshall," said Clark's chief of staff, Brigadier General Alfred M. Gruenther.[4]

The message was actually sent to General Eisenhower. Clark had just started to read it when the red telephone, a direct scrambled line between Norfolk House and 20 Grosvenor Square, jangled impatiently. Clark snatched up the receiver and growled, "Hello!"

"Come over," Eisenhower directed. "Right now!" The supreme commander hung up without waiting for a reply.

Clark rushed the two miles to Grosvenor Square and soon was conferring with a grim Eisenhower.

"When do I go?" Clark asked.

"Right away," was the reply.

The text of the cable from Marshall relayed a message received from Robert Murphy (code name: Colonel McGowan), the American underground chief who was then in Algiers. (Murphy's formal title was Consul of Embassy on Special Mission, an impressive handle for a spy.) Murphy said that he had been contacted by General Charles Mast, chief of staff to the French corps commander in Algiers. Mast had urgently requested that an American delegation slip into North Africa to confer with him and other French officers on Allied plans for Torch. It had been General Mast who had assured Murphy a few weeks earlier that French army and navy leaders would rally behind General Henri Giraud if Giraud were to appear in Algiers on the eve of D-day for Torch.

Mast had specified that the American delegation should come to Algeria by submarine and that it should be headed by a senior general officer. Mark Clark was itching to be that senior general; Eisenhower already had Clark in mind for the perilous task.

Mast had stipulated as the rendezvous date the night of October 21, only three days away. Clark selected the U.S. officers to accompany him: Brigadier General Lyman L. Lemnitzer,[5] Colonel A. L. Hamblen, U.S. Navy Captain Jerauld Wright, and Colonel Julius C. Holmes, a political expert who spoke French fluently.

Clark was mindful that the summons to Algiers could be a trick, perhaps orchestrated by the German Abwehr to capture him and obtain the invasion plans. Before leaving, the general left a note to be delivered to Mrs. Clark in Washington in the event he did not return.

Early on the morning of October 19, Clark and his party climbed aboard a B-17 Flying Fortress, the *Red Gremlin*, piloted by Major Paul Tibbets. Clark had replaced the two stars on his uniform with the silver leaves of a lieutenant colonel. Should he fall into hostile hands, he might have a better chance of escaping if his captors did not know immediately that they had bagged a top American general.[6]

It was not reassuring to any of the delegation to note that all the secret documents were being carried in a tube heavily weighted to sink in the event the Flying Fortress was shot down over the sea.

Lifting off from an airfield at Polbrook, seventy-five miles northwest of London, the B-17 set a course for Gibraltar, the huge British rock at the mouth of the Mediterranean Sea. While the flight was in progress under strict radio silence, Dwight Eisenhower received an alarming message from Robert Murphy in Algiers, who said he had been invited to a secret rendezvous with the chief of Vichy French intelligence, a session held in a dark, lonely farmhouse. Murphy was shocked by what he had learned: The French intelligence officer had been told by both the Germans and the Japanese that French Northwest Africa was about to be invaded by the Allies.

Hitler, the French officer had told Murphy, was vigorously "urging" French leaders to resist the Americans and British to the utmost. Otherwise, Hitler's spokesman threatened, the Wehrmacht might be rushed in to seize the French colonial territories of Morocco and Algeria.

At Gibraltar, the *Red Gremlin* touched down at the airstrip and the delegation was whisked by automobiles with drawn blinds to the house of Gibraltar's governor, Lieutenant General F. N. Mason-McFarlane. There, a solemn conference was held with three British admirals. Clark, customarily resolute, gained no solace from the talks. There were too many unknown factors; the mission had been mounted with too much haste.

Later that night, the American party scrambled aboard the British submarine *Seraph*, skippered by Royal Navy Lieutenant Norman Ambury Auchileck Jewell. Brimming with confidence and enthusiasm, the young officer buoyed the spirits of Clark and the others. Also in the underwater craft were British Commando Captain Godfrey B. "Jumbo" Courtney and a few of his men, who would go ashore with the landing party.

That night, the *Seraph* ran on the surface. Clark had never been in a submarine, so he maneuvered his way through cramped spaces and was impressed by the cheerfulness and efficiency of the crew, most of them youngsters. None knew Clark's identity, and he was not wearing any insignia of rank.

"Do you know what the *Seraph* is up to?" Clark asked a pleasant, tow-headed teenager.

"Oh, yes, sir," was the prompt reply. "We were told that we're taking a bunch of crazy Americans on some crazy mission."[7]

Nearing the Algerian coast, the submarine slipped below the waterline for the remainder of the journey. Just before dawn on October 21, Lieutenant Jewell surfaced *Seraph* off the rendezvous point. The sea was calm. On shore, a flashing white light was spotted. But it was too near daylight to land, so the sub went down again, and the passengers had to spend another day underwater.

Suddenly, the boat's radio crackled. It was "Colonel McGowan" calling from Algiers, sixty miles away. Before shoving off from Gibraltar, Mark Clark had arranged for Robert Murphy to contact the French conspirators on shore and set a new date for the rendezvous if the Clark party did not arrive in time. "McGowan" reset the session for the next night.

Just after midnight of October 22, a white light again flashed from a house on shore. Silently, the Americans began scrambling into tiny folboats, frail and tippy craft, for the long paddle to the beach. Reaching shore, Clark and the others made a dash for the cover of some woods a hundred yards inland. There were ominous rustling noises ahead. Several dark figures were picking their way down the incline. The Americans pulled their pistols and froze.

Out of the darkness a low American voice from the unknown group called out softly, "Welcome to North Africa!" It was "Colonel McGowan." With him were officers of the French underground.

Rapidly, the two groups climbed up the steep path to the rendezvous, a red-roofed French colonial villa of white stone enclosing a courtyard. Only a hundred feet away was the main highway to Algiers. The villa's wealthy owner, Jacques Tessier, had sent five Arab servants away for several days to protect the secrecy of the conference.[8]

"Where's General Mast?" Clark asked.

"General Mast is driving from Algiers," a French officer replied. "He will be here at about 5:00 A.M."

At the anticipated time, Mast drove up. Clark, Mast, and Robert Murphy immediately launched into a discussion of military strategy. Not knowing where Mast's true allegiance lay, Clark talked only in generalities—most of them lies. He conveyed the impression to Mast that the Allies were only in early planning stages for an offensive "somewhere in the Mediterranean." Actually, General Patton's task force already had sailed from the United States.

It was an uncomfortable moment when General Mast, a pleasant and courtly soldier, asked, "How large will the force be?"

"More than half a million men," Clark responded with his fingers figuratively crossed. "And we can put in about two thousand aircraft and hundreds of warships."

Mast was deeply impressed by such awesome power. Actually, there would be about 112,000 troops coming ashore, supported by 160 aircraft.

Mast repeatedly insisted that General Henri Giraud must be the supreme commander of the operation. What's more, Mast declared, the invaders must have nothing to do with Admiral Jean Darlan, the leader of Vichy France's armed forces.

At noon, Mast had to depart for Algiers. Nazi agents had been tailing him, he explained, and he did not want to arouse suspicions by his prolonged absence.

It was about 4:00 P.M. when the telephone rang in the villa. Monsieur Tessier answered, then whirled around and shouted, "Get out! The police will be here in a few minutes!"

French officers dashed away in every direction, jumped into cars, and sped off to Algiers. The Frenchmen's lives would be in jeopardy if they were caught conspiring with the enemy.

Tessier motioned the Americans through a trapdoor from the patio into a dark, damp wine cellar. Clutching musette bags loaded with incriminating documents of coastal defenses and French troop dispositions obtained from Mast, Clark and the other Americans hustled into the chamber. Moments later, a police car pulled up in a swirl of dust. Four French policemen leaped out and barged into the house. Down below, Clark held his carbine in ready position.

Tessier greeted the policemen warmly, offered them drinks, and clanked bottles around. Down in the wine cellar, the grim intruders huddled; they could hear footsteps as the policemen searched the premises. Finally, they told Tessier that they would have to drive back to town to check with their chief for further instructions. But, the stern policemen assured Tessier, they were convinced that something suspicious was afoot.[9]

"We'd better get the hell out of here!" Clark whispered after the police had driven away. His companions needed no urging. The Americans hid in a nearby woods until darkness, then stole to the beach, recovered the folboats that had been concealed, and paddled out to the *Seraph*, three-quarters of a mile offshore.[10]

Arriving back in London, Clark was greeted like a conquering hero. Winston Churchill insisted on a private session to hear from Clark the details of the incredible venture. Then, Eisenhower took the general to Buckingham Palace to meet King George, who told Clark, "I know all about you. You're the one who took that fabulous trip!"[11]

Despite the huzzahs poured on Clark, the bold mission had achieved almost nothing. Only one French general—Charles Mast—was contacted and, as a staff officer, he commanded no troops. The "goddamned French political mess" remained just that on virtually the brink of D-day for Torch.

A few days later, on the morning of November 5, a heavy rain was pounding an airport near Bournemouth, England. Wind gusts rocked the six four-engine Flying Fortresses that squatted like ducks on a pond, waiting to take off. These aircraft would carry Eisenhower, Clark, and other brass to the Torch command post at Gibraltar.

Major Paul Tibbets, pilot of the *Red Gremlin* and flight commander, approached Eisenhower, who would ride in Tibbets's plane. His professional opinion was that it would be highly dangerous to take off in the driving rainstorm, but it was up to the supreme commander to make the crucial decision. Eisenhower had no choice. He had to reach Gibraltar with his key officers or Torch could fall apart.[12]

"Go!" the general ordered, strapping on his seat belt.

The Flying Fortress wave-hopped, seldom rising more than a hundred feet above the water. Rain, fog, and virtually zero visibility plagued the pilots. A sudden downdraft could plunge the airplanes into the ocean, leaving Torch rudderless and in chaos. Finally, the Rock of Gibraltar neared, and the *Red Gremlin* began climbing. Tibbets called from the pilot's compartment to Eisenhower, "General, this is the first time I have ever had to *climb* to get into a landing pattern after a long trip!"

Eisenhower's underground command post on Gibraltar, though safe from the heaviest bombings, was cold, damp, and dismal. Cut out of solid stone in recent months, the supreme commander's office was a half mile inside the Rock. Almost immediately, Eisenhower called in his key officers. The subject: Henri Giraud, the French four-star general on whom the Western Allies were depending to halt or minimize the bloodshed when the invasion hit. Just before departing England, Eisenhower had received an urgent message from "Colonel McGowan" (Robert Murphy) in Algiers: "Unless Kingpin [Giraud's code name] lends his name to the invasion, the French may resist desperately."

Dwight Eisenhower was now a powerless commander. His three task forces already had sailed from the United States and from the British Isles. All the ships were maintaining strict radio silence, so Eisenhower had no way of influencing the Torch plan. The Rubicon had been crossed.

While the conference—actually more of a bull session—was going on in Eisenhower's office, British Admiral Andrew Cunningham, naval commander for Torch, stuck his head into the cubbyhole with significant news: General Giraud had been spirited out of southern France on the HMS *Seraph*, the same submarine that had carried Clark and his party to Algeria for the supersecret rendezvous with General Mast two weeks earlier.

Giving orders to his crew was the same self-assured young skipper, Lieutenant Norman Jewell. Technically, however, he was not in charge of the boat once Giraud was safely aboard. The French general had specified that he was to be picked up by an American submarine. The British had shelled the French fleet to keep it out of German hands in 1940, and Giraud refused to ride in a British submarine.

No American submarines were present in the Mediterranean, so to preserve General Giraud's honor, an American officer, Navy Captain Jerauld Wright, was placed in technical command of the *Seraph*. Wright had a pronounced handicap: He knew virtually nothing about submarines, so Norman Jewell ran the show. During the trip, however, Giraud refused to speak with Jewell; anything the Frenchman had to say was told to Wright, who relayed the verbal message to Lieutenant Jewell.[13]

A few hours later, Gibraltar received a radio signal from a Catalina flying boat. It had picked up Giraud from the submarine and was bringing him to Gibraltar.

That message triggered a renewal of Giraud discussions in Eisenhower's office. Admiral Cunningham suggested that since Giraud would soon be "in hand," the Allies should issue statements in the Frenchman's name. Translation: Giraud, in essence, would be arrested once he reached Gibraltar and held incommunicado indefinitely.

Eisenhower thought that was a marvelous scheme. On reflection, however, he finally rejected the machination as being "too double-crossy."[14]

In the meantime, two thousand miles east of Gibraltar in Egypt, General Bernard Montgomery was finalizing plans for Operation Lightfoot, a British Eighth Army offensive against Erwin Rommel's Afrika Korps and Italian troops. Montgomery intended to drive westward along the Mediterranean for hundreds of miles and link up with Torch forces that, if things went well, would be attacking eastward. If Torch and Lightfoot were successful, Rommel would be trapped in Tunisia. Montgomery's all-out effort would kick off from the hard sand, stone outcroppings, and camel scrub of the desert near a small group of Arab huts known as El Alamein.

Even before the crucial battle began, Rommel's army was doomed. Confronted by larger, better-equipped British Empire forces, denied accurate intelligence, bombed and shelled by day and by night, betrayed in each major move he made by Ultra (a supersecret British wireless monitoring operation), Rommel was a general without hope.

A deep purple dusk was settling over El Alamein on October 23, 1942. It was strangely quiet. Then, at precisely 9:40 P.M., the eastern sky was lit with the mightiest tornado of man-made fire that had occurred so far in the war. Several thousand shells were raining down every minute. Lightfoot had been launched.

CHAPTER 9

Dealing with "Selfish, Conceited Worms"

ON GIBRALTAR AT MIDAFTERNOON ON NOVEMBER 7, 1942—D-day minus one—General Henri Giraud was escorted into Dwight Eisenhower's office. Although dressed in rumpled civilian clothes and sporting a dark growth of beard, Giraud maintained a precise military bearing. Eisenhower and the Frenchman shook hands. Almost at once, the scenario went haywire.

Although Giraud was thought to understand and speak English, he insisted that a French interpreter be used. With time at a premium, it was a maddening request and stretched out the discussions. Eisenhower briefed the visitor on the invasion plan: H-hour at some beaches was less than ten hours away. It was explained that what was wanted was Giraud's signature on a letter stating that the United States, anticipating Adolf Hitler's intention of seizing French Northwest Africa, was beating the Germans to the punch and was calling on all French fighting men to rally to the Americans. The letter concluded by stating that Giraud would "resume my place in combat among you."

Giraud's reaction was a prolonged, icy silence. "Now," he finally said through the interpreter, "let's get it clear as to my part. As I understand it, I am to assume command of all Allied forces and become the supreme commander in North Africa."

Eisenhower and Mark Clark were stupefied. Then the Frenchman dropped another bomb. He insisted that the invasion target be shifted to the coast of southern France. Eisenhower, hard-pressed to keep his temper under control, argued with Giraud for an hour. He promised the Frenchman the governorship of French Northwest Africa, plus ample finances to build an army. To all of the offers, Giraud replied, "Non!" Unless the target was switched to southern France and he was designated Allied supreme commander, he would not cooperate or participate.

Speaking through the interpreter, the Frenchman said, "General Giraud cannot accept a subordinate command position. His honor as a soldier would be tarnished."

After seven exhaustive hours of wrangling, Clark, who had a sharp tongue when riled, took over the persuasion efforts. Always it was the same: "*I* am General Henri-Honoré Giraud! My prestige! My family!"

Only because Robert Murphy had insisted that Giraud's name was "something to conjure with" and could be used to avoid much French and American bloodshed did the ridiculous dialogue continue. Eisenhower was convinced that Giraud, who didn't command a single soldier, was stalling and planned to sit on the fence for forty-eight hours to see how the invasion was progressing before committing himself to the Allies.

Finally, Clark said, "We would like for the honorable general to know that the time for his usefulness to the Allies is *now*. After tonight we have no need for the honorable general."

Giraud bristled. "Then I shall return to France immediately!" he vowed.

"How are you going back?" Clark asked.

"By the same means that I got here."

"Like hell you will!" the American general snapped. "That was a one-way submarine you were on!"

Giraud, stone-faced, made no reply. An exasperated Clark instructed the interpreter: "Tell him this—if you don't go along, honorable general, you're going to be out on your ass in the snow!"[1]

Again, the Frenchman remained silent. All parties were pretty well exhausted, so it was decided to break up the session. D-day was only two hours away.

On reaching the office door, the Frenchman turned and spoke in English. "General Giraud will be a spectator at this affair!"[2]

At the precise time the American generals were arguing with the recalcitrant Giraud at Gibraltar, across Northwest Africa the intricate coup that Robert Murphy had orchestrated with pro-Allied French officers was set in motion. Its purpose was to establish Henri Giraud as undisputed leader of French forces in Morocco and Algeria to ensure that the American and British invaders would be greeted as liberators.

Just before midnight, with the first American soldiers to storm ashore in two hours, Murphy climbed into his dusty old sedan and raced to the hillside home of General Alphonse Juin in suburban Lambiridi. Juin, whose arm had been badly mangled in previous fighting, was the senior French officer in Northwest Africa. His ultimate loyalty was unknown to Allied headquarters, so he had not been told in advance of the invasion.

At 12:30 A.M. on D-day, Murphy talked his way past the platoon of Senegalese guards protecting Juin's villa and banged loudly on the front door. Moments later, a sleepy general, clad in striped pajamas, slowly opened the portal. Without preamble, the American told Juin that a mighty American armada was lying offshore and that assault troops would land within the hour.

Juin, who had graduated from St. Cyr (the French West Point) at the top of a class that included Charles de Gaulle, was furious to learn what was transpiring without his prior knowledge. Murphy tried to calm him down, but the fifty-four-year-old general refused to be placated, even when Murphy assured him that the United States was invading French territory at the specific request of General Henri Giraud.

Juin bristled. "Where is Giraud?" he snapped.

Murphy had to admit that he didn't know. At that moment Giraud was far away, fast asleep on Gibraltar.

Recovering from his shock and anger, Juin pledged his loyalty to the Allied cause. Then Murphy was in for a jolt: Juin would not announce his decision until he had checked with Admiral Jean-François Darlan, commander of all French armed forces and number-two man in the Vichy regime.

After the fall of France in 1940, Admiral Darlan, as commander of the powerful French Fleet, had wormed his way to the post of vice president of the Council of Ministers in the Vichy government. He had collaborated with the Germans and had run the government of the aged Henri Pétain from February 1941 to April 1942.

Darlan, Juin told Murphy, happened to be in Algiers at the present time, holding vigil at the bedside of his young son Alain, who had been stricken with polio.[3] Despite Darlan's connection with Hitler's puppet Vichy government, Winston Churchill had felt all along that the admiral was the one French leader who could prevent bloodshed during the Torch operation.

Juin telephoned the residence where Darlan was staying and told him that the American consul was at his villa with startling news. Speeding through the streets of blacked-out Algiers in his limousine, Darlan arrived within twenty minutes. Upon hearing the news, the admiral exploded.

"I have known for a long time that the British were stupid," he bellowed at Murphy. "But I've believed the Americans were more intelligent. Apparently you have the same genius as the British for making massive blunders."

After Darlan's tirade had run its course, Murphy asked whether the admiral would cooperate with the invaders should Marshal Pétain approve. Of course he would, Darlan replied. The admiral called in an aide and dictated a message to Pétain in Vichy. When Darlan started to leave the villa to send the message, however, he discovered that General Juin's Senegalese guards had been replaced by fifty pro-Allied French aspirants (officer candidates), who earlier had been alerted by Robert Murphy.

Darlan erupted in a new fit of anger, declaring that Murphy had committed treachery by placing the aspirants around the villa and, in essence, making the Vichy leader a prisoner. His suspicions were reinforced when the aspirant leader declared that he had orders to allow no one out of the villa except Murphy. Juin, of course, was also a prisoner.

While awaiting developments, Murphy got up to look out the front door. Now it was his turn to be stunned. The aspirants had vanished; in their place were members of the national police, whose allegiance was to Juin.[4] The tables had been turned again. Now Murphy was the prisoner.

Murphy continued to urge Darlan to send cease-fire orders to Algiers, Casablanca, and Oran. Darlan refused to do so until he held a face-to-face meeting with General Eisenhower. Impossible at this time, the American declared. Then Darlan swore that he would in no way cooperate with General Giraud, who earlier had stressed to Eisenhower that he would not work with Darlan.

Elsewhere in Algiers, General Charles Mast, who had held the secret rendezvous with Mark Clark two weeks earlier, flashed an order to the sixteen thousand soldiers in the region: "Do not, repeat not, oppose but assist American landings."

In less than thirty minutes, however, Lieutenant General Louis-Marie Koeltz, commanding the 19th Région Militaire in Algiers, countermanded Mast's order: "Resist any invasion by foreign troops with all the means at your disposal."

The conflicting orders triggered enormous confusion among French forces in Algiers. Some units received Mast's order, but not that of Koeltz. Others received only Koeltz's directive. Others got both orders.[5]

Koeltz also ordered Mast arrested for treason and replaced him with Major General Pierre Roubertie. But Mast could not be found. At 12:45 A.M., he was perched on a cliff at Cap Sidi Ferruch, ten miles west of Algiers, to await the arrival of the Americans.

At the same time, more than one thousand miles west of Algiers in Casablanca, Major General Émile Béthouart, commander of the Casablanca Division and a confederate of Henri Giraud, hopped into a jeep and raced fifty miles to Rabat, headquarters of the French army in Morocco. Béthouart was escorted by a battalion of Colonial Moroccan Infantry, men who had fled France after the German occupation.

Béthouart confronted Major General Georges Lascroux, in charge of army headquarters, demanding that he cooperate with the invading Americans "in the name of General Henri Giraud." Lascroux balked, so Béthouart had him arrested and hauled away.

Next, Béthouart buttonholed the commander of French air forces in Morocco, Major General Louis Lahouelle. Confused by the sudden turn of events, Lahouelle hesitated, then said he would fight the invaders. Béthouart responded by having his Colonial Moroccans jail Lahouelle.

At the same time, Vice Admiral François Michelier, naval commander in Morocco and a die-hard Vichyite, was approached with a virtual ultimatum by Lieutenant Colonel Eugène Mollé, General Béthouart's chief of staff. It said, in essence, to cooperate with American landings—or else. Michelier was furious. He shouted at Mollé that Béthouart was stupid and a naive victim of an elaborate Allied hoax. He called in guards and had Mollé arrested.

In Rabat, five-star General Auguste Paul Noguès, resident general of Morocco, was handed a letter by General Béthouart stating that Henri Giraud, backed by American warships, troops, and planes, was taking command of all French forces in Northwest Africa. Giraud, the document declared, had appointed Béthouart to command the French troops in Morocco. Noguès also was informed in the letter that Giraud was issuing orders for French forces not to oppose imminent landings.

Noguès appraised the confusing situation as he saw it. Admiral Michelier had issued orders to resist, and a telephone check with the commanders of the Meknes and Marrakech garrisons confirmed that they were remaining under Noguès's orders and not going over to General Giraud.

Noguès acted. A heavily armed regiment disarmed Béthouart's Colonial Moroccans. Clearly, the coup had fallen flat on its face; Henri Giraud's name had not sparked the magic that had been anticipated. Noguès had Béthouart arrested and sent to Meknes to stand trial for treason.[6]

At 4:30 A.M. on D-day, an exhausted Dwight Eisenhower fell into a deep sleep on a cot in his office at Gibraltar. Two and a half hours later, he was up and conferring with his staff. Talk shifted back to Giraud. Staff members felt that something had to be done with the recalcitrant Frenchman, perhaps "a little airplane accident." A British general posted to Gibraltar allowed as how he had "a good body disposal squad if needed."[7]

Eisenhower rejected such extreme measures and, once again, in the interest of minimizing bloodshed, sent for Giraud.

A new technique of coercion was put into practice. Instead of bribes and threats, the Big Lie was used. As Giraud listened in silence, Eisenhower vastly exaggerated the size of the invading forces and reported that the three landings had been highly successful. Actually, only garbled messages had been received from Algiers and Oran, nothing from George Patton at Casablanca. For all Eisenhower knew, Torch may have been a disaster.

Giraud seemed impressed and agreed to Eisenhower's earlier offer to become commander of French troops in Northwest Africa. The Big Lie apparently had paid off.

A stirring proclamation, urging French soldiers and sailors not to resist the invaders, was drawn up by Eisenhower, and Giraud's name—without the Frenchman's knowledge—was signed to it. The exhortation was broadcast to Algiers, Casablanca, and Oran. Only later would Gibraltar learn that virtually no French officer or soldier paid heed to the Giraud proclamation. At each of the invasion locales, Frenchmen were fighting and dying. So were Americans.

As the hours ticked past, Eisenhower grew more angry and frustrated, especially after learning that French generals in Northwest Africa were arresting and counterarresting one another in what would have been a comic opera scenario had the stakes not been so enormous. "All those stupid Frogs have a single thought—*me!*" he barked to his staff.[8] His reaction was equally heated when told that Admiral Darlan refused to talk to any Allied general other than him: "What I need around here is a damned good assassin!"

While anxiously awaiting more information from his invasion forces, Eisenhower vented his anger against French leaders in a cable to his chief of staff, Beetle Smith, in London: "Giraud wants to be a big shot, a bright and shining light, and the acclaimed savior of France. So does Darlan."[9] He concluded his outburst to Smith by declaring, "It's the petty intrigue and the necessity of dealing with little, selfish, conceited worms that call themselves men."[10]

Early on the morning of November 9—D-day plus one—Mark Clark lifted off in the *Red Gremlin* from Gibraltar's airstrip to fly to Algiers on a crucial assignment as Eisenhower's troubleshooter. He would meet with Vichy French leaders in Northwest Africa in an effort to halt the bloodshed, secure the French Fleet (based across the Mediterranean in southern France), and get on with the war against Nazi Germany. Clark held no illusions that his task would be a simple one. He would be going into a lion's den of feuding Frenchmen.

Earlier that morning, Clark had asked Gibraltar Governor General Mason-McFarlane to draw out Henri Giraud's views on Admiral Darlan. Giraud bristled at the mention of Darlan's name, but finally conceded that in order to stop the fighting and get the French Fleet, a place for Darlan "might be found." Under Giraud's command, of course.

At almost the same time in Algiers, Robert Murphy sounded out Admiral Darlan's views on Giraud. The Vichyite screwed up his face, then grudgingly huffed that Giraud, who had commanded the French Seventh Army against the Wehrmacht in 1940, "might be capable of leading a division."

Less than an hour after Mark Clark had set a course for Algiers, Henri Giraud lifted off in a Hudson bomber, bound for the same destination. Giraud had refused to ride with Clark and demanded his own aircraft for the trip.

A few minutes after 5:00 P.M., Clark's B-17 bomber, escorted by thirteen Spitfire fighters, touched down at Maison Blanche Airport on the outskirts of Algiers. In his briefcase he carried a tersely worded document signed by Eisenhower, so that there would be no misunderstanding of Clark's authority to speak and act for the supreme commander.

Shortly after Clark's arrival at the fashionable St. George Hotel, he received shocking news: General Giraud, on whose name the Americans had counted to halt the fighting, was being rejected by all the French leaders in Northwest Africa. None would even meet with him, and many considered him a traitor to France.

After dinner, Clark, who had slept only briefly during the past sixty hours and was near exhaustion, decided to retire in order to be ready for the next morning's anticipated fireworks with the French. Before entering his bedroom, the general said to an aide, "What a mess! Why do soldiers have to get mixed up in [political] things like this?"[11]

Just past 9:00 A.M. the next day, a refreshed Clark strode into a large, ornate conference room in the St. George to confront a galaxy of French generals and admirals. Customarily gracious and friendly, Clark had changed personalities. He was deliberately stone-faced in order to impress upon the would-be allies that America meant business.

Clark took his seat at the head of a long, polished table. Arrayed along each side were the grim French officers. Tension was high. For nearly a minute, Clark said nothing. He sat ramrod straight in his chair, glancing up and down the two rows of French officers, most of whom were much older than the American and all of whom outranked him. The Frenchmen squirmed uncomfortably under the scrutiny of the lanky officer. Until the previous day, they had never heard of him.

To Clark's left sat Admiral Darlan, who, the American noticed, had watery eyes and seemed nervous, uncertain, and ill at ease. On Clark's right, General Alphonse Juin, commander of French forces in Northwest Africa, sat silently, staring straight ahead. Among the other French leaders was General Louis-Marie Koeltz, who two days previously had ordered his forces to resist the invasion and had locked up Giraud's protégé, General Émile Béthouart.

Staring coldly at the short, stubby, perspiring Darlan, Mark Clark said to Robert Murphy, the underground chief who was acting as translator, "Tell Admiral Darlan that we have work to do to meet the common enemy [Germany]. Is he ready to sign the terms of the armistice? It will cover all French forces in Northwest Africa. It is essential that we stop this waste of time and blood!"[12]

Darlan mopped his perspiring brow with a handkerchief. Finally, he stammered that he had to send a synopsis of the terms to Marshal Pétain in Vichy, but that there could be no reply until the Council of Ministers met there later that day.

Angered by this obvious stall, Clark banged the table with his fist. "Do you understand," the American asked icily, "that relations between France and the United States were broken off [by Pétain] in the last twenty-four hours?"

Darlan, fumbling with his papers, looked down at the table and said that he had no official confirmation. "I have been given strict orders [by Vichy] not to enter negotiations until orders arrive from Marshal Pétain," he said. Clark's fist again struck the table, and Darlan quickly added, "However, my associates and I feel hostilities are fruitless."

Clark's histrionics were calculated primarily to galvanize the French leaders into halting the bloodshed. The American was also frustrated by having to deal with Darlan, whom the Torch generals had dubbed the Little Fella. Clark, like Eisenhower, regarded the admiral with distaste, considering him to be a crass opportunist.

Now, with the Anglo-Americans ashore in strength and apparently gaining momentum, Darlan was showing signs of climbing aboard the Allied bandwagon as Mark Clark had hoped he would. With few exceptions, French commanders in Northwest Africa were refusing to bring their forces over to the side of the Allies without authorization from senile Marshal Pétain in Vichy.

Despite his nervous demeanor, the admiral proved to be a tough and nimble-minded adversary at the conference table. Darlan knew—as did Clark—that he held a number of aces in this close-to-the-vest verbal poker game. Darlan realized that the Torch invaders could not turn eastward and link up with General Bernard Montgomery's British Eighth Army while at the same time maintaining law and order among twenty-one million Arabs of unknown loyalty and hundreds of thousands of Frenchmen in Algeria and Morocco, most of whom were obedient to Marshal Pétain. Only a cooperative French establishment could maintain order behind Allied lines when Eisenhower began driving eastward.

As the morning wore on, the debate grew increasingly tense. Clark's fist was becoming raw. Still, Darlan refused to order French forces to cease fighting. Clark threatened to throw Darlan in jail. Then he made an even more drastic threat: He would lock up all the French generals and admirals in the room, and the Allies would form their own government. Darlan shrugged as if to say, "Go right ahead."[13]

Finally, Darlan asked to meet alone with his commanders. Clark and the other Americans left the room. When the general rejoined the conference, Darlan wordlessly handed over an order he was willing to send out over his signature: All ground, sea, and air forces in French Northwest Africa were to cease fighting immediately, return to their barracks, and remain neutral.

Mark Clark silently read the order without expression. Inwardly, he was elated.

Robert Murphy escorted Darlan to his waiting car. Before climbing in, the Little Fella turned to the American and said evenly, "Would you please do me a favor? Remind Major General Clark that I am a five-star admiral. He should cease shouting at me and treating me like a junior lieutenant!"[14]

At the same time that Allied troops were storming ashore in the darkness in French Northwest Africa, Adolf Hitler's private train was rattling through the Bavarian hills of southern Germany on its way to Munich, where Hitler would address a rally of the Nazi party faithful. Dawn was breaking when the train was flagged down at a small station outside Munich. After a night of military conferences, the Führer was asleep.

Walther Hewel, a civilian advisor to Hitler, was summoned to the stationmaster's office to receive an urgent telephone call from the Foreign Ministry in Berlin. An excited voice told him of the Allied landings.

Hewel rushed back to the train. A hurried conference was held with Hitler's top military advisor, General Alfred Jodl. They decided to awaken the Führer and tell him of the invasion. Although he had been aware for several days that large Allied convoys were sailing toward Gibraltar, Hitler had been hoodwinked by Allied deception machinations into believing that the convoys were bound for the eastern Mediterranean, hundreds of miles from Algiers and Oran.

It was in the eastern Mediterranean that a large number of German submarine wolf packs were lying futilely in wait.

Despite his surprise, Hitler immediately moved to counter the invasion. Dancing to the Führer's tune, Premier Pierre Laval of the Vichy government requested that the Wehrmacht "defend" the unoccupied (southern) half of France. Shifty-eyed and devious, Laval had long catered to his Nazi masters, acting in the name of white-haired Marshal Pétain. Laval had pushed through the puppet Vichy government every law that Hitler wished to enact.

On November 11, in response to Laval's request, German spearheads were racing southward to take over the Mediterranean coast of France. Hitler also had covetous eyes cast on the French Fleet based at Toulon.

When German forces descended on the port, French admirals gave an agonizing order: Scuttle the proud fleet, the world's fourth largest. Battleships, cruisers, destroyers, submarines, small craft—seventy-three in all—died by their own hand in Toulon harbor.

CHAPTER 10

Uproar over the Little Fella

AT HIS OFFICE in the capital building in Vichy, the elderly Marshal Henri Pétain was shakily holding the radio message from Admiral Jean Darlan in Algiers. The communication asked Pétain's permission for a cease-fire in French Northwest Africa. The old soldier gave his approval to Darlan's request. It was November 11, 1942.

At the same time, Pierre Laval was driving toward Munich for a conference with Adolf Hitler when he heard the cease-fire news on the radio. He rushed to the nearest telephone, called Pétain, and persuaded the befuddled marshal to reverse his own order. Pétain did Laval's bidding and ordered Darlan arrested for treason.

In Algiers, Darlan was devastated. Seeking to get back in Pétain's good graces, the Little Fella performed yet another flip-flop, telling Mark Clark, "I must revoke the cease-fire order I signed this morning."

"Like hell you will!" the American Eagle thundered.

"Then I must consider myself a prisoner."

"That's okay with me!"

Admiral Darlan, his face impassive, was hustled away to a comfortable villa in an Algiers suburb, where he was guarded by a platoon of American soldiers.

In the meantime, French commanders at the three invasion locales, unaware of Darlan's imprisonment, arranged cease-fires with local American generals, pending the signing of an armistice in Algiers.

During the four-day war, the bloodletting had been heavy, even though General Eisenhower sought to play down the casualties to keep French emotions from flaring into even more hostility toward the invaders. France, after all, was supposed to be a friend of the Anglo-Americans. American forces suffered 1,404 casualties, including 556 killed, 837 wounded, and 41 missing. The British sustained nearly 300 casualties, and the French estimated their losses at more than 700 killed, 1,400 wounded, and 400 missing.

On November 12, five-star General Auguste Noguès flew from Morocco to Algiers, where he and other French military leaders were to meet with General Clark in an effort to hammer out an armistice. In only three days, the angular American had absorbed a crash course in high-level intrigue, a subject absent from West Point textbooks.

Only minutes after Clark and the Frenchmen settled into their chairs in the St. George Hotel, a series of disputes broke out. General Noguès proposed appointing Admiral Darlan (who was still locked up) as head of government in Northwest Africa and insisted that the commander of all military forces in the two colonies be himself.

Predictably, Noguès's suggestions hit a sore spot with Henri Giraud, who also had his sights set on becoming commander of French forces in Morocco and Algeria. For his part, Noguès refused even to speak with Giraud, whom he regarded as a traitor to France.

While bitter words flew, Clark acted as a sort of referee. Eventually, General Alphonse Juin stepped into the breach and brought Noguès around to agreeing that Giraud could be military commander, but only if he took his orders from Admiral Darlan in the name of Marshal Henri Pétain in Vichy. Giraud bristled. He would not speak with Darlan, much less take orders from him.

Then the plot thickened. Noguès declared that he would agree to Giraud being military commander (the niche that Noguès had carved out for himself) under one condition: Charles de Gaulle, leader of the Free French in London, must be barred from even setting foot on the African continent. By now, the exasperated Clark knew precisely what was meant by the expression "the god-damned French political mess."

Wrangling continued for hours. Finally, an armistice agreement was reached whereby the fighting would halt. Admiral Darlan would be head of government in French Northwest Africa, and General Giraud would be commander of French armed forces in that region. The two were strange bedfellows.

The tinkling of champagne glasses and the litany of toasts that followed the armistice agreement by no means resolved the volatile situation in Northwest Africa. Soured by the turn of events, General Auguste Noguès proved to be vindictive. U.S. intelligence learned that he still had locked up General Béthouart and other French officers who had worked with the Allies prior to the invasion. He intended to have them brought to trial as traitors—and shot.

George Patton, who had fought against Noguès's forces in the Casablanca region a week earlier, was especially incensed. He fired off a message to Eisenhower: "I believe it to be of the greatest importance that any [French] officer who had acted to assist this expedition shall be protected and upheld."

As a result of the intervention of Patton and other outraged American generals, Noguès quietly dropped charges against Béthouart and the other pro-Allied French officers and released them from jail.

On the morning of November 13, Dwight Eisenhower's Flying Fortress touched down at Maison Blanche Airport outside Algiers after a flight from Gibraltar. For the first time in his twenty-nine-year military career, he was in a war zone, albeit a peaceful one. That afternoon, the supreme commander met with the feuding Frenchmen in the St. George Hotel. It was a frigid setting, the rival French generals and admirals glaring at one another with obvious distaste.

After prolonged discussion, political neophyte Eisenhower gave his blessing, in the interest of military expediency, to terms of the proposed armistice.

There would be no French surrender, no transfer of sovereignty, simply a permanent cease-fire. To a man, French ground, sea, and air commanders had obeyed Darlan's order to break off hostilities and to make their troops, weapons, and facilities available to the Allies for pursuit against a common foe: Nazi Germany. None of the French commanders had known of Darlan's desire to revoke the cease-fire order.

When Eisenhower awakened in his St. George suite the next morning, aides anxiously informed him that he was the target of a heated controversy that had erupted in England and in the United States over what was disparagingly branded the "Darlan Deal." Editorial writers and radio commentators were mostly hostile, berating Eisenhower for what one newspaper described as "climbing in bed with an arch Nazi collaborator." Eisenhower's political action to save countless Allied and French lives and get on with the fight against Adolf Hitler nearly cost him his job.

Eisenhower was shocked and hurt by the torrent of abuse being poured on his head by some of his own countrymen and those of his ally, England. From London, Beetle Smith informed the harried supreme commander that the British Foreign Office had chipped in with the view that Darlan's background—that is, his collaboration with the Nazis—was so repugnant that there was no way he could be installed as high commissioner of French Northwest Africa.

"There is above all our own moral position," the British declared. "We are fighting for international decency and Darlan is the antithesis of this."[1]

That remark by his British "friends" struck Eisenhower particularly hard. In their eyes, the general had acted immorally when he installed Darlan as high commissioner.

Eisenhower was not only hurt but also angered by the barrage of criticism. "I can't understand why these long-haired, starry-eyed guys keep gunning for me!" he exclaimed. "I'm no reactionary. Christ on the Mountain! I'm idealistic as hell!"[2] Writing to his son, John, a West Point cadet, he complained bitterly, "I have been called . . . almost a Hitlerite!"[3]

Fully aware that he had stirred up a hornet's nest, on November 14 Eisenhower fired off lengthy cables to General Marshall in Washington and to Winston Churchill in London, explaining his political arrangement. "There may be a feeling at home that we have been sold a bill of goods," he told Marshall. "But without Darlan we would have to undertake a complete military occupation of North Africa. . . . The cost in time and resources would be enormous."[4]

To Churchill, Eisenhower wrote, "Please be assured that I have too often listened to your sage advice to be completely handcuffed and blindfolded by all the slickers with which this part of the world is so thickly populated."[5]

Powerful figures soon rushed to defend Eisenhower and his Darlan decision. Secretary of War Henry Stimson barged into the Oval Office of the White
House and all but demanded that President Roosevelt get behind his beleaguered commander in North Africa. Roosevelt, who considered the political
ramifications of everything he did, was noncommittal.

Elsewhere in Washington, George Marshall, Eisenhower's mentor, called a
press conference and came to the Torch commander's defense. A Marshall aide
said, "I have never seen him so concerned as he is on this occasion."[6]

Indeed, Marshall had good reason to be concerned. In light of the brouhaha
raging over the Darlan Deal, it appeared quite likely that Eisenhower's promising career as a top military commander was about to conclude. In dark corners
of the musty old Munitions Building, it was whispered that Eisenhower would
be sacrificed for the sake of inter-Allied harmony, brought back to the Zone of
the Interior (the United States), and assigned to mundane tasks.

At the press conference, General Marshall, in the words of an aide, "took
the hide" off American reporters. Torch planners had estimated that American
losses in the invasion would be as high as eighteen thousand, a heavy price to
pay for French territory on the periphery of Adolf Hitler's Festung Europa
(Fortress Europe), Marshall declared. As a result of the Darlan arrangement,
only eighteen hundred American casualties were sustained. Therefore, Marshall
emphasized, the Darlan Deal had saved more than sixteen thousand American
fighting men from death or wounds.[7]

Marshall pulled no punches. He told the reporters that their criticism of
Eisenhower with regard to Darlan was "incredibly stupid" and that they were
playing into the hands of the British, who, with Eisenhower sacked, would
demand that one of their own replace him.

President Roosevelt's statement, issued on November 18, and Marshall's
lambasting of the American press failed to stem, or even slow, the flood tide of
criticism. If anything, the clamor over the Darlan Deal grew even more intense,
and hordes of reporters rushed to Algiers. Then Eisenhower committed a faux
pas: He imposed strict censorship on what was termed "political news." That
edict brought howls from some American reporters. Back in the States, editorial
writers, comfortably perched in ivory towers, even demanded that Eisenhower
be sacked as incompetent.

Repercussions from the Darlan Deal reached all the way to the Kremlin in
Moscow. Josef Stalin conjectured to confidants as to whether the agreement
reached with the Nazi collaborator Darlan meant that Roosevelt and Churchill,
neither of whom the Soviet dictator trusted, might cut a deal with Hitler when
the time was right.

Torch did not bring American troops into direct contact with Axis (German and
Italian) ground forces, but it placed them in proximity to the enemy. Privately,
American generals agreed that it had been providential that the French had
chosen to fight. Torch had been a gigantic combat laboratory where generals and

privates alike learned the bitter lessons of warfare before having to clash with the battle-tested Wehrmacht. Even the supremely self-confident George Patton, who committed his share of mistakes, learned that there was much more to leading a large fighting force than dashing about and swearing loudly.

Dwight Eisenhower had been just as green as other Torch officers, but he wasted no time in starting his forces in Algeria and Morocco on a tortuous trek eastward for hundreds of miles to link up with Bernard Montgomery's British Eighth Army, which was driving Erwin Rommel's remnants westward to Tunisia. The American journey across the forbidding terrain was painful, slowed by a shortage of vehicles, torrential rains, and the inexperience of commanders in moving large formations and their equipment.

The snail-like progress toward Tunisia and the verbal and printed barrages that continued to be hurled at Eisenhower resulted in making his existence "a living hell." He was "like a caged tiger" and was "snarling and clawing to get things done." He was annoyed by his superiors and barked at his subordinates.[8]

At a critical point in the Western Allies' war effort against Nazi Germany, Eisenhower could have used the moral support of George Marshall's old sparring partner, Field Marshal Alan Brooke. But nothing was heard from the chief of the Imperial General Staff. Brooke was monitoring the situation in North Africa closely, however. "Eisenhower is far too immersed in the political aspects," he wrote in his diary. "I have little confidence in his ability to handle the military situation confronting him, and he is causing me great anxiety."[9]

On December 18, Admiral Jean Darlan matter of factly told Robert Murphy, "You know, there are four plots in existence to kill me." Although the admiral did not elaborate, Murphy knew that plenty of factions would have liked to eliminate the highly controversial figure: Giraud's people, the Germans, de Gaulle's confederates, Vichy Frenchmen, the British, and the Americans.[10]

Less than a week later, on Christmas Eve of 1942, Darlan returned to his office from a luncheon and was approached by twenty-year-old Fernand Eugene Bonnier de la Chappelle, who had been a member of Murphy's underground. Without a word, Bonnier pulled out a pistol and shot Darlan at point-blank range. Bleeding profusely from the mouth, the admiral collapsed in the doorway of his office and died a short time later.

Bonnier was caught by guards as he tried to flee the building. Incredibly, General Henri Giraud, commander of French forces and long an arch-foe of Darlan, hastily convened a court-martial. Bonnier was found guilty of murder and was immediately executed by a firing squad.

Circumstances surrounding the Darlan murder were rife with mystery. Why had Giraud acted so quickly, before the assassin could be interrogated about his motives? Was the hit man involved in a conspiracy? Most likely. But who were the conspirators? Rumor held that those in high places were involved. Giraud, however, squashed any hope of getting to the bottom of the assassination. He promptly ordered all records concerning the case burned.

No one in an official position seemed to be too distressed over the "Little Fella's" removal from the scene. General Eisenhower had been in British General Kenneth Anderson's army headquarters in Tunisia when he received word of Darlan's murder. Mumbling to himself, the supreme commander climbed into his armored Packard and was driven for thirty hours through snow, sleet, and rain back to Algiers. There he was briefed on Darlan's death but apparently took no action to probe into the slaying.

Mark Clark summed up the view of the American and British commanders: "Admiral Darlan's death was, to me, an act of Providence. His removal from the scene was like the lancing of a troublesome boil. He had served his purpose."[11]

By mid-November Field Marshal Erwin Rommel realized that the Axis position in Africa was hopeless. Since Bernard Montgomery's Eighth Army had kicked off Operation Lightfoot a month earlier, Rommel's retreating force had lost five hundred tanks, and fifty-nine thousand men had been killed, wounded, or captured. Furious and disillusioned with Adolf Hitler, Rommel decided to leave his command without authorization and fly to the Führer's headquarters in East Prussia, behind the Russian front.

Rommel arrived at Hitler's underground command post on the afternoon of November 28. Ushered into the Führer's presence, Rommel minced no words. He described the situation in North Africa and declared that the German army would be destroyed if it remained.

Hitler exploded. He accused Rommel of defeatism and his troops of being cowards. He reminded the field marshal ominously, "Generals who ... made the same sort of [defeatist] suggestions in Russia had been put up against a wall and shot."[12]

Undaunted by the threat to his own life, Rommel stated that it was quite impossible to analyze the battle in North Africa from East Prussia. He suggested that either Hitler or his chief advisor, Field Marshal Wilhelm Keitel, go to Africa to see for themselves.

Hitler was red-faced with fury over the suggestion. "Herr Generalfeldmarschall, capitulate if you want to," he said contemptuously. "If you, as a field marshal, think that you can no longer carry on [in Africa], then there was no point in my having made you a field marshal. Now get out!"[13]

Rommel saluted, spun on his heel, and exited. Then Hitler came out, put an arm on Rommel's shoulder, and said, "Everything is going to be all right. It is impossible to think of the Afrika Korps being destroyed." The Führer promised to send reinforcements into Tunisia.

Hitler was true to his word. By the first week of January 1943, one hundred thousand German troops and an equal number of Italian soldiers had arrived in Tunisia for a showdown with Torch and Lightfoot forces.

CHAPTER 11

High Strategy and Low Tactics

With the arrival of new year's day in 1943, Franklin Roosevelt was holding White House discussions with George Marshall and Ernest King in preparation for a high-level conference (code-named Symbol) between the Americans and British in Casablanca on January 13. With Allied armies in North Africa about to administer the coup de grace to the remaining German and Italian forces bottled up in Tunisia, future strategy would have to be settled. Roosevelt was concerned that the Americans would be going to Casablanca divided on future strategy, whereas Winston Churchill and the British could be counted on to thrash out their differences in advance, present a specific plan, and stick to it resolutely.

Churchill had cabled an invitation to Josef Stalin to join Symbol, but the Soviet dictator turned it down. In his command bunker far below the pavement of St. George Street in London, the British Bulldog pored over Stalin's long reply. "I [hope] that you and the Americans do not relax preparations along the [English Channel] coast to keep the Germans pinned down in [northern] France," Stalin goaded. "I hope you have not changed your mind with regard to your promise given to me in Moscow to establish a second front in Western Europe in the spring of 1943."[1]

Clearly, the wily Stalin had no intention of letting Churchill off the hook.

Now, to Marshall and King, Roosevelt stressed that the American delegation should present a united front at Casablanca. "Do we all agree that we should meet the British united in advocating a cross-Channel operation [in spring 1943]?" the President asked.

Marshall, who had been the staunchest advocate for cross-Channel assault the previous year, had altered his viewpoint. With the Dieppe disaster presumably still fresh in his mind, the army chief now said he favored invasion of the Brest peninsula, the land mass that jutted into the Atlantic Ocean west of Normandy. Admiral King gave lukewarm support to Marshall's proposal, but reminded Roosevelt that a greater effort should be made in the Pacific so as not to give the Japanese a chance to consolidate their widespread conquests.

Field Marshal John Dill, the amiable British liaison officer in Washington, and George Marshall had become close friends during the past year and often exchanged confidences. From Dill, Marshall had learned that the British would propose extending operations in the Mediterranean and leaving the invasion of northern France to a much later date. Both Marshall and King were vehemently against further operations in the Mediterranean. "Nibbling on the edges of Hitler's empire," Marshall called it.[2]

American strategic concepts were still up in the air when Marshall (code-named Braid), air corps chief Hap Arnold, and Field Marshal Dill lifted off from Washington in a C-54 transport on January 9. So that the U.S. military brain trust would not be wiped out in the event of a crash, Ernest King, services of supply head General Brehon Somervell, and two American planners, Brigadier General Albert C. Wedemeyer and Rear Admiral Charles M. "Savvy" Cooke, followed in a second C-54.

These two groups were flying ahead to work out a strategy with Field Marshal Alan Brooke and the other British chiefs before Roosevelt and Churchill arrived in Casablanca. That same night, the President (code-named Admiral Q) and his troubleshooter, Harry Hopkins (Mr. P), boarded a private train in Washington for a rail trip to Miami. From there they would fly to Morocco.

The two C-54s steered a roundabout course to their destination, hopping from Washington to Miami and then on to Puerto Rico. King's plane was the first to arrive over Puerto Rico, but Marshall's aircraft radioed that King was to remain airborne until the army chief had landed. Marshall was senior in rank (he had received his fourth star before King), so the navy boss had to circle the Puerto Rico airport for twenty minutes.

After the two service chiefs were on the ground, King angrily complained to Marshall about wasting airplane fuel. But to his own aides, King made known his real gripe: Marshall's pettiness in pulling rank.[3]

Winston Churchill, a cagey operative, had told Roosevelt that this would be a "little meeting" with "very small staffs." However, when Marshall and King arrived at the fashionable seaside Anfa Hotel four miles outside Casablanca, they discovered to their dismay that they had been outmaneuvered and outgunned. Only two planners, Wedemeyer and Cooke, had been brought along. Alan Brooke and his cohorts had arrived not only with a horde of planners but also with a communications ship anchored offshore—a floating library of hundreds of strategic studies, plans, and maps.

Around the Anfa Hotel, George Patton had placed antiaircraft guns. Men of Major General Ernest "Gravel Voice" Harmon's U.S. 2nd (Hell on Wheels) Armored Division ringed the facility with machine guns and bazookas. Casablanca, it was believed, was chock-full of Nazi spies, so an attempt might be made by the Luftwaffe or German commandos to wipe out the Anglo-American hierarchy in one fell swoop.

On the first night after the arrival of Churchill and Roosevelt, the moans of air-raid sirens caused lights to be extinguished in the sumptuous villa on the neatly manicured hotel grounds where the President and the Prime Minister were gathered with their military chiefs. Apparently, the Luftwaffe was approaching. For a half hour, the heads of state, generals, and admirals engaged in chitchat by candlelight that illuminated the whiskey bottles on the table. No bombs fell. The all-clear was sounded.

Casablanca provided the setting for family reunions of sorts. Major Randolph Churchill flew in from his post with the British Eighth Army in Tunisia. Sergeant Robert Hopkins arrived from his Signal Corps job in Algeria. Navy Lieutenant Franklin D. Roosevelt, Jr., somehow made it from his destroyer in the Atlantic, and his brother, Captain Elliott Roosevelt, winged in from his air corps reconnaissance assignment in Algiers. Army Lieutenant Hank Arnold, an artillery forward observer, came from a foxhole in Tunisia.[4]

When the first meeting of the Combined Chiefs of Staff convened the morning after the false air raid, there was give-and-take on both sides about global strategy. The British chiefs, following Churchill's suggestion, let the Americans "get their views off their chests without comment." Then the British counterattacked, supported by the avalanche of documents and reports they had brought along.

It soon became obvious to the Americans that they were at a distinct disadvantage. Admiral King would note, "Every time [we] brought up a subject, the British had a paper ready [to refute] it."[5]

If a needed British study or document was not immediately at hand, a courier rushed to the communications ship offshore to fetch it. America's only two planners, Al Wedemeyer and Savvy Cooke, were soon buried under a blizzard of British paper.

It was not long before old antagonisms burst forth. Alan Brooke declared that operations in the Mediterranean was the only course to follow, that this strategy would threaten southern Europe and force Hitler to spread tens of thousands of soldiers along the northern shore of the Mediterranean. This would help the Soviet army much more than definite commitments to northern France.

For the next two days, the Americans, chiefly George Marshall, presented their views. They claimed that definite decisions would have to be reached about global operations in 1943 and also in 1944. That would permit accurate establishment of priorities in the United States' awesome production potential. Marshall still leaned toward using the armies in Africa to invade the Brest peninsula.

The American arguments fell on deaf ears. Brooke snorted that it would be impossible to map out a detailed plan for winning the war at this stage. He claimed that extended operations in the Mediterranean might knock Italy out of the war and "undoubtedly leave Germany in a most serious position."[6]

Brooke grew increasingly angry at what appeared to be the Americans' refusal to see reason after he suggested that the Allied forces in North Africa should be used to invade Sicily, an island off the toe of Italy and only 150 miles across the Mediterranean from Tunisia.

Marshall snapped back that the Combined Chiefs would have to decide what was the "main plot." He argued that "every diversion [meaning Sicily] or side issue from the main plot acts as a suction pump."[7]

Then, on January 16, Admiral King, with Marshall's backing, presented his own suction-pump strategy: A series of operations in the Pacific that assuredly would siphon off troops and precious landing craft from the Mediterranean.

While the Combined Chiefs were wrangling, Roosevelt and Churchill were enjoying each other's company, temporarily freed from the incessant pressures of crucial decisions. Harold Macmillan, Britain's foreign secretary, noted in his diary, "There was a curious mixture of holiday and business. The charming Emperor of the West [Roosevelt] was the genial master of Villa Number 2. There was a great deal of joking. There was an enormous quantity of highballs, talk by the hour, and a general atmosphere of extraordinary goodwill."[8]

But that aura of goodwill did not extend to the conference of the Combined Chiefs. Ernest King declared that a balance had to be struck between resources to defeat Germany and Japan. When the British began expressing their views on the Pacific, King growled, "Details of operations in the Pacific must be left to the U.S. chiefs of staff, and is not a matter for the Combined Chiefs."

When the meeting adjourned for lunch, Alan Brooke was near despair. "It is no use," he moaned to Field Marshal Dill. "We shall never get an agreement with them."

Dill pointed out that George Marshall appeared willing to make concessions. "How far will you compromise to reach an agreement?" Dill asked.

"Not one inch," Brooke replied.

"Oh, yes, you will!" Dill shot back. "You know you must reach an agreement, that you cannot bring the unsolved problem to Churchill and Roosevelt. You know as well as I do what a mess *they* would make of it!"[9]

As the Combined Chiefs continued to argue, the Americans found themselves on the losing end of the verbal dueling. "I think the Mediterranean is a kind of dark hole into which one enters at one's own peril," Marshall said. "But under present circumstances, I'll support [an invasion of Sicily], but I'm opposed as much as ever to interminable operations in the Mediterranean."

The die was cast. Sicily would be the next target. Roundup, the proposed cross-Channel assault against Normandy in the spring of 1943, was dead.

Now it would be necessary to explain to Stalin why the Western Allies would have to renege on Churchill's impetuous promise of an invasion of northern France in 1943. President Roosevelt cabled Stalin that General Marshall would fly to Moscow to explain the Sicily decision. Back came a blistering message from the Soviet boss: A visit by Marshall would accomplish nothing. Stalin did not want an emissary bringing lame excuses as to why a second front could not be established in northern France.

Except for Marshall himself, the American delegation was furious over Stalin's high-handed message. They saw it as a slap in the face to the U.S. chief of staff, who had been brushed off as an "emissary."

In the meantime, General Henri Giraud, at the invitation of President Roosevelt, had flown to Casablanca for discussions. The prolonged hassles with the Frenchman prior to and in the early days of Torch were ancient history. Now the commander of all French forces in North Africa, Giraud was a portrait of congeniality and cooperation.

While meeting with Roosevelt and the Combined Chiefs, Giraud asked that his troops, now inactive, be equipped by the Anglo-Americans so that they could fight alongside the Allies against the Germans. Within a few weeks, Giraud estimated, he could form ten infantry and three armored divisions. If provided the planes, he could activate thirty bomber and fifty fighter squadrons.

Giraud's unexpected offer was greeted with delight by the Combined Chiefs. George Marshall pledged that American resources would be used to equip the French.

At the same time the invitation had been issued to Giraud, Winston Churchill had asked Charles de Gaulle to fly from London to Casablanca. De Gaulle bluntly refused, stating that it was a matter of honor that he, the leader of the Free French, not discuss topics of importance to France with "foreigners," meaning Churchill and Roosevelt.

Churchill was angry. Only after he impressed upon de Gaulle that England was paying his salary and underwriting most of the expenses of the Free French organization did the reluctant general agree to come to Casablanca. There he haughtily listed a series of demands, foremost of which was that a French provisional government be established—with Charles de Gaulle as its head.

Roosevelt and Churchill rapidly shot down de Gaulle's latest grasp-for-power balloon. They wanted the French people to choose their own government after the war, rather than impose de Gaulle's on them. Smarting from what he considered to be yet another slight by the Anglo-Americans, the tall Frenchman flew back to London.

With the conference winding down, Alan Brooke orchestrated a scheme designed to get Dwight Eisenhower out of the way. Brooke admired Eisenhower's skill at welding a mix of nationalities into a smooth team at AFHQ, but he held the supreme commander in low regard for his knowledge of tactics and strategy. Ike, Brooke felt, was a political general.

It was evident that Eisenhower, who had become a folk hero back home and was the protégé of army chief George Marshall, could not simply be booted out as supreme commander. So as part of Brooke's intrigue, he and his British colleagues joined with the American chiefs not only to retain Eisenhower in command of Torch forces, but also to place Bernard Montgomery's British Eighth Army under him.

The key component of Brooke's maneuvering was to restructure the Allied high command to insert three British deputies just below Eisenhower. The American chiefs agreed to the new setup. General Harold R. L. G. Alexander would be in charge of ground operations, Admiral Andrew Cunningham would command naval forces, and Air Marshal Arthur Tedder would oversee the air forces.

Brooke felt that these three experienced and capable combat officers would squeeze Eisenhower out of the strategic picture. Brooke (and presumably Churchill) expected Eisenhower to be the "political general" and the three British deputies to be the "strategic commanders." Making the arrangement more difficult for the three-star general would be the fact that he was outranked by his deputies, all of whom wore four stars.

Brooke admitted his scheming to his diary: "We [the British] were pushing Eisenhower up into the stratosphere as supreme commander where he would be free to devote his time to the political and inter-allied problems, whilst we inserted under him our own commanders to deal with the military situation and to restore the necessary drive and coordination which has been so seriously lacking."[10]

After Roosevelt and Churchill approved the new command structure, the Combined Chiefs issued a January 20 directive that stated control of all Allied operations would be in the hands of the three British deputies.

Eisenhower was furious. Even his mentor, George Marshall, had gone along with the plan to dilute his duties as supreme commander. He fired off a blunt message to Marshall, stating that as long as he was in charge, he would exercise full authority. "Responsibility falls directly on me," he told Marshall.[11]

On January 24, a day after the conclusion of Symbol, Roosevelt and Churchill agreed to meet with reporters. Roosevelt spoke in general terms about the war situation for about five minutes, then, in an off-the-cuff manner, loosed a thunderclap. With scores of journalists avidly taking notes, the President casually observed, "Prime Minister Churchill and I have determined that we will accept nothing less than *unconditional surrender* of Germany, Italy, and Japan!"

Seated next to the President, Winston Churchill was stunned. That was the first time that he had heard the phrase "unconditional surrender" used with regard to the current war.[12]

Churchill was deeply alarmed. With the Third Reich and its Wehrmacht still a powerful force to be reckoned with, he felt that the posture to be assumed by Allied leadership was one of defiance. He was convinced that it was a blunder of the first magnitude to be dictating harsh terms to the enemy nations at a time when victory and defeat still hung in the balance.

But the damage was done. Churchill could not, in the face of the free world's press, take issue with his war partner. He assured reporters that he concurred with the unconditional surrender ultimatum. Within minutes, the news was flashed around the globe.

Later, a shaken Stewart Graham Menzies (code-named "C"), the cerebral chief of MI-6, the British intelligence branch of the War Office, told Churchill, "Unless those terms are softened, the German army will fight with the ferocity of cornered rats."

Already on public record, Churchill merely shrugged.[13]

When George Patton heard about Roosevelt's remark, he confided to a close friend, "Our President is a great politician, but goddamn it, he's never read history. [He] and the people in our government can't understand the Germans. Look at this goddamn fool 'unconditional surrender' shit. If the Hun [German] ever needed anything to put a burr under his saddle, that's it. Now he'll fight like the goddamned devil. It will take much longer, cost us far more lives, and let the Russians take more territory!"[14]

Dwight Eisenhower was flabbergasted. "If you are given the choice of mounting the scaffold or charging thirty bayonets, you might as well charge the bayonets!" he told an aide.[15]

In Berlin, top Nazis rejoiced. Paul Josef Goebbels, Hitler's cunning minister of propaganda, trumpeted to a gathering of party leaders in Berlin: "Since the enemies of Germany are determined to enslave our nation, the war has become an urgent struggle for national preservation in which no sacrifice is too great!" Cheers echoed from the rafters.

In Junkers bombers over England and in Messerschmitt fighters above the Fatherland, in U-boats beneath the cold, murky waters of the North Atlantic, in snow-covered foxholes in the frozen tundra of Russia, at dispersed outposts along the underbelly of Europe, the German military man inwardly reaffirmed his vow to fight to the end—with courage, tenacity, and a growing feeling of desperation.

Had Franklin Roosevelt, a cerebral politician long accustomed to speaking in the global spotlight, truly been so incredibly muddleheaded as to make the offhand unconditional surrender ultimatum? Or had this press conference been the platform for a carefully calculated scenario, cooked up by the President and a few key advisors in the White House to trap Winston Churchill in a situation where he could not disagree?

There were indeed top figures in the Roosevelt administration who were promoting the theme that the war in Europe should not be concluded until the Third Reich had been not only crushed, but also dismantled. Chief among these hard-liners were Secretary of the Treasury Henry Morgenthau, Jr.; Assistant Secretary of State Harry Dexter White; Bernard Baruch, a moonlighting advisor to Roosevelt (whom a White House staffer described in his diary as "a pain in the ass"); and Alger Hiss of the State Department.[16]

Henry Morgenthau, who lived near the Roosevelt estate in Hyde Park, New York, had particular access to the ear of the President. Earlier, Morgenthau had drawn up a top-secret plan for dealing with a defeated Germany. It called for the destruction of German heavy industry and the flooding of mines, thereby denying the postwar nation the raw materials needed for producing consumer goods. In essence, the Morgenthau plan would reduce Germany to an agricultural entity, its ninety million citizens to be kept in a gigantic ghetto with armed guards posted around the borders with orders to shoot any German who tried to get out. The plan included a list of thousands of German officers and government officials who were to be summarily executed.

Conceivably, Morgenthau's plan had been created with the knowledge and approval of Franklin Roosevelt. Against this background, had the President's stunning unconditional surrender ultimatum at Casablanca been a slip of the tongue, or had it been the result of a subtle scheme to ensure that there would be no negotiated peace with Germany, no matter what the cost to young Americans doing the fighting?

Perhaps only Roosevelt, Morgenthau, and a few in the White House inner circle knew the true answer.

CHAPTER 12

Ike's "Neck Is in the Noose"

As JANUARY CLOSED IN ON FEBRUARY 1943, the rumor mills were grinding in Washington and in London. Dwight Eisenhower, it was whispered, was about to be sacked. The Darlan Deal still cast a shadow. Torch units seemed to be in disarray while trying to make the long, miserable trek eastward to Tunisia. Weather conditions were abominable—cold, torrential rains and gusting winds. Even so, bellyaching was heard because Eisenhower had not launched attacks to knock out Erwin Rommel's trapped force.

A flood of criticism was heaped on Eisenhower when he appointed Marcel Payrouton as governor of Algeria; Payrouton had been Vichy's minister of the interior. "Payrouton's appointment has been received with howls of anguish at home," Eisenhower wrote in his diary. "Who'd they want? He is an experienced administrator, and God knows it's hard to find many of them among the French in Africa."[1]

Then a firestorm of outrage erupted in Washington and London when General Henri Giraud, whom Eisenhower had appointed commander of all French forces in North Africa, jailed scores of suspected Vichy supporters, along with many of Charles de Gaulle's disciples. At this point, Eisenhower seemed to be a goner. Wife Mamie wrote to him from Washington: "The big boys are preparing to give you the boot." Mamie should have known; she had contacts in both the War Department and the White House.[2]

Scuttlebutt had even identified Eisenhower's successor: British General Harold Alexander, who had extensive combat experience in Burma against the Japanese and in the North African desert against Rommel's Afrika Korps and who was now Ike's deputy for ground operations.

Reports from Washington and London had it that Eisenhower would be assigned to an obscure desk job in England or that a post would be found for him in the War Department in Washington. In either event, he would be branded an incompetent, a failure. His aide, Harry Butcher, recorded, "I told him his neck is in the noose, and he knows it."[3]

In Washington, George Marshall was fully aware of the "bounce Eisenhower" rumors that were swirling on both sides of the Atlantic. As a tangible symbol of his backing, Marshall recommended that Eisenhower be promoted to four-star general so that he would be at least equal in rank with his three British deputies.

On February 10, Harry Butcher was listening to a BBC (British Broadcasting Company) news report from London and learned that his boss had been elevated to the highest rank in the U.S. armed forces at the time. He burst excitedly into Ike's office and blurted out the news. Ike had mixed emotions: Delight on one hand, annoyance on the other. Why did he have to learn of this milestone in his career from a radio broadcast instead of from the War Department?

Meanwhile, Eisenhower was having more of his customary headaches with the French. An army under General Alphonse Juin, who had been visited at his villa in Algiers by Robert Murphy ("Colonel McGowan") hours before D-day for Torch, was on the front line in Tunisia, between the British to the north and the U.S. II Corps to the south. Eisenhower issued an order that General Kenneth A. N. Anderson, commander of the British First Army, was to exercise tactical control over the forces of all three nationalities. Juin balked. So did Henri Giraud in Algiers. The French, they declared, would not take orders from a British general.

Eisenhower was a staunch advocate of unified command, but to placate the French he withdrew his order and permitted Juin's army, in essence, to fight its own battle. Ike personally would coordinate the battle against the beleaguered, but still formidable, German and Italian forces in Tunisia. Partly because of the long distance from his headquarters in Algiers, Eisenhower's coordination was largely ineffective.[4]

Four days after Eisenhower pinned on his four stars, wily Field Marshal Erwin Rommel struck with fury against the green U.S. II Corps. His veteran panzer forces plunged through Kasserine Pass and badly mauled the 1st Armored and 34th Infantry Divisions. Some Americans, under heavy attack for the first time, stood and fought until they were killed or captured. Many others fled in panic.

Eight days after kicking off the Kasserine Pass assault, the Germans had driven through American positions for 120 miles. II Corps was in total disarray. Then the advance ran out of steam and Rommel ordered a halt.

It had been a humiliating and devastating defeat for the Americans, jolting them out of their overconfidence gained largely through the relatively easy victories over the French. Rommel had captured 2,459 befuddled GIs, killed 192, and wounded 2,624 others.

The Desert Fox's crushing blow at Kasserine Pass triggered renewed strife and finger-pointing in the Anglo-American high command. British generals claimed that the U.S. debacle proved what they had been saying all along: The Americans did not have the ability to train and command combatworthy soldiers. They even suggested that American training techniques be scuttled in favor of British methods.

George Marshall would say in an off-the-record interview, "General [Harold] Alexander was particularly bitter on this subject. One might even say he was actually contemptuous of the U.S. infantry and did not believe it could ever be an effective force against the Germans."[5]

Marshall had his own explanation for the American debacle: "Stupid British generalship." His blunt barb was aimed at Kenneth Anderson, leader of the British First Army, under whose command the U.S. II Corps was fighting.[6]

Eisenhower had been having serious doubts about the ability of Major General Lloyd Fredendall, the II Corps commander, even before Rommel's Kasserine Pass victory. When Torch leaders had been selected the previous fall, Fredendall had been given II Corps on the recommendation of George Marshall, who had labeled him "one of the best."

Earlier in the Tunisian fighting, Eisenhower had gone to the front and found Fredendall in his command post, a man-made fortress of sorts located far up a canyon in a gulch many miles behind the battle. Fredendall had taken two hundred engineers from the front to spend nearly three weeks blasting underground shelters for him and his aides. The general seldom left his gloomy subterranean chambers.

Although Eisenhower tactfully instructed Fredendall to make certain that his *subordinates* moved up front from their command posts to personally reconnoiter the ground and assess the morale of their troops, the II Corps leader remained buried in his excavations.

For some time, Eisenhower had contemplated replacing Fredendall with Mark Clark, who had been promoted to three-star rank and given command of the new U.S. Fifth Army, which was in training far to the rear. Clark, however, declined the offer, not wanting to be reduced from leading an army to being a corps commander.

Now Eisenhower could wait no longer. Shortly after March 1, Fredendall was bounced with the explanation that he would be more valuable back in the United States using his combat experience to train troops. Replacing him was the colorful George Patton, who had been in Morocco for several months and was itching to get back into action.[7]

Patton roared into the II Corps area with all the stealth of an exploding bomb. Wearing his "battle face" and standing in an open command car, klaxons blaring and motorcycle escorts leading the way, Patton dashed about his command giving countless profanity-laced speeches. His mission was to instill strict discipline into his troops, who had been badly shaken at Kasserine.[8]

Even Patton's enormous energy, drive, and motivational skills could not transform a dispirited corps into an aggressive outfit overnight. When the 34th Infantry Division fell flat on its face attacking a key objective, a British commander sharply criticized the Americans' lackluster effort to reporters. Through a slipup in the censor's office, this damaging story reached the United States and was plastered on newspaper front pages.

George Marshall was furious with the British. He wired Eisenhower that such stories "create unfortunate impressions to our national disadvantage," and he warned Ike to "watch this very closely." The veiled admonition seemed plain: Marshall was tactfully faulting his protégé for letting the inflammatory piece slip through the censor's net.[9]

When word reached Patton that British generals were making insulting remarks about the fighting ability of American GIs, he roared, "And where in the hell were those Brit bastards at Kasserine!"

What had started as verbal skirmishing between George Patton and the British soon escalated into a full-scale war of words. On April 1, Patton's operations officer (no doubt with the connivance of Patton) issued a situation report in which he complained that the "total lack of air cover for our units permitted the [Luftwaffe] to operate almost at will."[10]

Since the Royal Air Force was responsible for air cover over II Corps positions, British Air Marshal Arthur Coningham fired back in a report that Patton was singling out the RAF "as an alibi for lack of success on the ground." What's more, Coningham declared, "it can only be assumed that [Patton's] personnel are not battleworthy."[11]

Both reports were widely circulated, gaining far more attention than would ordinarily have been the case with military documents because of the explosive nature of their contents. Eisenhower was anguished by the latest brouhaha, so much so that he wrote out a message to Marshall stating that he, Eisenhower, should be relieved because he could not control his subordinates. Beetle Smith, Ike's alter ego, talked him out of sending the cable.[12]

His composure restored, Eisenhower spoke with his deputy Air Marshal Arthur Tedder. Tedder contacted Coningham and ordered him to withdraw the anti-Patton document. It was a move akin to locking the barn after the horse had been stolen: Everyone from the rank of colonel on up already had read Coningham's blast.

As part of the damage control, Tedder took the unrepentant Coningham to Tunisia to meet with an equally unrepentant Patton. The suave Tedder, acting as referee, soon smoothed matters over—at least for the present. Patton and Coningham shook hands, and the three men sat down for a drink. As if on cue, three German fighter planes swooped in low and strafed the building.

Tedder looked at Patton, who was grinning broadly. "I always knew you were a good stage manager," Tedder told the American. "But this takes the cake."[13]

"If I could find the sons of bitches who flew those planes," Patton replied, "I'd mail each of them a medal!"[14]

Patton's anger toward the British soon boiled over again when Harold Alexander, in charge of ground operations, rejected his suggestion that II Corps launch an attack eastward to sever Erwin Rommel's line of communications to the south. Alexander was concerned that the Americans would take a fearful beating. Earlier, Bernard Montgomery had written Alexander: "Don't let them be too ambitious and ruin the show."[15]

When Eisenhower refused to intercede with Alexander and involve American troops in the final drive to crush Rommel, Patton exploded, convinced of a conspiracy to let Montgomery be proclaimed the Victor of Tunisia. "Goddamn all British and so-called Americans who had their legs pulled by them," Patton fumed in his diary. "I will bet that Ike does nothing about it. I would rather be commanded by an Arab. I think less than nothing of Arabs."[16]

Predictably, the volatile Patton regarded Alexander with disdain, viewing him as an aloof, distant figure, a fence-sitter who failed to support Patton in tactical arguments. "Alexander has an exceptionally small head," Patton told an aide. "That may explain things."

Newspaper headlines in the United States and in England focused on Montgomery's drive up the east coast of Tunisia. Patton, meanwhile, went virtually unnoticed by the media. The flamboyant general could stomach just about anything except being ignored. Angry and frustrated, he wrote in his diary, "Of course, being connected with the British is bad. So far, this war is being fought for the benefit of the British Empire and for postwar considerations. No one gives a damn about winning it for itself now."

George Patton had minimal understanding of politics and global strategy. Nor did he have the slightest conception of the demons tugging almost incessantly at the heavily burdened Eisenhower, who had been saddled with a seemingly impossible task: Massage the towering egos of Allied military and government leaders, keep the coalition together, and win the war. In Patton's view, wars were fought for individual glory on the field of battle.

Two days after Patton wrote that the conflict was being fought for the benefit of the British Empire, he exploded again in his diary with a vitriolic outburst against Dwight Eisenhower. "It appears to me that Ike is acting a part and knows he is damned near a Benedict Arnold, and the British have got him completely fooled. He is nothing but a Popinjay—a stuffed doll. The British are running the show on the sea, on the land, and in the air."

Indeed, it did appear that what Field Marshal Alan Brooke had hoped to achieve by his machinations at Casablanca had come to pass: The three British deputies, not the supreme commander, were "running the show."

Patton was galled by the prospect of being forced to step aside as supporting player in order to permit the star, Bernard Montgomery, to reap the laurels and global applause. He requested that Eisenhower send him back to Morocco, where he could form the nucleus of the new Seventh Army and finalize plans for Husky, the invasion of Sicily, which would be launched as soon as possible after Tunisia had been cleared of Axis troops.

On April 15, without fanfare, George Patton slipped out of Tunisia and flew to Morocco. Replacing him was Major General Omar N. Bradley, Patton's deputy at II Corps. An angular, soft-spoken Missourian, the forty-eight-year-old Bradley had been at II Corps when Patton took command, having been sent there by Eisenhower to be the supreme commander's "eyes and ears."

Patton had been irate. He roared that he didn't need "any goddamned spies running around" and insisted that Bradley be appointed his deputy, responsible directly to Patton and not to Eisenhower. The demand was approved.

While the switch of II Corps commanders was being implemented, General Alexander issued orders for the final offensive to crush the Germans and Italians, who had their backs to the sea near the major ports of Tunis and Bizerte. After reading the directive, George Patton was apoplectic. Omar Bradley was alarmed. Dwight Eisenhower was shocked. Alexander planned to virtually exclude the Americans.

The plan called for Bernard Montgomery's British Eighth Army to attack northward up the east coast of Tunisia until his left flank linked up with the right of Kenneth Anderson's First Army, which would be driving generally toward the northeast. This maneuver would pinch out the II Corps, which was in the line between Montgomery and Anderson.

Ever since Kasserine Pass, Eisenhower had been letting Alexander call most of the shots in the grueling battle in Tunisia. Now, the supreme commander took direct control once again: He rushed to Alexander's headquarters and drastically revised the plan for the final offensive. Alexander was to bring Omar Bradley's corps around the rear of Anderson's First Army and put it into the line along the north coast. Eisenhower also instructed the British general to assign a specific major objective to II Corps: Bizerte.

Alexander protested. Moving an entire American corps northward across First Army supply lines would be too difficult. Then Alexander raised Eisenhower's hackles by declaring that since the Americans had failed miserably at Kasserine Pass, their proper place was in the rear.

Eisenhower ignored the insult to America's fighting spirit and told Alexander to carry out his instructions. Again the British general protested, but Eisenhower cut him short. Within hours, Alexander issued revised orders: II Corps would be moved into position along the coast, with Bizerte as its primary objective.

The all-out offensive to crack the German-Italian bridgehead at Bizerte-Tunis would kick off on April 30. But Erwin Rommel would not be there. Seeing the handwriting on the wall, Adolf Hitler recalled the Africa Korps leader, whose popularity in the Third Reich rivaled that of the Führer. Hitler did not want the youngest field marshal in German history to be killed or wind up a prisoner of the Western Allies.

In England, Charles de Gaulle had set up his own radio station and newspapers, all of which spewed out incessant criticism of the British and Americans. On February 3, 1943, while the fighting was raging in Tunisia, de Gaulle made a secret speech to Free French paratroopers. "Although it is now necessary for the French to make pro-English statements, the British, like the Germans, are hereditary enemies of the French," he reportedly remarked. "It is the Russians who will win the war. After I gain control of France, I will not stand in the way of allowing the Russians to occupy Germany."

Winston Churchill was furious with de Gaulle for wreaking havoc with the Allied war effort and providing Josef Goebbels with fuel to fan the flames of inter-Allied discontent. In a face-to-face confrontation, Churchill again reminded the Free French leader that England continued to pay his salary and subsidize his organization. What's more, the British Bulldog declared, de Gaulle was not regarded as indispensable.

On the morning of April 23, a few weeks after the tension-packed encounter, de Gaulle arrived at Hendon airfield, a short distance outside London, to fly to Scotland to inspect members of the Free French navy. The trip would be made in his personal plane, a four-engine Wellington bomber that had been put at his disposal and maintained by the British.

Taking off at Hendon was a tricky endeavor. The runway was short, with an embankment at one end. A pilot had to rev up his engines to full speed, keep his wheel brakes on, and raise the tail by using the elevator controls. Then he would release the brakes and zip down the runway, much like a rocket being fired from a bazooka.

When RAF Flight Lieutenant Peter Loat, pilot of de Gaulle's plane, began the normal routine and headed down the runway, the tail suddenly dropped. Loat could not adjust it; the elevator control was loose in his hands. A skilled pilot, Loat managed to halt the aircraft shortly before it would have crashed into the embankment.

General de Gaulle was assigned a lighter aircraft, and Loat flew the Frenchmen and his party to Glasgow. Presumably suspecting British perfidy and perhaps feeling that discretion was the better part of valor, de Gaulle returned to London by train.

In the meantime, de Gaulle's Wellington bomber was inspected by mechanics at Hendon, who found that the elevator control rod had separated. The damaged piece of crucial equipment was sent to a laboratory for examination. Back came the report: The metal rod had been cut through with acid.

Flight Lieutenant Loat was informed by British authorities that German saboteurs had committed the deed. Loat didn't buy that explanation. Throughout the war, the British secret service had apprehended every Nazi spy in Great Britain and, through "turned" enemy agents, had learned of the arrival of new spies in time to greet them when they landed.

What's more, the Hendon aircraft maintenance crew was a closely knit outfit. It would have been almost impossible for a Nazi saboteur to even reach de Gaulle's Wellington, much less pour acid onto a critical piece of equipment without being observed.

Half-hearted efforts by the British secret service to identify the Wellington-bomber saboteur bore no fruit. Soon the investigation was quietly dropped.

There seemed to be no doubt in Charles de Gaulle's mind as to who had tried to kill him. A month later, he told a French colleague that henceforth he would base his policies on Germany and Russia.

For their part, Winston Churchill and Franklin Roosevelt were fed up with the French general. Churchill told the President that de Gaulle could no longer be trusted. On June 17, Roosevelt wrote to Churchill, "I am absolutely convinced that [de Gaulle] is injuring our war effort and that he is a very dangerous threat to us."

British, American, and French forces had been slugging it out with the Axis powers in Tunisia for five miserable, bloody months. Finally, on May 13, 1943, the resistance collapsed. A human deluge of 130,000 German and 120,000 Italian soldiers—more prisoners than the Soviets had taken in their trumpeted victory at Stalingrad earlier in the year—streamed into Allied enclosures.

A heavy price in Allied blood had been paid. In six months Eisenhower's forces had 10,820 men killed, 39,575 wounded, and 21,415 captured or missing. But the Western Allies were masters of the shores of North Africa.

CHAPTER 13

Dueling with Joan of Arc

THE BRITISH OVERSEAS AIRWAYS STATION in London knew that the weather had roughened over the Bay of Biscay, the vast body of water west of Nazi-held France and north of neutral Spain and Portugal. But there was no cause for worry over the fate of the regularly scheduled civilian commercial flight of a two-engine Douglas airplane bound from Lisbon to London. Among the thirteen passengers on board was celebrated British actor Leslie Howard. It was June 2, 1943.

The unarmed airliners had been flying on a regular basis between Lisbon and London since 1940. There had been an understanding on both sides that while the airplanes operated at their own risk, they would not be attacked by the Luftwaffe because they carried only civilian passengers.

These civilian flights were nerve-racking, however, because they involved flying uncomfortably near to Luftwaffe airfields in the Bordeaux region of western France. But the blue Douglas aircraft carried red, white, and blue identification stripes on their wings, and their civilian aircraft registration markings were painted on their fuselages in huge letters. It would require a myopic German pilot indeed to mistake one of the civilian airliners for a British or American military plane.

In Lisbon, the German Embassy had on its staff (under the guise of official diplomatic titles) some 125 men and women whose function was to ferret out Allied military secrets. It was important to the Third Reich that the British Overseas Airways service between London and Lisbon continue to function, for the afternoon plane from England brought the current daily newspapers and weekly magazines, prime sources for Nazi intelligence gathering.

Within minutes after the plane carrying Leslie Howard and the others had lifted off from Portela airfield outside Lisbon, eight long-range fighter planes took off from an air base at Kerlin, near Bordeaux. These speedy aircraft, led by Lieutenant Fritz Bellstedt, intercepted the Douglas. Closing in, the fighters opened fire. Moments later, the Douglas's fuel tanks were in flames and the plane plunged into the sea. The bodies of the victims were never found.

Few other World War II casualties induced in the British public such an acute sense of shared personal loss as did the death of fifty-year-old Leslie Howard. He was far more than just a popular actor who had starred in a number of successful American movies, including *Gone with the Wind, The Petrified Forest,* and *Of Human Bondage.* In an odd way, he stood for all that was deeply rooted in the British character. He was "typical"—a typical gentleman with guts.

When the war broke out in late 1939, Howard came home from Hollywood to make films for the British government at a time when others in the British film industry were scurrying in the other direction to the sanctuary of the United States.

Why, the outraged British public demanded to know, had the Germans broken an unwritten guarantee of safe conduct for the airliners on the Lisbon-London service? Speculation surfaced that Howard, a patriot to the core, actually had been in Portugal and Spain on an undercover mission for the British secret service.

The actor's curious actions lent some credence to this theory. Two months before he vanished over the Bay of Biscay, Howard had been in the middle of making a new film, *The Lamp Still Burns,* in England. Suddenly, he flew to Portugal and Spain for what was announced as "a lecture tour on how films are made," a rather strange and trivial endeavor for a loyal British citizen whose country was at war.

Those who held to the spy-mission theory pointed out that such a tour would be a typical, and ideal, role for an undercover operation. Had Howard's airplane been shot down by the Luftwaffe because Nazi spies in Spain and Portugal felt that he had stumbled onto vital intelligence and was bringing it back to London?

It was also speculated that Josef Goebbels, the Third Reich's propaganda genius, had learned of Howard's presence in Portugal and Spain and had ordered that his plane be shot down on its return to England. According to this theory, Goebbels's action resulted from a number of anti-Nazi films that Howard had starred in as well as produced and directed.

One of these movies was *The First of the Few.* Howard portrayed R. J. Mitchell, designer of the Spitfire, the fighter plane that had played such a critical role in defeating the powerful Luftwaffe in the 1940 Battle of Britain. Such movies provided an enormous morale boost to the home front, this school of thought held. In Goebbels's scheme of things, Howard had to go.

Other Britons were convinced that the breach of the implied safe-conduct rule had been a case of mistaken identity. In their opinion, the Luftwaffe attack was really an effort by the Nazis to assassinate Prime Minister Winston Churchill, who was winging to England at about the same time on generally the same route after visiting the British armed forces in North Africa. Churchill's visit had been widely reported in the Allied and neutral world press, so Nazi agents no doubt had been alerted to keep a vigilant eye open. In this theory, which was subscribed to by Churchill himself, a Nazi spy had mistakenly signaled the Wehrmacht that the British leader had boarded a civilian airliner at Portelo airfield outside Lisbon.

"Stupid Nazi agents!" Churchill would later remark. "It is difficult to understand how anyone could imagine that with all the resources of Great Britain at my disposal I should have booked a passage in an unarmed and unescorted plane and flown home in broad daylight. Our plane, of course, made a wide loop out by night from Gibraltar into the ocean, and arrived home without incident."

The truth of the airliner shoot-down would never be learned from the German side. But for Leslie Howard, being mistaken for Winston Churchill might well have been an exceptionally rewarding final curtain call.

Early on the morning of June 10, seven days after Leslie Howard's plane went down, Dwight Eisenhower strode into a roomful of reporters in the St. George Hotel in Algiers. Knowing that the Western Allies had a powerful war machine lying dormant since the capitulation of Axis forces in Tunisia the previous month, the correspondents were expecting a routine announcement—perhaps the appointment of an officer or two to key posts in the Allied coalition. What the reporters received instead was a bombshell.

Eisenhower, far too heavily burdened to engage in preliminary prattle, got right to the point. "We will assault Sicily early in July, with the British Eighth Army under General Montgomery attacking the eastern beaches near Syracuse and the U.S. Seventh Army under General Patton attacking the southern beaches," he said.

Everyone was silent. An official announcement to thirty reporters one month in advance of D-day for the invasion code-named Husky, including the target and time? The correspondents were stunned.

Eisenhower held back virtually nothing. Reporters ceased to scribble notes. The top-secret information they were receiving could not be transmitted to their newspapers, magazines, or radio stations. Each correspondent realized that thousands of Allied lives would be the price paid for any inadvertent leaks of this incredible briefing.

As the supreme commander neared the conclusion of his remarks, he stated, "We will use airborne troops on a much larger scale than has yet been attempted in warfare."

Eisenhower left the room. The reporters remained seated in silence. Then, individually and in small groups, they drifted away. Many resisted the impulse to glance back over their shoulders. Was anyone following them—perhaps German spies?

The supreme commander's top-secret disclosure had not been loosed impetuously; it had been extensively debated with staff officers. Curiously, the purpose of briefing reporters a month in advance was to maintain secrecy about Husky. During periods when no major operation was in progress, correspondents had to continue to send back regular reports to their publications or radio networks. Most of these stories were speculative, the correspondents seeking new angles. Eisenhower feared that a flood of conjectural articles in U.S. and British media could be pieced together by crafty German intelligence agencies to pinpoint Sicily as the target for invasion.

Some reporters were hesitant to go to bed at night, fearful that they might talk in their sleep. Others cut back on their drinking for the same reason.[1]

While Dwight Eisenhower and his commanders were feverishly preparing to bounce across the Mediterranean and invade Sicily, Allied leaders were bedeviled by Charles de Gaulle's relentless machinations to seize power in France after the war. His actions and intrigues brought him into conflicts of ever-intensifying gravity with Roosevelt and Churchill. "We call him Joan of Arc," Churchill said, "and we're looking for some bishops to burn him." In exasperation, Roosevelt recommended that de Gaulle be arrested and held in exile.[2]

Earlier in London, de Gaulle had created his own secret service, the Bureau Centrale de Renseignements et d'Action (BCRA), largely with the help and financial support of MI-6, the British secret service. Soon the French general viewed BCRA not as an agency to fight the Nazis but as an instrument to ruin his political opponents and obtain postwar leadership of France. By early 1943, BCRA and MI-6 were at war with one another.

De Gaulle had appointed André Dewavrin, an energetic and articulate escapee from Nazi-held France, to head BCRA. The thirty-seven-year-old Dewavrin was cunning, brainy, and ruthless, a man prepared to stop at nothing to reach de Gaulle's goals. He was accused of using Gestapo-like methods; opponents of de Gaulle had a knack for finding themselves dead in dark alleys in London.[3]

The British secret service regarded Dewavrin and de Gaulle as revolutionary exiles who would establish and maintain covert communications with their homeland for personal political gain. Consequently, BCRA was kept under surveillance by the British secret service, which even infiltrated agents into Dewavrin's headquarters as key staffers. De Gaulle, suspicious by nature, came to believe that the British secret service had paid French exiles handsomely to spy on him personally, a hunch that no doubt had merit.

De Gaulle was particularly mistrustful of the Special Operations Executive (SOE), a cloak-and-dagger outfit created early in the war by Winston Churchill with the order: "Set Europe ablaze!" SOE was under Major General Colin McV. Gubbins, a forty-five-year-old Scotsman regarded as Britain's foremost expert on guerrilla warfare. Over the months, Gubbins had slipped scores of spies into France, and de Gaulle was convinced that SOE operations were nothing more than Churchill's scheming for the postwar spread of British imperialism.

André Dewavrin at BCRA also had been sneaking agents into France by submarine, parachute, and swift motor torpedo boats; as a result, Charles de Gaulle's popularity among the French resistants was spreading rapidly. "De

Gaulle is busy furthering his political ends," Gubbins warned Churchill. "His agents do not appear to be making any attempt to fulfill their primary role of executing an active sabotage and subversion policy."[4]

Field Marshal Alan Brooke agreed. In his view, the Gaullists were creating an underground in France for the primary purpose of taking over the country after its liberation by the Allies. For its part, BCRA (particularly Dewavrin) constantly criticized Gubbins and SOE, accusing them of "bad faith and sharp practices."[5]

No doubt de Gaulle had his eye on postwar power when he established the Conseil National de la Résistance (CNR), a central organization of key Gaullist underground leaders headed by Jean Moulin, who was constantly on the run from the Gestapo in France.

Against this seemingly endless scenario of backstage skirmishing between supposed allies—the United States and Britain versus Gaullist forces—influential Frenchmen in Algiers demanded that de Gaulle replace General Henri Giraud, whom Eisenhower had appointed commander of all French forces in North Africa after Torch. Giraud, many Frenchmen felt, was a puppet of the Anglo-Americans, one who had no real following among "true" Frenchmen.

Consequently, Giraud bowed to heavy pressure and agreed to meet with his arch-foe de Gaulle. On June 10, the same day that Eisenhower was briefing the correspondents on the looming invasion of Sicily, the two French generals huddled in Algiers to discuss creation of a unified front.

Almost from the first stiff handshake between Giraud and de Gaulle, artful intrigue surfaced. It was agreed that a seven-member French Committee on National Liberation (FCNL) would be formed, with de Gaulle and Giraud as copresidents. Giraud, meanwhile, would retain his command over the armed forces—at least for the present.

The FCNL was established shortly thereafter. Immediately, de Gaulle demanded that former Vichy government officials in Algiers be replaced with his own people. Then the Free French leader connived to get Giraud booted out and replaced with a reliable officer—de Gaulle himself. When a majority of the FCNL, aware of de Gaulle's barefaced grasp for total control, failed to back him, he petulantly declared that he was resigning from the group.

Four thousand miles away in Washington, Franklin Roosevelt was delighted to learn that Joan of Arc had removed himself from the French political scene. In a message to Eisenhower, the President stated that "this de Gaulle situation was bound to come to a head sooner or later," because the French general had become "well nigh intolerable."[6]

But Roosevelt, an old pro in political machinations, had been outfoxed. De Gaulle covertly arranged for prominent Frenchmen in Algiers to loudly demand that the FCNL be expanded from seven to fourteen members (with most of the new members being staunch Gaullists, of course). In a magnificent gesture of loyalty to the French cause, de Gaulle agreed to come back into the fold as copresident of the committee.

With a majority of his supporters now on the FCNL, de Gaulle manipulated proceedings to vastly dilute Henri Giraud's clout. Control of the French armed forces was vested in the hands of a subcommittee: Giraud, General Alphonse Juin, and de Gaulle.

Roosevelt was enraged by this turn of events in the "French political mess." He cabled Winston Churchill: "I am fed up with de Gaulle. . . . The time has arrived when we must break with him."[7]

Churchill, who had a far better grasp of intricate French political maneuverings, disagreed, and said a way would have to be found to work with de Gaulle. That "way" was Dwight Eisenhower.

Like the British Bulldog, Eisenhower was convinced that de Gaulle could not be swept from the scene via AFHQ edict. On all sides of him in Algiers, the supreme commander could see signs of great support for de Gaulle. With preparations under way for the invasion of Sicily, Eisenhower feared that a civil war could erupt in North Africa if de Gaulle was bounced from the FCNL, resulting in violence and chaos.

In an effort to calm the agitated Roosevelt, Eisenhower cabled the President that much of the blustery talk between Giraud and de Gaulle had been merely "typical local French politics." He pledged to meet with the two French combatants and insist that Giraud remain in control of the armed forces.

The showdown was scheduled for June 19—only three weeks before D-day for Husky—in Eisenhower's office in the St. George Hotel. De Gaulle, in a calculated ploy, arrived several minutes late. In full uniform complete with decorations, he swept regally into the room and insisted on speaking first.

"I am here in my capacity as president of the French government," de Gaulle declared. It was an absurd pronouncement: There was no French government. Turning to Eisenhower, who was struggling to control his temper, de Gaulle continued, "If you wish to address a request to me, be sure that I will give you satisfaction."[8]

Again, a preposterous statement. The Frenchman's condescending demeanor toward one of the most powerful men in the Allied camp was a gambit intended to convey that de Gaulle was the man in charge in North Africa.

Eisenhower politely asked that Henri Giraud be left in control of the French armed forces. Outraged, de Gaulle snapped, "The organization of the French command is the province of the French government, not *yours!*" Again, de Gaulle projected himself as president of a nonexistent entity.[9]

The face-to-face confrontation between Dwight Eisenhower and Charles de Gaulle ended in a standoff.

In a cable to George Marshall in the Pentagon, Eisenhower claimed that he could "control" de Gaulle (which may have been wishful thinking) and asked the army chief to urge Roosevelt not to precipitate a crisis over the "de Gaulle situation." Giraud, he pointed out, had minimal backing among the French. In the interest of preventing widespread violence on the brink of Husky, Eisenhower intimated that Roosevelt should give "some kind of limited recognition" to the de Gaulle-dominated FCNL.[10]

Roosevelt was infuriated. Bypassing General Marshall, he fired off a blunt cable to Eisenhower, stating that "under no circumstances are you to recognize [the FCNL]." Eisenhower was shocked by the President's inference that Ike might take it upon himself to "recognize" the FCNL. Eisenhower assured the President that he was fully aware of Roosevelt's authority in such matters.

A few weeks later, Roosevelt reversed his position—to a degree. Stressing that he did not want to furnish de Gaulle "a white horse on which he can ride into France and make himself master of a government there," the President recognized the FCNL as the governmental entity of "those French overseas territories which acknowledge its authority."[11]

Until the spring of 1943, the careers of Bernard Montgomery and George Patton ran on separate tracks. Now, with the Sicily invasion nearing, they were about to converge. A personality clash was inevitable.

The son of an Anglican missionary bishop, Montgomery was a perfectionist who drove himself with a tight rein. Except for the men in his own Eighth Army—the self-proclaimed Desert Rats—Monty had managed to make himself roundly disliked in the British services. Soon he would irritate American generals, especially George Patton, as well.

Perhaps Montgomery was suspect in the U.S. hierarchy because he did not smoke or drink or play poker. He chose to live alone in a small trailer (captured from the Afrika Korps) and had a tiny headquarters manned by only a few aides and planners. Montgomery conveyed the impression of setting himself apart from his fellows.

Montgomery was aware of his personality quirks and knew that he annoyed both his superiors and his equals. He unwittingly intensified the irritation of other generals, British and American alike, by his habit of sending his chief of staff, the amiable Major General Francis W. "Freddie" de Guingand, to represent him at conferences.

Regardless of his eccentricities, Montgomery retained the trait that had caused Winston Churchill to rush him to the North African desert to bail out the collapsing Eighth Army—supreme self-confidence.

Planning for Husky had been under way for weeks in the École Normale (Normal School) at Bouzerea, a suburb of Algiers. Known as Force 141, the planners were headed by British Major General Charles H. Gairdner, a forty-five-year-old polo and yachting enthusiast. Under Gairdner, the staff produced seven Husky plans; one after the other, each was discarded as unacceptable. Time was growing short. Days and weeks slipped past. D-day for Sicily drew nearer.

Finally, Force 141 produced Husky Eight, and to the top brass—Eisenhower, Air Marshal Arthur Tedder, and Admiral Cunningham—it appeared to be an excellent invasion plan. But Husky Eight was scrapped, because Bernard Montgomery disliked it. A highly individualistic general, he could not adapt himself to strange plans created by "outsiders."

Harold Alexander, a fellow British general who would command Husky ground forces, confided to his staff that what bothered Monty was that his veteran Eighth Army and George Patton's untested Seventh Army were assigned objectives that would result in equal publicity. Husky Eight called for Patton to land in the northwest corner of Sicily and seize the major port of Palermo while Montgomery captured Syracuse one hundred miles away in the southeast. Two major ports were crucial at the outset to supply troops fighting inland.

Palermo was a glittering gem, and its capture by Patton would have detracted from Montgomery's own triumphs at Syracuse and, conceivably, at Messina, the island's major port in the northeast tip of Sicily. Montgomery, even as fighting raged in North Africa, dropped everything and flew to Algiers for an urgent conference with Eisenhower and Alexander. Although he had not actually seen Husky Eight and knew of it only in generalities, his goal was to discredit the plan. Monty declared that he could not accept Husky Eight and would draw up his own plan. He instructed his staff to create a counterplan in which his Eighth Army would "carry the ball" in Sicily and Patton would go ashore on Monty's left flank in a supporting role.

On April 16, only one day after reaching Rabat, Morocco, having been relieved at II Corps by Omar Bradley, Patton received an urgent telephone call from General Alexander: Could he fly to Algiers the next day for a crucial conference about Husky to be held in the St. George Hotel? It was especially important that Patton attend, Alexander said, because Bernard Montgomery would be present.

Patton was there, precisely on time, only to be told that Montgomery had been stricken by yet another brilliantly timed influenza attack and that Freddie de Guingand would take his place. Then came a message that de Guingand's plane had been forced down because of engine trouble, so General Oliver Leese, a corps commander, would represent Montgomery. Nothing was accomplished. Patton, fuming and damning Montgomery, winged back to Rabat.

Patton was especially upset by what he believed to be the hidden reason for the meeting. It appeared to him that Alexander and Montgomery had connived to rig Husky in Montgomery's favor, to lay the groundwork for giving the Eighth Army leader everything he wanted on a silver platter. Patton also was annoyed that Eisenhower was not present, an absence that he equated with tacit approval of Monty's connivances. This was another instance, Patton felt, of Eisenhower selling out to the British.

Now Eisenhower let it be known that he had changed his mind about Husky Eight and was leaning toward Montgomery's "Easter Plan," so-called because he had ordered his Eighth Army staff to prepare it in Cairo over the Easter weekend.

Patton was outraged by the "British plot." It may have been a plot, but it was not a British one. Air Marshal Tedder, Eisenhower's pipe-smoking British deputy, was vehemently opposed to the Easter Plan because it left thirteen airfields in the hands of the Germans. Another British deputy, Admiral Andrew Cunningham, spoke against the Montgomery plan in even stronger terms, insisting that those airfields had to be secured to protect the mass of ships that would be lying off the invasion beaches.

"Worse, the Easter Plan will throw the Americans [on Montgomery's western flank] to the wolves," Cunningham said.

A few days after the deadlocked Algiers conference, General Alexander flew to Tunisia to brief Montgomery on the progress of the Easter Plan. The two then discussed tactics to force it down the Americans' throats.

Another Husky conference was called for May 2. Apparently believing he had the momentum, Montgomery himself was present. Only this time, Alexander, for whatever reason, could not attend. While in Algiers, Monty attempted to meet with Eisenhower to lobby for the Easter Plan. Curiously, the supreme commander could not be found. No one at his office knew where he was or when he would be back—or so they said.

Undaunted, Montgomery, wearing his trademark nonregulation sweater and maroon beret, sauntered through the St. George headquarters in search of Beetle Smith, Ike's chief of staff. He found him in the men's toilet. For the next ten minutes, Allied strategy was discussed amid the washbowls and urinals.

Monty persuaded Smith to call a staff conference in Alexander's absence so he could boost his case. Smith had not consulted Patton, nor was he invited to attend, so Monty dominated the meeting. He bluntly issued a virtual ultimatum: "I must state here very clearly, and beyond any possibility of doubt, that I will never operate my army dispersed in this operation"—the term "dispersed" meaning if he landed near Syracuse in the southeast and Patton went ashore at Palermo in the northwest.[12]

Monty was plunging ahead full steam, and in the absence of protests from other invasion leaders, he apparently felt it was time to cut Patton down to size. "I consider that the answer to the problem is to shift the U.S. effort from Palermo and to use it in the Gulf of Gela [just west of his own landing beaches]," Montgomery explained.[13]

After the conference broke up, Montgomery returned to his headquarters in Tunisia. Forty-eight hours later, Harold Alexander was on the phone to notify him that he had won. Eisenhower approved of the Easter Plan. Cunningham caved in. So did Tedder.

It now fell to Alexander to notify Patton that his own plan for the Palermo landings had been scrapped. Outwardly, the American took the astonishing news calmly. Actually, he was furious. "This is what you get when your commander-in-chief [Eisenhower] ceases to be an American and becomes an Ally!" he barked to his aides.[14]

While Anglo-American forces in North Africa were coiled to spring, it was obvious to the high command on both sides that Sicily was the next logical target. Sicily, a mountainous, triangular-shaped island the size of the state of New Hampshire, was long regarded as a stepping-stone to continental Europe. The problem facing AFHQ was: What could be done to hoodwink Hitler into believing that the impending Allied blow would hit elsewhere?

An ingenious deception scheme was hatched by MI-6, Great Britain's intelligence branch, under the guidance of Stewart Menzies, an energetic, fifty-three-year-old aristocrat. Menzies and his clever associates constituted the XX-Committee, whose function was to mislead and confuse the enemy. The Sicily stratagem was code-named Mincemeat and was designed to suggest to the Führer and his generals that, because Sicily was such an obvious target, the Allies would strike instead at the large island of Sardinia, northwest of Sicily, or in Greece, several hundred miles to the east of the true invasion site.

It took eight weeks of intensive planning, study, and effort before the XX-Committee was ready to spring Mincemeat on the Germans. Should it succeed, hundreds, perhaps thousands, of British and American lives could be saved.

In London, the deception agents located the body of a young civilian male who had just died from pneumonia. After securing permission from the deceased's family, the corpse was dressed in an officer's uniform of the Royal Marines. A phony card was placed in the dead man's billfold identifying him as Captain (Acting Major) William Martin, 09560. Authentic-looking official documents, all painstakingly crafted, were put in a dispatch case attached to the officer's wrist.

"Captain Martin" was placed in a large container, packed with dry ice, and taken by submarine to the Gulf of Cadiz off southern Spain. On the morning of April 20, 1943, the body of a Royal Marine officer floated ashore at Huelva, where it was known that the Abwehr had an enterprising agent.

It seemed obvious to Spanish authorities that Martin was a British courier who had been delivering top-secret documents to Allied commanders in the Mediterranean when his plane crashed into the Gulf of Cadiz off Huelva.

As the XX-Committee had anticipated, the Abwehr spy, through collusion with pro-German Spanish officials, was permitted to thoroughly examine and make copies of the top-secret documents from the highest levels of the British military found in the dead officer's dispatch case. These papers seemed to indicate conclusively that the Anglo-Americans were going to invade Sardinia or Greece, not Sicily.

Ecstatic over his intelligence bonanza, the Abwehr agent rushed copies of Captain Martin's documents to his chief, Admiral Wilhelm Canaris, Hitler's spymaster, in Berlin. There the papers were meticulously tested as to authenticity. Canaris promptly informed the Führer that the documents were genuine and that the Allies planned to invade Sardinia or Greece. Consequently, German forces were shifted from elsewhere in the Mediterranean and southern Europe to Greece and Sardinia.[15]

Finally, Dwight Eisenhower was able to nail down a date for D-day: July 10. Husky would be the largest combined operation that had yet been undertaken, involving the land, sea, and air forces of two nations. The initial assault would involve 160,000 men, nearly three thousand ships and landing craft, fourteen thousand vehicles, six hundred tanks, and eighteen hundred guns. Spearheading the gargantuan blow to crack open Hitler's vaunted Festung Europa would be paratroopers of the U.S. 82nd Airborne Division, newly arrived and untested in battle, and glidermen and parachutists (known as the Red Devils) of Britain's 1st Airborne Division.

PART TWO

Turning of the Tide

CHAPTER 14

Plot and Counterplot

As D-DAY FOR HUSKY DREW CLOSER and tension thickened in the Allied camp, Major General Matthew B. Ridgway, the forty-six-year-old commander of the 82nd Airborne Division, and British Major General Frederick A. M. "Boy" Browning, the airborne advisor to Dwight Eisenhower, had for weeks been feuding over the allocation of resources. Divergent national interests and a personality clash between the two strong-willed airborne generals had fueled the controversy.

Ridgway and other American airborne commanders were often irritated by remarks made by Browning, who conveyed the impression that the "Yanks" were newcomers to war and thus should listen to his advice. Browning, who was married to the famous novelist Daphne du Maurier, was known as "the Father of the British Airborne," a designation he quite naturally relished.

In one-on-one meetings, Matt Ridgway's neck would turn red when Browning condescendingly responded to his comments: "Now, my dear Ridgway, what you Americans fail to understand is . . . ."

For his part, the brusque, no-nonsense Ridgway was no paragon of tact. His blunt remarks roused the ire of Boy Browning, even in minor matters.

Personalities aside, the core of the two generals' ongoing dispute was that Ridgway and his commanders resented the fact that American C-47 troop-carrier and glider-tug planes were steadily being taken away from allocations for the 82nd Airborne and turned over to the British for their use in Husky. Since orders for the transfer of these precious aircraft came from AFHQ, where Browning was the airborne advisor, Ridgway and his officers were convinced that the British general was the culprit.

Just past midnight on D-day, July 10, scores of gliders carrying grim soldiers of Brigadier P. H. W. Hicks's British 1st Air Landing Brigade cut loose from tug planes offshore and headed for the high-arched Ponte Grande bridge, the Red Devils' primary objective, outside Syracuse. Within hours, the crucial span was in British hands, paving the way for Bernard Montgomery's Eighth Army to storm ashore.

A short time after the British gliders crash-landed, one hundred miles to the west, men of the U.S. 505th Parachute Infantry Regiment, led by Colonel James

M. Gavin, bailed out behind the beaches along the Gulf of Gela, where George Patton's Seventh Army would land. Gale-force winds, inexperienced pilots and navigators, darkness, and the fog of war had resulted in Gavin's troopers being scattered along the coast for sixty miles instead of dropping close together.

Operation Husky had been launched.

On the morning of D-day plus one, Omar Bradley, leader of the U.S. II Corps which had assaulted the Gela beaches, was handed an urgent message from George Patton: "Notify all units, especially AA [antiaircraft], that parachutists 82nd Airborne will drop about 2330 (11:30 P.M.) tonight on Farello landing field west of Gela."

Although Colonel Rueben H. Tucker's 2,304 men of the 504th Parachute Infantry Regiment would bail out behind American lines on the abandoned airfield, great danger loomed. The sky armada of 144 C-47s would have to fly, at low altitude, over hundreds of navy vessels, then turn westward and wing along thirty-five miles of "friendly" beach, packed with guns manned by jittery GIs, to reach the demilitarized zone at Farello.

Bradley promptly issued instructions for all units on shore to be notified. "We don't want our guys being shot down by our own AA," he told Brigadier General William B. Kean, Jr., his chief of staff. An hour later, Kean reported back: Everyone had been warned of that night's paratroop reinforcing drop.[1]

At his makeshift headquarters on the beachhead, Matt Ridgway was worried. What if a lone, frightened GI happened to cut loose with his antiaircraft gun against the low-flying lumbering C-47 sky armada? Would other guns join in?

Ridgway contacted his old antagonist General Boy Browning, the airborne advisor to Eisenhower. The American demanded assurance that Rube Tucker's flight would not be fired on by the navy. In his usual condescending manner, Browning replied that the navy could make no such promise. Every precaution would be taken, but because many merchant vessels and smaller ships were in the area, it would be impossible to give an absolute guarantee.

Ridgway considered Browning's explanation vague and uncertain. It only served to increase his alarm. He rushed to Seventh Army headquarters on the beachhead and issued what amounted to an ultimatum to George Patton's staff: "Unless you give some assurance that the navy won't open up on Tucker's planes, I'm going to officially protest this follow-up drop!"[2]

Patton needed Tucker's paratroopers on shore. His aides approached the navy once again and, this time, obtained the needed assurance that friendly fire would be withheld. Ridgway departed for his command post only partially relieved.

That night, as Rube Tucker's sky armada neared the embattled shore of southern Sicily, American troops on land and scores of navy vessels anchored in the Gulf of Gela had just received the fourth heavy pounding in the past eighteen hours by Luftwaffe JU-88 bombers. Shortly after 11:00 P.M., the hum of German engines faded in the distance. Antiaircraft guns ceased firing. A hush fell over the region.

Minutes later, the ears of the fidgety soldiers and navy men again picked up the faint purr of airplane motors off in the distance. Most thought the Luftwaffe was returning. Actually, the lead flight carrying Rube Tucker's paratroopers was approaching. Suddenly, somewhere in the darkness below, a lone machine gun sent a fountain of tracer bullets into one of the lumbering C-47s as it knifed over the shoreline. Almost immediately, another automatic weapon, either on a navy vessel or on shore, followed suit. Then another and another. Gunfire increased to such an intensity that a curtain of explosives appeared to have been draped across the sky as if to bar entrance to Sicily by outside intruders, be they friendly or enemy.

At Farello airfield, George Patton and Matt Ridgway stood side by side and looked on in horror as plane after plane tumbled in flames out of the sky. "My God!" Patton muttered over and over. Tears welled in Ridgway's eyes.

Within minutes, twenty-three transport planes had been shot down by friendly gunfire, taking to their deaths 318 American paratroopers and air crewmen. Scores of other C-47s had been damaged, with many of those on board killed or wounded.

In the wake of the sky holocaust, finger-pointing erupted. Efforts were made to blame someone else or another branch of the service. General Boy Browning, who had played a major role in planning the parachute operations, was vitriolic in his remarks concerning the U.S. Troop Carrier Command for scattering Colonel Jim Gavin's paratroopers over a sixty-mile stretch of southeast Sicily and for plunging into the maelstrom of friendly antiaircraft fire. By implication, Browning absolved himself of culpability.

Air Marshal Arthur Tedder, Eisenhower's air advisor, was strongly critical of the flight plan that took Rube Tucker's 504th Parachute Regiment over many miles of American beaches bristling with weapons manned by largely inexperienced soldiers. Tedder's criticism seemed to be aimed at his fellow countryman, Browning.

Lieutenant Colonel William P. Yarborough, a battalion commander in the 504th, survived the disaster, although C-47s all around his plane were blown out of the sky. He was stridently vocal in condemning a faulty flight plan for the tragedy, a plan, he declared, that had been drawn up largely by officers unknowledgeable about airborne operations. So caustically did Yarborough make his views known to top generals that he was removed from his battalion command.[3]

In far-off Washington, George Marshall was appalled on receiving word of the dreadful misfortune in Sicily. For two years, he had been a solid booster of airborne forces. Now he was having second thoughts about their future usefulness, so he sent an aide to Sicily to bring back a firsthand report on the "friendly fire" tragedy.

At his battle headquarters on Malta, a tiny Mediterranean island seventy miles south of Sicily, Dwight Eisenhower also was shaken and expressed skepticism as to the future deployment of large airborne formations (a view he would later reverse). However, he refused to indulge in pointing a finger at others. "Blame is about equally divided among the several services," he wrote in his diary, "and with a large measure falling on me because of my failure to make better provisions against misunderstandings."[4]

Within a few days of the British and American armies getting ashore, the original plan was virtually scrapped. George Patton and Bernard Montgomery began improvising their own tactics, competing with each other, scrambling for individual honors. Plot was met with counterplot.

Montgomery's Eighth Army, according to plan, was attacking up the eastern shore toward Husky's primary objective, the glittering prize of Messina. If the port was captured rapidly, Monty could cut off and trap some 190,000 Axis troops in Sicily, denying them an escape valve. On D-day plus four, however, stubborn German resistance was encountered south of Mount Etna, and his attack bogged down well south of Messina.

One of the world's most famous volcanoes, Etna rises 10,705 feet. Part of its base, which is about one hundred miles around, lies on the Mediterranean Sea. Montgomery, therefore, could not skirt the frowning edifice on the east, so he decided to send part of his forces swinging around the left side of Etna. He intended to shift the weight of his advance to Road 117. There was a catch. Road 117 was in Patton's area, and the U.S. 45th Infantry Division already was moving northward on it.

Undaunted, Montgomery put in a call to General Alexander, who was in direct charge of the ground operation, and demanded that the Americans using Road 117 be halted and evicted, and the road turned over to Eighth Army for what Monty called "my left hook." Alexander promptly agreed, without consulting George Patton.

Patton first learned that the two British generals had evicted his forces from a crucial road when Alexander sent out a routine directive. Ordinarily, the volatile Patton would have exploded. His response to Montgomery's "pirating my road," however, was merely to light a cigar. Now he hatched his own counterplot.

Alexander's directive had limited the Seventh Army to acting as "Monty's nursemaid," as Patton put it. In Patton's mind, that meant that he was free to do anything he wanted in the western two-thirds of Sicily as long as he did not infringe on Montgomery's effort to seize Messina or get bogged down in a major battle.

Consequently, on his own initiative, Patton sent spearheads barreling toward the northwest in a mad, hundred-mile dash for Palermo, which had no real military significance but enormous publicity value.

On Malta, Dwight Eisenhower was furious on learning of the unpredictable Patton's tactical improvisation. Advancing largely against Italian troops who would fire a few shots, kill a few Americans, and then surrender, Patton entered Palermo a conquering hero. In view of the flood tide of publicity the capture of the large city was given in newspapers and on radio back home, there was nothing Eisenhower could do about his "bad boy" other than to gnash his own teeth.

While ensconced like a medieval monarch in an ornate palace in Palermo, Patton found out that Montgomery had been halted near Mount Etna and was cautiously regrouping and bringing up supplies before renewing the attack to capture Messina. That information triggered yet another plot in Patton's fertile brain: He would launch spearheads eastward along the northern coast to reach Messina ahead of Montgomery.

In the meantime, momentous events were in motion backstage in Italy. Mild little King Victor Emmanuel III booted out Adolf Hitler's close crony, the bombastic Benito Mussolini, as premier, a post the squat Il Duce had held for twenty-one years. Then, as part of the conspiracy, the monarch had Mussolini arrested and locked up in an undisclosed locale. He appointed the aging Field Marshal Pietro Badoglio in Mussolini's place.

Twenty-four hours later, Badoglio took to Radio Rome to announce Mussolini's downfall to the bewildered Italian people. "The war continues," Badoglio declared. "Italy will keep faith to its pledged word."

Eisenhower was in Tunis eating breakfast when he heard the radio report about Mussolini's downfall. Elated, he called in aides and excitedly ticked off means of getting the Italians to renounce their longtime relationship with Hitler and hop over to the side of the Grand Alliance. Although the aftermath of the Darlan Deal was still indelibly etched in his mind, Eisenhower was willing to seize this unexpected opportunity to get Italy out of the war, even if it meant conniving with an enemy general.

Then bickering broke out among the Allied hierarchy. President Roosevelt insisted that the Italians be held to terms "as close as possible to unconditional surrender." The pragmatic Winston Churchill wanted to handle the Italians more gently. "Now Mussolini is gone," he wired the President. "I would deal with any non-Fascist Italian government which can deliver the goods."

Shortly after reading the Churchill cable, Roosevelt broadcast a saber-rattling statement, firmly declaring that "our terms to Italy are still the same as our terms to Germany and Japan—unconditional surrender. We will have no truck with Fascism in any way, shape, or matter."

That was the "political President" speaking for public consumption. Privately, he expressed his true position in a cable to Churchill: "There are some contentious people here [in Washington] who are getting ready to make a row if we seem to recognize the House of Savoy or Badoglio. They are the same element that made such a fuss [over the Darlan Deal]."[5]

Now Eisenhower proposed making an immediate radio appeal to the Italians, pledging an honorable peace and declaring that the Anglo-Americans "will come to your country as liberators to rid you of the Germans and deliver you from the horrors of war."[6]

Before taking to the airwaves, Eisenhower called in his chief political advisor, Robert Murphy, who told him that the supreme commander had no authority to make a "political broadcast." It would have to be cleared by the governments of the United States and Great Britain.

Disappointed that an enormous opportunity to hold down Allied casualties might be slipping away, Eisenhower submitted his broadcast text to the Combined Chiefs of Staff in Washington. As he had feared, they argued over the wording for an entire week. By the time the butchered text was returned to the supreme commander, it was too late. While the Western Allies were hassling with one another, Adolf Hitler had sent several divisions racing southward from the Alps into northern Italy. German soldiers immediately began disarming the Italian units, a task that was achieved with surprising ease.

The incessant squabbling between London and Washington and Eisenhower's headquarters continued, and no formal action was agreed upon. The supreme commander grew increasingly frustrated. Bulletins from Ultra, the supersecret British electronic monitoring system, kept him advised on the Wehrmacht buildup in Italy, and he cabled the Combined Chiefs: "I do not see how war can be conducted successfully if every act of the Allied supreme commander must be referred back to home government for approval."[7]

During late July and early August, Allied generals in Sicily were convinced that they were driving Axis forces back into the northeast tip of the island through a series of brilliant tactical strokes. Actually, when the Germans and Italians had been unable to smash the seaborne landings, a decision had been reached in Berlin to abandon Sicily.

Northeast Sicily, with its rugged mountains and deep defiles, was ideal for an orderly Axis withdrawal into Messina. Pursuing forces under Patton and Montgomery were canalized to the coastal roads, where small units of German soldiers, fighting a stubborn rearguard action, made the advancing Allies pay dearly in blood.

Beginning on the night of August 10, Lieutenant General Hans Hube, a grizzled and shrewd tactician who had left an arm on a Russian battlefield, began Operation Lehrgang, the evacuation of German and Italian forces across the two-mile-wide Strait of Messina to mainland Italy. A total of 39,569 German troops (including some forty-five hundred wounded), forty-seven tanks, ninety-four large guns, two thousand tons of ammunition and fuel, and more than fifteen thousand tons of equipment and supplies were ferried across—without a shot being fired at the escaping force.

At noon on August 16, just as Patton's leading elements charged into Messina from the west, only an hour ahead of Montgomery's spearheads coming up from the south, a motorized raft carried the last detachment of Italian soldiers to Italy. This completed the transfer of 62,182 Italian troops, forty-one artillery pieces, 227 vehicles, one thousand tons of ammunition—and fourteen mules.[8]

General Hube's trapped armies had made a clean getaway.

At the same time Patton's tanks roared into Messina, a jubilant General Alexander cabled Winston Churchill: "The last German soldier [has been] flung out of Sicily." Actually, the Germans had hardly been flung out. The Allies had 475,000 men in the invasion to the Axis's 190,000, many of the latter being Italians who despised the Germans and only wanted to go home. Alexander could have added that just three tenacious German divisions had carried the brunt of the fighting and that they had skillfully held up the two Allied drives toward Messina for five weeks, then pulled off a daring escape under the noses of the powerful Anglo-American navy and air force. What's more, the invaders suffered more dead than did the Germans.[9]

Back in Algiers, Dwight Eisenhower was handed a report by a headquarters surgeon who said it was from one of his army doctors in Sicily. On August 10, the document stated, George Patton had visited the 93rd Evacuation Hospital and slapped an enlisted man who had no visible injuries. The supreme commander was reading the report on the same afternoon that Patton barreled into Messina.

Basking in the mellow glow of victory in Sicily, Eisenhower was only mildly disturbed. "I guess I'll have to give Georgie a jacking up," he remarked. Recognizing the uproar that would follow if the slapping episode became public, however, the supreme commander ordered his chief inspector, Colonel Herbert S. Clarkson, to go to Sicily and conduct a full investigation—and to keep it hushed up.

"If this thing ever gets out," Eisenhower said, "they'll be howling for George's scalp."

With great battles looming in the Mediterranean and in Europe, Eisenhower needed Patton, his most audacious commander and one indispensable to winning the war.[10]

At first, Patton's cronies hushed up the unseemly episode. Omar Bradley, the II Corps commander, who had received the first report, filed it away. Eisenhower's deputy, Major General Everett Hughes, a longtime friend and drinking buddy of Patton, also did nothing when he was told of the incident by Lieutenant Colonel Perrin H. Long of the U.S. Medical Corps.

Eisenhower did write a personal letter, in longhand, to Patton. "I clearly understand that firm and drastic measures are at times necessary in order to secure desired objectives," he wrote. "But this does not excuse brutality, abuse of the sick, nor exhibition of uncontrollable temper in front of subordinates."

Eisenhower closed by telling Patton that no copies existed of the surgeon's report on the slapping episode or of the letter of rebuke the supreme commander had written. The originals would be stashed in Eisenhower's "secret file."

Colonel Clarkson, the inspector general, handed his report to Eisenhower on September 1. It contained rather startling details. George Patton, it appeared, had gone totally berserk. The general, the document stated, had approached a private who was huddled up, shivering and whimpering, and had asked him what was wrong.

"It's my nerves," the man sobbed.

"What did you say!" Patton exclaimed.

"It's my nerves. I can't stand the shelling any more."

According to the report, the general retorted: "Your nerves, hell. You're just a goddamned coward, you yellow son of a bitch!"

Then Patton slapped the man, some witnesses said, with the gloves he held in one hand.

"Shut up that goddamned crying!" he screamed. "I won't have these brave men here who have been shot seeing a yellow bastard sitting there crying!"

By now, a group of nurses and patients had gathered from nearby wards. Again Patton turned to the soldier. "You're going back to the front lines and you may get shot and killed, but you're going to fight. If you don't, I'll stand you up against a wall and have a firing squad kill you!"

Then the irate general reached for his ivory-handled revolver, declaring, "Why, I ought to shoot you myself, you goddamned whimpering coward!"

At that point, doctors hustled Patton out of the ward.

Now the high-level cover-up began in earnest. Aides advised Eisenhower to secretly tip off George Marshall about the incident at once. Ike disregarded the advice, hoping that word would never leak out. All reports of the slapping were locked in Eisenhower's personal safe.

However, much of Sicily was buzzing about the affair, and it soon reached the ears of correspondents. On August 19, only forty-eight hours after Patton's triumphant entry into Messina, Quentin Reynolds of *Collier's*, Merrill "Red" Mueller of the NBC radio network, and Demaree Bess of the *Saturday Evening Post* called on Beetle Smith. Someone had leaked Colonel Clarkson's top-secret report.

The three correspondents, all of whom were highly regarded in and outside the media world, told Smith that they did not want to embarrass General Eisenhower or disrupt the war effort. However, they believed that the hotheaded Patton deserved punishment. They proposed a deal: If the general was booted out and sent home, they would hold back the blockbuster story.

Eisenhower thought quickly. He called in Reynolds, Bess, and Mueller and all but begged them to withdraw their demand and let him keep Patton. So emotional was his plea that, it seemed to the correspondents, victory could be assured only if Patton was retained. They agreed to sit on the story.[11]

In the meantime, Eisenhower gave Patton "the skinning of his life." He wrote the offender a blistering letter of reprimand and ordered Patton to personally apologize to the soldier he had struck, to the doctors and nurses at 93rd Evacuation Hospital, and to each unit in the Seventh Army where possible. It was a galling penance for the proud George Patton. But he carried it out.

Patton was hardly repentant, however, only bitter. He vented his frustration in his diary: "It is rather a commentary on justice when an Army commander has to soft-soap a skulker to placate the timidity of those above." No doubt the barb was aimed at Dwight Eisenhower, the very man who had saved Patton from being sacked and sent home in disgrace.

Patton was baffled by Eisenhower, his old friend of thirty years. "I can't make Ike out," he wrote to his wife, Beatrice, in Boston. "He's a strange person, and I feel he has an inferiority complex."

CHAPTER 15

Stormy Weather over Château Frontenac

While fighting continued in Sicily, the majestic British ocean liner, *Queen Mary*, sailed into the harbor at Halifax, Nova Scotia. On board were Winston Churchill, Field Marshal Alan Brooke, and their customary entourage of 250 conference delegates—advisors, analysts, typists, clerks, and statisticians. Also along was Brooke's floating library, the Special Information Centre, containing, as at Casablanca, a mountain of position papers for every conceivable contingency to rebut American arguments. It was August 9, 1943.

As usual, the British had fully prepared for the top-level strategy conference (code-named Quadrant), which would be held in the stately Château Frontenac overlooking the broad expanse of the St. Lawrence River in Quebec. On reaching the site, however, they were astonished to find an even larger American delegation similarly equipped with position papers and intelligence reports. Clearly, the American "newcomers to war" were learning quickly about techniques in salesmanship after floundering in previous strategy confrontations with the British.

Almost from the beginning of the American-British relationship, George Marshall and his advisors had sought to determine why Churchill, Brooke, and the British service chiefs always appeared to accept American demands for a cross-Channel assault against northern France, and then, through clever manipulation, talked Marshall and his colleagues into operations in the Mediterranean and other locales on the periphery of Adolf Hitler's empire.

Perhaps out of frustration, George Marshall had asked General Stanley D. Eimbeck, a former deputy chief of staff and a sort of elder statesman and kingmaker in the United States Army, to draft what could be called psychological profiles of Churchill and Brooke. Assisting the highly respected Eimbeck would be his son-in-law, Brigadier General Albert Wedemeyer, chief of the U.S. Strategy and Policy Group. These two officers had the task of assessing the truth behind the excessively intricate personality and oratory of Winston Churchill and the British point of view.

Eimbeck and Wedemeyer produced a document that claimed that for more than a century the British had not deviated one iota from their efforts to maintain the balance of power in Europe. It was Great Britain's intention, the psychological report declared, "to delay Germany's defeat until military attrition and civilian famine had materially reduced Russia's potential toward Europe."

Extended operations in the Mediterranean, therefore, served the British purpose of marking time with a minimum expenditure of British blood and resources, of dispersing and diverting German forces, and of ensuring a British presence in the Mediterranean and Balkans in the postwar world. In conclusion, Eimbeck stated what Marshall and his advisors no doubt had already discovered for themselves: Winston Churchill was a skilled and sometimes devious orator, a master salesman.[1]

Marshall was especially leery of the British again outwitting the Americans after hearing a powerful U.S. senator, Arthur Vandenberg, state before a Senate subcommittee that he and some of his fellow legislators were "disturbed" because the British "usually ended up on top."[2]

While the Combined Chiefs of Staff did the donkeywork at Quebec, Churchill traveled to Hyde Park, Franklin Roosevelt's estate overlooking the Hudson River, to meet with the President before the two leaders moved on to the conference. Churchill soon realized he was facing a "new" Roosevelt. The President's mind already was made up: He was resolved to concentrate every available soldier in England for a cross-Channel attack in the spring of 1944. Roosevelt added that he wanted to abandon all further operations in the Mediterranean, and he would insist that Marshall command the massive assault over the English Channel, now code-named Overlord.

Churchill may well have been taken aback by Roosevelt's firm stand. The British Bulldog also had been placed in an embarrassing position: He already had promised the command of Overlord to Alan Brooke.

Wily as always, however, Churchill heartily agreed with both of Roosevelt's proposals. After all, when it was time for Overlord, the Americans would be providing most of the troops after the assault phase, so it was only proper that Marshall be the supreme commander. On the other hand, Churchill continued, since the Mediterranean would be reduced to a secondary theater after Overlord, should not the commander there be a Briton? That made sense to Roosevelt, provided that the British stuck to Overlord as the *maximum* effort. Of course, of course, the Prime Minister purred.

While Roosevelt and Churchill were chatting at Hyde Park, the Combined Chiefs opened their conference in Quebec on August 14. From the start, the mood of the Americans was less amiable and far more determined than had been the case at Casablanca. George Marshall, Ernest King, and Hap Arnold were totally committed to Overlord and wanted no more adventures in the Mediterranean, especially not in Italy.

Both sides knew that there would be a no-holds-barred clash over Overlord—and it was not long in coming. Marshall, no doubt with Stanley Eimbeck's psychological profile of the British in mind, took the offensive immediately and stated that Alan Brooke and his colleagues must now give the cross-Channel strategy priority over any other operations in 1944. Marshall spoke in sharp tones and seemed to be angry.

Brooke appeared to be angry as well. He replied that Churchill and the British chiefs agreed that Overlord should be the major operation in 1944, *but* . . .

Marshall and King winced. There was that "but" again, the one the British always threw in after seeming to agree with American ideas for strategy. But, Brooke continued, the success of Overlord depended on achieving "three main conditions": Reducing the strength of the Luftwaffe, diminishing the ability of the Wehrmacht to bring up reinforcements after the invasion, and solving the awesome problem of supplying the Allied armies over the invasion beaches.

And how might a situation favorable to Overlord be obtained? Brooke said the answer was by leaping across the narrow Strait of Messina and invading Italy to contain the maximum German forces and by air action from Italian bases to whittle down the Luftwaffe.[3]

Now the session turned stormy. Admiral Ernest King, red-faced with anger, pounded the table and employed blunt, profanity-laced language to refute Brooke's viewpoints.[4]

When King's rebuttal had run out of steam, Marshall continued the attack. Unless the British honored their earlier pledges to give priority to Overlord, he stressed heatedly, "the entire [Allied] strategic concept would have to be revised." It was a direct threat, for Marshall was implying that the Germany-first concept would be altered by the Americans to a Japan-first doctrine, leaving Great Britain and the Soviet Union to fight the still powerful Wehrmacht.[5]

Tension still hung in the conference room when the sun began to sink into the horizon behind the St. Lawrence River, and the two sides adjourned. That night, Brooke wrote in his diary: "A gloomy and unpleasant day. Quite impossible to argue with [Marshall] as he does not understand a strategic problem. . . . The only real argument he produced was a threat."[6]

Worse was yet to come for Brooke. Churchill and Roosevelt had arrived in Quebec, and the Prime Minister took Brooke for a stroll on the terrace of the Château Frontenac. There the Prime Minister casually told the field marshal that he was out and Marshall was in as supreme commander of Overlord.

"Not for one moment did he realize what this meant to me," Brooke would write bitterly. "He offered no sympathy, no regrets at having had to change his mind, and dealt with the matter as if it were one of minor importance."[7]

Brooke had no time to lick his wounds. Early the next morning, electrifying news reached the conference: An Italian general had made contact with Eisenhower's headquarters to discuss the surrender of the Italian armed forces, after which Italy would turn against the Third Reich and join the Grand Alliance. Then came disturbing news by way of Ultra: A large German army under Field Marshal Erwin Rommel was massing in the Alps of northern Italy to reinforce the thirteen Wehrmacht divisions already on the peninsula.

Immediate action was necessary. Italy was quickly crumbling. Brooke rushed to the conference table and told Marshall in a conciliatory tone that "the root of the matter is that we are not trusting each other." America and Great Britain must take advantage of the Italian collapse and launch an invasion of Italy at once, Brooke said. In preparation for Overlord, it would now be possible to suck not only German divisions but entire armies into the areas of Italy and the Balkans formerly occupied by the Italian armed forces.

After three contentious hours of point and counterpoint, Marshall agreed to an invasion of Italy, even though he had many times sworn he would not get involved deeper in "the interminable black hole of the Mediterranean." In rapid order, the two sides whipped up an invasion concept. Bernard Montgomery's Eighth Army would cross the Strait of Messina in fourteen days, and the nucleus of a new U.S. Army, Mark Clark's Fifth, would land at Salerno, one-third up the boot of Italy, and capture Naples as a major supply port.

Alan Brooke was euphoric. In the moment of his greatest personal despair over losing the command of Overlord, he had triumphed at the conference table.

As a final order of business, Brooke and the British chiefs agreed to Marshall's demand that Overlord be the primary operation of 1944. The invasion date was set for May 1. The target would be Normandy, along the same beaches from which Duke William had sailed in 1066 to conquer England. To alleviate Brooke's concerns about supplying the armies across the open invasion beaches, two good-sized artificial ports (code-named Mulberries) were to be built, towed across the Channel, and anchored off the Normandy shore.

History's mightiest military endeavor, Overlord, had been nailed down. Or had it? Although he had agreed to the cross-Channel attack in 1944, Winston Churchill had not changed his mind. He could never forget the fearful price in blood that England had had to pay for the great frontal offensives of the First World War.

The days of endless friction at the Château Frontenac had occasional lighter moments. One of these came when Vice Admiral Louis Mountbatten, a relative of England's royal family and chief of Britain's Combined Operations, asked for permission to demonstrate a "revolutionary new weapon." Mountbatten—young, handsome, and with a distinguished record in the Royal Navy—liked Americans and got along especially well with Dwight Eisenhower.

Mountbatten's secret weapon was the brainchild of British scientist Geoffrey Pyke, who toiled for Combined Operations. Pyke had discovered that water mixed with sawdust and then frozen produced a substance six times stronger than ice. He called his substance Pykrete. Mountbatten, to the probable annoyance of the Combined Chiefs, delivered an enthusiastic spiel about building two-thousand-foot vessels of Pykrete as floating, virtually unsinkable, aircraft carriers.

Anticipating the skepticism of his hard-bitten audience, Mountbatten signaled two aides to wheel in a block of Pykrete and a chunk of ice for a demonstration. An ax was produced, and the Combined Chiefs chose Hap Arnold to conduct a test. Removing his jacket, the U.S. Air Corps chief picked up the ax and whacked the cake of ice, splitting it in two. Then he took a hefty swing at the Pykrete, and wrenched his arm when the blade bounced off the tough substance.

Mountbatten, a master showman, still was not satisfied. He pulled a pistol from his waist and announced that he would demonstrate Pykrete's resistance to gunfire. The Combined Chiefs discreetly rose from their chairs and took up defensive positions out of the line of fire.

Crack-k-kk-kkk! The sound of the pistol discharge reverberated through staid Château Frontenac. The bullet bounced off the Pykrete and ricocheted around the room as the Combined Chiefs instinctively ducked. Smiling smugly, Mountbatten replaced his weapon.

Outside the room, a voice called out, "First they argued, then they began hitting each other, now they've started shooting!"[8]

A few days after the Quebec conference broke up, an intricate, clandestine melodrama was unfolding in the Mediterranean. It began when Dwight Eisenhower received a mysterious telegram from the Pentagon, directing him to send a pair of top officers to meet with a certain Señor Raimondi in neutral Lisbon, Portugal. Clad in ill-fitting clothes borrowed from Italian civilians, Beetle Smith and British Brigadier Kenneth D. Strong, Eisenhower's intelligence chief, sneaked into Lisbon after dark.

The mood was that of a Hollywood spy thriller. Smith and Strong rendezvoused with Señor Raimondi in a shabby, dimly lit café on a Lisbon back street. Raimondi, it turned out, was the nom de guerre of General Guiseppe Castellano, King Victor's emissary, who also was wearing a tattered civilian suit, a widebrimmed hat pulled down over his eyes.

The confrontation was tense. Lisbon was saturated with German spies and informers. Castellano wished to negotiate a peace favorable to Italy, but his hopes were quickly dashed. Smith sternly told the Italian that he, as Eisenhower's envoy, was not there to negotiate, but to lay down terms that Italy would have to accept.

Smith made it clear that if by August 30 Eisenhower's headquarters had not heard of acceptance of the terms by the Italian government, it would be assumed that the Allied proposal had been rejected. Shaken by the unexpected turn of events—Castellano had thought he would be welcomed with open arms—the Italian emissary left for Rome. His luggage concealed a clandestine radio and a codebook provided by Smith and Strong for contacting Allied headquarters in Algiers.

On August 30, Castellano radioed Algiers that he would fly to Sicily the next day to discuss armistice terms. Reaching Cassible, near Syracuse, Castellano had startling news for Beetle Smith: Because of heavy German reinforcements rushed into Italy, King Victor and Pietro Badoglio would be unable to announce an armistice until the Allies invaded Italy and were firmly ashore.

An argument raged all day. It became obvious to Smith that the Italians were far more frightened of the Germans than they were of flaunting the Allies. Finally, in exasperation, the sharp-tongued Smith blurted, "Well, then, just what in the hell will it take to get your government's cooperation?"

Castellano replied that, at a minimum, the Allies would have to drop one airborne division on Rome, with a strong armed force to land by sea near the mouth of the Tiber River to link up with the paratroopers and glidermen. The airborne force was to secure Rome, 130 miles north of Salerno, just before a public announcement of Italy's surrender was made over the radio.

Dwight Eisenhower agreed to the terms and selected Matt Ridgway's 82nd Airborne Division for the perilous mission.

On September 3, a day after the Italians agreed to surrender terms, Bernard Montgomery's Eighth Army leapfrogged from Sicily across the narrow Strait of Messina onto the toe of mainland Italy under cover of darkness. Code-named Baytown, the operation had little military value. It did have enormous psychological impact, however, for it vastly increased the pressure on King Victor and Pietro Badoglio to comply with armistice terms and cooperate with the Allies.

Announcing the Italian armistice and subsequent moves by the Allies would have to be delicately timed. Dwight Eisenhower would read the surrender terms over Radio Algiers at 6:30 P.M. on September 8, and Field Marshal Badoglio would follow thirty minutes later with a statement over Radio Rome, only hours before Mark Clark's Fifth Army was to storm ashore at Salerno. Matt Ridgway's paratroopers were to lift off for Rome from airfields in Sicily as soon as they heard the start of the radio broadcast by the supreme commander.

As the hours slipped by, Ridgway and his regimental commanders began to have serious doubts about the Rome mission, code-named Giant II. It called for dropping a few thousand lightly armed paratroopers—without artillery, antitank guns, tanks, tactical air cover, or a reasonably certain method of resupply—into the midst of Wehrmacht concentrations in and around a sprawling city of three million people, 250 miles from the nearest armed Allied soldier in Sicily. Giant II had all the ingredients of a classic suicide mission.

In the meantime, shortly after dawn on September 6, Mark Clark's command ship, the *Ancon*, edged out of Algiers harbor to join a convoy of some seventy vessels escorted by the U.S. cruisers *Philadelphia, Boise,* and *Savannah* and fourteen destroyers for the trek to Salerno. As the *Ancon* was moving out to sea, it passed a small native vessel. The Algerian civilians on board waved vigorously and called out, "Have a good time in Salerno!"

Men on the *Ancon* were shocked. If these Algerians knew the target of the looming assault, did the Germans also know it?

Despite his early enthusiasm for Giant II, Eisenhower became increasingly disturbed that the mission could result in a calamity for the American airborne men. He was particularly worried about the true intentions of the Italian government, whose assistance would be crucial to the success of the drop on Rome. With the hours ticking away, he decided to send two American officers on a dangerous mission to Rome to determine firsthand the situation there and whether the Italian armed forces could provide the cooperation assured by General Castellano, King Victor's armistice emissary.

Selected for the secret mission were Brigadier General Maxwell D. Taylor, commander of the 82nd Airborne artillery, and Colonel William T. Gardiner, commander of a troop carrier squadron in Sicily. Each man could speak and understand Italian.

Taylor, the senior officer, was told that he had total authority to radio back from Rome any changes in the parachute operation he felt were vital. He also was empowered to cancel the drop if he determined that conditions in Rome might result in disaster for the paratroopers. If Taylor's decision was to cancel the airborne operation, he was to radio a single word: "Innocuous."

Boarding a British motor torpedo boat for the first leg of their mission, Taylor and Gardiner left Palermo harbor at 2:00 A.M. on September 7. Speed was vital: Ridgway's parachutists were to jump in only forty-one hours. Two hours later, the Americans transferred to an Italian-manned corvette, the *Ibis*, which docked at Gaeta, Italy, seventy-five miles below Rome, at 5:30 P.M.

Wearing disguises, Taylor and Gardiner rode in the backseat of an Italian navy car through the streets of Gaeta. Outside the city, they transferred to an ambulance for the two-hour run up the twisting coastal road to Rome. En route, the ambulance was halted at two German roadblocks, but was permitted to continue after the guards peeked casually at the two "patients" in the rear of the vehicle.

It was not until 8:30 P.M. that Taylor and Gardiner reached the Palazzo Caprara in Rome. The large, old stone building was part of the Italian war office. It soon became obvious that the Italians were stalling. With time slipping away, it would be two more hours before a few Italian generals showed up, bringing bad news with them.

Generale di Corpo d'Amata Giacomo Carboni, chief of Italian army intelligence, explained nervously that there had been only twelve thousand German soldiers in the Rome region. "Now they have reinforced the area and there are 125 heavy tanks and 150 light tanks and thirty-six thousand soldiers just north and south of Rome," Carboni declared. In the vicinity of the 82nd Airborne drop zones were an additional twelve hundred German troops and one hundred pieces of artillery.

In light of this shocking disclosure, Max Taylor insisted on meeting with Field Marshal Badoglio at once. It was then nearing midnight. Accompanied by the nervous General Carboni, the two Americans were driven through dark and lonely streets to the sumptuous mansion of marble and tile occupied by the seventy-four-year-old Badoglio.

A servant awakened the premier, and fifteen minutes later he greeted Taylor and Gardiner. It was a tense confrontation. Ridgway's men would be taking off from Sicily in only seventeen hours. Badoglio spent several minutes explaining his great desire to cooperate with the Allies.

"But if I declare an armistice now, the Germans will take Rome and put in their own government," he said almost tearfully. "I am helpless to do anything."[9]

At 8:10 A.M. that same day, a decoded message from Badoglio was handed to Eisenhower at his office atop the St. George Hotel in Algiers. The premier merely outlined the circumstances as to why he could not fulfill the agreements he had previously proposed—the radio announcement of the armistice and armed assistance to the 82nd Airborne Division.

Deeply disturbed by this news, a furious Eisenhower fired off a blunt radiogram to Badoglio: "I intend to broadcast the existence of the armistice at the hour originally planned [6:30 P.M. that day]. If you or any part of your armed forces fail to cooperate, I will publish to the world the full report of the affair."[10]

Confused, alarmed, frightened, caught in the center of a situation for which there seemed to be no solution, Badoglio wired back that he would read the armistice terms over Radio Rome as planned.

Elsewhere in Rome, at 11:55 A.M., only twelve hours before American paratroopers were to lift off from Sicily, Max Taylor sent a one-word message to Eisenhower: "Innocuous." Giant II was promptly canceled.[11]

At 6:25 P.M., nine hours before American and British assault troops sailing on the Tyrrhenian Sea were to storm ashore at Salerno, the men aboard the USS *Samuel Chase* were snapping fingers and tapping toes to the melodic strains of the Glenn Miller orchestra's popular tune "In the Mood," which was blaring over the loudspeaker. Suddenly, the amplifier fell silent. Curses rang out.

Moments later, a solemn voice intoned over the loudspeaker, "Stand by for an important announcement." Another voice followed, "This is General Dwight D. Eisenhower, commander in chief of the Allied forces. The Italian government has surrendered its armed forces unconditionally. . . . "

Bedlam erupted on the *Chase*. Cheers drowned out the remainder of the two-minute statement. There was backslapping. Shouts of joy. Men rolling on the deck in glee. "Home for Christmas!" they called out. "The war's over!" Similar scenes broke out on the other vessels in the convoy.

The first Allied invasion of continental Europe might, they thought, be unopposed. One of the overjoyed troops would recall, "We were convinced we would dock in Naples harbor unopposed, with an olive branch in one hand and an opera ticket in the other."[12]

CHAPTER 16

Rejection of an Anti-Hitler Conspiracy

AT 3:00 A.M. ON D-DAY, an earsplitting roar erupted from a line of American and British warships lying in the Gulf of Salerno. The sky was aglow with the brilliant muzzle flashes of large-caliber guns sending an avalanche of death-dealing shells onto the shoreline. Mark Clark's army—two American corps and one British—would storm ashore along a thirty-one-mile crescent of beaches.

In the blackness, Clark's men wriggled down rope ladders slung over the sides of squat transports and dropped into tiny assault boats. Guided by small inshore submarines flashing colored beacons, the boats formed into skirmish lines and headed toward the silent unknown on land.

Unaware that tough German soldiers were lying in wait, the assault troops scrambled out of their boats into waist-deep water and began wading to the beaches. Suddenly, the dark sky was illuminated with bright flares, and moments later came the angry chatter of scores of concealed machine guns and the cracks of German 88-millimeter shells exploding among the helpless men struggling to get ashore.

All the landing beaches were converted into a bedlam of fire, death, and confusion. The Germans, through wireless intelligence and aerial reconnaissance, knew that Fifth Army was coming—and where it would hit. By nightfall, after vicious fighting, Clark's men were hanging on by their fingertips. There was a twenty-five-mile gap between the British and American beaches. Worse, the invaders were confronted by two first-rate German divisions. Disaster loomed.

In the meantime, the legally constituted government of Italy had fled during the chaotic hours of darkness. King Victor Emmanuel, aged, pathetic, physically infirm, and nervous, had piled into an old Italian car at his palace. Field Marshal Badoglio, also elderly and shaky, had climbed into another vehicle, as had other government officials and the chiefs of the army, navy, and air force. With lights extinguished, the little convoy began weaving its way out of Rome. Even before the escapees departed, two veteran German divisions had raced into Rome and would soon have the Eternal City under control.

King Victor and his party traveled on the Via Tiburtina, one of the few exit roads not blocked by the Germans. Their detection no doubt would have resulted in their instant execution, following orders handed down by Adolf Hitler, who had been infuriated by Italy's treachery. Leaving the shadowy silhouette of Rome in the background, the escaping group drove eastward toward the Adriatic coast, arriving at the harbor at Pescara while it was still dark. There the group boarded an Italian navy ship and sailed southward to the coastal town of Brindisi, in the heel of the Italian boot, where King Victor would establish his government.

On D-day plus one at Salerno, the Allied situation worsened. Now the Luftwaffe hit at the invasion fleet offshore using a revolutionary new weapon: Wireless-controlled, rocket-propelled, armor-piercing bombs known as FX-1400s. Two U.S. cruisers and one British cruiser were badly damaged, and the mighty British warship *Respite* was jolted by bombs that nearly sank her. Five transports and a hospital ship were sent to the bottom.

Field Marshal Albert Kesselring, the highly capable German commander in Italy, rapidly ringed the beachhead with six divisions, which he launched in a coordinated counterattack. The Americans were almost driven into the sea. The GIs, battling desperately, held on, however, until the Wehrmacht assault was finally halted by an enormous deluge of shells and bombs from navy ships and clouds of aircraft. Finally, on September 16, the German front crumbled and the beleaguered invaders slowly began pushing inland.

A gargantuan Allied catastrophe had been narrowly averted. The operation demonstrated once again the perils of amphibious warfare and the fact that the Wehrmacht was still a highly efficient, mobile, and battleworthy force—perhaps the world's best.

All of this was not lost on Winston Churchill, whose deep-rooted anxieties about Overlord, the cross-Channel invasion, were authenticated. When the casualties at Salerno were counted, it was found that the Allies had lost fifteen thousand of their best troops, when only a fraction of that figure had been projected. If this was the cost of a comparatively small amphibious operation, Churchill reflected, what would be the price paid on D-day in Normandy in the spring of 1944?

In Germany, backstage machinations that could conceivably end the war were taking place. In late August 1943, Karl-Friedrich Goerdeler, an economist and the former mayor of Leipzig, and Jacob Wallenberg, a Swedish banker, held a clandestine meeting in bomb-battered Berlin. Gaunt, old Goerdeler was a leader in the Schwarze Kapelle (Black Orchestra), a tightly knit secret group of prominent German military officers, government officials, and church and civic leaders, who, for more than two years, had been conspiring to get rid of Adolf Hitler and his Nazi regime. Wallenberg, who in his role as an international banker had known Winston Churchill for many years, also was in on the plot. Once the

Führer was eliminated, Wallenberg was to make contact with the Prime Minister and ask for an armistice with the British and Americans, after which a new German government would be formed.

It was the sixth meeting between Wallenberg and Goerdeler since the outbreak of war, and the German told the Swede that plans were in place to kill Hitler in September. Just before the coup was carried out, Goerdeler said, German Major Fabian von Schlabrendorff would be sent to Stockholm to meet with British and American emissaries. Goerdeler asked Wallenberg to "persuade [Churchill] to send a suitable contact man to meet Schlabrendorff."[1]

"I will be glad to do this," Wallenberg replied, "as soon as the coup occurs. I will inform [Churchill] that a German, representing the new leaders, is in Stockholm not to negotiate but merely to obtain Allied advice as to how the new government should go about obtaining peace."[2]

Back in Stockholm, Wallenberg passed this information on to his banker brother, Marcus, who sneaked it to the British.

Curiously, nothing was heard from Churchill. So Jacob Wallenberg and Goerdeler met again in Berlin three weeks later. At the Swede's request, Goerdeler had prepared a memorandum on the Schwarze Kapelle's intentions to eliminate the Führer for transmission to Churchill. Again a request was made for British support in return for, in essence, calling back home German troops manning defenses along the English Channel, where, presumably, the Anglo-Americans eventually would strike. Again, Goerdeler did not receive a reply— strange behavior for the British Prime Minister, who long had anguished over the blood that no doubt would be shed in a cross-Channel invasion.

Churchill's lack of interest in dealing with the German conspiracy cabal was curious. Back in May 1943, while calling on Franklin Roosevelt in the White House, the Prime Minister had indicated a willingness to secretly deal with the Schwarze Kapelle if its actions would bring down the Nazi regime without an Allied bloodbath on the coast of northern France. Churchill indicated to the President that the Schwarze Kapelle could be manipulated in the same way that Britain was using underground organizations in occupied Europe for the purpose of weakening or destroying Nazism from within.[3]

Roosevelt, perhaps influenced by the "crush Germany" clique headed by Secretary of the Treasury Henry Morgenthau and State Department official Alger Hiss, steadfastly refused even to acknowledge the existence of the Schwarze Kapelle. In the U.S. view, Hitler and his Third Reich were to be destroyed by direct confrontation in battle. There would be no room for a political settlement of any kind.

Still trying to impress Roosevelt and Churchill with the sincerity and determination of the conspiracy, the Schwarze Kapelle initiated three attempts to kill Hitler between October and December 1943. Each effort was painstakingly planned and contained an element of ingenious creativity. A young German officer, who had access to the Führer at Adlerhorst (Eagle's Nest), Hitler's Alpine retreat in southern Germany, suggested that he smuggle a pistol into the

Führer's conference room at a staff meeting, whip out the weapon, and shoot him right between the eyes. Unfortunately, the would-be assassin was of junior rank, so when the meeting was convened, he found himself in the back of the immense room standing next to a sharp-eyed SS bodyguard, whose mission was to prevent Hitler from being shot by one of his own men. The junior officer could not even pull out a handkerchief, much less a pistol, and the plan was aborted.

A few weeks later in November, another assassination opportunity surfaced. A young officer, Major Axel Baron von dem Bussche, had been selected to model a new army overcoat for Hitler. His scheme was to conceal two small explosive devices inside the bulky garment. When Hitler neared, he would pull the safety pins, blowing both men to smithereens. An Allied bombing in the region resulted in the baron's demonstration being postponed, and it was never reset.

When Hitler called a manpower conference for December 26, 1943, thirty-six-year-old Colonel Klaus Philip Maria Count von Stauffenberg conceived and insisted on carrying out yet another effort to kill the Führer. Stauffenberg, the son of a German nobleman and a devout Catholic, had been badly wounded while fighting in North Africa, and now had but one eye, one arm, and three fingers.

On the day of the conference, Stauffenberg placed a small bomb in his briefcase and managed to reach the anteroom to the meeting place. There he was told that the conference had been postponed indefinitely. Hitler's evil guardian angel was watching over him.

In Washington and London, Roosevelt and Churchill were unaware of these assassination attempts. The two Anglo-American leaders continued their policy of lending no support or encouragement to the Schwarze Kapelle.

Within a week of the Allied landing at Salerno, George Marshall, in far-off Washington, sent his protégé, Dwight Eisenhower, a rather blunt statement criticizing the supreme commander's tactics and lack of boldness. A sort of father-son spat erupted.

Marshall's comments suggested his own unawareness of the true facts of life in the Mediterranean. The army chief expressed disappointment over Eisenhower's failure to seize Rome with Ridgway's 82nd Airborne Division. Yet Ridgway, his staff, and his battle leaders, to a man, privately held that had the airborne operation been mounted, the entire elite division would have been wiped out.

Marshall also was critical of a failure to grasp battlefield opportunities. Had Eisenhower given any thought to making an all-out dash for Rome, perhaps skirting German defensive positions by amphibious means?

Eisenhower, an aide would report, was "hot under the collar" over Marshall's denunciation of his generalship and lack of audacity. Struggling to control his anger, Ike dictated a reply. He stressed that he had given much thought to a division-sized amphibious assault (behind German lines) south of Rome, but he did not have the landing craft needed for such an operation. Tactfully, he reminded the older man that even if he had the landing craft, an amphibious end run possibly could meet with disaster. The Germans had a panzer division in the region Marshall had suggested as a site for going ashore, another panzer division in nearby Rome, and a third division being held in mobile reserve that could rush to the invasion beach to support the two panzer outfits.

What's more, Eisenhower declared in self-defense, "I do not see how any individual could possibly be devoting more thought and energy . . . to attacking boldly and with admitted risk than I do."[4]

A short time after Eisenhower's message was dispatched to Washington, he received unexpected moral support. Winston Churchill cabled his congratulations to Eisenhower on the Salerno landings, adding that he was proud of the supreme commander for his willingness to "run risks."

Eisenhower, no doubt gleefully, shuttled Churchill's message to Marshall with the following notation: "I feel certain that the [prime minister] looks upon me as a gambler."[5]

In early October, the Allies had a continuous line across the waist of the Italian peninsula in the tangled mountains south of Rome. Mark Clark's Fifth Army was on the left, General Oliver Leese's British Eighth Army was on the right. Leese had succeeded Bernard Montgomery, who was elevated to command the 15th Army Group in Italy.

The Italian campaign was a sacrifice made in the interests of Overlord. Eisenhower's eleven divisions were confronted by twenty-five German divisions, which otherwise could be in France to oppose a cross-Channel invasion. All through October and November, the Allies slugged forward, yard by bloody yard. Eisenhower had expected to capture the jewel that was Rome by the end of October. However, torrential rains, sleet, and snow, along with towering mountains and vicious German resistance, slowed and then halted the advance. Field Marshal Kesselring, known to Allied leaders as Smiling Al, had inflicted a stalemate on the Anglo-Americans.[6]

In Algiers, Dwight Eisenhower was such a long distance from Italy that he was having a difficult time keeping in touch with Montgomery, Clark, and Leese, so he instructed Beetle Smith to find an advance headquarters in the Naples region. For whatever reason—perhaps a reluctance on the part of the customarily speedy Smith to leave the comfort and pleasures of Algiers—an entire month passed before Eisenhower was able to move into his office in the magnificent Caserta Palace north of Naples.

When Eisenhower reached his new headquarters, he exploded, directing most of his anger toward Beetle Smith. His generals and aides had set themselves up in magnificent mansions that would have been the envy of ancient Chinese potentates. On a short cruise around the nearby fabled Isle of Capri, the supreme commander pointed to a huge villa.

"Whose is that!" he demanded to know.

"That's yours, sir," a timid voice responded.

Gesturing toward an even larger and more ornate mansion, Eisenhower asked, "And that?"

"Belongs to General Spaatz."

A string of curses followed. "Damn it!" Eisenhower exclaimed. "That's *not* my villa! And that's *not* General Spaatz's villa. None of those will belong to any general as long as I'm the boss around here!"

Still furious when he returned to Caserta Palace, Eisenhower sent a blistering message to Carl Spaatz: "This is directly contrary to my policies and must cease at once!"[7]

In late November, news of the George Patton "slapping" incident became public. Drew Pearson, a muckraking newspaper columnist and broadcaster in Washington, aired a garbled and exaggerated account of how Patton had struck an enlisted man in a Sicily hospital. Taking its cue from Pearson, newspapers around the United States erupted in a barrage of blaring headlines. The *New York Sun* ran a three-column front-page picture of a scowling Patton under the headline STRUCK SOLDIER.

In the Third Reich, Nazi propaganda minister Josef Goebbels reflected the delight of Adolf Hitler and the Oberkommando der Wehrmacht that the Allied general the Germans feared most was in deep trouble. Radio Berlin embellished Drew Pearson's account: "When the hospital personnel interfered, [Patton] pulled his pistol and was disarmed."

Goebbels's broadcast concluded by declaring that George Patton had been booted out of the United States Army. Based on the Nazi propaganda broadcast, many American media also reported that the beleaguered general had been sacked.

Eisenhower, the Pentagon, and the White House were bombarded by a blizzard of angry letters demanding that Patton be kicked out of the service. Patton himself received hundreds of pieces of mail—most of it in his support—from parents of young men in battle around the world.

Almost to a man, the war correspondents assigned to Eisenhower's headquarters did what they could to halt the bleeding. John Daly of the CBS radio network broadcast that Patton had made personal apologies to his men, "in most cases to thunderous ovations from his troops."[8]

Daly added that the Patton affair was closed. But it was far from over. In Washington, George Marshall, who must have known through the grapevine of the slapping episode but had never been officially informed by Eisenhower, directed the supreme commander to promptly submit an explanation. Like Eisenhower, Marshall did not want to lose the U.S. Army's boldest general for the savage campaigns ahead in Europe.

In a lengthy report, Eisenhower wrote that he had taken "corrective action" that was "adequate and suitable," meaning a blistering personal letter to Patton. Eisenhower said that the proper course of action now was to remain silent in the hope that the hullabaloo would blow over. "I will take the brunt of the affair myself," he declared.[9]

Even before the Marshall query, Eisenhower had sent Beetle Smith to call on Patton and inform him to keep his mouth shut. Ike followed his own advice and refused to make a public defense of his own decision not to summarily sack the old cavalryman.[10]

In the meantime, gossip was rampant in Washington, London, and Allied Force Headquarters in Caserta Palace as to who would be selected as the supreme commander for Overlord. Opinion was virtually unanimous: President Roosevelt would tap George Marshall for the coveted post. Marshall apparently held the same impression, for he had given instructions for his favorite desk to be shipped to London, and Mrs. Marshall was packing for his move across the Atlantic.

If Marshall was to be supreme commander, a post would have to be found for Eisenhower. Rumor prevailed that he would return to Washington and take over for Marshall as chief of staff. So certain was Eisenhower that his mentor would get the top Overlord slot that he wrote to Marshall requesting to be assigned command of a corps for the looming cross-Channel assault.

Despite the need to resolve the question of a supreme commander for Overlord, Roosevelt put off making the decision. Ideally, he would like Marshall to get the post as a reward for years of faithful and productive service in a desk job as chief of staff, with Eisenhower as his replacement in the Pentagon. However, such a shuffle would create an absurd situation. Eisenhower, the protégé, would become the boss of Marshall, his mentor. Worse perhaps, Eisenhower would have to give orders to Douglas MacArthur, who no doubt would resent them. MacArthur had been a four-star general back when young Eisenhower was a major and his aide.

Privately, Eisenhower was most unhappy over the quite real possibility that he would return to Washington to take over for Marshall. In a conversation with his confidants Beetle Smith and Commander Harry Butcher, he expressed the belief that appointing him chief of staff would be a "tremendous mistake." He said he would have to "deal with politicians who continue to argue even after logic has made their positions untenable."

"This uncertainty takes the pep out of everyone," Butcher wrote in his diary. "[Eisenhower] is sweating it out in big drops."[11]

Now, with momentous military decisions to be made, politics entered the equation. Back in the States, Republican leaders were ballyhooing General Douglas MacArthur as the GOP candidate to take on President Roosevelt in the 1944 fall election. MacArthur's silence implied acquiescence to the campaign to draft him.

Then those in the media began gazing into their crystal balls. If MacArthur challenged Roosevelt at the polls, they decided, then the President would have to counter that move by naming Eisenhower as his vice presidential running mate. When media heavyweight Walter Winchell reported that Eisenhower might team up against his former boss, MacArthur, Ike commented privately, "I can scarcely imagine anyone in the United States less qualified than I am for any type of political work!"[12]

CHAPTER 17

Brawls in Cairo and Teheran

WITH THE YEAR 1944 DRAWING NEAR, leaders of the Grand Alliance were still at loggerheads over final strategy for the defeat of Nazi Germany. Consequently, a summit of the Big Three—Franklin Roosevelt, Winston Churchill, and Josef Stalin—was scheduled for late November in Teheran, Iran. Before engaging in debate with the Soviets, however, the Americans and British agreed to meet in Cairo to thrash out their strategic dispute. General George Marshall intended the Cairo confab to be a final bare-knuckle showdown with the British. For despite the firm commitment made by Churchill and Field Marshal Alan Brooke at Quebec, the British seemed to be again wavering over what Marshall felt would be the decisive military action of the war against Germany: Overlord.

British Lieutenant General Frederick Morgan, who had been drawing up preliminary plans for Overlord in London, paid calls on Marshall and Roosevelt in Washington, after which he cabled Brooke: "Cairo and Teheran going to be tough. In comparison, that at Quebec was child's play."[1]

Marshall had received information that Churchill and Brooke would argue against Overlord, claiming that the war situation had changed drastically since Quebec. Italy had been knocked out of the conflict, the Soviet army was on the offensive, and intelligence disclosed plots inside the Third Reich to eliminate Adolf Hitler. If Allied strategy was realigned, in the British view, cheap victories could be earned until Germany collapsed.

This British strategy had gained considerable credence in recent weeks after Allied big-bomber barons boasted that no massive invasion of northern France would be necessary. "Give our bombers thirty days of clear weather and we'll wipe the Third Reich off the face of the earth!" they exclaimed.

There would be another bone of contention at Cairo. Churchill and Brooke were drastically opposed to Operation Anvil, an American plan to invade southern France from the Mediterranean Sea sixty days after Overlord to keep German divisions pinned down and away from Normandy. Brooke held that the Wehrmacht in southern France could be tied up by Allied machinations—feints, menace, and deceptions. Rather than mount a huge invasion apparatus for Anvil, in Brooke's view, these Allied divisions could be more productively used to reinforce the Italian campaign or to conduct operations in the Balkans.

George Marshall was agitated. Since the major Normandy port of Cherbourg would most certainly be destroyed by the Germans, he contended, it was crucial to resupplying huge Allied armies that Marseilles, in southern France, be secured. Marshall, in fact, was so angry that he swore he would resign rather than to commit American forces to further costly and indecisive land operations in the Mediterranean.[2]

Just past midnight on November 13, 1943, angry storm clouds hovered over dark Chesapeake Bay as the 45,000-ton *Iowa*, America's newest and speediest battleship, lifted anchor and prepared to set a course eastward to Gibraltar and beyond to Oran. On board were Roosevelt and his Joint Chiefs: George Marshall, Hap Arnold, Ernest King, and William Leahy.

The Joint Chiefs huddled to sharpen their claws for the confrontation with the British at Cairo. The Americans had at their disposal a vast collection of position papers to back up their strategic claims or to refute those of the British. Although the U.S. Chiefs were often racked by personality clashes and interservice disputes, they now agreed on one crucial point: Churchill and Brooke had to be rebuffed: The American strategic concept (Overlord) had to prevail.

George Marshall, to whose opinions Roosevelt gave the greatest weight, advised the President to adopt "a very cautious stand" on any British schemes to suck the Western Allies into the Balkans. Flashing his lopsided smile, the President snapped, "Amen!"[3]

Out on the bounding sea and away from the suffocating political climate of Washington, Roosevelt was filled with enthusiasm for the looming showdowns, first with the British, then with the Soviets. During one session on the *Iowa*, the President, in the presence of the army chief, declared that "George Marshall should be the C-in-C [commander in chief] against Germany and command all the British, French, Italian, and U.S. troops."[4]

Each week for many months, the American chiefs had lunched together, but they never became friends and often were bitter adversaries. During official sessions, George Marshall and Ernest King were the most frequent combatants. King seemed to have mixed feelings about Marshall. On occasion, he described the army leader as "an able man," yet one who could be "stupid." Hap Arnold, the air corps chief, "didn't know what he was talking about" and was a "yes-man" for Marshall, according to King. William Leahy, the President's trusted confidant and fourth member of the U.S. Joint Chiefs, was labeled a "fixer" by King. Perhaps the others' views of the navy chief were similar.[5]

While the nine-hundred-foot-long *Iowa* was knifing through the heavy rollers of the wintry Atlantic, the HMS *Renown*—old, salt stained, battle weary, but still majestic—was plunging through the ocean toward the Mediterranean Sea and Oran. The British ship was carrying Winston Churchill and his military chiefs: Field Marshal Alan Brooke; Admiral Andrew Cunningham, now the First Sea Lord; Air Marshal Charles Portal; and General Hastings "Pug" Ismay, the Prime Minister's personal chief of staff.

Like their American counterparts on the *Iowa*, the British chiefs met regularly to plot war, not only against the Germans but also against the American chiefs. On the second night at sea, Brooke scrawled in his diary, "I wish our [Cairo] conference was over. I despair of getting our American friends to have any strategic vision."[6]

President Roosevelt and his entourage disembarked from the *Iowa* at Oran and flew on to Cairo in the *Sacred Cow*, the chief executive's personal airplane. A caravan of Buicks drove the Americans to their quarters, a collection of comfortable villas, where, under the keen-eyed scrutiny of the Great Sphinx and Field Marshal Brooke, they were greeted effusively by Winston Churchill, nattily dressed in a white suit and brandishing a cigar.

Despite his bubbling facade and display of comradeship, Churchill was deeply concerned, with the near catastrophe at Salerno that boded ill for D-day in Normandy weighing on his mind. His personal physician, Lord Charles Wilson Moran, told confidants, "On the way here, it became plain that he was brooding on the extraordinary difficulties of this prodigious undertaking. He has grown more and more certain that an invasion of [northern] France as planned must fail."[7]

On the following morning, the American and British delegations came together in Cairo's fashionable Mena Palace Hotel. George Marshall immediately seized the initiative: Instead of discussing Overlord and Anvil, he proposed landing British and American troops in the Bay of Bengal to aid General Chiang Kai-shek, the Chinese leader.

Alan Brooke became angry, convinced that the Americans were stalling in order to avoid a discussion of Overlord and Anvil until the meeting with Stalin in Teheran. Stalin, the British knew, favored the two invasions of France. Tempers flared. Sharp-tongued Brooke snorted that the Bay of Bengal operation was a gross waste of time and effort. Words became increasingly heated, finally touching off an explosion.

Hard-bitten General Joseph W. "Vinegar Joe" Stilwell, who long had been battling the Chinese on a shoestring, wrote in his journal that night, "Brooke got good and nasty and [Admiral Ernest] King got good and sore. King almost climbed over the table at Brooke. God, he was *mad*! I wish to hell King had socked him!"[8]

Hap Arnold scribbled a similar sentiment in his diary: "I thought a brawl was going to break out."

For three more days, accusations flew back and forth. When the groups prepared to break up for the long flight to Teheran—fortunately, in separate airplanes—Harry Hopkins, Roosevelt's advisor, told Lord Moran bluntly, "Sure we are preparing for a battle at Teheran. You will find us lining up with the Russians."

"What I find so shocking is that to the Americans the P.M. [Churchill] is the villain of the piece," Moran noted that night. "They are far more suspicious of him than they are of Stalin."[9]

Although the mood was stormy when the Cairo sessions adjourned, Roosevelt and Churchill were in firm agreement on one point: The meeting with Stalin would be a touchy one. Stalin long had been convinced that the United States and Great Britain were conspiring to let the Germans and the Russians bleed each other dry. Then the Western Allies would strike in western Europe and occupy that vast region almost unopposed.

Churchill did not trust the Soviets and would have to carefully choose his words. Through British intelligence, the Prime Minister knew that while the Russian and German armies were slaughtering each other on the Eastern Front, clandestine contacts were being made between members of the Soviet and Reich general staffs. If it served Stalin, Churchill was convinced, secret British and American plans for invading Europe would not be long in reaching Hitler's ears.

Shortly after Franklin Roosevelt reached his room behind the protective walls of the U.S. Embassy in Teheran, a breathless delegation dispatched by Josef Stalin arrived. There were reports afloat that the American President was a German assassination target, the Russians explained. Since the U.S. Embassy was two miles across the city from the Soviet and British Embassies, which were side by side, would it not be more prudent for Roosevelt to occupy one of the villas on the tightly guarded Soviet Embassy grounds where the summit would convene?

Roosevelt saw no point in the move, but Michael Riley, the conscientious chief of the U.S. Secret Service, whose job it was to protect the life of the President, bundled Roosevelt into an old Ford and sped to the Russian Embassy.

Roosevelt soon was ensconced behind Soviet walls in a comfortable villa, just as the cagey Stalin had planned. The Soviet dictator long ago had staked out the Balkans as a major preserve for the Moscow-directed Communist empire, and the British had their eyes on the same target. Now he would have the ear of Roosevelt all to himself.

President Roosevelt had just settled into his villa when a suitor came calling. It was Josef Stalin. He amiably assured Roosevelt that he firmly backed a cross-Channel invasion by the Anglo-Americans and, in essence, expressed the hope that the President would persuade Churchill and the British to stay out of the Balkans.

When Alan Brooke learned of the secret Stalin-Roosevelt confab, he wrote gloomily in his diary, "This conference is over before it even begins."[10]

Soviet soldiers stood guard outside the embassy walls as the Big Three summit convened in a large drawing room at 4:30 P.M. on November 28. Stalin, who was outside Russia for the first time since the 1918 revolution that had toppled the czar, was turned out in a field marshal's uniform that appeared to have been tailored precisely for the summit. Lord Moran, Churchill's personal physician, later observed, "Stalin's outfit looked as if the tailor had put a large shelf on each shoulder, and on them dumped a lot of gold lace and stars."[11]

Armed with a cigarette in a long opaque holder, President Roosevelt kicked off the discussions by reminding those present that the previous August the Americans and British had agreed upon May 1944 as the period for a cross-Channel invasion of northwest Europe. Then Winston Churchill and Josef Stalin did most of the talking.

After speaking at length about what apparently was his determination to carry out Overlord, Churchill, in the next breath, launched into a long, drawn-out plea for expanded military operations in the Balkans. Then he asked Stalin what Russia would like to see the Western Allies do. Attack across the English Channel was the prompt reply.

That night at dinner, Roosevelt's aides centered their conversation on Stalin. Prior to this day, most of them had thought he was a bandit leader, a thug, who had slashed his way to the top of his government. While that description may have had merit, now they were aware that they were dealing with a highly intelligent and cunning man who knew precisely what he wanted and was ruthlessly determined to get it.

Early the next morning, Churchill, having heard of the private, forty-five-minute Roosevelt-Stalin talk and perhaps believing that the two men were ganging up on him, sent a courier with a note to the President. Would Roosevelt be his guest at lunch? Sorry, the President lied, he had an important meeting scheduled with his staff. Actually, Roosevelt was holding another secret discussion with Joe Stalin.

Churchill was both angry and disturbed by his old friend Roosevelt's backstage conniving with the premier of the Soviet Union. The Prime Minister did not entirely trust the President and thought that Roosevelt might be concocting some mischief against Great Britain. So Churchill arranged for his own private meeting with Stalin. He was shocked by what he was told. The Soviet army already had suffered four million casualties and his soldiers were war weary, Stalin said. If Overlord did not take place in May 1944, he intimated, then the Soviet Union might have to "do business with Hitler"—that is, surrender.

In the afternoon session, George Marshall made a pitch for Anvil, the proposed invasion of southern France. Anvil, he claimed, was crucial to Overlord. Nonsense, Brooke replied. Those forces could be better used elsewhere in the Mediterranean and the Balkans. It would be folly to get bogged down in the Balkans, Marshall countered. Joe Stalin puffed on his pipe and grunted in agreement.

At dinner that night, Brooke was in a foul mood. Clearly, he and Churchill were fighting a rearguard action. Roosevelt and Marshall, he was convinced, were incredibly naive, mere pawns in the hands of Stalin. Pecking at his salad, the field marshal looked at Lord Moran and muttered, "Doc, I shall come to you to send me to a lunatic asylum. I cannot stand much more of this. Seven hours' conference today, and we are not an inch farther along."[12]

On November 30, at the final session, tempers flared anew. At one point, Stalin turned to Churchill and growled, "Do you really believe in [Overlord] or are you stalling on it?"[13]

Churchill's face flushed crimson. Fingering his cigar, he replied that he did indeed support Overlord, but he felt that other operations the British were suggesting would help to ensure the success of the invasion of France. Then he recommended that the political aspects of his Mediterranean and Balkans proposals be referred to the foreign ministers of the three nations for their advice.[14]

"Why do that?" Stalin snapped. "We are the chiefs of government. We know what we want to do. Why turn the matter over to some subordinates to advise us?"

In the wake of the barrage of harsh charges and countercharges that had rocked the conference room for three days, a strategy agreement was reached. Marshall had won; Brooke had lost. American, British, French, and Canadian forces would assemble in England and strike across the Channel in May 1944. Anvil would hit southern France as soon afterward as possible. Overlord would coincide with a massive Soviet offensive to pin down German divisions in Russia until the Western Allies were solidly ashore.

Stalin was not satisfied and demanded to know precisely where the blow would fall. Churchill lied that a specific locale was "still under study." Actually, Normandy had been selected as the site months earlier.

Now Churchill took the floor to brief the gathering on Plan Bodyguard, an incredibly intricate and devious deception scheme created largely by ingenious British minds to hoodwink Adolf Hitler as to the location and date of the cross-Channel invasion.[15]

Never had warfare known the scope and complexity of this colossal stratagem, which, in essence, would be a Trojan horse to mask Allied intentions. Despite the mighty invasion force the Allies would muster in England, Overlord would be a success only if Bodyguard kept D-day secrets from the Germans.

As Churchill began his Bodyguard briefing, he was confronted by a challenge that would sorely test his widely recognized guile and skills as an orator. He did not trust the Russians, so he would reveal only generalities to allow Stalin and his generals to grasp the deception theme so that the Soviets could fill their roles in the plan. The Russians would be kept in the dark about specific techniques—which one day might have to be used *against* the Soviets.

Stalin, inscrutable as always, puffed on his pipe and listened intently as Churchill described Bodyguard, a witches' brew of plots, subplots, and counterplots, a tangled web of spoofs, fraud, deceit, camouflage, stealth, misdirection, skulduggery, fakery, lies, and occasional mayhem—collectively known to the British as "special means."

Stalin, certainly no amateur in the fine arts of deceit, conniving, and double-dealing, seemed to be fascinated by the machinations of the deception plan, and he readily agreed to Churchill's proposal that members of British and American intelligence agencies fly to Moscow in February to coordinate deception operations with their counterparts on the Soviet general staff.

November 30 was the final night of the summit, as well as Winston Churchill's sixty-ninth birthday. In order to celebrate both milestones, the Prime Minister played host at a lavish dinner party in the British Embassy. Russian custom was followed, which meant that toasts were offered to nearly all of the thirty-four persons at the banquet table. Roosevelt, Churchill, and Stalin made speeches. Churchill, anti-Communist to the core, droned on about Britain's abiding friendship with the Soviets.

After enduring the speeches, the revelers turned to idle repartee. Suddenly, Stalin grew serious and declared (through his interpreter) that after the war, fifty thousand German officers would be rounded up and shot. Silence descended. Roosevelt carefully positioned another cigarette in his holder and said nothing.

Rising from his chair, an irritated Churchill paced about the banquet room and replied, "The British government and people will never tolerate mass executions. They would turn violently against those responsible after the first butchery had taken place."[16]

Unmoved, Stalin continued to insist: "Fifty thousand must be shot!"

Churchill, now even angrier, retorted, "I would rather be taken out into the garden here and now and be shot myself than sully my own and my country's honor by such infamy!"[17]

Again a strained hush followed. To ease the tension, Franklin Roosevelt made what he thought was a joke. He suggested that, as a compromise, only *forty-nine* thousand be shot.

The President's attempt at humor fell flat. His son, Air Corps Colonel Elliott Roosevelt, tried to smooth over his father's remarks. Unsteadily, a glass of champagne in his hand, the younger Roosevelt said that he was in agreement with Premier Stalin's proposal and that he was confident that the United States Army would back it.

Winston Churchill was livid. He detested Elliott Roosevelt, who, he felt, was a "pompous, spoiled brat." The Prime Minister was astonished that the President would remain silent while his offspring committed the U.S. Army to executing fifty thousand German officers.[18]

Churchill stomped out of the room, slamming the door behind him. Allied harmony had reached the breaking point.

Stalin realized how serious the discussion had become. He and Vyacheslav Molotov, his young foreign commissar, rushed after the Prime Minister and caught up with him in an anteroom. Stalin assured Churchill that it had all been a big joke and asked the Prime Minister to return to the party, which he agreed to do.

Festivities continued into the early morning hours, when, in a haze of champagne and vodka, old pals Churchill, Stalin, and Roosevelt swore undying friendship and bade one another good night.

At noon the next day, Franklin Roosevelt, perhaps nursing a throbbing head, and his aides lifted off from the Teheran airport in the *Sacred Cow* and headed for Cairo on the first leg of the return trip to Washington. Before departing, the President wired Dwight Eisenhower to meet him in the city by the Nile.

When Eisenhower entered Roosevelt's car, the President turned to him and offhandedly remarked, "Well, Ike, you are going to command Overlord."[19]

Eisenhower struggled to mask his surprise and astonishment. He had been certain that General Marshall would be given the command plum.

"Mr. President," he finally said, "I realize that such an appointment involved difficult decisions. I hope that you will not be disappointed."[20]

At the British Embassy in Cairo that night, Alan Brooke was crushed by news of Eisenhower's appointment. During the Roosevelt-Churchill conference in Quebec in the late summer of 1943, the Prime Minister had promised Brooke the coveted Overlord post.

"Ike has a very limited brain," Brooke confided to his diary. "[He] has only the vaguest grasp of strategy and tactics."[21]

CHAPTER 18

The Pacific "Political Front"

WINSTON CHURCHILL HAD BEEN STRICKEN with pneumonia while on his way home from the Teheran conference. Lord Moran, his physician, ordered him to take a long bed rest in Tunis—and to cease smoking cigars. The scrappy Prime Minister ignored the medical advice and instead summoned Dwight Eisenhower and other Mediterranean generals and admirals to Tunis. It was December 26, 1943.

Churchill was at his eloquent best. Jabbing the air for emphasis with his cigar, the British Bulldog regaled the assembled Allied brass with tales of the military wonders to accrue by taking advantage of Anglo-American naval superiority to launch an amphibious end run far behind what the Germans called the Gustav line in Italy. This would cause Field Marshal Albert Kesselring to panic and withdraw from his seemingly impregnable winter defensive positions, leaving the road to Rome "wide open."

Arrayed before Churchill in a huge drawing room in the stately mansion that was being used as an impromptu convalescent center were General Harold Alexander, now leader of the 15th Army Group in Italy; British General Henry M. "Jumbo" Wilson, who would soon be Eisenhower's successor in the Mediterranean; Admiral Andrew Cunningham, the First Sea Lord; Air Marshal Arthur Tedder; and, of course, Eisenhower.

At Teheran, Franklin Roosevelt and Josef Stalin had shot down Churchill's proposal to "continue to set the Mediterranean ablaze" with diversionary operations, even if it meant weakening or postponing Overlord. Typically, the Prime Minister refused to take "no" as an answer.

Now, clad in pajamas, bathrobe, and slippers, his face still ashen from his bout with pneumonia, Churchill was ready to spring a pet military scheme on the leery commanders. His timing was perfect: How could the gathered brass take issue with a sick man?

"It would be folly to invade France in the spring with Rome still in German hands," Churchill said. "The Italian campaign must not be allowed to languish." He puffed on his Havana Corona momentarily to allow the audience to digest

146

his opening words, then added solemnly, "He who holds Rome, holds the title deeds to Italy!"[1]

Americans in the room, fearful that the Prime Minister was still bent on sidetracking Overlord and continuing a strategy of peripheral nibbling on Adolf Hitler's empire, had their suspicions confirmed. "Overlord remains on top of the bill, of course," Churchill said, "but it should not be such a tyrant as to rule out every other activity in the Mediterranean."

The Americans shifted nervously in their chairs. The Prime Minister toyed thoughtfully with his cigar.

Then the portly Churchill, relishing his self-designated role as chief strategist in the Mediterranean, unfurled his scheme for breaking the stalemate in front of the Gustav line and rapidly seizing Rome. His plan was to land at least two divisions of Mark Clark's Fifth Army at a small Tyrrhenian port known as Anzio, some sixty miles behind German lines and only thirty miles south of Rome.

"We will be hurling a raging wildcat onto the beaches to rip the bowels out of the Boches [Germans]!"[2]

Hearing Churchill out, Eisenhower, a lame-duck supreme commander who soon would be leaving for London, immediately protested, foreseeing the Anzio venture as a continuing drain on manpower, shipping, and other resources that should be husbanded in England for the cross-Channel attack. What's more, the general doubted whether the Germans would abandon the Gustav line and withdraw to the north. Instead, they probably would fight it out there while trying to contain an Anzio beachhead. His prophetic words were drowned in a flood of Churchillian oratory.

General Alexander deferred to his boss, but nearly every other top commander—British and American—protested the wildcat-hurling at Anzio. Brigadier Kenneth Strong, the tall, black-haired Briton who was chief intelligence officer in the Mediterranean, painted a gloomy portrait. He pointed out that Rome was of the utmost political importance to Hitler. The German dictator could not afford to let the city fall in the wake of Italy's recent defection.

The highly skeptical Strong stressed that many Wehrmacht divisions lying idle in France and eastward across the Adriatic Sea in Yugoslavia could be rushed to northern Italy and that other German formations under Field Marshal Erwin Rommel were available even closer on the German-Italian border.

All of these factors added up to a perilous venture, Strong summarized. Churchill listened quietly, then brushed off the intelligence expert's arguments. The hazards of Anzio would have to be accepted as a calculated risk due to the prize to be gained: Rome.

Churchill continued to speak out forcefully for the Anzio end run and succeeded, as usual, in imposing his will on others. Come hell or high water, an Anglo-American amphibious force would be hurled onto a beach far to the rear of the Gustav line. Anzio would be the Prime Minister's particular "baby."

D-day for the amphibious landing (code-named Shingle) was tentatively set for January 22, 1944.

Having emerged victorious in the strategy skirmish against almost solid opposition by the Allied military leaders, the Prime Minister immediately set about consolidating the hard-earned triumph. He cabled President Roosevelt: "Unanimous agreement has been reached on [the Anzio operation] and everyone is in good heart."[3]

In the meantime, after the Teheran conference had adjourned, George Marshall kept a secret from President Roosevelt: The army chief had decided to board a C-54 transport plane at the Cairo airport and wing halfway around the world to pay a visit to Douglas MacArthur, his antagonist for more than a quarter century. Had Roosevelt known of his itinerary, Marshall was certain, he would have scotched the long, dangerous, and exhausting journey.

Twice before since Pearl Harbor, Marshall had planned to call on MacArthur. Twice pressing business had forced cancellations. The army chief decided to go to the Southwest Pacific now because he "wanted to show MacArthur that he had not been forgotten."

No doubt the meeting would be a touchy one. Not since 1935, when war hero MacArthur retired as the four-star chief of staff and Marshall was an obscure colonel, had the two strong-willed men seen each other. Now Marshall was MacArthur's boss, and MacArthur was but one of six theater commanders in the army.

At several high-level conferences in 1943, where the Anglo-American generals and admirals and political leaders argued over who should do what to whom and when, the vast Pacific always got short shrift. The British insisted that the Americans limit their role in the Pacific and send nearly every rifleman who could be spared to Europe. General Marshall and Ernest King, on the other hand, were convinced that the British were underestimating the Japanese threat. They demanded that the American commitment in the Pacific be doubled from 15 percent of Allied manpower and resources to 30 percent.

Finally, a Pacific strategy had been reached with the reluctant British. A twin offensive was approved. Douglas MacArthur, based in Australia, would leapfrog northwestward up the spine of 1,500-mile-long New Guinea. Admiral Chester Nimitz, from his Hawaiian headquarters, would drive his marines and army troops westward across the central Pacific, capturing tiny, strongly fortified coral islands with names such as Tarawa, Kwajalein, Eniwetok, Saipan, and Peleliu. Both thrusts were to converge on the Philippines, from where an invasion of the Japanese homeland would be mounted.

Once the Pacific strategy had been settled with the British, the American leaders began arguing among themselves. Admiral King demanded that most of the emphasis be given to Chester Nimitz in the central Pacific. No way, Marshall replied heatedly, MacArthur's offensive should be the primary effort.

Sniping between the services grew intense, especially in Washington. At one point, Admiral King's verbal assault against MacArthur was so vicious at a meeting of the Joint Chiefs that Marshall banged a fist on the table and, in an uncharacteristically loud voice, declared, "I will not have any meetings carried on with this hatred!"[4]

Staff officers representing MacArthur and Nimitz were flown in and asked to outline their cases. Nimitz's emissary suggested that the waters around New Guinea, where MacArthur was conducting his hit-'em-where-they-ain't campaign, were too crowded for America's growing fleet of aircraft carriers and that the flattops would be vulnerable to Japanese land-based bombers. There was another, unspoken motive: To keep the carriers out of MacArthur's clutches.

General Richard Sutherland, MacArthur's chief of staff, presented the case for the Southwest Pacific. Seizing the Japanese island strongholds in Nimitz's path would be a bloody affair, Sutherland said. (Later events would substantiate his prediction.) On the other hand, MacArthur's route to the Philippines would deprive the Japanese of crucial oil and raw materials from Southwest Asia.

Although MacArthur's case was a solid one, he had sent a dubious salesman. Tall, thin, dour Dick Sutherland was a Yale graduate and the son of a West Virginia senator who became a Supreme Court justice. Sutherland was ruthless and tactless, although an able chief of staff. Clark Lee, a noted war correspondent in the Southwest Pacific, regarded Sutherland as "brusque, short-tempered, and of a generally antagonizing nature." George Marshall labeled Sutherland "the chief insulter of the Navy."[5]

MacArthur lost out in this squabble. Nimitz would get most of the manpower and resources allocated to the Pacific, but only a fraction more than would MacArthur. The war against Japan would continue to remain at the bottom of the Combined Chiefs' list of concerns.

Now, in late 1943, General Marshall's C-54 landed at an airport near Brisbane, Australia, where MacArthur's main headquarters had been located for months. Marshall was tired; the last leg of the flight from Ceylon—thirty-five hundred miles—had taken sixteen hours. At the bottom of the ladder leading down from the aircraft, Marshall was greeted by Colonel Lloyd A. Lehrbas, a MacArthur aide. MacArthur, who had been in Brisbane for six weeks, had chosen this time to fly to the front in New Guinea.[6]

While awaiting word of MacArthur's whereabouts, Colonel Lehrbas escorted the army chief on a wild jeep chase after kangaroos, a recreational sport the distinguished visitor did not especially relish. A waste of time.

Finally, Marshall and MacArthur met privately on Goodenough Island, off the eastern tip of New Guinea. The confrontation could best be described as "correct." Although they had known each other for more than forty years, they did not use first names. It was *General* Marshall and *General* MacArthur. Presumably, the Southwest Pacific commander was surprised that they were holding a one-on-one confab: MacArthur had predicted that Marshall would "find a way to have someone else present."[7]

They held a long, candid discussion. "Admiral King claims the Pacific as the rightful domain of the Navy," Marshall said, "and . . . seems to regard *all* operations there as almost his own private war."[8]

Marshall also spoke of King's constant criticism of MacArthur and said that the navy chief had considerable clout, being held in high regard by President Roosevelt. Two other members of the U.S. Joint Chiefs, Hap Arnold and William Leahy, often sided with King against MacArthur, the army boss confided. So when it came to allocating resources to the Southwest Pacific, he was often outvoted three to one.[9]

General Arnold, in particular, had defected from MacArthur since the development of the B-29 Superfortress, a huge craft that dwarfed America's current big bombers, the B-24 Liberator and B-17 Flying Fortress. Arnold and other air corps officers envisioned that Japan could be bombed out of the war by the B-29s.

Much of the conversation between the two four-star generals sounded like adversaries negotiating a truce. At one point during lunch on Goodenough, MacArthur started a sentence with, "My staff . . . " Marshall cut him off. "You don't have a staff, General," Marshall said evenly, "you have a court." It may have been an attempt at good-natured humor, a trait not usually associated with the army chief. Reportedly, the host did not know how to take the remark. After a few moments of silence, he continued with his comments.[10]

Despite the hatred between Admiral King and General MacArthur, many of the other navy gold braid in the Pacific found MacArthur to be quite congenial. They even liked him. On one occasion, Secretary of the Navy Frank Knox requested that the soft-spoken Chester Nimitz, the other Pacific theater commander, have a get-acquainted session with MacArthur. In November 1943, without concern for protocol, Nimitz flew to the Southwest Pacific. The talks were friendly and cordial.

Although MacArthur's rapport with Nimitz had been enhanced, William "Bull" Halsey remained the general's favorite admiral. Halsey, the embodiment of the old sea dog, had trounced the Imperial Navy in several sharp engagements that slowed the progress of the Japanese toward Australia. Halsey's peppery manner and fighting heart endeared him to the general.

Halsey had found himself in a peculiar command arrangement. Although he was subordinate to Chester Nimitz in Honolulu, he was under MacArthur's operational control. Known as The Bull, Halsey would recall, "Five minutes after I reported to [MacArthur] I felt as if we were lifelong friends. I have seldom seen a man who makes a quicker, stronger, more favorable impression."[11]

MacArthur was also impressed by The Bull. "He was of the same aggressive type as John Paul Jones, David Farragut, and George Dewey," he said. "His one

U.S. General Douglas MacArthur (left) arrives in Australia after his escape from Corregidor. At right is his chief of staff, Richard Sutherland. (U.S. Army)

Backstage skirmishers Admiral Ernest King (left) and General George Marshall. (National Archives)

French General Alphonse Juin.
(National Archives)

French General Jean de Lattre de
Tassigny. (National Archives)

French General Henri Giraud.
(National Archives)

French General Émile Béthouart.
(National Archives)

Supreme Commander Dwight Eisenhower (left), French Admiral Jean Darlan ("Little Fella"), and U.S. General Mark Clark shortly before Darlan was murdered. (National Archives)

British Admiral Andrew B. "ABC" Cunningham. (National Archives)

U.S. General Walter "Beetle" Smith. (U.S. Army)

President Franklin Roosevelt and Prime Minister Winston Churchill (left) at the Casablanca press conference, where Roosevelt sprang the unconditional surrender ultimatum. (National Archives)

British Field Marshal John Dill. (National Archives)

British Field Marshal Alan Brooke. (National Archives)

The Big Three—Josef Stalin, Franklin Roosevelt, and Winston Churchill—at Teheran. (National Archives)

U.S. Army Air Corps Chief Henry H. "Hap" Arnold (left) and British Air Chief Marshal
Charles Portal. (U.S. Army)

British Air Chief Marshal Trafford
Leigh-Mallory. (National Archives)

U.S. Secretary of War Henry L. Stimson.
(National Archives)

British Field Marshal Harold
Alexander (left). (National
Archives)

Eisenhower and his SHAEF deputy, British Air Chief Marshal Arthur
Tedder. (National Archives)

Dwight Eisenhower lied to Charles de Gaulle (right) about the time and place of the Normandy invasion. (U.S. Army)

British General Henry "Jumbo" Wilson. (National Archives)

U.S. Generals George Patton (left) and Omar Bradley (center) and British Field Marshal
Bernard Montgomery. (U.S. Army)

U.S. General Carl "Toohey" Spaatz.
(U.S. Army)

British General Miles Dempsey.
(National Archives)

French General Charles de Gaulle leading the parade he organized after the liberation of Paris
by the Allies. (National Archives)

Planning to storm the Rhine River. From left: Canadian General H. G. Crerar, British Field Marshal Bernard Montgomery, U.S. General William Simpson, and British Air Marshal Arthur Coningham. (National Archives)

British General Frederick "Boy" Browning. (National Archives)

U.S. General Courtney Hodges. (U.S. Army)

U.S. General Claire Chennault (left), Madame Chiang Kai-shek, and Chiang Kai-shek.

U.S. General Joseph
"Vinegar Joe" Stilwell.
(National Archives)

U.S. Admirals (from left) Chester Nimitz, Ernest King, and William "Bull" Halsey. (U.S. Navy)

U.S. General Jacob "Jackie" Devers. (U.S. Army)

After the German surrender, Bernard Montgomery decorates Soviet Marshal Grigori Zhukov. At the same time, Montgomery was stacking captured German weapons in a way to rapidly issue them to Wehrmacht troops should war erupt between the Western Allies and Russia. (National Archives)

Showdown at Honolulu over conflicting strategies. From left: Douglas MacArthur, Franklin Roosevelt, William Leahy, and Chester Nimitz. (U.S. Army)

Douglas MacArthur signs the Japanese surrender document on the battleship *Missouri* as other Allied brass watch. (U.S. Army)

thought was to close with the enemy and fight him to the death. The bugaboo of many sailors, the fear of losing ships, was completely alien to his conception of sea action."[12]

Now Douglas MacArthur found himself entangled on another front, this time a political front. A few months earlier, Arthur H. Vandenberg, a conservative Republican senator from Michigan, had penned an article for *Collier's*, a widely read weekly magazine, entitled "Why I Am for MacArthur [for President]." Vandenberg then lined up an impressive list of conservative newspaper publishers and political leaders, most of whom had long been disenchanted with Franklin Roosevelt's liberal New Deal domestic policies and were hell-bent on unseating the President in the 1944 election.

The "MacArthur for President" boomlet drifted to the Southwest Pacific. Lieutenant General Robert W. Eichelberger, who would soon take command of MacArthur's new Eighth Army, wrote in his diary, "My Chief talked of the Republican nomination—I can see that he expects to get it, and I sort of think so, too."

Admiral Bill Leahy, the President's personal military advisor and hardly a dues-paying member of the MacArthur fan club, was worried. "If the general should get the nomination he would be a very dangerous antagonist for anybody, including Roosevelt," he noted.[13]

Although the MacArthur bandwagon was small, a lot of influential leaders were trying to scramble onto it. That upset numerous liberal columnists, who began to take potshots at the general. John McCarten, in the *American Mercury*, wrote that "the worst elements on the political Right, including its most blatant lunatic fringe, are whooping it up for MacArthur."[14]

The implication was clear: In McCarten's view, America's most popular hero was a member of the lunatic fringe.

The *American Mercury* broadside triggered a firestorm. In the Southwest Pacific, General Eichelberger wrote his wife that MacArthur said he had "never read such lies," but regarded the article "as the type of cross" which was "necessary for him to bear."

Then, amazingly, an obscure civilian bureaucrat in the army's library service recommended the *Mercury* tirade for reading by the troops. Senator Vandenberg blew up, roundly blasting the War Department for endorsing a "smear of one of American history's greatest soldiers." Thereupon, the lords in the Pentagon assumed a peculiar stance. A scholarly analysis of the "MacArthur for President" movement in *Harper's* magazine was suppressed "for security reasons."[15]

Franklin Roosevelt, the consummate politician, was watching all this with a sharp eye. If MacArthur won the Republican nomination, the President predicted, he would run on a Pacific-first platform, in contrast to the Germany-first policy that Roosevelt had adopted shortly after Pearl Harbor. He instructed his aides to begin stockpiling anti-MacArthur political ammunition, including the general's report, made shortly before the outbreak of war in the Pacific, confirming that he could hold the Philippines in the event of a Japanese attack.[16]

A Roosevelt-MacArthur presidential campaign would have been rough—and probably dirty.

By early 1944, MacArthur was ready to take another great leap on the jungle-and-ocean road to the Philippines. It would be a risky venture. His target was the Admiralties, whose two islands, Manus and Los Negros, were reported by intelligence to be "lousy with Japs." The Admiralties were some three hundred miles north of the eastern tail of New Guinea and near the dividing line between MacArthur's Southwest Pacific theater and Nimitz's Pacific Ocean Area.

At dawn on February 29, GIs of the 1st Cavalry Division stormed ashore on Los Negros. Fighting was savage. Six hours later, MacArthur, in a pouring rain, landed on the beach and casually strolled inland. Assault troops were lying prone with streams of Japanese bullets whizzing past their steel helmets. Many peeked up in amazement as MacArthur, conspicuous in his salmon-colored trench coat and gold-braided hat, sauntered past. An excited lieutenant, his camouflaged battle dress spattered with mud, pointed up a path and called out, "Excuse me, General, but we killed a Jap sniper in there just a few minutes ago!"

MacArthur, lighting his famous corncob pipe, flipped away the match and replied, "Fine, that's just the thing to do with them!"

A week later, Los Negros and Manus had been captured. MacArthur had attacked the Admiralties against the advice of numerous officers. They had argued that the nearest Allied base for reinforcing and supplying the islands was three hundred miles to the south at Finschafen, New Guinea.

Praise from around the world was showered on MacArthur for his latest bold conquest. Winston Churchill cabled, "I send you my warm congratulations on the speed with which you turned to good account your first entry into the Admiralty Islands."[17]

Not everyone was impressed by MacArthur's bold gamble. Rear Admiral William M. Fechteler, deputy commander of the U.S. amphibious force that put the GIs ashore, said, "Actually, we're damned lucky we didn't get run off the islands."[18]

Hardly had the Admiralties been secured when MacArthur learned that the navy planned an expansion of the anchorage of Manus. Seabees were already at work. MacArthur was furious; he had not even been consulted. Manus was in his theater and his troops had captured it. He summoned Bull Halsey.

As soon as Halsey walked into MacArthur's office, he could tell that the furious general was struggling to control his temper. "Unlike me," Halsey would later note, "strong emotion did not make him profane." MacArthur got right down to business. He said he had "no intention of tamely submitting to such interference by the Navy."[19]

When the theater commander had run out of steam, Halsey replied firmly that if MacArthur took that position, he would be "hampering the war effort." MacArthur's aides gasped. "I imagine they never expected to hear anyone address him in those terms this side of the Judgment Throne," Halsey would later recall.[20]

It was a prolonged squabble, lasting into the next day. Then, suddenly, MacArthur smiled, clasped Halsey around the shoulder, and said evenly, "Well, you win, Bill."[21]

CHAPTER 19

A Stranded Whale
at Anzio

DWIGHT EISENHOWER, who as supreme commander for Overlord would soon become one of the most powerful figures in history, was furtively slinking around Washington like a fugitive with a price on his head. He had arrived from the Mediterranean by plane at 1:30 A.M. on January 2, 1944. Wary that German spies might be lurking in the nation's capital, the general had removed the stars from his uniform. He looked like an aging private in an officer's uniform, or perhaps a Red Cross field-worker.

Eisenhower was greeted at the airport by a soldier wearing civvies and driving an unmarked Chevrolet sedan. The general had secretly returned to Washington for a round of conferences in the Pentagon before plunging into his awesome assignment as supreme commander of Overlord in London. After a brief reunion with wife Mamie at her apartment in the Wardman Park Hotel, Eisenhower was driven by the plainclothes GI to the massive Pentagon on the banks of the Potomac.

A lieutenant colonel led Eisenhower though a secret passage to the office of Secretary of War Stimson. Gathered in the room was an imposing galaxy of top generals, scientists, and government officials. The subject of Italy was broached, and the general told the assemblage what was already evident: The Germans were resisting ferociously along the Gustav line.

Then Eisenhower gave a rundown on the forthcoming Anzio operation, scheduled to hit on January 22, and told of Winston Churchill's dominant, even dictatorial, role. Secretary Stimson remarked grimly, "Churchill is dead set on making this offensive for political reasons." He later added, "Of course, Churchill is banking on pulling off the Anzio operation quickly."[1]

None of the Pentagon generals endorsed Anzio. They considered it to be merely an infuriating sideshow that would sop up manpower, landing craft, and resources from the main event, Overlord.

In the days ahead, Eisenhower learned that two of the Allied bomber barons in England, General Carl Spaatz, who would command the U.S. Eighth Air Force, and Air Marshal Arthur Harris, leader of the Royal Air Force Bomber Command, felt that Overlord would not even be necessary. Harris was convinced that the Third Reich could be crushed through heavy bombing of German cities, whereas Spaatz believed that the selective destruction of key oil production and armament plants would bring surrender. Spaatz was overheard by subordinates boasting that if he had only twenty or thirty clear days over western Europe, the heavy bombers could finish the war on their own.[2]

On January 12, shortly before his departure for London, Eisenhower called at the White House for a private discussion with President Roosevelt and found the leader in bed with the flu. Despite his weakened condition, the President talked with the general for two hours. Eisenhower said that he was quite concerned by the widespread anti-de Gaulle sentiment that he detected in Washington.

Prior to leaving the Mediterranean, Eisenhower had invited Charles de Gaulle to meet with him at the St. George Hotel in Algiers in what Commander Harry Butcher described as a "love fest." Ike, in fact, was indeed the suitor, wooing the egomaniacal leader of the Free French. "I must have your help, and I ask you for it," Eisenhower told him.

Peacock proud, the Frenchman glowed. "Splendid! You are a real man," de Gaulle responded. "For you know how to say, 'I was wrong!'"[3]

Actually, what Eisenhower was saying was that the Allies would be counting on underground bands to raise merry hell with the Wehrmacht just before and on D-day for Overlord. He knew that most of the French Resistance would respond only to de Gaulle.

Perhaps overstepping his authority, Eisenhower then worked out an arrangement that delighted de Gaulle. In return for the Resistance obeying the instructions of Eisenhower, de Gaulle was promised that his Free French forces would take part in the liberation of Paris and that the FCNL committee, which de Gaulle dominated, would assume control of governmental affairs in the areas of France overrun by Allied armies.

Now, in Washington, Eisenhower was appalled because no one wanted to deal with de Gaulle. Roosevelt felt that any effort to impose de Gaulle and the FCNL on the French people would trigger a bloody civil war. The general tried to dissuade the President from this view, but failed.[4]

At the same time, four thousand miles from Washington, mild-mannered Major General John P. Lucas, the bespectacled, fifty-four-year-old leader of the U.S. VI Corps, was undergoing the torments of the damned at his headquarters in Caserta, Italy, twenty miles north of Naples. Lucas, known to his troops as Foxy Grandpa, had been selected to command Operation Shingle, the assault at Anzio.

No one could know it, but the appointment of Lucas to lead the tricky operation, a task that would require nerves of steel and an audacious spirit, would be a tragic one. The intelligent, white-haired general had performed well at Salerno, but he was not an inspirational leader.

Lucas was deeply concerned about the men he was required to send into battle. It troubled him to be in a job where young Americans were sent to their deaths at his order. "I am far too tenderhearted ever to be a success at my chosen profession," he confided to his diary.

As hasty planning for Shingle progressed, Foxy Grandpa began to fret. "They plan to put me ashore with inadequate forces and could get me in a serious jam," he scribbled in his diary. "Then, who will take the blame?"[5]

Lucas had good reason to be jittery. He would be sent ashore with an initial assault force of only forty thousand men—about half the number Mark Clark had at his disposal when he hit Salerno in a similar operation and was nearly driven back into the sea.

Fifth Army leader Clark was hardly the portrait of confidence, either. At a staff meeting at Caserta, he stated, "We are supposed to go up there [to Anzio], dump two divisions ashore without resupply or reinforcements, and wait for the rest of Fifth Army to catch up with us!"[6]

Major General Lucian K. Truscott, who led the U.S. Third Infantry Division that would make the assault, was also concerned. A tough, bold, and resourceful commander, his courage and fighting spirit were beyond question. But he was worried. "If [Anzio] is to be a 'forlorn hope' or a 'suicide sashay,' then all I want is to know that fact," he wrote to Mark Clark. "I will carry out my duty."

Gloomy reports about the disaster awaiting the Allies at the popular peacetime resort of Anzio reached the ears of General George Patton, who was still in Eisenhower's doghouse because of the slapping incident six months earlier. "Gainfully unemployed," as he termed his situation, Patton flew to VI Corps headquarters to cheer up his longtime friend John Lucas.

Patton's manner of cheerfulness, of course, was peculiarly his own. Beaming broadly, he bellowed, "John, there's no one in the army that I'd hate to get killed as much as you, but you can't get out of this thing alive!" Then he added thoughtfully, "Of course, you might only get wounded. No one ever blames a wounded general!"

Turning aside to a Lucas aide, Patton suggested, "If things get too bad at Anzio, shoot the Old Man in the ass. But be sure not to kill him, only wound him."

Early in the afternoon of January 9, John Lucas walked out of the headquarters of General Harold Alexander, the 15th Army Group leader, after a planning session for Shingle. "I felt like a lamb being led to the slaughter," he wrote that night. "The whole affair has a strong odor of Gallipoli and apparently the same amateur is still on the coach's bench."[7]

The "amateur" was Winston Churchill, and Gallipoli had been a military scheme of his as First Lord of the Admiralty in World War I. That operation had ended in disaster when a force of British, French, Australian, and New Zealand troops was routed in an amphibious assault on Turkey.

Just after midnight on January 22, Lucas's convoy arrived off Anzio and dropped anchor. By noon, the U.S. 3rd and British 1st Divisions, along with other units, had control of Anzio and a nearby seaside town, Nettuno. Resistance had been astonishingly light and Allied casualties were low: Thirteen dead, ninety-seven wounded, forty-four missing.

As Lucas had expected a bloodbath, his spirits soared. From his command ship offshore, he radioed a coded message to Mark Clark in his trailer at Caserta: "Paris—Bordeaux—Turin—Tangiers—Bari—Albany." That terse wording was filled with meaning: "Weather clear, sea calm, little wind, force's presence not discovered, more landings in progress."

For two days, hardly a shot had been fired on the beachhead, which was seven to eight miles deep in places and extended for sixteen miles along the Anzio shoreline. Lucas and his men dug in while he awaited reinforcements and built up supplies and ammunition. Small patrols probed the "front."

On D-day plus one, Lucas wrote in his daily journal, "I must keep my feet on the ground and my forces in hand. I must not do anything foolish. This is the most important thing I have ever tried to do and I will not be stampeded."[8]

One who was all for a stampede to be launched toward Rome was the father of Shingle, an impatient Winston Churchill. He was enraged at what appeared to him to be a failure to exploit the surprise landing far behind German positions. He fired off a message to General Jumbo Wilson, who had succeeded Eisenhower as supreme commander in the Mediterranean, demanding to know why the Allied troops were not now racing for Rome.

Wilson shifted the blame onto Foxy Grandpa, claiming in his response that "there has been no lack of urging from above," meaning Generals Alexander and Clark, as "both had visited the beachhead during the first forty-eight hours to hasten the offensive."

Pacing about in his London bunker, the Prime Minister rasped to confidants, "I thought we were throwing a wildcat onto the beach to rip the bowels out of the Boche. Instead we have a stranded whale."

Far north of Anzio on the night of D-day plus three, Field Marshal Albert Kesselring, always imperturbable, was now breathing easier. He had been quite worried over the situation at Anzio since the Allied landings; the Germans had virtually nothing between the beachhead and Rome. Now, in a masterpiece of logistics, Kesselring had elements of eight divisions ringing the Allied enclave, with five more divisions rushing to the new battleground. He told his chief of staff, Colonel General Siegfried Westphal, that the Anglo-Americans had missed their golden opportunity.

Nearly all the top brass in the Allied camp—except for John Lucas—agreed with that lost-chance assessment. Shingle was stalled, with some forty thousand troops packed sardinelike in what a German radio announcer would call "the world's largest self-sustaining prisoner-of-war compound."

Now the finger-pointing and search for a scapegoat began among the British and Americans. Much of the dispute centered around *one* word that Mark Clark had altered in Fifth Army's battle orders. In his directive to Clark, General Alexander wanted Fifth Army to launch a full-blooded attack against the Gustav line to draw down German reserve divisions positioned near Rome.

When it was determined that these reinforcements had been committed, Lucas's VI Corps was to land at Anzio, take the Alban Hills only ten miles south of Rome, and link up with Fifth Army elements that were to break through the Gustav line. Then Rome would be captured.

Clark had been skeptical about Alexander's directive, however. Salerno was etched in his mind. So the Fifth Army leader instructed Lucas to *advance on*—not *take*—the Alban Hills. Before doing that, Lucas was to "secure the beachhead" and "advance as soon as possible." There was no mention of exploiting the landing rapidly.

In any event, Lucas did not launch a major assault until January 30—D-day plus eight. The fighting was savage. The attack failed. Then Anzio settled down to a relentless, murderous battle of attrition. Allied soldiers were being killed or wounded at the rate of two thousand per week—a staggering price for a piece of drained Italian marsh.

Massed German artillery ringed the beachhead and constantly poured a deluge of shells into the huddled Allied troops and onto the support installations along the shore. So concentrated were the men (and one hundred female nurses in the tent hospital) and installations that it was nearly impossible for a German shell not to find a target.

Winston Churchill would say, "I held no illusions. It was life or death."

After a visit to the beachhead, Harold Alexander was convinced that he had located the required scapegoat: Mild-mannered John Lucas. Alexander sent a message to Field Marshal Alan Brooke in London, seeking to replace VI Corps headquarters with a British corps headquarters—or to replace Lucas with a British general.

A copy of Alexander's message to Brooke was sent to Dwight Eisenhower, now in London at the headquarters of SHAEF (Supreme Headquarters, Allied Expeditionary Force). Ike was alarmed. Not only was an Allied debacle looming at Anzio, but it appeared that an American general might have failed—at least in the eyes of some of the Allied leaders.

On February 18, Eisenhower forwarded Alexander's message to George Marshall in the Pentagon. Unusually stiff security precautions were taken in sending the cable in order to keep official Washington in the dark about the looming Anzio catastrophe. In a sharply worded statement, Eisenhower told his boss that he was opposed to replacing Lucas with a Briton, pointing out that changing command in the midst of a crisis—especially from one nationality to another—could result in crushing the morale of troops fighting for their lives at Anzio. It would also provide enormous propaganda fodder for the Third Reich. Eisenhower added, however, that if a change in command was made, he would be willing to send George Patton "to take command of the forces in the beachhead until the crisis is resolved."

While the Anzio cauldron continued to boil and the issue remained in doubt, Harold Alexander called at Mark Clark's headquarters at Caserta. The British general said that he was "deeply concerned" about the command situation on Anzio and proceeded to sharply criticize John Lucas. Clark bristled at Alexander's rebuke of a fellow American general (whom Clark had appointed), and a sharp exchange of angry words ensued.

Clark found himself in an ambivalent position. He too had gnawing concerns over Lucas's handling of the Anzio situation, yet he felt compelled to defend Foxy Grandpa. The man had been saddled with an extremely difficult operation.

As the discussion became more heated, Clark's blood pressure soared. He was particularly resentful that Alexander appeared to be serving as Winston Churchill's mouthpiece. The Prime Minister, Clark felt, was endeavoring to direct the battle of Anzio from an armchair in London. Churchill seemed to want a mad dash to Rome—and he was unconcerned with the enormous tactical and logistical problems confronting General Lucas.

In the meantime, a backstage campaign to pin the blame on Lucas was gaining momentum. George Marshall signaled Lieutenant General Jacob L. "Jakie" Devers, now the senior American commander in the Mediterranean and Alexander's deputy, that "Washington estimates that the drive and leadership of [Lucas's] corps appear below the stern standards required in the existing situation." Then the army chief suggested that Lucas be thrown to the wolves. "Let nothing stand in the way of procuring the leadership of the quality necessary."[9]

While the Allied generals were exchanging caustic words and messages about Anzio, Field Marshal Kesselring launched an all-out assault to drive the Anglo-Americans into the sea. It may have been the most furious fight between the Wehrmacht and the Allies in the war to date. For three days, both sides fought with enormous courage and tenacity. In his dank underground command post, John Lucas wrote in his diary, "The strain of a thing like this is a terrible burden. Who the hell wants to be a general?"

Finally, the Allied soldiers, aided by a gargantuan rain of shells and bombs, broke the back of the German assault. Lucas's victory seemed to vindicate his seemingly early caution. Had he not built up supplies and ammunition on the beachhead, it was doubtful whether the Anglo-Americans could have resisted the overwhelming onslaught.

As far as is known, Foxy Grandpa received not a single word of praise from the Allied alliance of generals for his epic triumph—one of the most significant of the war. Congratulations for Lucas would have called attention to the salient fact that he had been right and those who had been clamoring for a mad dash to Rome had been wrong.[10]

Yet, the brutal fact remained: John Lucas had not seized Rome as envisioned in Winston Churchill's grandiose strategic scheme. So the backstage onslaught against the Anzio commander resumed. Harold Alexander thought that the VI Corps leader looked harried and concluded that he would be unable to "stand up to the hard long struggle which it was clear the Anzio operation would involve."

General Jakie Devers, Alexander's deputy, had been campaigning for Lucas's relief for some time. After visiting Anzio, Devers concluded that Lucas was tired. Mark Clark agreed that the beachhead commander, after prior months of fighting in Italy, was worn out physically and emotionally.

Exactly one month to the day after the Anglo-Americans went ashore at Anzio, General Lucas's head rolled, just as he had predicted it would in his diary. Mark Clark, who had long been fond of the friendly, pipe-smoking Lucas, had the painful task of informing him that he was being replaced by Lucian Truscott, leader of the U.S. 3rd Infantry Division.

Lucas departed from Anzio a broken and bitter man, convinced that he had performed as well as anyone had the right to expect given the resources he had been allocated. A secure beachhead had been established, and his troops had smashed two full-blooded assaults to drive the Anglo-Americans into the Tyrrhenian Sea. Lucas was kicked upstairs to the newly created and hollow post of Fifth Army deputy commander.

In Lucian Truscott, Clark had the ideal man for the task at hand. Bold, decisive, and vigorous, the new VI Corps leader, unlike the unfortunate Lucas, looked and acted like a two-fisted fighting man. At this point in the ongoing death struggle at Anzio, those traits were vital for the beachhead's commander.[11]

The spotlight now shifted to the British Isles, where feverish preparations were under way for the decisive operation of the war: Overlord.

CHAPTER 20

An Ultimatum to Ireland

WITH THE ALLIED INVASION OF NORMANDY just over the horizon, the Irish Question, as Franklin Roosevelt called the dispute, which had been simmering on the back burner for months, now boiled over. William "Wild Bill" Donovan of the American OSS and officials in Great Britain's MI-6 warned Roosevelt and Churchill that "a great deal of information pertaining to Allied activities in England . . . comes from the German Embassy in Dublin. . . . This embassy is heavily staffed, and has succeeded in infiltrating agents into England. . . . The Germans attribute great importance [to intelligence] obtained from Irish sources."

Hard on the heels of that jolting disclosure, it was learned that Nazi agents with two-way radios had parachuted near Galway, where they were arrested by Irish police. How many more enemy spies had parachuted into Eire and not been caught, Roosevelt and his aides wondered.

After consulting with Churchill, the President decided it was time for firm action. With one of history's mightiest armies massing in the British Isles for the looming cross-Channel assault, Nazi spies snooping from nearby Eire posed a serious threat.

On February 21, 1944, American minister David Gray in Dublin presented Prime Minister Eamon de Valera with what amounted to an ultimatum. No doubt the United States took the potentially explosive action alone because of the feud between Ireland and Britain that had been ongoing for seven hundred years. If Eire continued to operate in favor of the Axis powers against the Western Allies, "on whom your security and the maintenance of your national economy depend," the document declared, "serious consequences could result." The United States demanded that the Irish shut down the large German and Japanese missions in Dublin (which were thriving espionage nests), seize their wireless equipment, jail all German and Japanese agents, and break off relations with Berlin and Tokyo.

Eamon de Valera, long an Irish patriot, found himself cornered. If he rejected President Roosevelt's ultimatum, his tiny country of three million might be invaded and taken over for the duration of the war by U.S. forces.

De Valera, who had been born in New York City of a Spanish father and an Irish mother, had spent his early years in Ireland and, at age fourteen, became a leader in the unsuccessful Easter Rebellion against British rule. A British court sentenced him to death, but the term was changed to life imprisonment because he was American-born.

Now, de Valera seemed to be stonewalling the U.S. ultimatum. An exasperated David Gray fired off a message to Washington with a stern recommendation: Unless the Eire Prime Minister rapidly complied with Roosevelt's terms, U.S. troops, already in the British Isles, should storm into Eire, arrest the German and Japanese spies masquerading as diplomats, and close down the two enemy missions.

Across the English Channel, the German Y Service, a highly sophisticated and extremely efficient wireless monitoring operation, picked up Gray's message, decoded its contents, and rushed them (through the German Embassy in Dublin) to the beleaguered Eamon de Valera.

Gray's signal had hardly reached the White House in Washington when the Irish army was put on full alert. All leaves were canceled, bridges mined, outposts fully manned, and troops deployed along the frontier.

De Valera had the courage to oppose what seemed to be an American invasion threat. "Irish neutrality will be protected at all costs," a grim Prime Minister told his cabinet. Irish-American relations had never been worse. Tension gripped Eire.

Despite the seriousness of the situation, de Valera took more than two weeks to respond to the American ultimatum, which infuriated Franklin Roosevelt. Finally, on March 7, the Prime Minister's reply was handed to David Gray, who promptly relayed it in a wireless message to Washington. De Valera expressed deep surprise at the harsh terms of the American demands, but said that the Irish government would "continue to safeguard the interests of the United States" and at the same time "protect the neutrality of the Irish state."

De Valera, long skilled in the nuances of politics, hinted that any invasion of Eire could result in Roosevelt's offending the large Irish-American electorate. Such an eventuality could result in the President's defeat at the polls in his bid for an unprecedented fourth term.

Now Roosevelt was in a corner. Not only would armed intervention call forth the wrath of the Irish population in the United States, but an invasion of the Eirean "David" by the American "Goliath" also would provide fodder for Josef Goebbels's high-powered Nazi propaganda machine. With the Normandy operation looming, Roosevelt did not want U.S. forces bogged down in Eire for what could be prolonged guerrilla warfare. On the other hand, could the Anglo-Americans risk having Adolf Hitler gain access to history's most profound military secret—the time and place of Overlord—from Nazi spies operating in Eire?

Had Roosevelt truly intended to invade the small island off England? Or had he been engaging in a bluff? Only the President and a tiny clique around him knew his true intentions.[1]

On January 16, 1944, Dwight Eisenhower arrived in London aboard his private railroad coach, *Bayonet*, which had whisked him through the thick fog from Prestwick Airport in Scotland. From that moment, Overlord began to dominate every aspect of the war against Hitler. Within hours of settling down in familiar surroundings, 20 Grosvenor Square, the affable general felt the weight of the tremendous burden.

Plans for Overlord were not settled. Landing craft were Eisenhower's biggest problem. Neptune, the code name for the assault phase, required sufficient landing craft to carry five divisions ashore on D-day, with two follow-up divisions. Therefore, Ike needed 271 landing craft in addition to those already assigned to Neptune. Because he did not have them, he decided, within a week of his arrival in London, to push back D-day from May 1 to early June to allow time for the additional craft to be manufactured or scrounged.

Landing craft were indeed precious. There was a global shortage. "The destinies of two great empires seem to be tied up in some goddamned things called LSTs," Churchill grumbled.[2]

Eisenhower, in his frustration, was complaining bitterly about the U.S. Navy, especially Admiral Ernest King, who he believed was keeping the number and location of landing craft in the Pacific a dark secret. The general said that King looked on the Pacific as the "navy's private war."[3]

In Washington, George Marshall realized that more assault craft would be hard to obtain from King's secret Pacific stockpile. Angered by the navy chief's refusal to cooperate, Marshall complained to his close friend Field Marshal John Dill. As Marshall had intended, Dill passed the remark on to Alan Brooke in London. "The U.S. Chiefs of Staff are engaged in a fresh battle regarding Pacific strategy. It really is the Navy, and Admiral King in particular, *versus* the rest," Dill explained to Brooke. "King does not get any easier as time goes on. He does not trust us [the British] a yard. I believe King's war with the U.S. Army is as bitter as his war with us."[4]

On the other side, Ernest King and his chief of staff, Savvy Cook, were convinced that the British and Eisenhower were conspiring to steal his landing craft by deliberately underestimating the number of usable landing craft already stashed in the British Isles.

As the Battle of the Landing Craft raged, Churchill had grown disenchanted with Field Marshal Dill, whose job it was to interpret American moods and positions for the British, and vice versa. Through his spies in London, Marshall learned that Churchill was going to order Dill's recall. The British Bulldog, secret reports informed Marshall, felt that Dill had become "too American," that he was taking Marshall's side too often in disputes with the British.

Jack Dill was tall, thin, and invariably polite, and possessed a dry sense of humor. Ever since his arrival in Washington two years earlier, he and Marshall had hit it off. In fact, some Americans grumbled that the army chief was far closer to Dill than he was to his own generals. Dill and Marshall had much in common, and they often went horseback riding together. Dill and his wife, Nancy, lived in comfortable lodgings that Marshall had made available at Fort Myer, just outside Washington.

Dill was invaluable to Marshall not only as a friend and confidant. Early in his Washington assignment, Dill discovered from covert sources that Franklin Roosevelt and Winston Churchill often exchanged cables without Marshall's knowledge, even though these messages could, and often did, have enormous impact on the military situation.

By a circuitous route, Dill obtained copies of these Churchill-Roosevelt top-secret cables. "Then Dill would come over to my office, and I would get Mr. Roosevelt's message," Marshall would later recall. "Otherwise I wouldn't know what it was."[5]

This arrangement was kept supersecret, its security almost akin to that surrounding D-day for Overlord. Marshall would remember, "I had to be very careful that nobody knew this—no one in the War Department—and certainly not the British Chiefs of Staff, because Dill would be destroyed in a minute if this was discovered."[6]

The clandestine sharing of secrets of their own government leaders cemented the bond of affection and mutual trust between Marshall and Dill. Although the "spying" arrangement was unorthodox, it was the only means the army chief had for cracking the wall of secrecy that Roosevelt had erected around himself with regard to military matters.

Now, in the wake of transatlantic reports that Churchill was going to yank Dill out of Washington, Marshall set into motion a series of connivances to slyly coerce the Prime Minister into changing his mind. Covertly, Marshall contacted Harvey Bundy, a prominent Boston lawyer before the war and now special assistant to Secretary of War Stimson.

"We're going to lose Dill," the general told Bundy. "An honorary degree from your friends at Harvard might impress the old man in England."[7]

Bundy contacted Harvard but was rejected. No honorary doctorates without a special convocation. Marshall suggested he try Yale. He did, with the same results. However, Yale President Charles Seymour came up with a clever angle that would achieve the same goal. Seymour proposed that John Dill be named the first recipient of the newly established Charles P. Howland Award for contributions to international relations. General Marshall thought it was a great idea.

Seymour went all out, laying on a full-dress academic parade and related pomp and circumstance. Scores of Pentagon public relations officers and photographers descended upon the Ivy League campus in New Haven, Connecticut. Marshall saw to it that British media were flooded with photographs and news of John Dill's prestigious award at Yale.

A few weeks later, Marshall again spoke with Bundy: "My underground tells me that the prime minister said, 'You know, that fellow [Dill] must be doing quite a job!'"[8]

The British field marshal would remain in Washington, presumably still conspiring with the army boss on crucial matters related to the conduct of the war.[9]

Across the Atlantic, Dwight Eisenhower was inundated with a conveyer-belt series of seemingly insolvable problems, not the least of which were towering egos and jealousies among his top commanders.

On February 12, when Dwight Eisenhower presented his Overlord command arrangement to the Allied air leaders, a strident controversy broke out. The plan called for all aircraft to be under the control of Air Chief Marshal Trafford Leigh-Mallory, who had led the Royal Air Force Fighter Command. Leigh-Mallory was regarded by most as being testy and difficult.

Until Eisenhower's command plan was unveiled, Carl "Toohey" Spaatz, leader of the U.S. Eighth Air Force, and Arthur "Bomber" Harris, who was in charge of the RAF Bomber Command, had independent control of their strategic bombers. Now Spaatz and Harris were incensed. What would Leigh-Mallory, whose background was in fighter planes, know about strategic heavy bombers?

Bomber Harris and Toohey Spaatz had much in common. Both were convinced that if given free rein, they could make Overlord unnecessary by pulverizing the Third Reich in massive bombing raids. Soft-spoken and unassuming, Harris kept an arm's length from the men he was sending daily into hostile skies over Germany. Already forty thousand of his airmen had been casualties. Harris planned his strategic strikes from a bunker near High Wycombe, outside London, and never visited his bomber stations.

Harris sent his bombers over Germany at night; Spaatz's heavies pounded the Third Reich by day. Spaatz ran what the navy brass would call "a loose ship." Immaculately tailored American ground force generals, such as George Patton, frowned on Spaatz's untidy, and often unshaven, appearance. When Eisenhower hinted that Spaatz should get his airmen to salute properly, Spaatz was said to have replied that he didn't care how his fliers saluted as long as they carried out their duties properly.

Unlike Bomber Harris, Spaatz detested "flying a desk." On one occasion in early 1943, he scrambled into the nose of a Flying Fortress and went on a mission over German-occupied France, during which his tail gunner shot down a pair of Messerschmitts that had attacked the formation. Also unlike Harris, Spaatz never missed a chance to speak his mind, be it to Eisenhower or to Winston Churchill, whose friendship he had cultivated.

Now, after disclosing his air command structure for Overlord, Eisenhower was acutely embarrassed by the vehement outbursts from Spaatz and Harris against Leigh-Mallory. Seeking to reassure his two miffed heavy-bomber commanders, Eisenhower said that he, along with Arthur Tedder, would personally supervise the Overlord air campaign. Now it was Leigh-Mallory's turn to be annoyed.

That night, Spaatz was still upset. "Ike tried subtly to sell Leigh-Mallory [to me], saying that he felt that maybe proper credit had not been given to the man's intelligence," he wrote in his diary. "I told him that my views had not and would not change." What's more, Spaatz had been unwilling to concede that Leigh-Mallory was intelligent.[10]

A few days later, Spaatz's feud with Leigh-Mallory erupted anew. On the morning that the air marshal was to present his air campaign plan for Overlord to British and American air commanders, Spaatz rushed to see Eisenhower to complain before he had even seen the plan. Ike was frustrated when his efforts to gain Spaatz's cooperation were ignored.

At the conference, Leigh-Mallory proposed to shift the heavy-bomber emphasis from industrial targets in Germany and occupied northwest Europe to pounding the railroad network all the way into the Third Reich. In his opinion, the German air force would fight to defend the rail system and could be decimated prior to D-day.

Leigh-Mallory had no sooner concluded than Spaatz bitterly disagreed. "What if they don't fight?" he snapped. He declared that he had to have the opportunity to pulverize anything else that would make the Luftwaffe come up and fight in large numbers. Otherwise, he would not be able to accomplish his primary task: The defeat of the German air force.

A thoroughly angry Arthur Harris "lowered the boom"—as it would later be described by one of the Americans present—on his fellow countryman. Leigh-Mallory's plan was based on a fallacy, he charged. "Railroads cannot be sufficiently interrupted by bombing to impede the Germans from moving troops [toward Normandy]."

Now Leigh-Mallory brought forward Professor Solly Zuckerman, who was billed as an "expert on the European rail network," to back his bombing theory. Zuckerman, a British anatomist, spoke at great length, presenting a bombing scheme intended, in military jargon, to isolate the battlefield (meaning Normandy). His plan called for the destruction of eighty key railroad targets in northwest Europe in the period between March 1 and D-day in early June.

Air Marshal Harris was unimpressed. "I'll give a written guarantee that [this railroad destruction] plan will not succeed," he snapped. "Then the army will blame us, the air forces, for the army's failure."

Despite the fireworks among the Allied air barons, Eisenhower stuck to his guns: Trafford Leigh-Mallory would command all aircraft for Overlord.

A few nights later, the supreme commander discovered that a new figure had entered the controversy: Winston Churchill. At a dinner at 10 Downing Street, the Prime Minister kept Eisenhower up until nearly 2:00 A.M., haranguing him about the choice of Leigh-Mallory as air chief for Overlord. Perhaps Churchill had been coached by Bomber Harris, because the Prime Minister pointed out time and again that Leigh-Mallory was a fighter-plane commander.

When Eisenhower refused to budge, Churchill sulked. Later, Ike would tell Arthur Tedder, "I told him if I needed any help, which I did not anticipate, I'd come to him promptly."

In the days ahead, Eisenhower became exhausted and exasperated by the air controversy and finally raised the white flag of surrender. Churchill's tenacity and guile had triumphed. Arthur Tedder, Ike's deputy, would continue with his present duties at SHAEF headquarters and also command the Overlord air campaign. Leigh-Mallory would remain in his post, but take his orders from Tedder, a clumsy situation that rankled Leigh-Mallory.

The hassle over air commanders refused to die, however. Eisenhower complained to confidants that each time he felt that he had the problem settled, someone else's tail feathers got ruffled or feelings got bruised.

On March 5, SHAEF headquarters moved from crowded Grosvenor Square to Bushy Park, a group of Quonset huts on a private estate a short distance from London. One of Eisenhower's first callers was George Patton, who was ushered into his office while the supreme commander was engaged in a loud telephone conversation with Tedder.

"Now, listen, Arthur," Eisenhower snapped testily, "I am tired of dealing with a goddamned bunch of prima donnas. By God, you tell that bunch that if they can't get together and stop quarreling like children, I will tell the prime minister to get someone else to run this war. I'll *quit!*"[11]

Patton broke out in a broad grin as if to say, "Give 'em hell, Ike!"

A month later, on April 7, Bernard Montgomery, who would command initial ground operations in Normandy, held a meeting to review Overlord in its final version. Even before the session got under way, while the officers were milling about, Omar Bradley and Montgomery had a spat. Bradley had noticed a large relief map of Normandy on a tilted platform. What caught his eye and raised his hackles were the carefully drawn phase lines on the map.

In keeping with his tactical concept of a neat, set-piece battle, Montgomery had insisted that phase lines be set for expansion of the bridgehead, lines scheduled to be reached on designated days. Bradley had always strongly opposed what he considered to be a timid approach to the battle, believing that commanders should enter an action with the expectation of breaking through the enemy for long gains if the opportunity arose.

"At least I do not want phase lines in the American sector," Bradley had stressed to Monty a few weeks earlier. At the time, he thought that the British general had reluctantly agreed with him. Now he spotted the phase lines on the big map. He approached Montgomery and demanded again that the lines be erased, "at least in the American sector." Montgomery, flushed with anger, finally agreed. Or had he?

CHAPTER 21

Patton: Frame-up
Target?

WHEN SWASHBUCKLING GEORGE PATTON had arrived in England from
Italy—"fresh from Ike's doghouse," as he put it—in late January 1944, he landed in
a thick fog at Cheddington airfield, thirty-two miles northwest of London.
Alighting from his airplane, he was irritated to see that Eisenhower had sent
Major General J. C. H. Lee to greet him. It was no secret that Patton detested
Lee, and that the sentiment was mutual.

Lee was two years junior to Patton, but they had graduated together at
West Point. Lee had stood twelfth in a class of 103; Patton was far down the
totem pole in forty-sixth place. A sharp-eyed, balding, blond man, Lee had the
face Hollywood usually typecasts in the role of a glad-handing small-town
clergyman. A soldier of the old school, he had a reputation for being pompous
and a martinet. His not-too-adoring subordinates privately called him, after his
first three initials, Jesus Christ Himself.

At Cheddington, Patton's face brightened when he saw that Commander
Harry Butcher, Eisenhower's naval aide, was also on hand. He liked the outgoing Butcher and appreciated Eisenhower's thoughtfulness in sending him.
Moments later, Patton's ego was deflated: Butcher had met the airplane to
welcome another passenger: Tiny Caacia, one of Eisenhower's pet dogs. She had
flown in from North Africa.

A day after reaching London, Patton paid a call on his old friend Eisenhower and was told that he would command the Third Army in Overlord. Third
Army components were still in the United States and would not arrive in the
British Isles until February or early March. Then the supreme commander dealt
the proud Patton a crushing blow: Third Army would not be in the initial assault
on Normandy.

Eisenhower, who was Patton's junior in both age and permanent rank and
was keenly conscious of it, looked sternly at his friend and proceeded to give the
older man a lecture. Ike and nearly every other Allied leader knew that a Washington newspaper editorial had described Patton as "Chief Foot-in-the-
Mouth," and all agreed with that assessment. At the same time, the dashing

168

cavalryman was the Allies' boldest and most audacious battle commander—and the war effort needed him. Eisenhower needed him.

"Georgie, I don't mean to sound like a Dutch uncle, but I told you innumerable times to count ten before you take any abrupt action," Eisenhower said. "Think before you leap, or you will have no one to blame but yourself for your rashness."[1]

Like a penitent schoolboy, the chastised Patton promised that he would watch his step and "keep my big mouth shut."

After leaving Eisenhower's office, Patton was stricken yet again by paranoia, angry about being excluded from the Overlord initial assault. He railed to confidants that "they" were out to get him, to halt him, to gag him, to prevent him from earning laurels on the battlefield. "They" included Eisenhower, Jesus Christ Himself Lee, most of the SHAEF staff, all other Allied generals, most newspaper correspondents, a large number of senators and congressmen—and the entire British nation.

Along with paranoia, Patton was racked by a confused mental state. He considered himself to be far superior to other American battle commanders, yet he had not even been told what role his new Third Army would eventually play in Overlord. Nor was he being called on to express his views during invasion planning. In essence, Patton was persona non grata at SHAEF.

When the outcast did learn a bit about plans for Third Army, he was galled. He would eventually be commanded by Omar Bradley, who was in charge of American ground forces for the invasion and later would command the 12th Army Group. As recently as Sicily, Bradley had been taking orders from Patton; now their roles would be reversed.

Since the beginning of America's direct involvement in the war, Patton had come across as being anti-British. He had feuded with Bernard Montgomery, the idol of the British home front, whom he privately referred to as "that arrogant little fart." Patton had also crossed swords with another British war hero, Harold Alexander. Patton described the reserved Alexander as "an incompetent cold fish." There was no known instance of any British general, admiral, or air marshal speaking out in praise of George Patton.

Hoping to erase his anti-British image, aides prodded Patton into accepting an invitation to speak at the opening of a ladies' welcome club in Knutsford, a town in the Third Army region, on April 25. As a few hundred women listened in rapture, the general, in his high-pitched voice, told them how "lovely" they were. Actually, Patton long had held the view that Englishwomen were "ugly as sin."

Then Patton wandered into the delicate realm of politics. "It is the evident destiny of the British and Americans [*long pause*] and of course the Russians, to rule the [postwar] world," he told the cheering ladies.

Although he had been assured in advance that his remarks were off the record, within hours a British news agency, despite a pledge of confidentiality, broke the story to the world. In so doing, it omitted the key words *and the*

Russians. Convinced that the outspoken fighting man had pulled a monumental boner, SHAEF officers tried to get the British news organization to include the words "and the Russians" in the release. Too late, was the reply, despite the fact that it was routine for news agencies to send follow-up alterations or corrections on major stories.

In the wake of the controversy, left-wing segments of the American press launched an assault against the general. PATTON INSULTS RUSSIAN ALLIES, one headline blared. A few liberal members of Congress took to the floor to denounce Patton, and his pending promotion to permanent major general was held up.

In the Third Reich, Josef Goebbels ordered all German media to play up the remarks in the hope of driving a deep wedge between the Soviets and their western Allies.

George Patton, fearless and decisive on the battlefield, was stupefied and shaken by events. Eisenhower, who had, at the risk of his own career, stood by Patton in his previous scrapes, now considered inflicting on him the worst fate that could befall a born warrior: Relieving him of command of Third Army and shipping him back to the States to become a paper-shuffler.

Who or what had triggered the global uproar? Patton thought he knew the answer: "It's a frame-up!" Who had perpetrated the frame-up? "The goddamned British!"

While nabobs on both sides of the Atlantic called for Patton's scalp, Winston Churchill dismissed the matter. "I don't see anything wrong with his remarks—he simply told the truth," the Prime Minister said.

Could it have been that a covert British agency known by the innocuous name London Controlling Section (LCS) was the knowing instigator of the international hubbub in the wake of the Knutsford affair? It was the function of LCS to coordinate deception schemes designed to hoodwink Adolf Hitler and his Oberkommando der Wehrmacht into believing that the looming Allied invasion of France would hit at the Pas de Calais (in England, known as the Strait of Dover).

As a key component of the intricate deception scheme, code-named Quicksilver (a component of Bodyguard), the phony First United States Army Group (FUSAG) was supposed to be forming in southeastern England, across from the Pas de Calais. The idea was to convince the Germans that FUSAG spearheads would bolt across the Channel at its narrowest point, some two hundred miles northeast of the actual landing beaches in Normandy, thereby keeping the defending Fifteenth Army in place along the Calais coast on D-day.

A crucial requirement for the Quicksilver stratagem was an actual, authentic commander of FUSAG. That commander was at hand: George Patton, whom the German generals regarded as America's most gifted and boldest combat leader and, therefore, a logical choice to command U.S. assault forces for *der Grossinvasion.*

Patton had been playing his mock role to the hilt, dashing all over England inspecting his supposed units. "I'm a goddamned natural-born ham!" he told aides. With his ramrod posture, lacquered helmet liner, fifteen gleaming stars (on headgear, shirt collar, and shoulders), ivory-handled revolver, and tendency to roar profane commands, Patton should have been highly visible to hostile eyes.

However, it was conceivable that the Germans had not grasped the fact that the American general they most feared was in England and commanding FUSAG. So, perhaps the LCS, a consortium of Britain's most brilliant and devious minds, seized on the Knutsford affair to trumpet to Hitler and his generals that Patton would lead the charge across the Channel against the Pas de Calais. Even the most nearsighted Nazi spies could hardly miss the headlines about Patton.

Had Patton truly been framed? Or had Fleet Street, London's newspaper row, merely seized an opportunity to discredit an American general it hated? Or had Patton been the sacrificial pawn in Allied deception machinations? Answers to those questions would be lost in the haze of passing time.

In the days ahead, George Patton could not shake his paranoia. In late April, he complained in his diary: "I have a feeling that neither Monty or Bradley are too anxious for me to have a command. If they knew what little respect I have for the fighting ability of either of them, they would be even less anxious for me to show them up."[2]

As preparations for Overlord became steadily more hectic, demanding, and nerve-racking, Dwight Eisenhower was beginning to show signs of the enormous strain. Only his intimates knew that he had been undergoing secret medical treatment for an eye that was inflamed and sore, resulting in blurred vision on occasion, and for ringing ears. Most nights, as only his confidant Harry Butcher knew, the general was so exhausted he could barely undress and get into bed. Even then, he was haunted by visions of seemingly unsolvable problems, including the skirmishes among the Allied alliance of generals.

No detail of Overlord planning was too small to find its way to the supreme commander. He had even been forced to settle a low-level dispute over the amount of toilet tissue to be taken ashore on the first day of the invasion. Buck-passing halted at Eisenhower's desk.

Reflecting the anxiety that gripped SHAEF, Eisenhower wrote to his old friend General Brehon Somervell, chief of the Army Services of Supply, in Washington. "As time goes by, tension grows and everybody gets on edge," Ike admitted. "This time, because of the stakes involved, the atmosphere is probably more electric than ever before. . . . We are not merely risking a tactical defeat— we are putting the whole works on one number."[3]

There was ample reason for SHAEF jitters. British General Fredrick Morgan, who had drawn up the original invasion plan, warned, "If the Germans have even a forty-eight-hour advance notice of the time and place of the Normandy landings, we could suffer a monstrous catastrophe!"

By mid-April, chances for a security leak had multiplied many times. Hundreds of American and British officers now were privy to the innermost secrets of Overlord—including the projected D-day and the locale of the invasion. They were known as Bigots, which took its curious name from the stamp "To Gib" that had been imprinted on the papers of officers traveling to Gibraltar for the invasion of North Africa in November 1942. To confuse the Germans (and Allied personnel not in the know), the "To Gib" letters had been reversed.

Only a Bigot could see secret documents marked "Bigot" in large red letters. He had a special pass to enter certain offices that others could not enter, however high their ranks. When one Bigot spoke to another Bigot over the wire, a special green telephone equipped with a scrambler was used so that the conversation would sound like gibberish to hostile eavesdroppers.

Ever since the Big Three summit at Teheran in late 1943, Soviet Premier Josef Stalin had never ceased trying to unlock the Anglo-American secrets for D-day. In April 1944, Major General Brocas Burrows, chief of the British military mission to Moscow, cabled London that Stalin was demanding to know the precise date and locale of Overlord. A few days later, the Russian ambassador to England, Feodor Tarasovich Gousey, a stoical figure the British had dubbed Frogface, also badgered British diplomats for precise information.

British intelligence knew of Gousey's true role: He was a high-ranking official in the NKVD, the Russian intelligence agency. Straight-faced British and American officers briefed Gousey on many details of Overlord, most of them phony. They lied that George Patton's FUSAG, in southeastern England, would assault the French Pas de Calais.

Subsequently, General Burrows in Moscow was instructed to inform Stalin only that D-day would be two or three days before or after June 1, depending on weather conditions. If the Soviet leader was to inform the Germans of the information he had secured from Frogface, as Winston Churchill thought he might, it would play right into the hands of Bodyguard—convincing the Germans that Patton would command the cross-Channel assault against the Pas de Calais.

Stalin was not satisfied with the information and wanted more details. General Burrows was ordered to keep his mouth shut. So that the military mission chief could plausibly deny that he was privy to Overlord secrets, he and his assistants were forbidden to return to London on leave. Actually, Burrows was a Bigot.

In the pressure-cooker climate at SHAEF, verbal clashes at high levels intensified. In mid-April, Bernard Montgomery was presiding at an airborne planning session at his headquarters at St. Paul's School, a large, red-brick Gothic building that stood beside the road leading to Heathrow Airport outside London. Fireworks were touched off when Air Chief Marshal Trafford Leigh-

Mallory made a stunning proposal: Cancel the parachute and glider assault by the U.S. 82nd Airborne and U.S. 101st Airborne divisions behind Utah Beach, where the green American 4th Infantry Division would land.

If any one of the five assault beaches was more critical than the others, it had to be Utah, at the base of the Cherbourg peninsula on the far west of the Neptune region. Once firmly ashore, the 4th Infantry Division was to attack northward and help seize the port of Cherbourg, the invasion's primary objective, twenty-two miles from Utah.

"I cannot approve your airborne plan," Leigh-Mallory told Omar Bradley. "Your losses will be far more than what your gains are worth. I cannot go along with you."

Bradley was shocked. "Very well, sir," the low-key American replied, "if you insist on cutting out our airborne attack, then I must ask that we eliminate the Utah assault. I am not going to land on that beach without making sure our airborne people have [captured] the four causeway exits behind it."

Now it was Leigh-Mallory's turn to be stunned. After a few moments of awkward silence, he responded, "Then let me make it clear. If you insist upon the airborne operation, you'll do it in spite of my opposition." Turning to Montgomery, he added, "If General Bradley insists upon going ahead, he will have to accept full responsibility for the operation."

Bradley flushed with anger and quickly cut in. "That's perfectly okay. I'm in the habit of accepting full responsibility for my operations."

Bernard Montgomery, who for two years had had more than his share of clashes with American and British generals alike, now found himself in the unaccustomed role of peacemaker. Monty rapped for order and declared, "Gentlemen! Gentlemen! That's not at all necessary. I'll accept responsibility."[4]

The American airborne assault behind Utah Beach was still on—at least for the present.

A short time later, Dwight Eisenhower summoned Omar Bradley. Leigh-Mallory had gone to the harried supreme commander to pursue his crusade to get the American parachute and glider attack canceled, and now Eisenhower wanted to get Bradley's view.

Hearing of Leigh-Mallory's refusal to accept his conference-table defeat at Montgomery's headquarters, Bradley exploded. "Of course the airborne attack is risky," he agreed, "but not half so risky as a seaborne landing at Utah without it!"[5]

Again Bradley stressed that those risks must be subordinated to the early capture of Cherbourg. Unless the Utah Beach invaders could quickly seize that port to bring in reinforcements, guns, tanks, artillery, ammunition, and fuel, the Allies would be in danger of withering on the vine and being cut to pieces by German panzer forces converging on the Normandy bridgehead.

Eisenhower, confronted with divergent views from top air and ground commanders, later pondered the dilemma and ruled in favor of Bradley. That ended the bitter dispute—or so Bradley thought.

On May 15, an extravaganza worthy of a regal coronation ceremony was held at St. Paul's School for a final review of Overlord plans. SHAEF had even sent out engraved invitations. The galaxy of Allied leaders included King George, Winston Churchill, and Dwight Eisenhower. George Patton greeted the British monarch warmly, although two weeks earlier, after attending a gala dinner at Buckingham Palace, Patton had confided to his diary, "The King is a pleasant little fellow—and one notch above a moron."

Eisenhower opened the show with a brief speech of welcome, then turned the spotlight over to the star performer, Bernard Montgomery. In deference to the chain-smoking Eisenhower and cigar-puffing Churchill, Monty broke his firm rule and permitted those in attendance to light up, a concession that brought muffled gasps from several of the Britons in the room.

Speaking in crisp, nasal tones, Montgomery reminded his listeners that the Germans had sixty divisions, ten of them panzers, in France. Field Marshal Erwin Rommel, an "energetic and determined commander," would do his level best to drive the invaders back into the sea, he declared. Rommel might well rush nine divisions around the beachhead by D-day plus two, and launch a coordinated counterattack with ten panzer divisions four days later.

Despite this haunting portrait of a looming disaster, Montgomery exuded confidence when he turned to the Allied situation. Storming the beaches was no real problem, he indicated, although heavy Allied casualties might occur. He spoke glowingly of getting far inland and "cracking about" on D-day. Falaise, thirty-two miles south of the beaches, might even be reached by British armored spearheads on the first night.[6]

After Montgomery concluded his briefing, King George spoke for a few minutes. He had to leave early. Then Winston Churchill made a lengthy, emotional speech, preaching on "bravery, ingenuity, and persistence as human qualities of far greater value than equipment."[7]

Omar Bradley, Toohey Spaatz, Bomber Harris, and British Admiral Bertram Ramsey, the Overlord naval commander, presented briefings on the roles of their forces. Field Marshal Alan Brooke was in a grumpy mood and unimpressed. That night he wrote in his diary that Spaatz was a bore, and he complained that Harris "told us how well he might have won the war if it had not been for the handicap imposed by the existence of the two other services."

Brooke also blasted the supreme commander: "The main impression I gathered was that Eisenhower is no real director of thought, plans, energy, or direction. . . . He's just a good coordinator, a good mixer, a champion of inter-Allied cooperation."[8]

Clearly, the chief of the Imperial General Staff was still smarting over having lost out to Eisenhower in the supreme commander sweepstakes.

Far from the pressures of SHAEF, plans were afoot for a breakout from the stagnant Anzio beachhead in Italy. On May 5, Harold Alexander, leader of the 15th Army Group, paid a visit to Lucian Truscott, who had succeeded John

Lucas as commander of the U.S. VI Corps. The American general proudly unfurled four alternative plans for the impending dash to Rome, each with an exotic code name: Crawdad, Buffalo, Turtle, and Grasshopper.

Truscott said that he could launch any one of the plans on forty-eight hours' notice. Alexander replied, "The only worthwhile one is Buffalo."

Buffalo called for Truscott to drive northeast from Anzio and seize Valmontone, just south of the Alban Hills. "This is the plan I want, and I reserve for myself the decision as to the time for launching it," Alexander told the American.

Twenty-four hours later, Mark Clark, the Fifth Army leader, arrived on the beachhead and was infuriated to learn that Alexander had bypassed the American chain of command and gone directly to Clark's subordinate, Truscott.

"Apparently Alexander has decided to move in and run my army!" Clark snapped.

Now Clark was convinced that there was a devious British plot afoot to deprive Fifth Army of its hard-earned glory of capturing Rome. The name of Winston Churchill popped up regularly at Fifth Army headquarters after Clark returned from Anzio.

Still furious, Clark telephoned Alexander and said that he was surprised to learn that Alexander had skirted him and gone directly to a Clark subordinate to issue orders contrary to those given earlier by Clark. The Fifth Army commander had told Truscott to be flexible and ready to launch any of his four breakout plans when Clark gave the signal, depending on the situation at the time.

Alexander told Clark that he understood and had no intention of interfering directly with the operations of Fifth Army, which was under 15th Army Group control.

Despite the high-level squabbling, all Allied commanders in Italy were united on one point: The Anzio breakout would be a difficult, bloody affair. Colonel General Eberhard von Mackenson had five and a half first-rate German divisions in his beachhead noose, and the 26th Panzer Grenadier Division was posted just south of Rome and could be rushed to the action on an hour's notice.

Sixty miles south of Anzio on the night of May 11, a drizzling rain was falling along the Gustav line. It was deathly still. Suddenly, the quiet was shattered. Nearly eleven hundred Allied big guns roared and flamed. After the German positions were deluged by thousands of shells, grim Allied infantrymen trudged forward to close with the enemy. As anticipated, the Gustav line became a bloody slugging match. There would be no rapid breakthrough to link up with the Anzio force.

On the bridgehead, Lucian Truscott was devouring every scrap of rumor that poured into his headquarters from the Gustav line violence. Truscott's force was like a star open-field runner sitting on the bench in a crucial football game, straining for a signal from the coach to leap into the fray and dash for a touchdown.

After six days of vicious fighting, General Alphonse Juin's French corps broke the Gustav line logjam and charged ahead for twenty miles. By May 21, the Germans were in full retreat all along the southern battlefront. With the attacking Allied spearheads only forty miles from Anzio, another controversy erupted between Mark Clark and Harold Alexander. Alexander instructed Truscott to prepare to launch Operation Buffalo. Clark violently disputed the order as premature. He pointed out that only the French corps had reached northward for twenty miles and that Oliver Leese's British Eighth Army was lagging far behind Juin's fighting men.

Clark was also angry over the fact that Alexander had again bypassed him and gone directly to Truscott. Privately, Clark felt that the British were making no real effort to advance, but were permitting the French to clear a path for Eighth Army.

Now the inter-Allied high-level jockeying got into gear. At stake was the honor of being the first army in fifteen centuries to capture Rome from the south. Clark made no secret of his goal to beat the British into the Eternal City.

Buffalo—the breakout from Anzio—began just before dawn on May 21, when five hundred Allied guns deluged German positions with thousands of shells. Then, through the haze- and smoke-covered battleground, reeking with the putrid smell of death, Truscott's tanks rumbled forward. Thousands of foot soldiers climbed out of their waterlogged slit trenches and followed. As expected, the Germans fought back tenaciously.

Two days after Buffalo kicked off, a Fifth Army task force driving up from the Gustav line and U.S. elements from the bridgehead linked up a mile northwest of Borga Grappa, a village which had, perhaps symbolically, been flattened by Allied bombers. Anzio beachhead no longer existed.

CHAPTER 22

The Unconditional Surrender Brouhaha

ALL THROUGH THE LATE WINTER AND EARLY SPRING OF 1944, an intense debate had been raging backstage in the Allied camp about the wisdom of the doctrine of unconditional surrender, the ultimatum that Franklin Roosevelt had blurted out at Casablanca a year earlier. Nearly all Allied generals were urging a softening of the policy, declaring that unconditional surrender was stiffening German resistance on all fronts, thereby causing heavier casualties among Allied soldiers and airmen.

On the other hand, a few powerful American politicians—including President Roosevelt, Secretary of the Treasury Henry Morgenthau, and State Department official Alger Hiss—claimed that any softening of terms would be taken as a sign of Allied weakness and seized upon by German propagandists to make the Feldgrau (field gray, the average soldier) fight even harder.

Consequently, a subtle, behind-the-scenes machination was launched by those seeking to modify the unconditional surrender demand prior to the looming invasion of Normandy. There were those who thought they detected the deft, invisible hand of Winston Churchill behind the movement. The British Joint Intelligence Committee kicked off the campaign by asking its counterpart in the Pentagon a series of pertinent questions about the wisdom of unconditional surrender and whether that policy would result in enormous casualties on D-day. After lengthy discussion, the U.S. Joint Chiefs (Marshall, King, Arnold, and Leahy) dispatched a document to Roosevelt on March 25. It read in part: "The Joint Chiefs are of the opinion that a restatement of the formula of unconditional surrender should be made at an early date so that it may establish a favorable condition precedent to Overlord."[1]

Then the Joint Chiefs gave Roosevelt a draft of a statement it suggested he broadcast to the Wehrmacht and the Herrenvolk (German people) just prior to D-day in Normandy. The thrust of the text was to give the Feldgrau and German home front some hope while reiterating the unconditional surrender demand. Key parts of the proposed presidential broadcast stated, "It is not our purpose to extinguish the German people or Germany as a nation. It will be a main task of Allied military occupation to create the conditions for rebirth of a peaceful German society. Only unconditional surrender can provide the necessary basis for a fresh start."[2]

Lieutenant General Frank N. Roberts, the Pentagon officer primarily responsible for directing American involvement in the Bodyguard deception scheme, was greatly in favor of the proposed presidential remarks. The modified thrust for unconditional surrender would be a "psychological blockbuster" that should "reduce German resistance to the cross-Channel attack," Roberts said.[3]

In London, Dwight Eisenhower was an enthusiastic backer of the presidential broadcast. Acting on the advice of Colonel Robert A. McClure, SHAEF's propaganda chief, Eisenhower urged that unconditional surrender be "restated" by Roosevelt shortly before D-day so that the German soldiers in Normandy would know that it would be "good business" not to resist but to capitulate.

For nearly a week, the Joint Chiefs waited eagerly for Roosevelt's reply to the proposed broadcast. Surely the President would not reject a course of action recommended by all of his highest military leaders. Might it not be possible that on the basis of the Roosevelt broadcast, the Allied assault troops would *waltz* ashore rather than encounter tenacious resistance?

On April 1, the President shattered the hopes of the leaders of his armed forces. In a letter to the Joint Chiefs, he rejected the broadcast proposal. His communication dripped with vengeance. "German philosophy cannot be changed by decree, law, or military order," Roosevelt stated. "I am not willing at this time to say that we do not intend to destroy the German nation. As long as the word 'Reich' exists in Germany, it will forever be associated with the present form of nationhood. If we admit that, we must seek to eliminate the very word 'Reich'. . . ."

Roosevelt's rejection seemed to reflect Henry Morgenthau's plan in capsule form: Crush Germany into a pastoral nation without industry and with Allied troops guarding her borders, and eliminate a long list of German military and government leaders.

Roosevelt's bitter declaration astonished and angered George Marshall. He complained to his confidant John Dill that "[we] are up against an obstinate Dutchman who had brought the phrase [unconditional surrender] out and doesn't like to go back on it."[4]

Subconsciously perhaps, Eisenhower held a faint ray of hope that Overlord and the savage battles to follow might even be prevented. He searched for a means to make a final attempt to obtain for the German armed forces what Harry Butcher called "a white alley," a path down which the enemy could surrender with honor intact.[5]

Eisenhower saw an opportunity to get Roosevelt to soften his stand when forty-three-year-old Edward R. Stettinius, a top executive with U.S. Steel who soon would be appointed Secretary of State, called at SHAEF. The supreme commander prevailed on Stettinius to cable Secretary of State Cordell Hull and relate Eisenhower's views on unconditional surrender, no doubt hoping that Hull would become an advocate in changing Roosevelt's mind.

Stettinius sent the cable, engaging in what apparently was an Eisenhower scheme to put the Germans in a capitulation mood. Stettinius's telegram stated that "General [Beetle] Smith, rather than General Eisenhower" had recommended that the supreme commander make his own appeal to Field Marshal Karl Rudolf Gerd von Rundstedt, the aristocratic, capable Wehrmacht commander in the West, to surrender. Eisenhower's broadcast appeal, Stettinius suggested, should be "recited in soldierly terms" and should be made *after* a bridgehead was established in Normandy.

Again attributing the opinion to Beetle Smith, Stettinius's telegram declared, "All available evidence, in default of declarations [by Roosevelt and Eisenhower], indicates it would be impossible to exploit the crisis in the German army which undoubtedly will arise immediately after a successful Allied landing."[6]

SHAEF apparently had been well informed, through secret contacts with the Schwarze Kapelle, that there was great unrest among Adolf Hitler's generals, who felt that the Bohemian Corporal, as von Rundstedt sneeringly called the Führer in private, was taking Germany hell-bent down the road to destruction.

British intelligence had received reliable information that the biggest name in the Schwarze Kapelle conspiracy, famed Field Marshal Erwin Rommel, was willing to negotiate a separate peace with the Western Allies. Rommel, who was directly in charge of repulsing the looming Allied onslaught, would seize the first opportunity to discuss terms with Eisenhower, according to clandestine information from an excellent source within the Third Reich. How many tens of thousands of lives could be saved if Rommel or his emissary could negotiate a German surrender that would be acceptable to both sides?

Perhaps acting at Eisenhower's direction, Colonel Robert McClure's Political Warfare Branch at SHAEF prepared a statement softening the unconditional surrender demand for the supreme commander to broadcast. The speech was to be a "fireside chat," much like the ones that Roosevelt had made famous on the home front. Routinely, the speech was sent to the White House for approval. Time for the bloodletting on the far shore was approaching, but Roosevelt provided only silence.

When the President did reply, he did not castigate Eisenhower, the soldier, for involving himself in an effort to change Anglo-American political policy. All Roosevelt said was that he continued to stand behind his unconditional surrender terms for Germany.

Although Winston Churchill shared Eisenhower's view on softening the unconditional surrender policy, he severely rebuked the supreme commander in a scathing letter on May 31, less than a week before D-day. For a considerable period of time, the Prime Minister had been concerned about the enormous power that had been placed in the hands of one man, Eisenhower. Now Churchill was irked because the supreme commander appeared to be trying to usurp the political functions of the President and the Prime Minister.

Churchill also was unhappy about the timing of Eisenhower's proposed broadcast, accusing him of "begging before we have won the battle."

"This is a matter which really must be dealt with by governments," Churchill wrote angrily, "and cannot be made the subject of fireside chats. I have never read anything less suitable for [German] troops."[7]

Eisenhower's broadcast was dead. Unconditional surrender would remain in force as the clock ticked inexorably toward D-day.

Late in May, Winston Churchill, a human dynamo despite his nearly seventy years, and King George traveled to Portland on the Channel coast to inspect American PT boats and their crews. In charge of the swift, sleek craft with the mighty sting in their tails was John Bulkeley, who had rescued General Mac-Arthur from Japanese-surrounded Corregidor in March 1942. Now a lieutenant commander, Bulkeley was in charge of all PT boats. They would spearhead the attack on the two American beaches, code-named Utah and Omaha.

Churchill and the King climbed aboard PT 504, Bulkeley's flagship. Seldom, perhaps, had such a small craft been invaded by so much gold braid: King George in the uniform of a five-star admiral of the fleet, U.S. Rear Admirals Alan G. Kirk and Arthur D. Struble, along with a few Royal Navy flag officers.

As soon as the VIPs were on board, each was approached by the PT boat's young quartermaster first class, whose task was to record the names and ranks of visitors. Pen and pad at the ready, the sailor passed from one admiral to the other, asking for names. When he reached the monarch of Great Britain, whom he did not recognize, he asked, "Sir, may I please have your first name?" Without changing expression, the King replied, "George." The sailor scrawled "George" on his pad.

"And your last name, sir?"

"Windsor," the King responded.

Again the hasty scribbling. The sailor read aloud: "Fleet Admiral George Windsor, Royal Navy."[8]

Then Churchill, the King, and their entourage were taken on a high-speed tour of Portland harbor on another PT boat that darted among the assembled warships, transports, and landing craft. While the torpedo boat was returning to its dock, the door to the chart room popped open and the beaming face of a young cook appeared.

"Would yer Majesty like a cuppa jamoke?" he asked.

The PT boat officers winced. King George looked puzzled. When the question was explained, the monarch went down the ladder to the small wardroom, where he drank two cupfuls of coffee and complimented the cook for "an excellent brew."[9]

Neptune, the assault phase of Overlord, was unmatched historically in scope and complexity. The printed plan was five inches thick, and even the single-spaced typed list of American units—fourteen hundred of them—required thirty-one pages. On D-day alone, the equivalent of five hundred trainloads of troops—57,506 American, 72,215 British and Canadian—along with their weapons, vehicles, ammunition, and supplies would be put ashore in Normandy. Thousands of Allied paratroopers and glidermen would jump and land behind the beaches.

There would be landings by five great naval task forces in the Bay of the Seine, which was divided into the American assault area on the west (Utah and Omaha beaches) and the British and Canadian assault area on the east (Gold, Sword, and Juno beaches).

A few days before D-day, invasion fever swept the British Isles when the gargantuan operation was activated. All over southern England, dusty roads and narrow-gauge rail lines groaned under the weight of the mighty army edging southward to the Channel ports. Seaborne assault troops, grim and tight-lipped, marched into seventeen assembly areas called "sausages" because of their oval shapes on high-level military maps. Men of the 82nd and 101st Airborne Divisions were sealed into encampments of long rows of pyramidal tents at airfields in the Midlands.

On May 30, Trafford Leigh-Mallory called on Eisenhower to protest a final time the "futile destruction of two fine American airborne divisions." The tune was the same; only the words were different.

"You can expect 70 percent casualties among American glider troops and 50 percent among parachute troops," Leigh-Mallory forecast. It was a heavy load to be dumped on Eisenhower's already sagging shoulders on virtually the eve of the mighty endeavor.[10]

Grim-faced and worried, Eisenhower went to his tent to ponder. It was his decision to make, and his alone. Eisenhower agonized for more than an hour, reviewing over and over each step in the Neptune plan. If Leigh-Mallory turned out to be accurate in his prediction, Eisenhower would one day go to his grave still burdened with the guilt of having disregarded the warning and sent thousands of paratroopers and glidermen to their deaths. But if he canceled the American airborne attack, the seaborne assault on Utah Beach might fail, Cherbourg would not be captured, and the entire invasion would be in the most serious peril.

Eisenhower rose from his chair, extinguished the tenth cigarette he had smoked during the past hour, returned to his combat headquarters at Southwick House overlooking Portsmouth, and placed a call to Leigh-Mallory. The American airborne attack was on as planned.[11]

With D-day fast approaching, Charles de Gaulle continued to be a heavy cross for Dwight Eisenhower to bear. The supreme commander was all for dumping the stubborn French general, but Winston Churchill was adamant: The French must be permitted to play a role in their own liberation. Churchill agreed with the Americans at SHAEF that French politics was a witches' brew, but it was not one, he argued, that could be ignored.

By May 1944, Allied intelligence estimated that some eighty-five thousand Frenchmen had been armed during the past three years by parachute drops and boats slipping ashore at night along secluded shorelines. Only about ten thousand of them, however, were believed to have enough ammunition for a day's fighting. And few of the resistants had any experience as guerrillas.

SHAEF was hesitant to provide the French underground any detailed information on Neptune. The Resistance was fractured by a bitter rivalry between those loyal to de Gaulle and the Communists, who were aligned with Moscow. In fact, a shooting war within a war erupted a few months earlier when the Communist underground launched an all-out attack on the Gaullists. Known as the French Forces of the Interior (FFI), de Gaulle's underground fought back.

Aware of the bitter strife between the Communists and the FFI, German counterintelligence sought to intensify the hatred. The Germans arranged to murder popular French leaders, derail civilian trains, and burn down buildings and homes—and then distributed phony printed sheets in which the FFI claimed credit for the mayhem and bloodshed. The Gaullists perpetrated similar actions and blamed them on the Communists, and the Communists followed suit and blamed their actions on the FFI, Dwight Eisenhower, Charles de Gaulle, or Winston Churchill.

Although detailed information on Neptune would be kept from de Gaulle in Algiers, Eisenhower cabled the Combined Chiefs of Staff in Washington on May 8 for permission to take General Pierre Koenig, de Gaulle's representative at SHAEF, into his confidence. "It is my intention to give Koenig personally but to *no* other member of the French mission, under pledge of secrecy, the name of the country in which the attack will take place and the month for which it is scheduled. . . ."[12]

Eisenhower proposed this drastic action out of deep concern that the French resistance groups would start battling one another on and just after D-day unless there was some sort of coordination, such as could be provided by General Koenig, who was highly regarded in France and by the Allied leaders. However, his cable triggered a sharp retort from the Combined Chiefs: He was to tell the French absolutely nothing about Neptune.

Eisenhower sent another cable in which he cautioned the Joint Chiefs that "the limitations under which we are operating are becoming very embarrassing and are producing a situation which is potentially dangerous." That situation was all-out civil war in France among competing resistance groups, thereby disrupting the Allied operations.

Apparently, the Joint Chiefs had bucked the hot political potato up the chain of command to the White House. Roosevelt replied to Eisenhower directly and made a small concession. The supreme commander could tell Koenig of the month in which the landings would take place. However, left unresolved was the tricky question of when Koenig should be told of an intricate broadcast schedule for the *messages personnels*, which were terse, seemingly meaningless phrases to alert the French underground that invasion was near and to launch

predesignated acts of violence and sabotage against the Wehrmacht. Nearly 350 messages already had been prepared and distributed to resistance groups throughout France so that they would understand what the broadcasts meant. These messages would go out over BBC on June 1 and continue up to a few hours before H-hour, which was set for June 5.

SHAEF security officers suspected, accurately, that de Gaulle's headquarters in Algiers was penetrated by German agents. If Koenig was informed about Neptune too far in advance, word would certainly reach de Gaulle. It was decided that Koenig would be told a limited number of Neptune secrets only a few hours before the first *messages personnels* were broadcast.

An even more delicate problem remained: When should Charles de Gaulle be informed of the invasion? If too soon, word would most certainly get to Algiers—and to the Abwehr, Hitler's efficient secret service. If de Gaulle was told *after* D-day, he would be highly offended and not cooperate with the Allies during the time of the heavy battlefield clashes that lay ahead after Neptune.

Churchill and Roosevelt reached a decision: De Gaulle would be left in Algiers until only a few days prior to the invasion, then the Prime Minister would personally invite the French general to London and send his private airplane to fetch him. On his arrival, however, de Gaulle would be told virtually nothing about the pending operation.[13]

CHAPTER 23

De Gaulle Threatens to Arrest Churchill

As THE WESTERN ALLIES were about to embark on the most complex, dangerous military operation that history had known, the British War Cabinet's focus
was upon one man: Charles de Gaulle. Although Winston Churchill and others
insisted that the leader of the Free French be in London when the invasion hit
to broadcast a message to his homeland for citizens to remain calm, there was a
maddening, seemingly insolvable catch: If de Gaulle did come to England, he
might be arrested and jailed on criminal charges.

Nearly two years earlier, an obscure Frenchman named Dufour was
charged by Gaullists with being an agent of the British secret service whose
mission was to infiltrate the French intelligence service in London. Dufour was
court-martialed by de Gaulle's men in London, found guilty of misrepresenting
himself when he tried to join French intelligence, and jailed at a French facility
outside London.

Within a couple of weeks, Dufour escaped, went into hiding, then filed
charges with the British courts against de Gaulle, claiming that he had been
beaten and maltreated while in French custody. That touched off a jumble of
technical legalities. Unless Dufour withdrew his charges, British courts had no
power to quash them, even in the extraordinary conditions of war and the
presumed need for de Gaulle to be in London just before D-day.

Since de Gaulle had no official status with any government at the time of
the alleged criminal offense, Britain could not grant him immunity or prevent
him from being arrested if he returned to England. Nor had the British courts
any authority to keep him from being tried and, if found guilty, jailed.

In Algiers in March 1944, de Gaulle had been enraged when notified by
British courts that he was about to be brought to trial on the Dufour charges.
He labeled the episode the "latest attempt to spatter me with filth."[1]

Through an emissary in London, de Gaulle contacted the British Foreign
Office and branded the Dufour affair "an infamy." Then the French leader
hatched a scheme to strike back at the British and Churchill, who he suspected
was the ringleader behind the "filth-spattering" episode. Centerpiece of de
Gaulle's machination was Stephane Manier, who had been making broadcasts

for the Gaullists to the French people on the BBC transmitter at Accra, the capital of Ghana in western Africa. When Manier returned to England as an alien, he was routinely detained for interrogation by British security authorities.

Within a few days, Manier died of natural causes, the British said. Then de Gaulle sprang his scheme. He announced that Manier's son was going to lodge criminal complaints against all British secret service officers in French territory, Winston Churchill, and the entire British government. If the British could arrest de Gaulle, the French leader declared, then he would arrest Churchill.[2]

On June 1, grim members of the War Cabinet met to consider what to do about the Dufour case, which was about to come to trial. A decision was reached to offer Dufour £1,000 ($5,000) to drop his charges against de Gaulle. Apparently, Dufour agreed to the settlement, and the way was clear for the leader of the Free French to fly to London.

That same day, the first of the *messages personnels* were flashed to the French underground over BBC: "The fox is hungry." "Mary loves Joseph." "The violins of autumn." "The doctor buries his patients." "The tomatoes are ripe." "Flora has a red neck."

There were sighs of relief at Southwick House when Ultra reported that the Germans on the far shore had displayed no reaction to this curious litany of messages read by a sinister-sounding voice.

In London, de Gaulle was fuming in the mansion he had been assigned by Churchill. With British security men discreetly surrounding the villa and tapping his telephone, the leader of the Free French was virtually an Allied prisoner. Most D-day secrets were kept from de Gaulle, much to his anger and humiliation.

On June 3, at the suggestion of Churchill, de Gaulle was invited to Southwick House. With the Prime Minister looking on, the supreme commander showed de Gaulle a draft of the speech that he intended to broadcast to the French people. In it Eisenhower urged the French to carry out his orders and told them that local administration would remain for the time being. That meant Vichy civilian officials would continue to function. The draft went on to say that once France was liberated, the French people themselves would choose their own government.

De Gaulle wanted the Vichyites kicked out immediately and himself installed as ruler of France. He loudly demanded that the speech be changed. Too late, Eisenhower replied, it already had been cleared by the governments of the United States and Great Britain. What's more, the supreme commander already had recorded the speech, which would be aired on the morning of D-day.[3]

Shifting to another crucial topic, Eisenhower explained that Washington had printed a large amount of occupation francs. He wanted de Gaulle to broadcast a short statement assuring the French people that he had authorized the occupation currency and would guarantee that it would be redeemed after France was liberated. De Gaulle declared that he alone, as President of the provisional government (Henri Giraud had been squeezed out as copresident in a de Gaulle power play) had the authority to issue currency.

Now the Frenchman demanded that he be briefed on invasion plans. Anticipating such an eventuality, SHAEF security men earlier had created a convoluted scenario featuring Dwight Eisenhower in the starring role. After explaining Neptune (the assault phase) in the broadest terms, Eisenhower led the French leader to the sacrosanct war room, where the really important items of information had been tucked out of sight.

Eisenhower performed his act beautifully. He showed de Gaulle maps with the words "Top Secret" stamped on them in red. These maps had been so sanitized, however, that they made no sense to Eisenhower, much less to the Frenchman. Never overburdened by humility, de Gaulle presumably did not want to admit that he failed to understand the cleverly doctored battle maps.

Then, almost casually, the supreme commander lied that the landings in Normandy were diversionary and that the main invasion would hit at the Pas de Calais under General Patton.[4]

Referring to his latest encounter with the recalcitrant de Gaulle, Eisenhower scrawled these words in his diary: "A rather sorry mess."

On Sunday, June 4, Eisenhower awoke at 3:00 A.M. to a foreboding weather picture. A violent storm was raging in the English Channel, clouds were thick, and winds were howling. Thousands of Allied assault troops were cooped up on transports ready to head for the far shore. How long would it take the Luftwaffe to detect the mighty invasion armada if a D-day postponement was necessary?

A grim, sleepy-eyed group of Allied commanders apprehensively gathered around the conference table at Southwick House at 4:15 A.M. The spotlight was focused on SHAEF's chief meteorologist, Group Captain John Stagg of the Royal Air Force, who felt as though he was carrying the weight of the world. His spirits had not been lifted by a well-meaning friend who earlier had called out to him, "If you don't read the omens right, they'll string you up on the nearest lamppost!"

While the commanders listened intently in stone-faced silence, Stagg offered a bit of optimism. Charts indicated that the weather might break long enough for the assault to hit on June 6. Eisenhower agreed that the group would meet again that night for a final decision.

At 9:30 P.M., Stagg weighed his words carefully, but told the Allied leaders that he believed that cloud conditions on June 6 would allow the air force to strike with accuracy and that bombardment ships could fire with accuracy. Stagg also predicted that the wind, shortly before midnight on June 5, would not be strong enough to interfere with the delivery of paratroopers and glider forces. He stressed that weather conditions, while not ideal, at least would permit the invasion to be launched.

When the meteorologist concluded, those in the room were silent. Then Eisenhower asked each officer to comment. Beetle Smith was in favor of launching the attack on June 6. Bernard Montgomery was decisive: Go! Arthur Tedder was cautious, describing a June 6 assault as "chancy." Trafford Leigh-Mallory doubted that the air forces could operate effectively in the cloud cover Stagg had predicted.

Deliberations were over. Again, a tense silence. Others could, and had, equivocated. Eisenhower had the burden of saying yes or no. All eyes were on the supreme commander. Finally, Eisenhower spoke, softly but firmly: "I am quite positive that we must give the order. I don't like it, but there it is. The question is, how long can we hang this thing out on the end of a stick? I don't see how we can do anything else but go."[5]

Within a few hours, the invasion juggernaut, its tentacles extending into scores of transports, airfields, harbors, estuaries, encampments, and towns, began slowly to unwind and edge inexorably toward the far shore. Of such magnitude was the war machine that it was beyond the capability of Eisenhower or other mere mortal to postpone or cancel Neptune. Now the Plan had taken over.

Never in history, perhaps, had one man been forced to shoulder such a gargantuan burden as had Eisenhower on the eve of Overlord. A telephone call from Beetle Smith in London added to the weight. Winston Churchill, whose treasury long had been paying Charles de Gaulle's hefty salary and financing his Free French organization, had been exerting tremendous pressure on de Gaulle, but the Frenchman adamantly refused to broadcast the SHAEF text to the French people.

"To hell with the bastard!" Eisenhower roared into the telephone. "If he doesn't come through, we'll deal with someone else!"[6]

It was a hollow threat, one made in frustration—and desperation. There was no other French leader with whom to deal. That night de Gaulle broadcast his own text over BBC.

"The orders given by the French government [meaning de Gaulle] must be followed precisely!" he told the French people.[7]

That evening, while 6,939 Allied vessels were plowing through the heavy swells of the Channel, Eisenhower was having dinner with Maxwell Taylor at an airfield near Greenham Common. In a few hours, Taylor and the Screaming Eagles of the 101st Airborne would be making their first combat jump.[8]

Outwardly buoyant and confident, Eisenhower drove after dinner with Taylor to nearby airfields where hundreds of paratroopers were donning combat gear, smearing Apache-style warpaint on their faces, and steeling themselves for the looming ordeal. Many troopers had partially shaved their heads and cropped the remaining strips of hair into freakish "warpath" designs. Grinning, Eisenhower whispered to Max Taylor, "I don't know if your boys will scare the Germans, but they sure as hell scare me!"[9]

Strolling from plane to plane and talking with troopers in his friendly, man-to-man style, the supreme commander concealed his torment. He was unable to forget Leigh-Mallory's haunting warning: "Your American para-troopers and glidermen will be slaughtered." Was he stupidly sending these cheerful, bright-eyed youths to their deaths in wholesale numbers?

Eisenhower shook hands with Taylor. "Well, good luck, Max," he said softly. As Ike walked toward his waiting staff car, an aide cast a fleeting glance. There were tears in Eisenhower's eyes.[10]

Elsewhere, other players in the drama also passed the evening. In the White House, Franklin Roosevelt quietly dined with First Lady Eleanor. At last the President was able to tell her the momentous secret he shared with few others in America: Allied forces would hit Normandy at dawn. The Roosevelts prayed.

George Marshall, in dress uniform, arrived at the Soviet Embassy in Washington, where Ambassador Andrey Gromyko would present him with the highest Soviet military decoration awarded to foreigners: The Order of Sauvarov. Marshall arrived at 7:30 P.M., knowing that at that precise time—1:30 A.M. on June 6 in France—Allied paratroopers were bailing out over Normandy.

Before and during the decoration ceremony, Marshall was his usual courteous self and gave no indication of his anxiety. He made his customary early escape and was driven to Fort Myer, where he climbed into bed. He could do nothing to alter or influence operations in Normandy.

In London, Marshall's old sparring partner, Alan Brooke, poured out his deep concerns to his diary: "I am very uneasy. At the worst, it may well be the most ghastly disaster of the whole war. I wish to God it was safely over."

Winston Churchill spent a subdued evening sipping brandy with Jock Colville, his longtime secretary. The Prime Minister was uncommonly quiet, even brooding. Churchill realized that all the chips were on the table.

In southern England, Dwight Eisenhower was returning to Southwick House from the paratrooper airfields in the Midlands. During the trek, he had written the following on a slip of paper: "Our landings [in France] have failed, and I have withdrawn the troops. My decision to attack at this time and place was based upon the best information available. The troops, the air, and the navy did all that bravery and devotion to duty could do. If any blame or fault attaches to the attempt it is mine alone."[11]

Praying that he would never have to release that terse statement to the press, Eisenhower shoved it into his pocket—just in case Neptune failed.

It was 1:15 A.M. when Eisenhower reached his trailer at Portsmouth. He knew that British and American paratroop pathfinders (those who jump first to mark the drop zones) already were on the ground. In the remaining hours of darkness until reports could be expected to filter in from Normandy, Eisenhower nervously paced the floor, smoking countless cigarettes and gulping down cup after cup of coffee. His only companions during this nerve-racking ordeal were his two aides, Kay Summersby and Harry Butcher.

Not far away, the one man in the Allied camp who seemed to be impervious to the tension was Bernard Montgomery. As was his habit, he was in bed and asleep by 10:00 P.M. Monty knew that he had done all he could do. Matters were now out of his hands, so he had seen no reason to sit up all night and fret.

At the same time, Adolf Hitler was relaxing with his mistress, Eva Braun, to the melodic strains of Wagner at Adlerhorst, his plush retreat on towering Obersalzburg in the Bavarian Alps. A night person, the Führer idled away the hours until 4:00 A.M. on June 6, when he swallowed several barbiturate pills and retired. Der Führer und Oberste Befehlshaber der Wehrmacht des Grossdeutschen Reichs—the grandiose title Hitler had bestowed upon himself by German law—fell asleep totally unaware of the thunderclap that was about to hit him in Normandy.

Four thousand miles from Hitler's Alpine retreat, the War Department in Washington received an electrifying cable from General Eisenhower. It was shortly after dawn, U.S. time. An excited colonel, clutching the message, rushed to Quarters No. 1 at nearby Fort Myer and banged on the front door. Katherine Marshall, the army chief's wife, sleepily responded but refused to awaken her husband.

Frustrated and not knowing what other action to take, the colonel thrust the Eisenhower cable into Mrs. Marshall's hands. Calmly, she scanned the text, which stated that, an hour and a half after the first American landing craft hit the beaches at Utah and Omaha, preliminary reports from Normandy were optimistic.

Mrs. Marshall looked up and asked, "And what would you have the general do about it?" Deflated and confused, the War Department colonel saluted and conducted a strategic retreat. George Marshall slept on.[12]

CHAPTER 24

Strategy Gridlock

MONTY'S TROOPS LAND IN FRANCE!

THE LONDON NEWSPAPER HEADLINE ON D-DAY infuriated American commanders. These were not Bernard Montgomery's troops, the Americans griped, but Allied troops fighting under Dwight Eisenhower and an Allied chain of command. However, the brief squawks rapidly vanished as the focus shifted to the death struggle raging on the far shore.

It was nail-biting time at Southwick House that morning. News in the early hours was fragmentary, sometimes contradictory, as is the case in all violent clashes of major magnitude. The huge invasion armada had crossed the Channel undetected, thanks to the Bodyguard deception plan and the inclement weather that grounded Luftwaffe reconnaissance planes and kept swift German E-boats (a craft similar to PT boats) penned up in Cherbourg.

Allied aerial sweeps far inland disclosed no unusual movement by German panzer divisions being held in reserve. The event that Eisenhower, his planners, and commanders had thought was impossible had occurred: Neptune gained total surprise. Hitler had been caught completely unaware.

Eisenhower would write to his chief weatherman, Group Captain John Stagg, "I thank the Gods of War we went when we did."[1]

Just before 10:00 A.M., the edgy Eisenhower received a telephone call from Trafford Leigh-Mallory, a man of personal courage who always spoke what was on his mind. The air chief reported that the 82nd and 101st Airborne Divisions had landed, apparently without heavy losses, and were in action. Leigh-Mallory voiced his delight over the "good news" and expressed regret that he had found it necessary to add to Eisenhower's personal burden during the final tense period before D-day.[2]

By noon, things were not going according to the Neptune plan. At Utah Beach, the U.S. 4th Infantry Division was ashore but failed to link up with the 82nd and 101st Airborne Divisions, which had been widely scattered. At Omaha Beach, assault elements of the U.S. 1st and 29th Infantry Divisions ran into a buzzsaw and were pinned down on the shoreline, suffering heavy casualties. Although

190

the British, Canadians, and French landed against sporadic opposition, the Germans succeeded in mounting local counterattacks that halted their progress.

None of the D-day objectives—especially Caen, which Montgomery called the gateway to Paris—had been achieved. However, when night wrapped its ominous cloak over the smoking Normandy battlefield, the invaders had bitten a large chunk out of Hitler's Fortress Europe. On shore were 75,215 British and Canadian soldiers and 57,506 Americans. But a heavy price in blood had been paid: More than nine thousand Allied soldiers, perhaps one-third of them killed, had been casualties.

No sooner had the first Allied soldier set foot in Normandy than Dwight Eisenhower found himself engaged, almost daily, in "one of the longest sustained arguments that I had with Winston Churchill throughout the war." The bone of contention was Operation Anvil, the projected invasion of southern France, which was intended to draw German divisions away from Normandy.[3]

Throughout the spring, Churchill had been badgering President Roosevelt to scuttle Anvil and conduct expanded operations in Italy and the Balkans. Roosevelt's military advisor, Admiral William Leahy, explained the argument in his diary: "The [controversy] is caused by American all-out concentration on an early defeat of Germany, and a British intention to combine with a defeat of the Nazis an acquisition of postwar advantages in the Balkans for Great Britain."[4]

Roosevelt, ever the politician, informed Churchill, "I can't afford to have American armies run the risk of bogging down in the Balkans in what the American public would consider support of British postwar interests."

Undaunted, the Prime Minister responded that he was disturbed by the "arbitrary reaction" of the Americans, and he asked the President to "hear both sides before making a final decision." Anvil was "bleak and sterile," he told Roosevelt, stressing that it would "do nothing to help Overlord forces."[5]

Roosevelt refused to become irritated over being talked to like a schoolboy and continued to rebuff Churchill, confiding to his son Elliott, "Our Chiefs [of Staff] are convinced of one thing. The way to kill the most Germans with the least loss of American soldiers is to slam them with everything we've got. [Anvil] makes sense to me."

Now Churchill demanded that the Combined Chiefs conduct a sweeping review of the entire strategy in Europe and the Mediterranean when that body convened in London on June 9.

Not unexpectedly, Field Marshal Alan Brooke sided with Churchill in demands to call off Anvil. Mark Clark's Fifth Army had captured Rome on June 5—less than twenty-four hours before Neptune hit—so Brooke and Churchill argued that with the Germans in retreat in Italy, new opportunities were present for the Allies to attack northward in the direction of Venice and Florence. As for George Marshall and Dwight Eisenhower, they looked on the seizing of

Rome as the conclusion of the Italian campaign, which had been largely intended to keep Wehrmacht divisions there away from Normandy.

Early in the morning of June 8—D-day plus two—George Marshall, Ernest King, and Hap Arnold lifted off from Washington in a C-54 four-engine aircraft and flew to Scotland. They rode by rail in a special coach to London, where they were greeted warmly at Euston Station by the British chiefs. All were encouraged by reports from Southwick House indicating that the Normandy buildup was progressing on schedule, with ten Allied divisions ashore and three more on the way. However, a haunting question remained: How long would it take Field Marshal Erwin Rommel to collect enough strength from northern France to launch an all-out counterattack against the bridgehead?

Early the next morning, the Combined Chiefs met in Churchill's command-post bunker far below Storey Gate. As the Prime Minister had demanded, they reviewed the global situation, including Admiral King's briefing on MacArthur's and Nimitz's two-pronged offensive toward the Philippines. King's was a harmless exercise, as Britain already had virtually conceded the Pacific war to the Americans.

With the thorny Anvil matter still to be discussed, the Combined Chiefs adjourned to leave for a visit to Normandy. Despite their decades of experience, Winston Churchill and the Combined Chiefs reacted like kids playing hooky, almost giddy and delighted to be going where there would be a hint of danger, where history's mightiest military endeavor had taken place.

Reaching Normandy on separate destroyers, they split up and headed for the American and the British sectors. Marshall, King, Arnold, and a few aides drove up the bluffs overlooking Omaha Beach, and along the way chatted with the fighting men who were marching up to the front. Eisenhower, who privately referred to the highest Allied leaders as the "Big Shots," would later note, "Their presence appeared heartening to the troops—possibly on the theory that the area was a safe one or the [high] rank wouldn't be there."[6]

At U.S. First Army headquarters, a collection of tents in an apple orchard, Marshall had a long talk with bespectacled Omar Bradley. Among other topics, they discussed Charles de Gaulle, whom Marshall hated almost as much as President Roosevelt did. "De Gaulle really messed things up for us," Bradley said, apparently referring to the French general's refusal to broadcast in advance the appeal to the underground leaders that SHAEF had prepared.

Meanwhile, Churchill, Brooke, and the British Joint Chiefs descended on Bernard Montgomery, who was temporarily wearing two hats as Neptune ground forces commander and leader of the British 21st Army Group. They were greeted by the famous Montgomery scowl. Barely civil, he managed to "push away" Churchill within two hours. That night, Monty wrote to James Grigg, his superior in the War Office with whom he had long exchanged confidences. "It is not a good time for important people to [come] sightseeing and visiting forward areas," he complained. "I have made this clear to the P.M. My corps and divisional generals are fighting hard and I do not want their eyes taken off the ball."

Back in Churchill's bombproof bunker the next day, the Combined Chiefs got down to the potentially explosive Anvil situation. Alan Brooke no doubt was bolstered by a cable he had just received from George Marshall's good friend Field Marshal John Dill in Washington: "It is odd how that charming person Marshall can fly off the handle and be so infernally rude. Also he gets fixed ideas about things and people which it is almost impossible to argue."[7]

Not unexpectedly, Brooke was aboard the Churchill bandwagon and called for canceling or postponing Anvil. Curiously, Marshall, who had been dueling with Brooke for two years, seemed to be siding with his British adversary.

Earlier, Marshall had told General Mark Clark, commander of the U.S. Fifth Army in Italy, "We ought to give it [calling off Anvil] a lot of consideration, because Eisenhower is doing well and the landing in southern France may not be worth that much to the overall picture."

Eisenhower, for once, was on the opposite side of the fence from his mentor. "I want all the insurance I can get," he said. "I always planned on a thrust into southern France, a one-two!"

During a break in the discussions, Marshall was chatting with Anthony Eden, the suave British foreign secretary, whom Churchill considered to be his successor should anything happen to the Prime Minister. Belying his classic features and stylish dress, Eden was a hard-nosed statesman, who had tangled several times with Josef Stalin.

During their conversation, Marshall felt that Eden was defending not only Churchill's decision to woo Charles de Gaulle but also the French general's behavior. Marshall's temper flared. "No sons of Iowa farmers would fight to put up statues of de Gaulle in France," the army chief retorted.[8]

Unimpressed, Eden persisted in speaking out on de Gaulle's behalf, touching off another Marshall outburst. Secretary of War Henry Stimson would recall, "[Marshall] said he couldn't talk politics but he said he knew more about the U.S. Army and more about the people of the United States than Eden did, and that if Eden went on in this way and things that had happened came out in the [media] in full, it would make a wave of indignation in the United States which would swamp the whole damned British Foreign Office!"[9]

Eden's face flushed. George Marshall, soldier, was laying down the law to Anthony Eden, foreign secretary and leader in Parliament. Both angry men stared at each other in silence for several moments; then Eden broke off the argument by turning on his heel and walking out of the room.

When the conference resumed, the Combined Chiefs continued to debate the merits of Anvil. The final session adjourned on June 13. Eisenhower had gained the impression that the invasion of southern France was still in the works, and that the squabbling over the operation had concluded.

Before returning to Washington, General Marshall flew to Italy to gain the
strategy opinions of British General Henry "Jumbo" Wilson, who had succeeded Eisenhower as Allied commander in the Mediterranean, and other top
officers. Large of frame and hearty in manner, Jumbo Wilson proposed that his
forces in Italy, instead of being diverted to Anvil, continue attacking northward
to Venice and then turn east around the Adriatic Sea and into the Balkans. It was
the standard British argument.

On the following night, Marshall dined with Mark Clark, an old friend ever
since the days when they were both instructors at the Infantry School at Fort
Benning. Marshall found that Clark endorsed the British strategy: Pressing
northward in Italy and then on into the Balkans. Although the Fifth Army
commander did not advocate canceling Anvil, he did have a novel approach:
Turn the entire southern France invasion over to the French. That scheme, of
course, would permit Clark to keep his three divisions earmarked for Anvil.

Meanwhile, Jumbo Wilson, perhaps at the instigation of Churchill, fired off
a message to the Combined Chiefs in Washington calling for yet another review of
strategy, with renewed emphasis given to continuing the Italian campaign northward. Snorted Henry Stimson, "[General] Wilson is never far from a bottle!"[10]

Gridlock had set in. The American chiefs in Washington insisted that Anvil
take place in mid-August. In London, the British chiefs strongly supported
Jumbo Wilson's strategy.

Consequently, a blizzard of messages blew back and forth across the Atlantic. Churchill zeroed in once more on his old friend Roosevelt: "Our first
wish is to help General Eisenhower in the most speedy and effective manner.
But we do not think this involves the complete ruin of all our great affairs in the
Mediterranean." Clearly, those affairs were intended to keep the Balkans out of
the clutches of Josef Stalin.

Roosevelt stood fast. "I really believe we should consolidate our operations
[in France] and not scatter them," he replied.

Twenty-four hours later, the controversy grew even more heated when the
British chiefs fired off a harsh message to their American counterparts in Wash-
ington: "We recognize General Eisenhower's responsibility for the success of
Overlord itself, but we cannot admit that he has any responsibility for European
strategy as a whole. This responsibility must rest with the Combined Chiefs of
Staff and cannot be delegated to any one commander in chief."

A day later, Churchill turned up the heat. In an unusual move, he invited
three-star General Beetle Smith—who was deemed (quite correctly) as being
most influential with his boss, Eisenhower—to lunch at 10 Downing Street. On
his arrival, Smith, a man not known for his humility, was received almost as a
visiting head of state. No doubt Churchill felt that Eisenhower's aide was the
key to breaking the strategy gridlock—in favor of the British Mediterranean
viewpoint. For nearly two hours, Churchill spoke eloquently and without in-
terruption. Beetle Smith held fast.

Forty-eight hours after Smith's regal reception, Churchill received a message from Roosevelt: "My dear friend, I beg you let us go ahead with our plan [Anvil]." Slyly, the President reminded the Prime Minister that they had both given their "solemn word" to Stalin that southern France would be invaded.

Aware that Roosevelt had a deep-rooted hatred of Charles de Gaulle, Churchill responded by declaring that only the leader of the Free French would profit by Anvil.

Continuing on the attack, Churchill lamented to the President the plight of British General Harold Alexander, leader of the 15th Army Group in Italy. Alexander, the Prime Minister moaned, was on the verge of tears and had anguished that "the ghost of Anvil hangs heavily over our battlefield." Alexander was complaining (according to Churchill) that Anvil was taking away American units that he badly needed in Italy, and he forecast doom for the impending venture into southern France.

Within a few hours, the British Joint Chiefs backed up Churchill's argument. If Anvil was scuttled and Alexander retained his American units, there was an excellent chance that the retreating Wehrmacht could be driven out of Italy.

Not so, the U.S. Joint Chiefs retorted. Ultra intercepts had disclosed that after the fall of Rome, Hitler had ordered Field Marshal Albert Kesselring, commander in the Mediterranean, to stand fast in Italy. Kesselring, regarded by the Allies as one of Germany's most capable commanders, had at his disposal a force almost as large as that of Alexander. And northern Italy's topography was ideal for the defense: Countless towering mountains on which a German machine gun or two could hold off an entire attacking battalion. Given these facts of life, the American chiefs rejected the theory that General Alexander could drive the Wehrmacht out of Italy.

Then Churchill committed an uncharacteristic debate blunder. In closing his relentless plea for dumping Anvil in favor of an accelerated campaign in Italy and the Balkans, he assured Roosevelt that the British would cooperate should the Combined Chiefs give the order for Anvil to be laid on, but that such compliance would be given "under the strongest protest."

Now strange doings took place. In Washington, George Marshall, who had been tinkering with the notion of abandoning Anvil because "Eisenhower is doing so well," performed an about-face and came out vigorously for the operation. In London, Field Marshal Brooke, Marshall's longtime foe who had strongly supported Churchill's Italy and Balkans scheme, also flip-flopped and endorsed Anvil. Consequently, the Combined Chiefs issued a directive for the southern France invasion: It would take place on August 15. It also was given the new code name of Dragoon.

A grumpy Churchill told confidants that the code name was most appropriate, that he had been "dragooned" into accepting the operation at the expense of his Balkans strategy. For his part, Dwight Eisenhower was elated that the Prime Minister had finally surrendered. Or so it seemed.

Meanwhile, Normandy had turned into a slaughterhouse. Mighty Allied air-power, huge naval guns offshore, and field artillery battalions lined up almost hub to hub were chopping the Feldgrau to pieces. Field Marshal Rommel informed Berlin that he was losing his army group at the equivalent of a regiment a day. Gasoline, ammunition, and oil shortages were plaguing the Germans. Orders from the Führer had filtered down to the lowest schütze (private): *"Don't give up a foot of ground!"*

The Allies, too, were suffering heavy casualties. Gains were measured in bloody yards. Nearly every pasture in western Normandy was hemmed in by thick earthen hedgerows, many of them eight to ten feet high. Long, snakelike roots packed the dirt together much like reinforcing steel in concrete. These thick hedgerows made each field a minifortress, behind which Germans fought with machine guns, rifles, and panzerfausts (bazookas).

Although the fighting was savage, by June 13—D-day plus seven—the Neptune beachheads were linked into a solid front. The invasion plan called for Cherbourg to be captured at that time, but U.S. spearheads were still twenty-two miles away from the crucial port north of Utah Beach.

On the eastern portion of the bridgehead, Bernard Montgomery remained bogged down outside the old cathedral city of Caen, his D-day objective. Eisenhower tried to subtly prod him into action, but Monty was unmoved. Before attacking again, he had to "tidy up the battlefield," an expression that maddened American generals. It meant he would move all his supplies forward before launching an assault.

Montgomery wanted to kick off his Caen attack by landing the paratroopers and glidermen of the British 1st Airborne Division in front of his spearhead, the 7th Armored Division. That operation would require the approval of Trafford Leigh-Mallory, who responded with a curt "No!" Monty was infuriated. "[Leigh-Mallory] sitting in his office there cannot possibly know the local battle form here," he wrote to an aide in England. "He could fly here in a half-hour, talk for an hour, be back in England an hour later. Obviously, he is a gutless bugger, who refuses to take a chance and plays for safety on all occasions. I have no use for him."

Without the paratrooper and glider support, the 7th Armored jumped off and suffered a bloody nose. Caen remained in German hands.

Perhaps as Montgomery had intended, the "gutless bugger" description reached Leigh-Mallory; on June 14, he flew to Normandy to confer with the general. Together, they arrived at a revolutionary decision: Allied heavy bombers would be used to pound the defenses in front of Montgomery's army advancing toward Caen. The proposal triggered an uproar among American bomber generals. Carl Spaatz was especially irate. "Fourteen half-baked Nazi divisions would contain the heavy bomber power of the Americans and British [along one narrow beachhead corridor]," he penned in his diary.[11]

Spaatz rushed to see Eisenhower to protest but received no satisfaction. The supreme commander was anxious to seize Caen, and if it took heavy bombers to get the job done rapidly, so be it. "Our forces [in Normandy] are now far superior to the Germans opposing us," Spaatz complained to his diary. "The only thing necessary to move forward is sufficient guts on the part of the ground commanders."[12]

In London, Charles de Gaulle was still angry over the failure of the Western Allies to officially recognize him as President of a provisional French government. So while Allied fighting men were sacrificing their lives in Normandy and in the skies above Europe to liberate France from the Nazi yoke, de Gaulle was doing all that he could to throw a monkey wrench into Allied plans.

Earlier, the U.S. government had printed French francs (that is, occupation money) to be redeemed by the French government after the Germans were driven from the country. Now, de Gaulle publicly branded that currency "counterfeit." Propagandist Josef Goebbels seized on the pronouncement to broadcast a warning to French merchants not to accept the "Washington counterfeit money."

Next, de Gaulle held a press conference at his headquarters in London and implied that General Eisenhower planned to administer France as though it was a "conquered nation." Goebbels latched onto that remark to sow seeds of doubt and fear among the French people.

Although the damage was done, SHAEF reacted to de Gaulle's latest charge against his "allies." Eisenhower issued an order to his public relations officers that French towns would no longer be "captured" by the Allies; instead, they would be "liberated."

In Washington, the fiery Secretary of War Henry Stimson was enraged by de Gaulle's latest antics. "It's as bad as if he were trying to steal our ammunition on the battlefield or turn our guns against us," he declared heatedly.[13]

Since D-day, de Gaulle had been badgering Southwick House for transportation across the Channel to visit what he called "my people." SHAEF had stonewalled his persistent demands. Then, on June 14, against Eisenhower's wishes and without his knowledge, de Gaulle climbed aboard a French destroyer and went ashore in Normandy on the French invasion beach.

With a few aides, de Gaulle set out for Bayeux, a picturesque little town ten miles inland that had been the home of William the Conqueror. Word of de Gaulle's imminent arrival quickly spread throughout Bayeux, and when the general rode in majestically like a Roman caesar in a chariot, the crowds responded with enthusiastic shouts and applause. Standing on the steps of the city hall, de Gaulle launched into a speech in which he declared that his forces, "with the aid of the Allies," were liberating French territory from the Germans.

In far-off Adlerhorst on the night of June 26, an aide handed Adolf Hitler a wireless bulletin: Lieutenant General Karl Wilhelm Dietrich von Schlieben, the hulking commander at Cherbourg, had surrendered to GIs of the U.S. VII Corps. The Führer was livid. "A disgrace to the uniform and the lowest form of German general!" he ranted about von Schlieben. Hitler had ordered him to defend the port "to the last man and the last bullet."

Probably through Ultra, the Allied high command had been aware that Hitler and his top generals were directing the battle of Normandy from Berchtsgaden. Plans were laid to wipe out the Führer and the Wehrmacht high command in a thunderstorm of bombs, an operation code-named Hellhound.

Since June 15, U.S. photoreconnaissance planes had been winging over Hitler's Alpine retreat in preparation for the Italy-based U.S. 15th Air Force to launch a massive air strike. Ten days later, the intelligence photomosaics had been pieced together and distributed to bomber groups. Air crews were ready to be briefed.

Then, mysteriously, headquarters of the Mediterranean Allied Air Force received orders to cancel Hellhound. No explanation was given. Adolf Hitler and his top generals were spared a deluge of high explosives that might have left the Wehrmacht in confusion and altered the course of the war in Europe.

CHAPTER 25

Bogged Down
in Normandy

A BOLD HEADLINE in the July 3, 1944, edition of the *New York Herald Tribune* told it all:

**ALLIES IN FRANCE BOGGED
DOWN ON ENTIRE FRONT**

Instead of breaking out of Normandy, racing for Paris, and then heading hell-bent for Germany, nearly 1.5 million American, British, Canadian, French, and Dutch troops and their equipment were bottled up in the narrow confines of a relatively small bridgehead eighty miles long and only twenty-five to thirty miles inland at its deepest points.

At cemeteries behind the lines, the bodies of young Allied soldiers, each shrouded in a mattress cover, were stacked up in long rows awaiting burial. Field hospitals in Normandy were swamped with thousands of wounded men.

Dwight Eisenhower anguished over the heavy casualties and the haunting stalemate that Field Marshal Erwin Rommel had managed to achieve. At Southwick House, tempers were short. Most of the anger was aimed at Bernard Montgomery, commander of ground forces, whom many held responsible for the stalemate. His most vocal critics were not American, but British.

Which general would replace Montgomery was being openly discussed. Arthur Tedder, deputy supreme commander, exploded, "We've been taken for suckers by Montgomery!" The British Tedder urged Eisenhower to sack his fellow countryman and replace him with a more aggressive commander—George Patton, for example.[1]

"Monty does a lot of personal publicity stuff," another British general at SHAEF complained. "I don't believe he's a general at all, just a film star!" Harry Butcher, Eisenhower's aide, referred to Montgomery as Chief Big Wind, a moniker that stuck at Southwick House.

Anger in the Allied high command erupted anew when Montgomery claimed that it had never been his intention to break out of the beachhead at Caen, on the direct road to Paris. It had been his strategy all along, he insisted, to pin down the Germans in front of Caen so that Omar Bradley's Americans could break loose in the western sector.

British Brigadier Kenneth G. McLean, a SHAEF officer, retorted that Monty's contention was "absolute rubbish" and a "complete fabrication," one hatched after he had been halted in his tracks short of Caen, his D-day objective.[2]

Then, Montgomery, who had a genius for escalating dissension within the Allied camp, identified his choice for the culprit responsible for the stalemate: Omar Bradley. While elements of Bradley's First Army were attacking northward from Utah Beach to capture Cherbourg, Monty explained, other First Army units should have been driving to the southwest to seize Coutances, a key road junction. "Bradley didn't want to take the risk," Montgomery wrote a confidant in England. "I have to take the Americans along quietly and give them time to get ready."[3]

American generals were infuriated by Monty's claim that he had to nursemaid Bradley to prod him into attacking. None was more angry than George Patton, the Allied general the Germans most feared, who had arrived "secretly" in Normandy on July 6 and was met by several hundred cheering GIs at a landing strip behind Omaha Beach.

Itching for immediate action, Patton instead had been "exiled," as he termed it, to an apple orchard near Nehou, south of Cherbourg, and far behind the front lines. "I *have* to redeem myself!" he would say time and time again, referring to the aftermath of the Sicily slapping affair. He had been given no specific assignment, however, and for two weeks paced furiously about the orchard. "My destiny in this war is to sit here on my ass and watch the cider apples grow!" he grumbled to an aide.

Patton's flamboyance made him what news reporters call "good copy." He could be counted on to spit out offhand remarks that, although considered harmless by him, would make headlines back in the United States. So two weeks after he arrived in France, an eager covey of correspondents, aware of his deep frustration, gathered around the general.

Flicking the ash off a cigar, Patton cautioned the newsmen, "No notes, no quotes." This time he was determined to put a zipper on his mouth. Asked what he would do to break the stalemate if he was in command in Normandy, Patton unzipped the zipper.

"I'd line up my tanks on a narrow front and in a couple of days we'd go through the Krauts like shit through a goddamned goose. We'd head straight for Avranches [forty miles to the south] and from there turn westward and bust out into Brittany and all over France," Patton exclaimed.

Pausing briefly for dramatic effect, the general added, "Of course, that would be too bold for some. We'd never do it with that little fart in charge!"

Patton's aides winced. All the reporters knew the identity of the "little fart": Bernard Montgomery.

In his anguish and frustration over being "exiled," Patton vented his wrath by lashing out at American generals in his diary: "Neither Ike nor Brad has the staff. Ike is bound hand and foot by the British and doesn't know it, poor fool. Brad and [General Courtney] Hodges are such nothings. I could break through in three days if I commanded. We actually have no supreme commander—no one who can take hold and say that this shall be done and that shall be done."[4]

At Southwick House and during periodic visits to the beachhead over the past two weeks, Eisenhower could not afford the luxury of sniping at fellow generals. He was far too busy trying to unsnarl the Normandy logjam. As military leader of an Allied coalition, it was Ike's style to ask and suggest to his subordinate commanders, rather than order them. So when Arthur Tedder and Beetle Smith urged Eisenhower to prod Montgomery to get moving, the supreme commander wrote a mildly worded letter to "my good friend Monty." In it he suggested that the British launch an early attack to seize Caen. Montgomery ignored him.

Snubbed by his ground commander, Eisenhower appealed to Churchill to "persuade Monty to get on his bicycle and start moving." Churchill complied. Montgomery responded by promising a "big show" on July 9. Although elements of his 21st Army Group received support from Allied heavy bombers, the attack floundered and Montgomery called it off the next day.

Perhaps sensing that Churchill was still breathing down his neck, the general promptly advised Eisenhower that another major push, code-named Goodwood, was being "cooked up," adding that "my whole eastern flank will burst into flames."[5]

Delighted, the supreme commander granted Montgomery's demand for the full Allied air forces to be hurled into the looming battle: Seventy-seven hundred tons of bombs would be dropped by 1,676 heavies and 343 mediums in what would be the most concentrated air explosives ever dropped in front of a ground attack.

Goodwood was launched on July 18. For three days, the British and Canadians slugged forward behind the massive air bombardment. Then the attack was stopped cold by tenacious German resistance. The small town of Caen, now a mass of rubble, had been captured. But the British and Canadians lost twenty-six hundred men killed, wounded, and missing, and more than four hundred knocked-out tanks, burned and twisted, dotted the pastures and forests. There had been no breakthrough. Montgomery told reporters that he was satisfied with the results.[6]

At Southwick House, Eisenhower was furious, snapping that it had required seven thousand tons of bombs for Monty to gain seven miles and that the Allies could not go through the war dropping a thousand tons of bombs per mile. Tedder, too, was irate and blamed Montgomery for "the army's failure." That night, Commander Butcher wrote in his diary, "[SHAEF] officers are wondering aloud whether Montgomery should be made a peer and sent to the House of Lords or given the governorship of Malta."[7]

While Bernard Montgomery was being verbally pummeled at SHAEF, he had staunch defenders high up the totem pole in London. Among them was Alan Brooke, chief of the Imperial General Staff, to whom Monty had looked for advice, sidestepping Eisenhower. Another Monty booster was Secretary of State for War James Grigg.

"Those bastard Yanks are beginning to crab Montgomery," Grigg wrote to his father. "It is an absolute outrage because I know for a fact that the plan is working out as he designed it from the beginning. But our own journalists fell into the [SHAEF] trap and I am afraid some of our jealous airmen help too."[8]

A few days later, Secretary Grigg ripped into British and American commanders alike. In a letter to Montgomery, he insisted that Monty have a face-to-face showdown with Eisenhower: "I am convinced that [Air Marshal Arthur] Coningham is continuing to bad-name you and the [British 2nd] Army and that what he says in this kind is easily circulated at SHAEF via Tedder and that Bedell [Smith]—who seems to have become very conceited and very dour—listens too readily to that poison."[9]

Grigg, clearly, was especially angry at forty-eight-year-old Air Marshal Coningham, who led the 2nd Tactical Air Force (British and Canadian). Coningham had long been closely associated with Montgomery. In North Africa, he had been commander of the Western Desert Air Force and conducted many joint air-ground operations in conjunction with Monty's Desert Rats.

"You will have no comfort until you have demanded and obtained [from Eisenhower] the removal of Coningham from any connection with Overlord whatever," Grigg continued in his letter to Montgomery. "He is a bad and treacherous man and will never be other than a plague to you."[10]

While the Anglo-American leaders were groping for a solution to the bloody stalemate in Normandy, they were beset by another crisis of equal portent. For six weeks, London had been under around-the-clock attack by German robots. Swarms of the Führer's "vengeance weapons"—pilotless aircraft packed with explosives—were being launched from ramps along the Pas de Calais on the French coast. With an airspeed of 440 miles per hour (far faster than any Allied plane), the robot's engine was timed to cut off over London, after which the frightening weapon would plummet soundlessly to earth and explode with the impact of a powerful bomb.

Code-named Target 42 by the Germans, the sprawling city of London had been in constant fear and chaos ever since the first robot exploded on June 12. Hundreds of the flying bombs had rained down on the British capital over the weeks. Thousands of Londoners had been killed, tens of thousands wounded, countless homes smashed. In dark corners of British government buildings, there was hushed talk that unless something was done about the robot assault, England might have to sue for peace.

In desperation, Winston Churchill proposed to the British chiefs of staff the all-out use of poison gas against the German home front. Then he began promoting an innovative scheme to halt the deluge of explosives on London. He would select one hundred small, undefended German towns, and Royal Air Force bombers would wipe them out, one at a time, until "Herr Hitler calls off his dogs."

Launching bacteriologic warfare against the Third Reich, with all its hideous consequences, also was seriously considered. British scientists had developed a top-secret bacteriologic agent against which there was no known remedy. Using the agent as a retaliatory weapon against Germany was ruled out, however. Large quantities could not be ready for at least a year.

General Eisenhower was being pressured to scrap strategic plans and cancel an Allied landing in southern France (Operation Dragoon) set for August 15, and instead use those troops and resources to invade the Pas de Calais and wipe out the robot launching ramps.

Frightful as was the carnage being heaped on embattled London's civilians, Hitler's vengeance weapons were not greatly affecting the prosecution of the war. London would have to endure the robot assault, and an all-out effort would be made to break out of Normandy and overrun the launching ramps.

In the meantime, on July 20, Omar Bradley (Omar the Tentmaker to correspondents) was in the operations tent of his First Army headquarters behind Omaha Beach. He and his G-3 (operations officer), Colonel Truman C. "Tubby" Thorson, were going over details of Operation Cobra, a daring scheme that, if successful, would break the Americans out of the swamps and tangled hedgerow country of Normandy and send tank-tipped flying columns as far south as Avranches, where the Cherbourg peninsula rounded into Brittany.

Rather than mount yet another maximum effort by infantry and tanks to break out of Normandy in frontal assaults, Cobra would concentrate gargantuan airpower on a tiny rectangle of countryside along the east-west Saint-Lô-Périers road, a few miles west of Saint-Lô. Now a pile of rubble, Saint-Lô had been captured on July 8 by the U.S. 29th Infantry Division after a bloodbath at its gate.

The targeted rectangle was three and a half miles long and one and a half miles deep. Hundreds of heavy and medium bombers would pulverize the rectangle with more than sixty thousand bombs, after which U.S. infantry divisions, closely packed along the northern side of the road, would immediately advance into the bomb-saturated area and clean up whatever resistance might survive. Then swarms of tanks of the U.S. 2nd and 3rd Armored Divisions would bolt through the gap and dash southward—all the way to Avranches. At least, that was the goal of Omar Bradley.

As a hedge against American bombs accidentally hitting American soldiers, Bradley's plan called for the heavies of the U.S. Eighth Air Force, flying from bases in England, to approach the rectangle on a course *parallel* to the arrow-straight road, resulting in any "shorts" dropped from twelve thousand feet landing on the German side of the bomb-line, not on the American side.

Despite this built-in precaution, the specter of American troops being slaughtered by "friendly" bombs haunted Bradley. "Those air fellows do a lot of boasting," he told Tubby Thorson. "But the truth is, they are not skilled in pinpoint bombing."

Consequently, on July 19, Bradley and thirty-nine-year-old Brigadier General Elwood R. "Pete" Quesada, whose fighter-bombers worked in close support of the U.S. First Army, flew to England to coordinate details of the massive Cobra air bombardment at Air Chief Marshal Trafford Leigh-Mallory's sumptuous headquarters at Bentley Priory near Stanhope. The lineup of bomber barons facing Bradley was formidable: Commander of Allied air forces for Overlord, Leigh-Mallory—argumentative, abrasive, disliked and distrusted by American commanders; leader of the U.S. Eighth Air Force, Lieutenant General James H. "Jimmy" Doolittle—hero of the Tokyo bombing raid in March 1942; Air Marshal Arthur Coningham—aggressive, his square jaw thrust out when confronting an adversary; U.S. Major General Lewis H. Brereton—diminutive, eyes peering coldly through horn-rimmed glasses; and commander of the U.S. Army Air Forces in Europe, Lieutenant General Carl Spaatz—shrewd and capable.

The confrontation—ground versus air—had hardly begun when a heated squabble broke out. Bradley, an inarticulate speaker, voiced his deep concerns over "shorts" falling on American assault troops and insisted that the heavies fly a course parallel to the Saint-Lô-Périers road. The bomber barons lashed back with pointed objectives: A parallel approach would expose the bomber stream to German flak over a much longer period. They held out for a perpendicular approach, which meant winging in southward directly over the heads of Bradley's assault troops and dropping bombs as soon as the planes reached the Saint-Lô-Périers road.

A customarily calm man, Bradley was angry. No way, he stressed, would he agree to a flight plan that called for hundreds of heavy bombers to fly in over the heads of his men. The tense session broke up with Bradley convinced that his parallel flight approach had been accepted by the others. He would soon learn how wrong this assumption had been.[11]

On the other side of the Channel, these were tense, hectic days for Erwin Johannes Eugen Rommel, revered on the home front as "Der Junge Marschall" (the Boy Marshal). While exerting enormous effort to strengthen Normandy defenses to make the Allies pay dearly so that he would have bargaining power during peace negotiations independent of Adolf Hitler, he also spent many of his waking hours wooing German generals in Normandy to revolt against the Führer.

By mid-July, Rommel had secured pledges of cooperation from most army and SS generals in France and felt that it was time to actively make contact with Allied leaders, especially General Bernard Montgomery. The two men had been battlefield foes ever since North Africa in 1942 and held each other in high esteem. Monty had a portrait of his Teutonic rival on his trailer wall. Rommel often referred to the British general as "my friend Montgomery." Their names and destinies had become indelibly intertwined.

At the same time that Rommel was ready to seek peace with the Western Allies, Montgomery, his great admirer, approved a plan to either kill or kidnap the famed German field marshal, who was the symbol of the Wehrmacht's skill, courage, and tenacity. Code-named Gaff, the clandestine operation had been in the works since March but had not been attempted because British intelligence could not pinpoint Rommel's headquarters.

In the middle of June, Lieutenant Colonel William Fraser of the elite British Special Air Service (SAS) and about 125 of his men parachuted into central France with the mission of harassing and spying on the Wehrmacht. Early in the war, Winston Churchill had ordered the British chiefs to create "troops of the hunter class" to make "butcher and bolt raids" against the Germans. One of these units was the SAS, whose benign title belied its hazardous mission.

A few days after jumping into France, Colonel Fraser discovered that Rommel's headquarters was located in the Château La Roche Guyon, fifty miles west of Paris along a bend in the Seine River. Based on this disclosure, Brigadier R. W. McLeod, the SAS commander whose headquarters was in a country mansion outside London, decided to proceed with Gaff.

McLeod's operational plan was simple: "Kill, or kidnap and remove to England Field Marshal Rommel." It added, "It is preferable to ensure the former rather than to attempt and fail in the latter. If it should prove possible to kidnap Rommel and bring him to this country the propaganda value would be immense. . . ."

In the days ahead, SAS intelligence gathered a thick dossier on the Château La Roche Guyon and on Rommel's habits and movements, all gained through spies on the ground, air photoreconnaissance, and electronic monitoring. It was learned that the field marshal went to the front nearly every day, returned at about 6:00 P.M., dined at 7:30 P.M., then often strolled through the surrounding woods.

In London, an SAS team of an officer and six men was selected for Gaff. They would parachute near the château under cover of darkness, take up positions near the woods, and either shoot or kidnap Rommel while he was on one of his walks. Should he be kidnapped, the field marshal would be smuggled out of France with the help of the French underground.

On July 15, the Gaff team was at an airport near London and ready to take off. Wireless reports from France indicated that the weather was cloudy over the drop zone, so the mission was postponed. Two days later, the SAS team bailed out of a transport plane not far from Rommel's château. Unbeknown to the intruders at the time, they were too late.[12]

Now, fate intervened to thwart a possible negotiated peace in the West. On the afternoon of July 17, Rommel was returning from an inspection of units in the Caen region. His powerful Mercedes sped along what was known as the Liverot road. Suddenly, two RAF fighter planes zoomed in at treetop level and riddled the Mercedes with 20-millimeter shells, killing the driver. The car went out of control, hit a tree stump, careened across the road, and halted in a ditch.

Rommel, who had been hit by shell fragments in the left cheek and temple, was thrown from the car and lay in the road as one of the aircraft came back and raked the macadam with bullets. Two aides, who had escaped serious injury in the attack, dashed out and carried the bloody field marshal, alive but unconscious, to cover in the roadside ditch.

Even now, Erwin Rommel could not escape the image of his longtime nemesis and friend. Near where Rommel lay was a sign announcing the name of the village the Mercedes had been about to enter: Montgomery.[13]

PART THREE

Road to Victory

CHAPTER 26

The "Friendly Bombs" Fiasco

AT NOON ON JULY 20, 1944, a black Trimotor Junkers transport plane lifted off from Rangsdorf Airfield outside rubble-strewn Berlin and set a course for Wolfsschanze, Adolf Hitler's battle headquarters set among thick woods outside Rastenburg, East Prussia. On board was thirty-eight-year-old Colonel Klaus von Stauffenberg, a tall, lean, and exceedingly handsome aristocrat. A year earlier in Tunisia, he had lost an arm, part of the other hand, an eye, and a piece of his scalp when strafed by American fighter-bombers.

Nothing about the demeanor of von Stauffenberg betrayed that he had embarked on a desperate and perilous mission. If all went well, within the next six hours he would violate his devout religious principles and murder a human being in cold blood. His target: Adolf Hitler. Von Stauffenberg was the hit man for the Schwarze Kapelle underground conspiracy.

Winging toward Wolfsschanze, the maimed colonel clung tightly to a briefcase on his lap. In it was a package containing a British-made bomb. Despite his physical infirmities, von Stauffenberg was confident that he could succeed in covertly placing the bomb-loaded briefcase under a conference table at the Führer's feet.[1]

Shortly after dawn the next day, Dwight Eisenhower was in France when he was told that German underground conspirators had set off a bomb at Hitler's conference table and that several officers had been killed or wounded. Miraculously, the Führer had escaped with only minor injuries.

"Holy smoke!" Eisenhower exclaimed. "There seems to be a revolt going on among the Krauts! What does that mean?"

Told that for three weeks secret Allied intelligence sources had been picking up reports of an assassination attempt, the supreme commander beamed. "Well, it sure looks good for Cobra!" The operation was scheduled to be launched that day.

In his euphoria over the possibility of a quick end to the Normandy bloodbath, Eisenhower failed to grasp a crucial factor: Wehrmacht commanders in

France now would fight with the desperation of cornered rats to *prove* their loyalty to Hitler.

Across the Channel, Arthur Tedder, long a staunch critic of Bernard Montgomery, seized on the aborted Hitler assassination plot to get in a few licks at his fellow countryman. "Monty's failure to take action earlier has lost us the opportunity offered by the attempt on [the Führer's] life," he said.

Tedder also said that he would put his views on Montgomery to the British Joint Chiefs in the hope of getting the ground force commander sacked. When Eisenhower returned to SHAEF, Tedder told the supreme commander that "your own people will think that you have sold them to the British if you continue to support Montgomery without protest."[2]

At his orchard headquarters far behind the lines in Normandy, George Patton was both angry and despairing on the eve of Cobra. One of the momentous battles of the war was about to erupt, and he and his Third Army were being left behind. Patton was convinced that there was a conspiracy to deprive him of redemption after the Sicily slapping affair. To aides, he fingered the culprits: Bernard Montgomery and Omar Bradley, with an assist from Beetle Smith.

Deepening Patton's blue mood was the fact that he felt Bradley had stolen the Cobra concept from him. Two weeks earlier, he had submitted to Bradley an audacious plan for breaking out of Normandy: Concentrate tanks, backed by infantry, on a narrow front, punch a hole in German lines, and send armor racing south down a good road network to Avranches. His plan, Patton was convinced, had been the basis for Cobra—but Bradley had never mentioned his name.[3]

At Bushy Park outside London, Dwight Eisenhower paced the floor after learning that Cobra would be postponed for twenty-four hours because of the torrential rains pounding Normandy and the English Channel. Presuming that the awesome air bombardment would blow open a huge hole in German defenses, he sent a message to Bradley: "Pursue every advantage with an ardor bordering on recklessness."[4]

Then Eisenhower climbed into a B-25 bomber and flew through heavy rain squalls to Bernard Montgomery's headquarters in Normandy. His plane may have been the only one in the air that day. While Monty frowned, Eisenhower urged him to be certain that the British Second Army, commanded by Lieutenant General Miles Dempsey, go all out in his attack in the Caen region when Cobra kicked off, to make certain that German panzers did not shift to the American front.

Eisenhower's exhortations irked both Montgomery and Field Marshal Brooke. "It is quite clear that Ike considers that Dempsey should be doing more than he does," Brooke wired Monty. "It is equally clear that Ike has the very vaguest conception of war."[5]

Still the rains came, and Cobra had to be postponed for three more days.

Early on the morning of July 24, Air Chief Marshal Trafford Leigh-Mallory, who had flown over from England, was with Omar Bradley at First Army headquarters behind Omaha Beach. Both men were worried; heavy clouds were socking in Normandy. In England, 2,246 Allied warplanes were preparing to lift off for the saturation-bombing mission, which was to begin at 12:30 P.M.

Just before 11:30 A.M., Leigh-Mallory put in an urgent call to England: "Cancel Cobra!" It was too late. Three hundred and eighty-five heavy bombers were burrowing through thick clouds over the Channel.

Fifty minutes later, the first flight of heavies approached the rectangle target at twelve thousand feet. American ground generals, gawking skyward two miles behind the front, were horrified. The bombers were not flying a course parallel to the Saint-Lô-Périers road, as Bradley had thought was the plan, but rather were coming in perpendicularly, directly over the heads of the American troops on the north side of the bomb-line.

Soon were heard the curious whines of hundreds of bomb clusters fluttering earthward. Explosives burst like giant firecrackers—on both sides of the road. Most of the bombs detonated on the German side, but errant "shorts" killed 25 men and wounded 130 others in the U.S. 30th "Old Hickory" Infantry Division.

The tragedy, bad as it was, could have been infinitely worse. At a small airfield west of Caen, Colonel William Macauley, a wing commander of the U.S. Ninth Fighter Command, was startled to receive radio reports of "shorts" landing among American ground troops. Acting on his own initiative, Macauley tried to reach the bombers over a frequency he thought they would hear. *"Stop the bombing! Stop the bombing!"* he shouted repeatedly into the transmitter. The frantic message got through to hundreds of heavies, and the big Liberators and Flying Fortresses turned away before reaching the target and headed back to England.

Minutes after the final bomb exploded, Major General Leland S. Hobbs, leader of the 30th Infantry Division, raced to a hill in the rear where the generals had gathered to watch the bombing. Charging up to Courtney Hodges, deputy to Omar Bradley, the infuriated Hobbs shouted, "The goddamned bombers came north-south, not east-west along the road like we were told!"[6]

At his headquarters, Bradley was shocked and enraged by the devastating bombing fiasco. Later, aides would say that they had never seen him so angry. "They broke faith with the plan!" Bradley ranted. "They're goddamned liars!"

For whatever reason, it later would be claimed, General Jimmy Doolittle, perhaps with the concurrence of the other bomber barons, had decided to fly a course directly over the heads of Bradley's ground soldiers in order to get his huge stream of heavies across the Saint-Lô-Périers road in the minimum possible time so as not to subject it to prolonged fire from German antiaircraft guns. Doolittle also felt that stray bombs would be more likely to crash into American positions by flying a parallel course.[7]

Bradley was left in a quandary by the abortion of the saturation bombing. It was obvious that the Germans knew that this sector had been targeted for an attack, and he feared the enemy would rapidly shift reserves to meet the threat. If Cobra was to succeed, the bombers would have to strike again—quickly.

Bradley asked Leigh-Mallory whether the bombing could be laid on around noon the next day, only this time with the heavies flying a course *parallel* to the road so that "shorts" would fall on the German side.

"Impossible!" the air chief marshal replied. Rearranging the complicated flight plan and briefing thousands of airmen could not be accomplished in the available time of less than twenty-four hours. Furthermore, Leigh-Mallory stressed to Bradley that if he insisted on a parallel approach, the air strike would be canceled.

Bradley struggled to control his fury. Who was Leigh-Mallory to be deciding whether a crucial air bombardment would be scrubbed? However, there was no time for lengthy wrangles over who was in charge of heavy bombers when tactical operations were involved. So he asked Leigh-Mallory whether the heavies could repeat the mission the next day by using the same approach. Leigh-Mallory replied that it could be done.

"It's a risky business," a worried Bradley remarked to aides. "But we've got to go!"

Just past 10:30 A.M. on July 25, a seemingly endless stream of Allied bombers flew over the rectangle of ground and began dropping their lethal cargo. Thousands of bombs followed. The ground shook and rumbled. Over the target, a thick pall of smoke and dust began drifting northward, covering the Saint-Lô-Périers road and thousands of American soldiers, who earlier had pulled back nine hundred yards.

Errant bombs fell as far as two miles behind the bomb-line on the American side. General Courtney Hodges heard the strident scream of approaching bombs and threw himself into a ditch. The blasts shook the ground and showered him with dirt. Picking himself up, shaken but unhurt, he began searching for the other generals who had been with him. He located all except Lieutenant General Lesley McNair, chief of army ground forces, who had arrived recently from the Pentagon and was in Normandy to witness the Cobra bombing.

McNair's aide was located. The last time he had seen McNair, the general was jumping into a foxhole. A search located the foxhole, which had been struck by a bomb. GIs began digging with entrenching tools, but nothing was there.

Within an hour, searching soldiers saw the remains of a man wearing the three stars of a lieutenant general lying alongside a narrow dirt road. There was not much left of General McNair's body.

At 11:32 A.M., the final bomb dropped. An eerie stillness fell over the smoking, pockmarked landscape. Four thousand tons of high explosives, fragmentation bombs, and napalm had poured down on Germans and Americans alike.

Meanwhile, Omar Bradley could only sit and wait at his headquarters until he learned how hard his three assault divisions had been hit by the "shorts." He hoped for the best, feared the worst. Cobra's ground attack, slated to jump off on the heels of the bombing, might have to be canceled.

An hour later, Bradley learned of the toll. It was horrendous. Leland Hobbs's 30th Infantry Division, which had been badly chewed up in the previous day's bombing, again took the brunt of the friendly bombs: Fifty-one killed and 374 wounded. Altogether in the three assault divisions, 601 GIs had been casualties, along with a few hundred more men who had been shaken so badly they would be unable to fight.[8]

Despite the staggering casualties, Bradley accurately reasoned that the Germans on the south side of the road had been hit infinitely harder, that their communications were snarled, artillery mangled, and tanks knocked out or incapacitated. Therefore, he contacted J. Lawton Collins, the VII Corps leader: "Attack as planned!"

Rallied by company officers and platoon sergeants, the dazed, demoralized, and shaken GIs shouldered their packs, picked up their weapons, and trudged across the Saint-Lô-Périers road and into the rectangle of death and destruction. Leading elements of the three assault divisions methodically wiped out scattered German pockets of resistance. Soldiers of Hobbs's 30th Infantry Division were edging down a narrow, hedgerow-lined dirt road when they heard the roar of powerful airplane engines. Instinctively, they leaped into ditches to escape the lethal streams of bullets aimed at them by a swarm of American fighter-bombers that had swooped over the cursing GIs at treetop level.

Collins's attack bogged down far short of the first day's objectives. Gloom hung heavy that night at Omar Bradley's headquarters. The big breakout, on which the Allied high command had placed enormous hopes, had fizzled. Flying back to England, Dwight Eisenhower was visibly depressed and furious at the bomber barons, vowing never again to employ heavies in close support of ground troops.

That night, Kay Summersby penned the following in her diary: "Attack not going too well. The Air bombed our troops. [Ike] says that we must press on with the attack and get going."[9]

Shortly before midnight, Winston Churchill telephoned Southwick House and asked to speak to the supreme commander. Although Eisenhower had been in bed for an hour, he was still wide-awake, turning over in his mind time and again what he might have done to avoid the "friendly bombs" tragedy.

Picking up the telephone, Eisenhower gave the Prime Minister a rundown on the day's events in Normandy, after which Churchill invited him to lunch at 10 Downing Street in London the next day at 1:00 P.M. He indicated that he had an important matter to discuss.

Early the next morning, word of Churchill's invitation swept through SHAEF. It appeared likely that the Prime Minister was seeking a scapegoat for the Cobra fiasco and perhaps wanted to see some high-level heads drop into baskets. Arthur Tedder rushed to see Eisenhower in order to discredit arch-foe and fellow countryman Trafford Leigh-Mallory, implying that the air chief marshal was responsible for the errant bombing.

Leigh-Mallory, who was skilled in the art of backstage infighting, apparently realized that he was a target for censure. He called at Eisenhower's office only minutes after Tedder had departed. Leigh-Mallory told the supreme commander that it was urgent he see him at once, for he was lifting off for Normandy in two hours. His talk with Eisenhower was presumably designed to show that the bomb "shorts" had not been his fault.

After Eisenhower departed for London, Harry Butcher scrawled in his diary: "Perhaps the Air is ganging up on Ike before he sees the P.M. this afternoon."[10]

Lack of coordination on the German side led Lightning Joe Collins, on the night after the bombing tragedy, to believe that the enemy had been damaged far more seriously than the GIs, slugging their way through the hedgerows, had realized. Collins, a bold combat leader, decided to take a gamble. In the morning, he would turn his 2nd Armored and 3rd Armored Divisions loose to exploit the turmoil in German defenses.

Collins's gut instincts proved to be accurate. On the heels of a thunderous artillery barrage, swarms of American tanks rumbled forward past the infantry and roared southward. Never in their wildest dreams had any of the SHAEF brass or the generals in Normandy visualized that the armored rampage would not halt until it had swept across France and penetrated the border of the Third Reich.

Early on the morning of July 28, Field Marshal Günther-Hans von Kluge was talking on the telephone to General Alfred Jodl, Hitler's closest military advisor, at the Führer's battle headquarters behind the Russian front. Known to some German officers as Hurrying Hans, the stocky sixty-one-year-old von Kluge was highly regarded by Hitler as the "master of victorious defense" against the Soviet army. On July 4, he had replaced aging Field Marshal Gerd von Rundstedt as Commander in Chief, West.

Von Kluge had arrived in France with spirits high and a firm resolve that the Allies could be defeated in Normandy. Within days, he had become totally disillusioned. The Feldgrau were being mindlessly butchered in a hopeless cause. Now, facing reality, von Kluge exclaimed, "Herr Jodl, everything here is *eine Riesensauerei* [one hell of a mess]!"[11]

In London, Alan Brooke was agitated. For three days, British newspapers and radio had been praising the American breakout and heaping criticism upon the head of Bernard Montgomery, Brooke's protégé. These media accounts implied that Monty was sitting idle at Caen on the eastern portion of the bridgehead while Omar Bradley's GIs were doing the bulk of the fighting and making stunning advances. It was a faulty rap. Montgomery's troops were pinning down most of the German panzers in Normandy to prevent them from shifting westward in front of the Americans.

Stung by the press stories, Brooke fired off a message to Montgomery: "[Eisenhower] seems to think that the British army could and should be more offensive. . . . It is equally clear that he considers that [General Miles] Dempsey should be doing more. Now as a result of all this talking [in the newspapers] and the actual situation on your front, I feel quite certain that Dempsey must attack at the earliest possible time on a large scale. We must not allow German forces to move from his front to Bradley's front or we shall give more cause than ever for criticism."

"Everything will be thrown in," Monty replied. "Gave orders to Dempsey that attack is to be pressed with the utmost vigor and all caution thrown to the winds and any casualties accepted."

At Bushy Park outside London, Beetle Smith read a copy of Montgomery's message. He seized on the word "caution" as proof of what Smith had been complaining about for weeks: Monty had been far too cautious.

While the spectacular Allied breakout from Normandy was capturing the world spotlight, dramatic events were unfolding in the Pacific. The U.S. Army and the U.S. Navy were butting heads in a bitter squabble over future strategy on the long and bloody road to Tokyo.

CHAPTER 27

A Meeting with "Mr. Big"

By THE SUMMER OF 1944, at the same time that General Eisenhower's armies were breaking out of the Normandy bridgehead, Douglas MacArthur had become convinced that the U.S. Navy brass intended to take over the war in the Pacific, relegate him to the backwaters, and administer the coup de grace to the Japanese. The suspicions of the supreme commander in the Southwest Pacific were intensified when his Eighth Army leader, General Robert Eichelberger, returned from a short visit to Honolulu and reported the current gossip in army circles there: The navy wanted the final crushing of Japan to be "their show and no one else's."[1]

MacArthur's spies in the Pentagon sneaked word to him that Admiral Ernest King had been lobbying President Roosevelt to bypass the Philippines and strike directly at Formosa (now called Taiwan), a mountainous island rising from the South China Sea a hundred miles off the China mainland and three hundred miles north of the Philippines.

Clearly, the army and navy were on a collision course to decide forthcoming strategy for delivering the knockout blow to Japan. For months, MacArthur's forces had been moving up the spine of 1,500-mile-long New Guinea. Now the general planned to turn north and invade the Philippines. There he would liberate eighteen million loyal Filipinos, avenge Bataan and Corregidor, and restore tarnished American pride throughout the western Pacific.

At the same time, U.S. marines (and a few army units), supported by carrier-based aircraft, all under Admiral Chester Nimitz, had been slugging it out with the Japanese in a brutal island-hopping campaign westward. By mid-1944, Nimitz's forces had seized the Mariana Islands—Saipan, Tinian, Guam, and Rota—only fifteen hundred miles from the Japanese homeland.

In the looming showdown over future strategy, MacArthur felt that he could not count on the support of his boss, George Marshall. In recent weeks, Marshall's position on where to strike next in the Pacific had become clear to MacArthur after the chief of staff cabled him: "Bypassing the Philippines is not synonymous with abandonment."[2]

216

MacArthur's blood boiled. He had never forgiven Marshall for what he considered to be the chief of staff's role in abandoning the Philippines in early 1942. Now this cable indicated that Marshall was prepared to again turn America's back on the Philippine people.

A few days later, Marshall again chastised MacArthur in another cable: "With regard to the reconquest of the Philippines, we must be careful not to allow our personal feeling and Philippines political considerations to overrule our great objective [winning the war against Japan]."[3]

The other general on the four-man Joint Chiefs, Hap Arnold, also was leaning toward bypassing the Philippines and striking at Formosa. He wanted Formosa as a base for his new B-29 Superfortresses, which dwarfed the workhorse B-17 bombers. From Formosa, the B-29s could be launched against Tokyo and other Japanese cities. So MacArthur would not have a strategy ally in Arnold.

Roosevelt, a patient man, finally grew weary of the ongoing dispute over Pacific strategy. "I know what everyone's opinion is in the Pentagon," he told Secretary of War Henry Stimson. "Now I am determined to meet face-to-face with MacArthur and Nimitz, get their views, and settle this thing once and for all!"

Much to the annoyance of the Joint Chiefs, Roosevelt would do some bypassing of his own, leaving Generals George Marshall and Hap Arnold and Admiral Ernest King behind in the Pentagon and traveling to Honolulu for the showdown with only two aides: Presidential speechwriter Sam I. Rosenman and Elmer Davis, head of OWI, America's propaganda arm.

Ernie King, the man Roosevelt called the Big Bear, was especially angry over the President's decision to take along only his speechwriter and "publicist." King labeled Roosevelt's safari a political stunt to help his reelection campaign, a trip designed to impress on the voters that he was the commander in chief and on top of things in the war.[4]

On July 20, the Democratic convention in Chicago nominated Roosevelt for an unprecedented fourth term. Twenty-four hours later, he was carried aboard the new heavy cruiser *Baltimore* by two husky Secret Service men and set sail for Honolulu.

On July 25, while the *Baltimore* was knifing westward through the swells of the Pacific Ocean, Douglas MacArthur's four-engine Flying Fortress, the *Bataan*, was winging its way through the clear blue Pacific skies bound from Brisbane, Australia, to Hickham Field, Hawaii, twenty-six hours and four time zones away. The Southwest Pacific commander had been in a foul mood through much of the lengthy flight, pacing the aisle and grumbling to aides about the indignation being inflicted on him by the big shots in Washington.

The main target of MacArthur's wrath was the commander in chief himself, Franklin Roosevelt, who he felt had betrayed him and his men on Bataan and Corregidor more than two years earlier by writing off the Philippines and concentrating on Nazi Germany. Now, "they" had forced him to leave his command post, where he was preparing to invade the Philippines, and fly to Honolulu for a "political picture-taking session." Roosevelt, MacArthur was fully aware, was up for reelection in November. He was convinced that the President's long trek from Washington had been contrived to let him bask in the reflected limelight of a popular national hero, Douglas MacArthur.[5]

As the *Bataan* neared Honolulu, MacArthur's irritation grew. The entire affair had been cloaked in mystery. A coded message from the Pentagon merely had said that he was to proceed to Honolulu to "meet with Mr. Big." MacArthur knew that had to mean the President, but he had been told nothing else. He had radioed Washington to inquire about the purpose of the conference and to ask which staff officers to bring. The reply had been terse—and evasive: "The meeting is top-secret and no information can be given." So MacArthur had left Australia without maps, charts, statistical data, or other materials that might help him to plead his case.[6]

Shortly before 3:00 P.M. on July 26, the *Baltimore* churned into sight of Hawaii's majestic Diamond Head. Franklin Roosevelt, a master showman, had made certain that he would receive a tumultuous welcome. His approaching warship was greeted by several squadrons of sleek fighter planes and a score of swift PT boats that dashed about the *Baltimore* like so many waterbugs on a farm pond. The populace had been alerted in advance to the arrival of the President, and when the *Baltimore* berthed, thousands of Hawaiians lined the docks and let loose with thunderous cheers.

Waiting at the gangplank were Admiral Chester Nimitz, along with his army commander, Lieutenant General Robert C. "Nellie" Richardson, and fifty-four other high-ranking officers in crisply pressed uniforms. They immediately boarded the *Baltimore* to pay their respects to the President. Douglas MacArthur was nowhere to be seen, his whereabouts unknown.

More than an hour before the *Baltimore* berthed, and in plenty of time for MacArthur to be on hand with the other brass to greet the President, the *Bataan* had landed at Hickham Field. Instead of heading for the docks, MacArthur had ordered his driver to take him directly to the house where he would be staying. There he bathed and leisurely unpacked.

On the *Baltimore*, Roosevelt was aware of his famous general's absence. Thirty minutes later, he questioned Chester Nimitz. Before the admiral could reply, an earsplitting siren pierced the air and two military policemen on shiny motorcycles paced an open limousine onto the dock. Those on the deck of the *Baltimore*, including Roosevelt, craned their necks to witness the arrival of an apparently exalted figure. With a raucous screeching of tires, the limousine lurched to a halt in front of the ship's gangplank. Perched on the backseat, wearing a leather jacket, outsize sunglasses, and a jaunty, gold-embroidered cap, was Douglas MacArthur.

Franklin Roosevelt had made a razzle-dazzle entry. MacArthur had upstaged him.

Cheers rang out as the Hawaiians recognized the general. Loud shouts could be heard: *"Mac-Arthur! Mac-Arthur!"* The general, four silver stars on each shoulder glistening in the sunlight, stood up in the limousine and acknowledged the adoring crowd with regal waves of his arm.[7]

Once the applause and shouts had subsided, MacArthur strode up the gangplank. Reaching the deck, he walked over to the seated Roosevelt. The President had been virtually ignored by the others during the sudden burst of excitement. The two men, who had not seen each other in seven years, shook hands warmly. If the President resented having been upstaged, he gave no indication.

"It's good to see you, Doug!" Few were ever that familiar with the general.

"Thank you, Mr. President," MacArthur replied. "It's good to see you, too!"

On the following morning, Roosevelt invited MacArthur to accompany him on a motorcade tour through downtown Honolulu. The President had insisted on riding in a bright red convertible. Thousands of Hawaiians crowded the sidewalks and cheered as Roosevelt and MacArthur rode past. During the jaunt, the general brought up a topic customarily off-limits for professional military officers: The approaching November election, in which the President would be opposed by Republican Thomas E. Dewey, the governor of New York.

MacArthur asked Roosevelt what he thought of Dewey's chances.

"I've been too busy to think about politics," the President replied.

MacArthur, knowing that the presidency *is* politics, laughed loudly.

Roosevelt broke into a wide grin. "I'll beat that son of a bitch in Albany if it's the last thing I do!"

Somewhere during the ride, MacArthur warned the commander in chief that if the navy's plan to bypass the Philippines in favor of Formosa was adopted, "I dare say that the American people would be so aroused that they would register complete resentment against you at the polls this fall." It was an audacious remark—even a thinly disguised threat. Roosevelt made no reply.

The showdown on Pacific strategy got under way that night in the spacious, book-lined living room of the palatial residence owned by Christian R. Holmes, overlooking Waikiki Beach. Even the President, born to wealth, was awed by the splendor and magnitude of the surroundings. Present, in addition to Nimitz and MacArthur, were Roosevelt's personal military advisor, Admiral William Leahy, and General Richardson, Nimitz's army commander.

The President opened the tense session by saying that alternative plans for the ongoing drive toward Tokyo had been narrowed to two: One was to hit Formosa and bypass the Philippines; the other was to invade the Philippines and bypass Formosa. Admiral Nimitz presented his Formosa case first.

It soon became evident to the sagacious Admiral Leahy that the low-key Nimitz, though sincere in his argument, was laboring under three handicaps: He was far from eloquent; he was articulating not his own views, but those of his boss, Admiral Ernest King; and he was either unprepared or unwilling to discuss the political and moral aspects of bypassing the Philippines, to which Mac-Arthur had sworn to return more than two years earlier.[8]

After Nimitz concluded his presentation, MacArthur set his pipe in an ashtray, rose, took up a pointer, and walked to a huge wall map of the western Pacific. He paused dramatically and glanced about at the small, silent gathering. Then the general began to present his case for invading the Philippines.

MacArthur spoke of his "high esteem and extraordinary admiration" for Admiral Nimitz and his naval associates. However, he stressed, the navy's strategic thinking was faulty. As President Roosevelt, in his role as referee, smoked a cigarette and listened impassively, MacArthur declared that abandoning the Battling Bastards of Bataan in 1942 had been a major blunder—by implication, Roosevelt's and George Marshall's. Had the United States had the will to do so, he said, it could have opened a way to reinforce Bataan and Corregidor and probably not only saved the Philippines but also stopped the Japanese advance toward Australia.

"To sacrifice the Philippines a second time would be neither condoned nor forgiven," MacArthur said.[9]

Roosevelt continued to puff on his cigarette. If the President of the United States and commander in chief of its armed forces was stung by the rebuke from one of his generals, he showed no sign.

MacArthur was at his eloquent best. Along with what he considered to be sound military logic, he stressed repeatedly the moral implications of bypassing the Philippines. "The Filipinos look on the United States as their mother country, and consigning them to the bayonets of an enraged Japanese army of occupation would be a blot on America's honor," he emphasized.[10]

At one point, the President interjected: "But, Douglas, taking the Philippines would demand heavier losses than we can stand."[11]

MacArthur knew that this was the pet argument of his rival in the Pentagon, Admiral King. "Mr. President," he responded, "my losses would not be heavy, no more than they have been in the past." In his "hit-'em-where-they-ain't" strategy of the past two years, his casualties had been relatively light.

As his presentation continued, MacArthur appeared to be winning over his audience—even Chester Nimitz. MacArthur shot down Admiral King's plan to put a naval blockade around the largest Philippine island, Luzon, after it had been bypassed. "Luzon is far too big," he declared. Admiral Bill Leahy cast a furtive glance at Nimitz and thought he detected a slight nod of agreement with MacArthur's view on the blockade.[12]

His arguments concluded, MacArthur walked through the silent room to his chair. Everyone realized that one of the major councils of the war had just been held. It had lasted only ninety-two minutes. Roosevelt adjourned the meeting and indicated that he would sleep on the matter before reaching a decision.

Before retiring that night, the President summoned his personal physician. It had been a long day, and Roosevelt was extremely tired. "Give me a couple of aspirin," he told the doctor. "In fact, give me another aspirin to take in the morning. In all my life *nobody* has ever talked to me the way MacArthur did today!"[13]

Seated on the immaculately groomed lawn the next morning, Roosevelt was confronted by a horde of newspaper and radio reporters and photographers. Having reached a decision on the thorny matter of Pacific strategy, the President was in a chipper mood.

Roosevelt got to the point promptly, telling the reporters, "We have had an extremely interesting and useful conference. We are going to get the Philippines back, and without question General MacArthur will [lead us] there."

Later, as MacArthur took his leave to fly back to Brisbane, Roosevelt said, "Well, Douglas, you win! But I don't know how I'm going to explain this to the Big Bear [Admiral King]!"[14]

Back in Brisbane forty-eight hours later, MacArthur was jubilant over Roosevelt's decision—and his own victory over the navy. "You know," he told Clark Lee, an International News Service correspondent, "the President is a man of great vision—once things are explained to him."[15]

Back in the United States, the Joint Chiefs who had been left out of the discussion had by no means accepted the order of the commander in chief, whose power over the Pentagon was supposed to be absolute. Marshall, King, and Arnold were still angry over Roosevelt having reached such a crucial decision without their presence, strategic advice, or guidance. On his return from Honolulu, William Leahy briefed his fellow Joint Chiefs on the discussions in the Holmes house. He stressed that both Roosevelt and he were especially impressed by MacArthur's moral and political arguments for invading the Philippines.

Marshall, King, and Arnold, however, were not impressed. They argued that the Philippines-or-Formosa debate should be decided strictly on military considerations. Consequently, the hot topic, which presumably had been settled by order of the President, continued to simmer. Battle lines had been drawn.

Admiral King still insisted on landing on Formosa. An invasion of Luzon, in the Philippines, would tie up the navy's fast carriers for at least six weeks, he argued. Hearing of these discussions, MacArthur responded in a cable to Washington: He would need only a small force of escort carriers for a few days until his engineers could scrape out strips for land-based airplanes.

The controversy continued through August and September. George Marshall and Hap Arnold slowly were converted to the Philippine strategy, but Ernest King stuck to his guns doggedly. Then, in the last week of September, King met in San Francisco with Chester Nimitz, who apparently had been leaning toward MacArthur's point of view even in Honolulu, when he had faithfully been presenting the navy's case.

Nimitz pointed out that the airfields in China, where King planned to base planes for a Formosa invasion, had been overrun by Japanese troops and were no longer available. Therefore, an invasion of Formosa would not be possible unless Luzon was captured first. Returning to the Pentagon, King capitulated and withdrew his objections to MacArthur's plans for invading the Philippines.

CHAPTER 28

A Gut-Wrenching Discussion

IN THE WAKE OF the Schwarze Kapelle's bungled attempt to assassinate him on July 20, 1944, Adolf Hitler now saw a traitor behind each bush and was suspicious of his field marshals and generals. He particularly mistrusted Field Marshal Guenther-Hans von Kluge, his commander in the West, who in the Führer's eyes had perpetrated the crime of allowing the Americans to break out of Normandy.

Meanwhile, in London, an important matter was being thrashed out at the highest levels: Should the Allies take up where the Schwarze Kapelle had failed and try to kill Hitler by aerial bombing or other means? Through the magic of Ultra, the Führer's whereabouts were constantly pinpointed, almost minute by minute. It was decided not to make the effort for fear of tipping off the Germans to the fact that their "unbreakable" Enigma code had been cracked nearly three and a half years earlier. "Besides," observed Winston Churchill, "they might put some other Nazi in there who is even worse than Hitler. With Hitler at the helm, we can't lose the war."

At midafternoon on July 28, while Omar Bradley's First Army tanks were charging ahead in Normandy, Captain Elliott R. Taylor, an aide to George Patton, burst in on the Third Army commander at a supply dump he was inspecting far behind the blazing battle. Such dull chores were humiliating for the man a major stateside magazine only the previous fall had labeled "one of the greatest fighting generals in history."

Taylor was visibly excited. "General, sir," he gasped, "you're wanted on the scrambler at headquarters. It's *General Bradley*! He's been looking all over for you!"

"Hot damn!" Patton shouted, smacking one of his polished boots with his riding crop. He raced back to his apple orchard base and called the commander of First Army.

"George," Bradley said, rolling out a time-honored phrase, "this is it!"

Patton's face flushed with excitement. But his elation quickly vanished. Bradley wasn't quite ready yet for Third Army to be made operational.

"You'll be deputy First Army commander and supervise operations in Middleton's zone," Bradley said. "You are to trail Middleton's columns and aid in unscrambling them should they become entangled." However, Bradley stressed, Patton was not to actively influence the course of Middleton's operations.

Bradley was referring to Major General Troy H. Middleton, in peacetime an educator at Louisiana State University and now leader of the U.S. VIII Corps. Middleton had jumped off on the right (west) flank of Joe Collins's breakthrough with the mission of seizing Avranches.

Patton had been given a vague assignment, but he did not quibble with Bradley. Keeping the general from "actively influencing" the course of VIII Corps' operations would be akin to hiding the rising sun from a barnyard rooster.

Bradley also told Patton that his presence in Normandy would be kept a deep, dark secret "to keep the Germans guessing." Patton, who lived for the spotlight, didn't even dispute that point.

Patton's zealously loyal staff, however, was furious on hearing of their boss's new assignment: Deputy army commander—a hollow title, a gimmick. Bradley, they were convinced, was merely afraid the dynamic Patton would steal the show. Why else would he throw a blackout curtain over the general the Wehrmacht most feared?

It was unfair criticism. Dwight Eisenhower, not Bradley, had decided to keep Patton under wraps. After the general had a few resounding victories under his belt, the home front would forget the uproar over the soldier-slapping incident in Sicily.

At one minute past midnight on August 1, Omar Bradley was elevated a notch on the command totem pole when he became leader of the newly activated U.S. 12th Army Group. Under him would be the First Army, whose reins he had turned over to his deputy, Courtney Hodges, and George Patton's new Third Army, whose divisions were still pouring across the English Channel.

Patton's Third Army would include Troy Middleton's corps, which had advanced down the west coast on Hodges's right and captured Avranches, where Normandy turns into Brittany.

With Third Army now officially operational, Patton told Major General Hugh Gaffey, his chief of staff, "Brad simply wants a bridgehead over the Selune [a river a few miles south of Avranches]. What *I* want and intend to get are Brest and Angers."

Gaffey was taken aback. Brest, the crown jewel of Brittany, was two hundred miles west of Avranches. Angers, the historic capital of the Anjou, was one hundred miles to the south. In between these two objectives were large numbers of Germans.

Early that afternoon, Major General Robert S. Grow, leader of the U.S. 6th Armored Division, was directing traffic at a road junction below Avranches. A jeep, trailing a plume of dust, roared up. Out jumped an excited George Patton. "Bob, I've bet Montgomery five pounds [twenty-five dollars] that we'll be in Brest by Saturday night!"

Startled by the audacious remark, Grow toted up the days. This was Tuesday. Saturday was only five days away. Patton was expecting the 6th Armored to barrel westward through enemy-held territory, without flank protection, and reach the port of Brest, two hundred miles away, in only five days. Grow swallowed hard. Within the hour, his tanks were charging toward the tip of the Brittany peninsula.

At noon the next day, August 2, Omar Bradley called on Troy Middleton and found him mad—plenty mad—at his immediate boss, George Patton. Without consultation, Patton had ordered Bob Grow to dash for Brest, leaving nothing between Middleton's extended columns and the main body of the German Seventh Army in Normandy.

Patton, Bradley now learned, had ignored his specific orders to firm up the base of the Brittany peninsula with infantry units before pushing on toward Brest.

"Damn it!" Bradley exploded. "George seems to be more interested in making headlines with the capture of Brest than in using his head!"

Bradley's long-held fears regarding Patton's impetuous habits emerged. Unbeknown to Patton or his staff, for weeks Bradley had had misgivings about calling the armor leader into the fight. "I'm afraid that if I bring in George, I will spend half my time watching him and the other half watching the Germans," he had confided to aides. He had struggled with his personal dilemma: Whether to have Patton in his command or get along without him. It was a difficult decision as to which was the lesser evil.

In the bloody slugfest in the hedgerows, there had been no critical need for a bold, slashing old cavalryman. But now, with the Wehrmacht in Normandy and Brittany beginning to fall apart, and American armor in position to slice up the Seventh Army, the situation *demanded* a George Patton.

At Bushy Park, the atmosphere was one of euphoria. The Normandy stalemate nightmare was over. Dwight Eisenhower was flashing his famous smile, which had been noticeably absent for weeks. "If the [Ultra] intercepts are right," he told Harry Butcher, "we are to hell and gone in Brittany and slicing 'em up in Normandy!"[1]

Back in the United States, all eyes were focused on the spectacular drives into Brittany. Newspapers were conjecturing that George Patton—who was still under wraps—was the moving spirit behind these daring armored thrusts.

If the American home front was trying to discover the identity of the armored leader, Adolf Hitler knew full well—and he was puzzled. "That crazy Patton," the Führer said to aides, "galloping along into Brittany with an entire army, not caring about open flanks or risks, as though he owned the entire world!"

Actually, only Troy Middleton's corps was galloping into Brittany. The remainder of Patton's Third Army soon would be utilized in one of history's most audacious feats.

At the same time, Winston Churchill's focus was on Dragoon, the impending invasion of southern France. If Eisenhower had thought that the Prime Minister had capitulated on Dragoon, he was in for a rude awakening when he attended dinner at 10 Downing Street on August 4.

At the four-hour showdown, Eisenhower was flabbergasted by his host's incredible new proposal. Churchill suggested that the large Allied force in Italy earmarked for Dragoon should disembark at Brittany ports instead. When the general regained his composure, he pointed out that these ports—Saint-Malo, Lorient, Saint-Nazaire, Quiberon, and Brest—were strongholds of the Germans. Churchill brushed aside that argument, declaring that the ports soon would be captured by George Patton.[2]

Early the next morning, Churchill resumed the attack to sink Dragoon. In an upbeat cable to President Roosevelt, he said that Eisenhower agreed with him that the Dragoon force should land at Brittany ports, from where the troops could reinforce Overlord troops in nearby Normandy. "Why should we bash in the back door [southern France], when we have the latch key to the front door [Brittany ports]?" the Prime Minister asked.

No doubt Churchill's contention that Eisenhower concurred in diverting Dragoon to Brittany came as a shock to the supreme commander. On returning from the exhausting dinner, Eisenhower had told aides that Churchill had nearly worn him out but that he had stuck to his guns on Dragoon.

Now, the Prime Minister rolled out his heavy artillery. Alan Brooke, who already had flip-flopped from being against Dragoon to being in favor of it, executed another somersault: He came out strongly for landing Dragoon troops in Brittany. The British Joint Chiefs echoed that sentiment.

Eisenhower and George Marshall were astonished by this amazing development. They looked on a Brittany landing as absurd, even bizarre. It would require transferring the Dragoon operation, which would be second in scope only to Normandy, sixteen hundred miles from its base in Italy. There was no written plan and no analysis on how such an eventuality would affect current operations in northern France.

Churchill, smelling victory in the latest dispute, telephoned Eisenhower just before midnight on August 5 and invited himself to lunch at Southwick House the next day. In the morning, Ike fired off a cable to George Marshall in the Pentagon: "I will not, repeat not, under any conditions agree to cancellation of Dragoon."[3]

After Eisenhower and Churchill engaged in an uneasy lunch, the Prime Minister unveiled two heavy hitters: Admiral Andrew Cunningham, the First Sea Lord, and British Admiral Bertram Ramsay, SHAEF naval commander.[4] Apparently outnumbered three to one, Eisenhower promptly sent for Beetle Smith.

Churchill said that history would accuse the supreme commander of passing up an enormous opportunity to shorten the war if he failed to shift Dragoon to Brittany. Eisenhower kept his temper in check, even though his friend Churchill was charging him with prolonging the war by his bullheadedness.

No doubt to the consternation of the harried Eisenhower, Beetle Smith sided with Churchill. Admiral Cunningham, who had usually been in Ike's corner in the past, also supported the Brittany scheme, even though only ten days remained before Dragoon was scheduled to hit. Then it was time for Churchill to be shocked. Rolling a black cigar in his fingers, the Prime Minister lifted an eyebrow when his own Admiral Ramsay spoke out against the shift to Brittany.

It had been a long, tedious, combative afternoon. When the visiting delegation departed, Eisenhower was limp and drenched with perspiration. However, he took time to rush a report to George Marshall, stating that he felt the Prime Minister "would return to the [Brittany] subject in two or three days and simply regarded the issue as unsettled."[5]

Harry Butcher, an awed onlooker at the confrontation, wrote in his diary that night, "[Eisenhower] said no in every form of the English language, continued saying no all afternoon, and ended saying no."[6]

As Eisenhower had suspected, Winston Churchill had by no means surrendered. On August 9, with the battle raging in Normandy and in Brittany, the supreme commander arrived at 10 Downing Street to accept a dinner invitation. Realizing that only five days remained to divert Dragoon to Brittany, the Prime Minister now changed his thrust. He argued emotionally for scrubbing the southern France invasion so that General Alexander in Italy could launch a powerful stab into the Balkans.

Earlier that day Churchill had remarked to confidants, "Good God, can't they see the Russians are spreading across Europe like a tide? They have invaded Poland, there is nothing to prevent them from marching into Turkey and Greece!"[7]

Now Churchill continued to bore in on Eisenhower, claiming that the Americans were "acting like bullies," rather than trying to see the British point of view.

"I am sorry that you feel we use our great actual or potential strength as a bludgeon," the general responded.

When Eisenhower stated that Dragoon was strictly a military decision and a correct one, Churchill replied that the correct military policy was to avoid a useless campaign in the south of France and push on in Italy toward the Balkans.

During the prolonged and intense argument, Churchill became upset, even despondent. Unless Eisenhower could see the strategy his way, the Prime Minister said, "I might have to go to the king to lay down the mantle of my high office."[8]

When the discussion—later described by Eisenhower as gut-wrenching—concluded, Churchill had tears in his eyes. As he viewed it, he was fighting for Great Britain's postwar security—and that of the United States as well. It was crucial, he was convinced, to keep the Soviets from spreading communism into the Balkans.[9]

Back at his advance headquarters in Normandy, which had been set up at Granville at the western base of the Cherbourg peninsula, Eisenhower was gripped by a haunting specter: Would Churchill, who was often highly emotional and unpredictable, really go to King George and resign? If so, that act could split the Western Allies asunder.

Early the next morning at 10 Downing Street, Winston Churchill finally admitted defeat, lamenting to aides, "Southern France may well prove to be another Anzio!" That is, a bloody stalemate.

On August 6, Charles de Gaulle launched an all-out effort to seize political control in France. Taking to BBC in London, he called on the French people to commence an insurrection. "Frenchmen, the hour of liberation sounds!" he exclaimed. "The national uprising will be the prelude to the liberation!"

Throughout France, a rebellion against the Germans erupted. Long-concealed weapons were brought out by the French underground, and the Wehrmacht found itself under siege from the shadows. While Bob Grow's 6th Armored Division was charging toward Brest in Brittany, thousands of maquis-ards—the shirtless, shoeless, underground warriors—were paving the way by keeping the roads open and the bridges intact, protecting the tankers' flanks, acting as guides, and riding herd over thousands of Feldgrau the American spearheads had captured. After Grow reached Brest in time for George Patton to win his bet with Bernard Montgomery, the underground fighters formed into infantry battalions and helped to encircle and then wipe out German forces holed up in several ports, including Brest.[10]

Now de Gaulle played another ace. On the night of August 8, ten RAF bombers towing ten Waco gliders flew to the region north of Vannes in Brittany, where the motorless craft were cast loose and skidded to jolting crash landings in pastures secured by a team of Jedburghs.[11]

Each team of Jeds, as they were known for short, consisted of one American, one Briton, and one Frenchman. Since D-day, Jed teams had been parachuted into many parts of France with the mission of organizing, rallying, arming, and training the French underground—and making certain that it fought according to Eisenhower's orders.

When the gliders' doors were opened, out hopped some twenty Gaullist bureaucrats. Carried inside the fragile craft were jeeps, communication radios, typewriters, folding desks, mimeograph machines, filing cabinets—all the equipment needed to establish a new regime, known as the Gouvernement Provisional de la Republique Française. Its president? Charles de Gaulle.[12]

This unique operation—labeled Mission Aloes—was the only time in history that an ambitious politician tried to gain political power in his country by sending in an advance guard of bureaucrats in gliders.

Across the Atlantic, meanwhile, a hubbub of excitement broke out in the high levels of the Roosevelt administration. On August 11, Bill Donovan's OSS released a top-secret report that indicated unknown circles in the Third Reich were trying to seek peace with the Western Allies. The OSS document was given only limited distribution—to the President, the secretary of state, and the Joint Chiefs.[13]

The OSS report said that Heinz Karl Weber, who was in charge of German mineral purchases in neutral Portugal, had received a message from unidentified German generals in Berlin. Weber had been requested to determine how the United States would react if Germany surrendered unconditionally to the Western Allies—provided that the Americans and British would rush into the Third Reich at once to keep out the Soviets.

Weber contacted Baron Oswald Hoyningen-Huene, the German ambassador in Lisbon, who, the OSS report stated, arranged for a three-way clandestine contact between American, British, and German diplomatic figures there. If the German peace overture was accepted, it might not be necessary for the Western Allies to fight their way to Berlin.

Apparently, the hierarchy in London and in Washington turned down the overture, making no reply. The bloodletting in western Europe would continue unabated.

In Normandy, while George Patton's tanks were galloping ahead in Brittany, Feldgrau of the Fifth Panzer and Seventh Armies, burrowed in the thick earthen hedgerows, were battling ferociously against Courtney Hodges's First Army and Bernard Montgomery's British and Canadians in the Caen region. Lashed on by Adolf Hitler to stand and fight "to the last man and the last bullet," the Germans fought as though the entire left flank of Seventh Army had not collapsed.

Field Marshal Guenther von Kluge considered the Führer's demand "strategic madness." He and every German general in France wanted to pull back to the natural defense barrier of the Seine River.

On the other side of the lines, Omar Bradley also recognized the vulnerability of von Kluge's two armies. He concocted a tactical scheme designed not only to inflict a calamitous debacle on the Germans but also to possibly end the war in the West.

Briefing his staff on details of the plan, Bradley declared in atypical bombast, "Let's talk big turkey! I'm ready to eat meat all the way!"[14]

Bradley's reputation among some generals as a cautious, methodical infantry plodder was about to vanish—in dramatic fashion.

Earlier plans to send Patton's entire Third Army into Brittany were scrapped; only Troy Middleton's corps—with the help of the French underground—would clean up that peninsula. The remainder of Patton's army would speed eastward for one hundred miles to Le Mans, then turn sharply northward to link up with Bernard Montgomery's troops attacking southward from the Caen region. That action would shut a gigantic trap, bagging both of the German armies in Normandy.

Patton was delighted. Sending spearheads racing toward Le Mans, he admonished his commanders: "Lead with your tanks—and go like the goddamned devil is chasing you!"

By August 12, Patton's spearheads had roared through Le Mans, turned northward, and reached Argentan, where Third Army had been ordered to halt so as not to collide with Montgomery's forces coming down from the north. Von Kluge's two armies were nearly encircled. Monty's Canadians, meanwhile, were having trouble reaching their objective, Falaise, twelve miles above Argentan, and closing the trap.

Frustrated and angry, Patton was damning Montgomery. Telephoning Bradley, he exclaimed, "Let me go on northward to Falaise and we'll drive the British back into the sea for another Dunkirk!" Bradley, fearful of a friendly-fire disaster, refused Patton's request.[15]

A short time later, Patton was contacted by Major General Wade Haislip, whose U.S. XV Corps was marking time at Argentan. Haislip pleaded with Patton to give him the green light to charge on to Falaise. "For chrissakes, George," the corps leader replied, "there's nothing in front of us but a company of Kraut bakers!"

Angrily, Patton again telephoned Bradley and urged him to contact Montgomery and tell him, in essence, "Patton is almost to Falaise. The stakes are enormous. Why don't we just dissolve the boundary line and let Patton close the gap?"

Bradley snapped, "If Monty wants my help, let him ask for it!"

For his part, Montgomery had no intention of calling on anyone for help, least of all Omar Bradley.

CHAPTER 29

High-Level Bungling

W HILE GERMAN UNITS WERE HEADING for the escape valve at Falaise to avoid capture, one of the most puzzling, enduring mysteries of the war in Europe was unfolding. The star of this curious conundrum was Field Marshal Guenther von Kluge, German supreme commander in the West. Shortly after dawn on August 15, 1944, von Kluge, clutching the jewel-encrusted field marshal's baton presented to him personally by Adolf Hitler three years earlier, climbed into the backseat of his Horch at the ornate Fontaine l'Abbe near the town of Bernay. Seated at his side was his son, Lieutenant Colonel Hans von Kluge.

Moments later, the party sped off for Necy, where the field marshal was to meet at a church with his two army commanders, SS General Sepp Dietrich and General Heinz Eberhard. In the lead were a motorcycle and sidecar, and a radio communications truck brought up the rear. It was a curious ensemble. Why was von Kluge taking a wireless communications vehicle along for a meeting with two of his generals? Would not the radio truck with its long antennae whipping in the breeze furnish a telltale clue to marauding Allied fighter-bombers that there was an important German commander on the road? Besides, units along the way had their own wireless equipment that the field marshal could have used. And why was von Kluge taking his son with him?

At Necy, Generals Eberhard and Dietrich waited three hours for von Kluge; then they concluded that he was not coming and departed. Staff officers at von Kluge's headquarters at Saint-Germain, a Paris suburb, and others at Fifth Panzer Army and Seventh Army headquarters were alarmed when no word was heard from the German supreme commander in the West. It was as if the battlefield had swallowed him. The greatest consternation was felt at Wolfsschanze, Hitler's headquarters behind the Russian front. Earlier that morning, the Gestapo had presented Hitler with evidence that von Kluge had been involved in the July plot to kill the Führer.

Hitler was now convinced that von Kluge had compounded his treachery by "deserting to the Anglo-Americans" and believed that he was trying to surrender the German armies in the West.

Throughout the day, a frenzied search had been in progress for the mysteriously missing field marshal. Acting at Hitler's direction, General Alfred Jodl, the Führer's confidant since the start of the war, made repeated telephone calls to various headquarters in France. Always the question was the same: Where is von Kluge?

No one had an answer.

At 8:00 P.M., Jodl was forced by the Führer to ask General Guenther Blumentritt, von Kluge's chief of staff, point-blank: "Has *der Feldmarschall* gone over to the enemy?"

At 10:00 P.M., a mud-caked Horch drove up to General Heinz Eberhard's battle headquarters. Slowly emerging from the vehicle was a tired Guenther von Kluge, together with his son. "Caught in the traffic," the haggard field marshal explained.

It was a curious explanation. The Wehrmacht commander in the West had vanished for more than seventeen hours.

Twenty-four hours later, von Kluge received a terse message from Hitler: "[You] are to leave [the battlefront] immediately and return to Berlin." No mention was made that Field Marshal Walther Model, a monocled, able commander faithful to the Führer, was already on his way to France to take over command. Hitler was taking no chances that von Kluge would, in his final hours as supreme commander in the West, surrender his battered armies to the Anglo-Americans.

Later, Field Marshal Wilhelm Keitel, Hitler's longtime confidant, would say that both he and the Führer were convinced that von Kluge had been in radio contact with the British on the day he disappeared. Keitel would maintain that von Kluge's radio messages had been intercepted by a special intelligence unit set up after Hitler became suspicious of his commander in the West.

At a staff conference at Wolfsschanze, the Führer threw a classic temper tantrum. "Field Marshal von Kluge planned to lead the whole of the Western Army into capitulation and to go over himself to the enemy," Hitler claimed. "It seems that the scheme miscarried owing to an enemy fighter-bomber attack. He had sent away his aides, British-American patrols advanced [to the designated rendezvous], but no contact was made."[1]

Von Kluge, after being recalled to Berlin on August 17, would take his own life by poison during the trip, and the mystery of the vanishing field marshal would never be entirely solved. It does appear, however, that fate—in the guise of Allied fighter-bombers—intervened at a crucial point. Otherwise, the war in the West might have concluded that month.

It was not until August 19, a week after George Patton's spearheads reached Argentan and he was demanding permission to close the gap himself, that the steel jaws of the sixty-mile-wide trap snapped shut. Due primarily to bungling in the Allied high command, the Germans had the escape valve open long enough for forty thousand soldiers—mostly SS and other crack formations—along with one hundred panzers and scores of artillery pieces, to slip through and head for the Siegfried line. With them were forty generals.[2]

Despite the Allied failure to achieve total victory, Adolf Hitler, by his stubborn refusal to heed the advice of his professional officers in Normandy, had doomed the bulk of two armies in the Falaise pocket. Ten thousand of his soldiers had been killed, and another fifty thousand dust-covered, bedraggled, exhausted Feldgrau shuffled into POW camps.

Privately, Dwight Eisenhower and Omar Bradley were mystified by Bernard Montgomery's tactics during the crucial period at the Falaise gap. Why did the British general employ the green Canadian First Army, spirited and game as it was, to try to close the trap? And after the raw Dominion troops failed repeatedly to break through to Falaise, why had Montgomery not substituted battle-tested British infantry and tankers to get the job done?

Eisenhower and Bradley were far from blameless for the escape of such a large force of Germans. The supreme commander bore ultimate responsibility for the prosecution of the war, but he did not intervene directly when it became obvious that a golden opportunity to snare two entire armies had arisen. Possibly he remained aloof in order not to offend Montgomery, the Allied ground commander. For his part, Bradley was infrequently in contact with his direct superior. Even before leaving England, the two generals had barely been on civil terms. As a result, Bradley and Monty remained apart in the Falaise operation, as though conducting separate wars.

On August 15—the same day that von Kluge disappeared—monumental events were unfolding along the French Riviera, four hundred miles south of the Falaise cauldron. It was D-day for Operation Dragoon. Early that morning, a thousand-vessel Allied armada was lying off the coast and discharging American and French assault troops. Ten miles offshore on the destroyer HMS *Kimberley*, Winston Churchill was staring avidly through binoculars at the military extravaganza unfolding before him. His two years of bitter opposition to Dragoon did not deprive him of a front-row seat for the invasion.

Long aware of Churchill's penchant for injecting himself into the thick of the action, the British admiral commanding in the Mediterranean had appointed a trusted naval officer to stand at the Prime Minister's side at all times. The escort's orders had been firm: "Don't let Mr. Churchill out of your sight for one minute!"

The protective measures were well taken. Almost immediately, the Prime Minister demanded that the *Kimberley* move in closer "to get a better look at things." On shore, American GIs and French commandos already were carving out a beachhead against sporadic resistance. Told that strict orders had been given against the *Kimberley* approaching any closer because of floating mines, the Prime Minister was unmoved. He reminded the beleaguered destroyer captain that he was the commander in chief of the armed forces, including the Royal Navy. So strict had been his orders not to subject Churchill to increased danger, the ship's skipper mumbled something to the effect that he would be cashiered out of the service if the *Kimberley* hit a mine. Before the morning was over, however, the skipper had been coerced into approaching to within only four miles of the invasion beaches.

Among the high-ranking Allied officers aboard was General Brehon Somervell, the War Department's supply chief in the Pentagon. "Met [Churchill] on *Kimberley*," he wrote in his diary that night. "He was lively and talkative. . . . Spoke of the main events of the war and of his opinion on operations. . . . Denied that he wanted campaign in the Balkans, except on guerrilla scale."[3]

There was good reason for Churchill's upbeat mood that day. Dragoon was a rousing success. It would be no Anzio. Less than one hundred American casualties and perhaps half that number of French dead and wounded had been suffered.

That night, the Prime Minister wired Eisenhower that he had "adopted" Dragoon and was delighted by the sporadically opposed landings. Ike, on receiving the message, recalled "all the fighting and mental anguish I went through in order to preserve [Dragoon], so I didn't know whether to sit down and laugh or cry."[4]

While the Allied generals were embroiled in controversy over who was to blame for the Falaise-gap command swoon, George Patton's tank-tipped columns were barreling eastward and reached the Seine River south of Paris. The old cavalryman was in a euphoric mood: Eisenhower had lifted the blackout curtain.

Patton, who had embarrassed fellow officers, angered the American public, and been indignantly rejected for promotion by the U.S. Senate, had suddenly burst from the shadows in a dazzling display of blazing newspaper headlines. Overnight he became America's most admired general. The British press idolized him, the American press forgave him his sins, and U.S. senators fell all over one another in quickly confirming his nomination to permanent major general.

Once Patton was revealed as the dynamo who had led the Third Army in its dash to the Seine, the fiery general could do no wrong. In the sudden new acclaim for Patton, Senator Albert "Happy" Chandler, who originally had helped block his promotion, rose hurriedly and intoned, "At this hour [Patton] is the greatest tank soldier in the world. . . . I have changed my mind!" Cheers rocked the august chambers.[5]

On August 19, with Patton on the Seine, Eisenhower sent Bradley and Montgomery a strategic plan for approaching Germany on a broad front. Montgomery's 21st Army Group would drive northeast toward Brussels and Antwerp, and Bradley's 12th Army Group would head due east in the direction of Metz, France. At the same time, the supreme commander said he was going to take over direct control of the land battle as of September 1.

Montgomery was furious over his demotion from Allied ground commander. He rushed his amiable chief of staff, Freddie de Guingand, to see Eisenhower and protest both the command change and the strategy plan. Speaking for Monty, de Guingand declared that the fastest and cheapest way to end the war was to hold Patton in the Paris region, hand over Courtney Hodges's First Army to Montgomery, and give control of all supplies to 21st Army Group. Then Montgomery would dash on to Antwerp, cross the Rhine River, and head with all speed for Berlin.

Moreover, said de Guingand, the Allies should continue to fight under a *single* ground commander. Eisenhower, as supreme commander, should "sit on a very lofty perch in order to be able to take a detached view of the whole intricate problem," and someone, meaning Montgomery, should run the land battle for him. Changing the command structure now, after the triumphs in Normandy, would prolong the war.[6]

If Eisenhower was incensed by the implication that the war might be prolonged because of his own ineptness if he took charge of the land battle, he kept his feelings to himself. After an exhaustive two-hour session with de Guingand, he said no to both of Monty's demands.

Montgomery refused to accept defeat, however. Instead of flying to Granville to meet with Eisenhower, he invited the supreme commander to his tactical headquarters at Condé. On August 21, Eisenhower and Beetle Smith arrived to see the British general. They had hardly set foot on the grounds when Montgomery said sharply that he wanted to see Eisenhower alone in his trailer. The proud Smith was angered to be, in essence, booted out of the conference. Although his chief of staff had been slapped in the face by Montgomery, Eisenhower made no protest.

Inside the trailer, Montgomery stood beside a wall map, hands clasped behind his back, while Eisenhower perched on a stool. Much like a schoolmaster lecturing a student, Monty explained to the supreme commander the tactical situation in France. If Eisenhower's plan to approach Germany on a broad front was adopted, it would result in "abject failure," Monty said.

Now Montgomery made new demands. Not only did he want Patton halted, Hodges's First Army put under his control, and all supplies handed over to 21st Army Group, but he also asked that the new First Allied Airborne Army (FAAA) be assigned to him for his single thrust to the northeast and on into Germany.

After a lengthy discussion, Eisenhower performed an about-face and agreed with Monty's single-thrust strategy. However, he refused to budge on his intention to take over the direction of the land battle from Montgomery.

A jubilant Montgomery wrote Alan Brooke that it had been an "exhausting day," but that he was "quite pleased" to have extracted key concessions from Eisenhower.[7]

Montgomery may have been quite pleased, but Omar Bradley and George Patton were nearly apoplectic. "Brad feels that Ike won't go against Monty," Patton wrote in his diary. "Brad was madder than I have ever seen him, and he wondered aloud what Ike amounts to. . . . Monty has a way of talking Ike into his own way of thinking."

Patton told Bradley that both of them should resign "if Monty continues to have his way." It would be a calculated risk, because Patton felt that Eisenhower would not dare accept the resignations of two of America's most successful generals. Bradley thought the threat would be going too far, but he was so angry that he hopped into his car and rushed to call on Eisenhower to vigorously protest giving his First Army to Montgomery.

Bradley's view was supported by three of Eisenhower's top aides: Arthur Tedder; Major General Harold "Pink" Bull, SHAEF's operations chief; and Brigadier Kenneth Strong, the chief of intelligence. Under this unanimous pressure, the supreme commander yielded. First Army would remain under Bradley.

That decision settled the Allied strategy dispute for the drive toward the Third Reich: A broad-front approach would be taken instead of Monty's single thrust. At least that's what Eisenhower thought.

No sooner had the supreme commander finished smoothing Omar Bradley's ruffled tail feathers than Charles de Gaulle barged in on him. The French leader demanded that Major General Jacques LeClerc's 2nd Armored Division, which had landed in Normandy in late July, be sent into Paris, which was still in German hands. Eisenhower intended to bypass the French capital in order to keep a large Allied force from becoming bogged down in street-to-street fighting. However, the situation had changed in the past forty-eight hours. French underground fighters had taken basic control of Paris, and the German commander agreed to an armistice.

Eisenhower infuriated de Gaulle by turning down his request. If he was going to charge into Paris, Ike declared, he would do it using American divisions already positioned much closer to the city. Rising to his feet, the French general saluted stiffly and stomped out of the office.

A few hours later, a note from de Gaulle was delivered to Eisenhower. He had ignored the supreme commander's wishes and issued his own orders for LeClerc to enter Paris.

Meanwhile, French Resistance leaders slipped out of Paris and reached Eisenhower's headquarters. They begged him to send troops into the city before the Germans broke the shaky truce. Under pressure from all sides, Eisenhower relented. Not only would the French 2nd Armored be bolting into Paris from the west, but Major General Raymond O. "Tubby" Barton's U.S. 4th Infantry Division, veterans of the D-day assault on Utah Beach, was ordered to charge into the capital from the south.

CHAPTER 30

"The War in Europe Is Won!"

THE FOUR MILLION CITIZENS OF PARIS, under the Nazi jackboot for nearly four years, were both hopeful and fearful in the early morning of August 25. It appeared to them that German soldiers were pulling out of the sprawling metropolis, and rumors were rampant that Allied forces were knocking at the gates.

When Jacques Le Clerc's French 2nd Armored Division rolled into the city from the west and Tubby Barton's U.S. 4th Infantry Division charged in from the south, one of history's most frenzied civilian celebrations was touched off. Parisians poured into the streets by the hundreds of thousands, engulfing the liberators. GIs and French soldiers were wined, dined, hugged, kissed, squeezed, applauded, and romanced.

Bedlam reigned in the City of Light.

In Paris that afternoon and night, wild shooting and chaos erupted among feuding French political parties, collaborationists, and anticollaborationists. An American captain was accidentally shot through the head and killed by a Frenchman.[1]

Major General Leonard T. "Gee" Gerow, leader of the U.S. V Corps to which Le Clerc's division had been attached, telephoned Omar Bradley. Gerow complained bitterly that many of the French drivers had become drunk on the way to Paris and were holding up traffic by halting at every town along the road to accept the huzzahs of the people and consume champagne and wine.

During the night, Bill Walton, a young correspondent for *Time* who had parachuted into Normandy in the early hours of D-day, established a beachhead at the Royal Fromentin Hotel in Montmartre, the bailiwick of shabbier elements of the Paris population. After a night of wild rejoicing, Walton awakened in his hotel room to the sounds of raucous cheering outside. He stumbled out onto the second-floor balcony, where, like a conquering Roman emperor, he bowed and waved regally to a screaming multitude of prostitutes, pimps, pickpockets, petty thieves, and other Montmartre habitués.

237

At the same time, Gee Gerow, whose West Point textbooks had failed to prepare him for the turmoil he encountered in Paris, barged into Bradley's headquarters at Chartres, west of the city.

"Who in the hell is boss in Paris!" he demanded to know. "The goddamned Frenchmen are shooting at each other, each party is at each other's throats. Who the hell is in charge? Koenig? De Gaulle? Me?"

Pondering these rapid-fire questions, Brigadier General William B. Kean, Bradley's chief of staff, as confused as everyone else, replied, "You are in charge."[2]

Bill Kean only *thought* Gerow was in charge. Actually, Charles de Gaulle had bolted into Paris and immediately ordered a parade through the city by the French 2nd Armored Division, appointed his confidant General Pierre Koenig military governor of the city, and personally taken control of the government buildings. Twenty-four hours later, de Gaulle, standing tall and masking his deep emotions, led a parade down the broad Champs Élysées to Notre Dame cathedral. There he directed several hundred thousand Parisians, many of them weeping, in singing the French national anthem.

Meanwhile, Eisenhower drove to Bradley's headquarters at Chartres. Although he had vowed to stay clear of the raucous Paris celebration, the urge to go into the historic city had overcome him. He suggested to Bradley that they drive into Paris the next morning. It would be a Sunday, Ike said, "so everyone will be sleeping late. We can do it without any fuss."

Eisenhower was wrong. The city was still on an unprecedented binge. Wildly cheering Parisians instantly recognized Eisenhower and Bradley, and all but smothered the two generals with hugs and, to the Americans' dismay, a rash of kisses.[3]

Eventually, Eisenhower's Packard wended its way through the maddening crowds and reached the Prefecture of Police, where de Gaulle received the two generals as though he had been the liberator of Paris and Eisenhower and Bradley had arrived to pay homage to him.

These were heady days in the ivory towers of SHAEF. Two German armies had been wiped out in Normandy, and Paris had been liberated. The Allied hierarchy was intoxicated by the sweet scent of victory. On August 23, a SHAEF intelligence bulletin stated: "Two-and-a-half months of bitter fighting, culminating for the Germans in a bloodbath big enough even for their extravagant tastes, have brought the end of the war within sight, almost within reach."[4]

In London, Field Marshal Alan Brooke also had been stricken with victory fever. Writing to Henry Maitland Wilson, the Allied supreme commander in the Mediterranean, Brooke said, "It has become evident that the Boche is beat on all fronts."

In Granville, Dwight Eisenhower advised the Combined Chiefs that he might have to face the occupation of the Third Reich much sooner than expected.

In Washington, George Marshall cabled top commanders in Europe to be prepared for the deployment of divisions to the Pacific. "While the cessation of hostilities against Germany may occur at any time, it is assumed that it will extend over a period between September 1 and November 1, 1944," he prophesied.[5]

In France, the field commanders also were euphoric. Patton boasted that he could charge across the German border in only ten days, and Montgomery declared that one full-blooded thrust could reach Berlin.

On September 2, General Beetle Smith bustled importantly into a room filled with reporters. His message was simple and direct: "Militarily, the war in Europe is won!"

There was ample reason for the Allied brass to exude a happily expectant attitude. Since D-day in Normandy, the German losses had been gargantuan: Four hundred thousand Feldgrau killed, wounded, or captured; thirteen hundred panzers, twenty thousand vehicles, two thousand pieces of artillery, and thirty-five hundred aircraft seized or destroyed.[6]

Despite defeat and disorder, the Wehrmacht in France began withdrawing eastward in orderly fashion after the fall of Paris. Its destination was the vaunted Siegfried line, the concrete-and-steel fortifications that stretched for some three hundred miles from the Swiss border to the Netherlands inside or near the western boundary of the Third Reich.

Along the way, the fleeing German columns were bombed and strafed by swarms of warplanes, and Allied spearheads were nipping at their heels. In four days, British forces covered a distance of two hundred miles in the direction of Brussels, and Courtney Hodges's First Army and George Patton's Third Army were charging eastward on the right of the British. Below Patton, General Jacob Devers's U.S. 6th Army Group, which had come over the Dragoon beaches, was approaching the German border near the Swiss frontier with the Third Reich.

In this climate of looming Allied victory, friction erupted once again when SHAEF announced publicly that the U.S. 12th Army Group had been activated and that Omar Bradley was now equal to Bernard Montgomery. London newspapers were outraged, claiming that Monty had been demoted. Then American media got into the act and demanded an apology from the British press. There were also complaints from the U.S. press that the British were dominating SHAEF, because the chiefs of air, sea, and ground commands were (or had been) British.[7]

George Marshall was extremely upset over the uproar. So was Eisenhower, who bitterly resented a suggestion in the *New York Times* that he was a figurehead. He asked Marshall to have the U.S. media informed that "no major effort takes place in this theater by ground, sea, or air without my approval."[8]

Then, on September 1, Winston Churchill further complicated the hassle over the Allied command structure by announcing that Bernard Montgomery had been promoted to field marshal. That meant that Monty outranked his boss,

Eisenhower, five stars to four. George Patton was hardly impressed, writing to wife Beatrice, "The field marshal thing makes us sick, that is Brad and me."

Bradley was far more furious than sick about Montgomery's promotion. "Montgomery is a third-rate general," he told Beetle Smith, "and he never did anything or won any battle that any other general could not have won as well or better."

Just prior to 7:00 P.M. on September 8, while many Londoners were having their dinner, a terrific explosion rocked the suburb of Chiswick. It sounded like a thunderclap, but the sky was clear. Terrified citizens dashed for basements, unaware that Adolf Hitler's first V-2 missile had arrived. The blast demolished nineteen Chiswick houses and gouged out a thirty-foot crater in the ground. Scores of dead and injured were dug out of the ruins.

Shaped like a cigar, the V-2 was forty-seven feet long and carried a one-ton warhead capable of leveling an entire block of buildings. Huge by contemporary standards, the missile could attain a height of ninety miles and such an enormous speed (nine hundred miles per hour) that those on the receiving end would not even see or hear it approaching.

In the days ahead, the V-2s continued to rain down on London. Allied intelligence ferreted out the fact that the missiles were being launched from the hearts of cities in Holland. If the Allies were to carpet-bomb missile-launching sites in the hope that an occasional explosive might hit the target, they would slaughter thousands of Dutch citizens. London was in deadly peril.

Forty-eight hours after the first V-2 wreaked havoc in Chiswick, Eisenhower asked Field Marshal Montgomery to fly from Belgium to Granville in western Normandy for a strategy consultation. At the time, the supreme commander was laid up in bed and in great pain after severely twisting his knee. Monty knew of the injury but insisted that he was too occupied to leave his command post and asked Eisenhower to come to Brussels instead.

Painfully climbing into a two-engine B-25 bomber, Eisenhower flew to Brussels. Unable to get out of the plane as it sat on the airfield, the supreme commander conferred inside with Montgomery, who accused Eisenhower of double-crossing him and implied that George Patton was actually running the war.

As always when dealing with the temperamental Montgomery, Eisenhower refused to get involved in a shouting match, but gently reminded Monty that it was unwise to speak in such tones to one's boss. Aware that he had overstepped his bounds, Montgomery mumbled a terse apology, then unfolded a bold plan of action to "bring the war to a quick end."

Eisenhower was astonished by the audacity of the proposed operation, code-named Market-Garden. Customarily cautious and methodical in battle, Monty now wanted to drop large numbers of paratroopers and land glider forces behind German units, like pieces on a checkerboard hopping over their opposition, to seize a number of key bridges over the multitude of waterways that crisscrossed the Netherlands.

But in war, unlike in checkers, the enemy pieces that have been hopped over are not thereby swept from the board but must be removed by force. It would be the job of Lieutenant General Brian Horrocks's British XXX Corps to dash along the sixty-mile-long corridor hacked out by the airborne troops and bolt over the Rhine (known in this region as the Neder Rijn) on the big bridge at Arnhem. Then Monty's spearheads could wheel eastward and head for Berlin.

Market-Garden, the field marshal stressed, would not only eliminate the V-2 launching sites on the Dutch coast but also permit the Allies to skirt the Siegfried line (which ended in the north at Cleve), thus avoiding the heavy bloodshed that would result if that menacing fortified belt had to be pierced by frontal assaults.

Eisenhower would later write, "Had the pious, teetotaling Monty staggered into SHAEF with a hangover, I could not have been more astonished than I was over the boldness of Market-Garden."

With one eye on the secret V-2 launching sites and the other on grabbing a bridgehead across the Rhine, Germany's historic water barrier to invasion from the west, Eisenhower bought the plan.

Although Montgomery seemed to have switched from caution to audacity, he had not acted impetuously: He would have at his disposal the First Allied Airborne Army, which had been activated only a month earlier (on August 8) amidst a storm of controversy.

The First Triple A, as the new command was called, consisted of the U.S. XVIII Corps (which included the 17th, 82nd, and 101st Airborne Divisions) and the British 1st Airborne Corps (comprising the 1st and 6th Airborne Divisions, a Polish brigade, and miscellaneous smaller units), along with several American and British air forces troop carrier commands.

Activation of the First Triple A had gained a unanimity of opinion: Nearly everyone involved was angry. Omar Bradley felt that this was an unneeded layer of authority insulating him from his three airborne divisions. Dwight Eisenhower indicated that the First Triple A top command should go to an American, a proposal that triggered a negative response from Alan Brooke. Sure, the Americans would have far more troops, aircraft, and air crews than would the British, but the British were far more experienced in this type of warfare, Brooke argued.

Brooke had a candidate in mind to command the First Triple A: One of his protégés, General Frederick "Boy" Browning. The dapper Browning did nothing to discourage the heavy drumbeating on his behalf. Air Chief Marshal Trafford Leigh-Mallory, who had predicted an American airborne debacle for the Normandy invasion, also was furious. He would lose authority over the U.S. IX Trooper Carrier Command.

Eisenhower had his own candidate: Thirty-four-year-old U.S. Air Corps Major General Hoyt Vandenberg, who was deputy to Leigh-Mallory. Just when it appeared that the young general would get the coveted command, someone backstage pulled the rug out from under him.

The rug-puller may have been George Marshall, who, at the age of sixty-three, may have considered Vandenberg to be too young for the job. A much older three-star general, Lewis H. "Louie" Brereton, leader of the U.S. Ninth Air Force, was selected for the post.

Surprisingly, the fifty-five-year-old Brereton, who had been a pilot in the First World War, was angry and frustrated. No doubt he felt that commanding lumbering transport planes and the soldiers they hauled or towed in gliders in relatively infrequent operations was a distinct comedown from his prestigious post as leader of the powerful Ninth Air Force, whose hundreds of swift fighter planes roamed the skies over Europe.[9]

Brereton—short in stature, hard-boiled, and hard-driving—was far from the only one displeased with his appointment. Omar Bradley was, too. He had clashed frequently with the bespectacled air corps general during the Normandy campaign. Bradley had felt that Brereton's fliers were not providing effective close-support for hard-pressed infantrymen.

Eisenhower, seeking to soothe frayed British feelings over the appointment of an American to head the First Triple A, named Boy Browning as Brereton's deputy. Browning was unhappy playing second fiddle to Brereton, a man who, Browning felt, knew nothing about airborne operations. He barely concealed his disdain for having to work under an air corps officer, especially one who was junior to him in rank.

General Matt Ridgway, the American airborne veteran of Sicily, Italy, and Normandy, agreed in one respect with Boy Browning, with whom he had clashed several times in North Africa and elsewhere. Like Browning, Ridgway felt that the First Triple A commander should have been an experienced airborne leader. Possibly, Ridgway had his own ideal candidate in mind: Matt Ridgway.

Ridgway's ego was assuaged to an extent when Eisenhower named him to command the new U.S. XVIII Airborne Corps, an appointment that left a vacancy at the helm of the 82nd Airborne Division. Filling that post would be Ridgway's deputy, James "Slim Jim" Gavin, who at the age of thirty-seven soon would be promoted to two-star rank and become the youngest major general in the U.S. Army since the Civil War.

By early September, rough-and-ready Louie Brereton had fidgeted for weeks. Seventeen times he and his staff had drawn up plans for a historic action: The landing of all or a major part of an airborne army, a huge force capable of fighting on its own behind German lines. Seventeen times he had had to scrap the plans; the Allied spearheads had advanced so swiftly across France and into Belgium and Holland that the First Triple A was not needed. Now, with Bernard Montgomery's daring operation, Market-Garden, Brereton's eighteenth plan would go through.

Shortly before the mighty airborne army lifted off for Holland, Brereton made a controversial appointment that rankled the American airborne brass: Boy Browning would land in Holland and take field command of operations in the narrow corridor.

Curiously, Bernard Montgomery, Louie Brereton, and their planners ignored several startling clues that the Germans might give the airborne invaders an unexpected reception. Ultra disclosed that the crack 9th Panzer and 10th Panzer Divisions were positioned near the drop and landing zones. Also ignored was Ultra's disclosure that the wily Field Marshal Walther Model, German commander in the West, had his headquarters near Arnhem, from where he could rapidly order countermeasures to the Allied assault from the sky.

Sunday, September 17, was bright and clear when the big sky parade began. Lifting off from twenty-four airfields in England, fifteen hundred transport planes crammed with paratroopers or towing gliders filled with soldiers set a course for Holland. A short time later, the skies over the land of the windmills were awash with parachutes and the terrain was clouded with dust from the crash landings of hundreds of gliders.

Undaunted by the awesome sight of an entire Allied airborne army descending on Holland, Field Marshal Model rushed swarms of panzers to each side of the corridor and at its nose around the Arnhem Bridge over the Rhine. Fierce fighting raged for nine days. A narrow passage fifty-five miles long had been carved out and key bridges seized over the Waal and Meuse Rivers. Brian Horrocks's British tankers, however, crunched to a halt only seven miles short of the Arnhem Bridge, where a large contingent of British paratroopers was trapped on the north bank of the Rhine.

Montgomery's bold gamble to grab a bridgehead over the Rhine had fallen agonizingly short, and the Allies suffered seventeen thousand casualties. Someone had to be blamed for the failure. Most American generals—among them Carl Spaatz, George Patton, and Matt Ridgway—pointed fingers at their favorite whipping boy, Bernard Montgomery. They claimed that the field marshal should have insisted that Horrocks's spearheads crash on to Arnhem regardless of losses.

Few, if any, of the Allied brass targeted the real culprits in Market-Garden's failure: Field Marshal Walther Model and the tenacious German fighting men.

CHAPTER 31

Frigid Reception for a Pentagon Inspector

EARLY AUTUMN OF 1944 found President Franklin Roosevelt deftly juggling a crowded agenda that included the global war, domestic issues, and his reelection campaign. His energetic Republican opponent, Governor Thomas Dewey of New York, was hammering away at the President's alleged culpability in the Pearl Harbor disaster, claiming that Roosevelt had failed to detect in advance Japanese intentions in the Pacific.

As the campaign heated up, Dewey charged that Roosevelt had engineered an intricate cover-up to conceal his own failure in the Pearl Harbor surprise and that Douglas MacArthur had been deliberately shortchanged on manpower and weapons in the Pacific because the general was a serious political threat to Roosevelt.[1]

George Marshall was a political eunuch, one who refused to even vote for fear of being accused of siding with this candidate or that one. As army chief of staff, however, he had been closely observing the presidential campaign with regard to its possible influence on the course of the war. One day in late September, Marshall received shocking news. An unidentified official in either the navy or the War Department had slipped information to Tom Dewey about supersecret Magic, code name for the interception and translation of Japanese messages, and the fact that the Japanese codes had been broken four years earlier, permitting the White House to have received advance indications that war was about to break out in the Pacific.

Marshall was fearful that Dewey planned to disclose the existence of Magic in a speech to prove that Roosevelt and his administration were at fault for the Pearl Harbor debacle. Once Magic was made known to the world, the Japanese would change their codes, thereby wiping out an enormous U.S. strategic advantage, costing thousands of American lives, and prolonging the war in the Pacific.

Marshall found himself in a dilemma. If he declined to contact Dewey and explain the crucial importance of keeping the Japanese from knowing about Magic, he would be grossly derelict in his duty as army chief. If he approached

Dewey, he would be accused of sticking his nose in partisan politics to curry favor with President Roosevelt.

Marshall discussed the critical matter with only one person: Admiral Ernest King. They agreed that some action would have to be taken and that no one else should be let in on the secret. This presented a problem: How could Marshall personally meet Dewey without attracting media attention?

The problem would be solved by a scenario worthy of a spy novel. Colonel Carter W. Clarke of the Pentagon's intelligence office was told only that he was to wear civilian clothes and deliver to the Republican presidential nominee a sealed, top-secret letter marked "For Mr. Dewey's Eyes Only." Clarke caught up with Dewey in Tulsa on September 26, and the two men met secretly in a hotel room.[2]

Donning horn-rimmed eyeglasses, Dewey scanned the first two paragraphs, which asked him to read no more unless he agreed to keep the contents secret, and then he put the letter down. He explained that he "did not want his lips sealed on things he already knew about Pearl Harbor, facts already in his possession."[3]

Dewey was leery. A seasoned political pro, he felt that this curious meeting may have been orchestrated by Franklin Roosevelt as a ploy to silence the Republican nominee on Pearl Harbor or to somehow discredit him. He asked Clarke to discuss the contents with him, but the colonel replied that he had no such authority. In fact, Clarke had not been privy to what was in the letter.[4]

Dewey said that if the Marshall letter merely advised him that American intelligence was reading Japanese codes there was no point in reading further. "Well, I know it and Franklin Roosevelt knows all about it," the candidate told Clarke. "He knew what was happening before Pearl Harbor and instead of being reelected, he ought to be impeached!"[5]

Dewey thrust back the letter unread, but said he would be willing to discuss it with Clarke when he returned to Albany in two days.

In the Pentagon, Marshall mulled over the situation, then decided to dispatch Clarke to Albany for a second encounter. Dewey, now thoroughly wary, had a witness on hand for the meeting, fearful that Roosevelt might later charge him with reading a letter different from the one he was really going to peruse.

After reading the letter, Dewey recognized that he had been caught in a trap. If he disclosed that Roosevelt had been reading translated Japanese messages since shortly prior to Pearl Harbor, the governor probably would be roundly condemned and hung out to dry by voters for callously spilling even more American blood in the Pacific. Frustrated and angry, Dewey raged that Roosevelt was "a traitor who had willingly or accidentally permitted more than two thousand American men, and most of the Pacific fleet, to go to a watery grave."[6]

Six weeks later at the polls, Dewey would go down to defeat, having never hinted that the Japanese codes had been cracked prior to Pearl Harbor.

Across the Atlantic, on September 20, SHAEF headquarters moved from bucolic, isolated Granville in Normandy to the lavish Trianon Palace in Versailles, a suburb of Paris. Aides ensconced Dwight Eisenhower in a nearby mansion that had been occupied a few months earlier by Field Marshal Gerd von Rundstedt, the former Wehrmacht commander in the West.

Two days after SHAEF set up shop in Trianon Palace, Eisenhower called together the largest collection of Allied brass since before D-day: Twenty-three generals, admirals, and air marshals. Noticeably absent was Bernard Montgomery, who sent Freddie de Guingand in his place.

Eisenhower had set up the conference to discuss strategy for the drive into Germany. His plan envisioned all Allied armies approaching the Third Reich on a broad front, then crossing the Rhine River above and below the industrial Ruhr (the arsenal of Hitler's armed forces). Once the Ruhr was encircled, whichever army's position was most promising would be sent charging toward Berlin.

De Guingand, speaking for Montgomery, was opposed to the broad-front strategy and championed a single thrust across the Rhine by the 21st Army Group north of the Ruhr. There would not be sufficient fuel, ammunition, and supplies to support all the attacking armies, Monty argued through his chief of staff.

Eisenhower bought de Guingand's sales pitch. A broad-front advance would be scuttled in favor of Monty's single-thrust concept. He ordered Omar Bradley to move Courtney Hodges's First Army farther north to support Montgomery's right flank, while George Patton's Third Army, below Hodges, would halt its advance and go over to the defensive.

Curiously, Patton, although he had been designated to mark time while Montgomery carried the ball to the goal line of Berlin, seemed to be happy with the outcome of the Versailles confab. "Things look better today," he wrote in his diary that night. "Ike still insists the main effort must be thrown to the British for the time being. However, he was more peevish with Montgomery than I have ever seen him. In fact, privately, he called Monty 'a clever son of a bitch!'"[7]

There was good reason for Patton's charitable outlook, for he and Bradley had no intention of standing by and watching Montgomery gain the glory for crossing the Rhine and dashing for Berlin. Now the two American generals began a subtle cat-and-mouse game with SHAEF. On September 25, Bradley wrote Eisenhower that he had directed Patton to halt in place and "to make only minor adjustments in his lines."

As Bradley knew would be the case, Patton seized on loopholes in the SHAEF directive to continue to attack, rather than to conduct a static defense. Patton's ruse de guerre was to reconnoiter with a battalion or even a regiment, instead of the customary squad or platoon. Once the larger unit had advanced a considerable distance, Patton would decide it was out on a limb and in danger of being cut off and destroyed; thus, he would reinforce the reconnaissance unit with another battalion or regiment. Then the Third Army leader would "sense" that the Germans were about to deal this reconnaissance force a heavy blow, so he would launch a full-blooded assault by an entire division to disrupt the enemy's attack preparations. That was Patton's interpretation of making "minor adjustments in his lines."[8]

Meanwhile, Bernard Montgomery was simmering over the failure of Market-Garden to catapult him over the Rhine. Had Eisenhower listened to him and appointed an overall ground commander—that is, Montgomery—the Holland setback never would have happened, he wrote to Alan Brooke.

In a letter to War Minister James Grigg, Monty claimed that the American armies had outrun their maintenance, supplies, and fuel, and, therefore, "flexibility has been lost along the entire front." Sourly, he added that "the whole show has been mucked up."

There was no doubt in Montgomery's mind as to who was the principal mucker-upper: The Allied supreme commander. "It is a great tragedy," Monty complained to Grigg. "I did what I could."

In early October, the rat race (as the GIs called it) from Normandy to the approaches to the border of the Third Reich slowed to a crawl. Eisenhower's mighty legion of 2.5 million men was bogged down along the 450-mile front, from the Swiss border to the North Sea. Wehrmacht generals had achieved a near miracle, establishing a firm defensive line in the wake of their calamitous debacle in Normandy. At SHAEF, the rose-colored eyeglasses worn in recent weeks disappeared.

Now Eisenhower was confronted by both stalemate and another haunting specter: A critical shortage of artillery ammunition, fuel, and other accoutrements of war. In brief, the Allied supply network had struck a snag of monumental proportions.

Most French railroads, which had been bombed heavily just prior to D-day, remained twisted wreckage. Nearly ninety trains loaded with artillery and mortar shells were stalled just east of Paris; no service troops were available to unload them.

Fifty percent of the ammunition, fuel, and other supplies badly needed at the front were sitting in Cherbourg or behind the gale-swept Normandy invasion beaches. To move these mountains of cargo for hundreds of miles to the front lines, a unique hauling operation called the Red Ball Express was created. Thousands of GI trucks, almost bumper to bumper, night and day barreled along a designated one-way road network, which was patrolled by military police to keep off civilian vehicles.

Although the Red Ball Express delivered thousands of tons of needed supplies, French thugs often hijacked trucks carrying food, cigarettes, and clothing earmarked for the fighting GIs and sold these goods on the thriving black market. Some American drivers deserted, taking their trucks and valuable cargo with them, and went into hiding after pocketing thousands of French francs by peddling their wares to native gangsters in Paris. Pilferage along the Red Ball route was gargantuan.

Under the round-the-clock pounding by the conveyor-belt stream of heavily loaded trucks, the designated roads, most of them constructed with cheap materials in the first place, became pockmarked with potholes—tens of thousands of them. Consequently, by late October, eight thousand trucks were sidelined with burned-out engines, broken axles, and other disabling defects.

Knowing that the Channel and Atlantic ports would be crucial to the Allies, Hitler had ordered their bypassed garrisons at Bordeaux, Dunkirk, Lorient, Brest, Saint-Nazaire, and Antwerp to hold them at all costs. So the Feldgrau, isolated hundreds of miles behind the front lines, were clinging tightly to these deep-water harbors.

Antwerp, the largest port in Europe and relatively close to the front lines, was crucial to Eisenhower. There would be no lessening of the supply logjam until Allied ships could dock there. Although the city had been captured by the British on September 4, its excellent dock facilities were useless because strong German forces were dug in for thirty miles along both sides of the Schledt estuary leading to the port.

At the urging of Eisenhower, General George Marshall flew to France on October 5 to seek a solution to the supplies crisis. After a two-day discussion with the supreme commander, Marshall flew to Brussels to confer with Bernard Montgomery. There the British field marshal abruptly told the American to leave his aides outside while the two men held a conversation in Monty's trailer.

Montgomery promptly launched a harangue against Eisenhower, claiming that "the armies [had] become separated nationally" since Ike had taken control of the land battles. Furthermore, Monty declared, "There is a lack of grip and operational direction. Our operations [under Eisenhower] have become ragged and disjointed, and we are now in a real mess."[9]

Marshall was irate. "I came pretty near to blowing off," he would write, "and overcame an urgent compulsion to whittle him down. It was very hard for me to restrain myself because I didn't think there was any logic in what [Monty] said but overwhelming egotism."[10]

At the same time, Eisenhower hoped to nudge Montgomery into ceasing his attacks in Holland and clearing the Schledt estuary. "Of all our operations along the entire front," he wrote Monty, "I consider Antwerp of first importance. Unless we have Antwerp producing by the middle of November, our entire operations will come to a standstill."[11]

British Admiral Bertram Ramsay, SHAEF's naval commander, then stirred up a hornet's nest by issuing a report claiming that Montgomery would be unable to clear the Schledt estuary until early November because of ammunition shortages. Ramsay's prognostication triggered a stinging reply from Montgomery to Eisenhower: "Request you ask Ramsay for me by what authority he makes wild statements to you concerning my operations, about which he can know nothing, repeat, nothing."[12]

Rumors of the supply-lines breakdown in Europe reached Washington, triggering a political scandal. There was the customary search for one or more scapegoats. So George Marshall, after his return from Europe, ordered his supply chief, Brehon Somervell, to send to France a top-notch officer to get the supply situation unsnarled and functioning efficiently. Somervell chose energetic Major General Henry S. Aurand for the troubleshooting mission.

Word that Aurand was on his way set off a flap in the inner clique at SHAEF. Officers who had been bickering with one another since before D-day now more or less forgot their squawks and joined ranks to stonewall the "outsider," whose task, it appeared, was to lop off some heads.

Aurand no doubt realized that he was to be given the cold-shoulder treatment when he arrived at Orly Airport in Paris late in October and found that no staff car was waiting to pick him up. The two-star general had to catch a taxi to Versailles. When he arrived at the Trianon Palace grounds, he had a hard time getting past the two military policemen.

Possibly as the result of staff intrigue, Eisenhower assigned the newcomer as deputy to Major General Henry Sayler, SHAEF's ordnance chief, even though Aurand outranked Sayler. The two men had been West Point classmates and longtime friends, but Sayler was cool toward Aurand.

Puzzled by the icy reception, Aurand left at the end of the day to go to the hotel he had been assigned. It was a ramshackle building far from the palace. His room was tiny, sparsely furnished, and unheated.

For the next two weeks, General Aurand toured supply depots of the American armies, seeking to remove the bottlenecks that were threatening Eisenhower's operations. On his return to Versailles, the inspecting officer issued a report that sent tremors through SHAEF: He suggested sacking a number of two- and three-star generals—including his old pal, Henry Sayler.

That startling report was the final straw for the SHAEF inside clique. On November 19, Aurand was summoned by Beetle Smith, who tersely told the unfortunate troubleshooter that, because of Aurand's stringent disapproval of the setup in Europe, he would be sent back home—as a colonel. No doubt Eisenhower had approved that action, because Smith did not have the authority to demote generals.

In the bewildered Aurand's moment of despair, Henry Sayler rode to his rescue. Aurand, no longer a threat to the SHAEF insiders, retained his two stars and was assigned a menial job as Normandy Base Section commander.[13]

In the meantime, Bernard Montgomery sent a harsh letter to Beetle Smith, declaring that Market-Garden had fallen short of its goal because of a lack of coordination between 21st Army Group and Omar Bradley's forces on his right. Monty implied that Eisenhower was to blame for that situation and renewed his demand that he be given control of land battles.

Eisenhower took the broadside to mean that the field marshal did not approve of his order to cease attacking in Holland and wipe out the German force blocking access to the port of Antwerp. Eisenhower, for the first time in his dealings with Montgomery, exploded. "The Antwerp operation does not involve the question of command in the slightest degree," he wrote to Monty. If the field marshal felt that Eisenhower's campaign plan was unsatisfactory, he added, "then indeed we have an issue that must be settled soon in the interest of future efficiency."

Therefore, the supreme commander continued, "It is our duty to refer the matter to higher authority for any action they may choose to take, however drastic."[14]

That higher authority was Franklin Roosevelt and Winston Churchill.

Perhaps influenced by the levelheaded Freddie de Guingand, Montgomery now realized that he had blundered. He rushed a written reply: "My dear Ike. I and all of us will weigh in one hundred percent to do what you want." Antwerp would be given the highest priority, Monty stressed, and he concluded his letter by saying, "You will hear no more on the subject of [ground] command from me."[15]

Within a few days, British and Canadian troops launched a series of amphibious assaults along the Schledt estuary, and some of the bloodiest, nastiest fighting of the war raged for two weeks before the German resistance was wiped out. Monty's men had paid a horrible price to open the port of Antwerp: 27,633 dead, wounded, or missing.

Dwight Eisenhower had been urging Franklin Roosevelt to officially recognize Charles de Gaulle—the man Roosevelt loved to hate—as President of the French provisional government, which de Gaulle had brought to France in the ten gliders that landed in Brittany the previous August. Eisenhower's recommendation was strictly a matter of military expediency; he wanted de Gaulle to take charge of liberated France to prevent rioting, looting, chaos, anarchy—even civil war—from erupting behind Allied lines.

Eisenhower, in essence, had undercut Roosevelt, who no longer could ignore de Gaulle or pretend that France was an occupied nation run by SHAEF. So on October 23, the United States announced that it was formally recognizing de Gaulle's provisional government. In the lengthy clash between two towering egos, the persistent French general finally had triumphed over the stubborn American President.

All the while, vicious fighting was raging at the front. Each day, hundreds of Allied soldiers were shipped to the rear in body bags for burial in temporary, makeshift cemeteries. Every twenty-four hours, two thousand more combat troops were evacuated with wounds.

Although the sea approach to Antwerp had been cleared, supply ships would be unable to dock until late November, because the Germans had extensively mined the Schledt estuary. Icy gales pierced the light field jackets of the Americans and British combat soldiers while a million overcoats lay in the holds of a ship lying off Antwerp. Torrential rains created oceans of mud, but the combat soldiers were deprived of galoshes, many of which had been stolen from Red Ball trucks and sold on the black market.

Meanwhile, in Paris, thousands of General J. C. H. Lee's Communications Zone soldiers had descended en masse. Lee had taken over 651 hotels. He ensconced himself in luxury at the posh Hotel Majestic, which had hot running water and impeccably tailored French flunkies. Just in case the need to entertain arose, Lee also reserved several suites in the palatial King George V Hotel.

Eisenhower's rear-area generals had staked out the finest Paris mansions for their own use and often could be found mingling at cocktail parties at elegant hotels and restaurants. An angry supreme commander ordered Lee to pull his thousands of men out of Paris to less exotic surroundings, then told his top combat commanders at the front that he was "chasing the SOS [Services of Supply] out of Paris" and making the City of Light a rest center for fighting men on brief leaves.

Lee ignored Eisenhower's order, and swarms of SOS men in neatly pressed dress uniforms continued to crowd Paris bistros and other nightspots. Nearly everyone—Lee's men and French civilians—smoked American cigarettes, which were intended for the GIs but had wound up on the French black market.

While most of the world focused on the war in Europe, halfway around the globe dramatic developments were unfolding in the China-Burma-India theater of operations. The situation involved bickering between a prominent American general and the Chinese strongman he had been sent to help.

CHAPTER 32

Vinegar Joe, Peanut, and Dragon Lady

"WHAT DO I THINK OF Generalissimo Chiang Kai-shek?" U.S. Lieutenant General Joseph "Vinegar Joe" Stilwell mused to Theodore White, a reporter for *Time* magazine covering the China beat. Stilwell, long known for his blunt opinions, peered through his thick lenses at the correspondent and exclaimed, "Peanut is an ignorant, illiterate, superstitious, peasant, son of a bitch!"[1]

Peanut was the derogatory nickname that Stilwell had pinned on Chiang, the Chinese strongman, after the American general had been sent to the Far East in early 1942 to train and inject discipline into the Chinese army. It was now October 1944, and Vinegar Joe had just been tipped off by General George Marshall, an old friend and staunch booster, that Chiang, after two years of effort, had succeeded in coercing President Roosevelt to sack Stilwell.

Roosevelt long had been aware of the friction between Chiang and Stilwell. At a 1943 strategy session in Washington, Roosevelt had felt compelled to admonish Stilwell to cease referring to Chiang as Peanut.

Many Americans in China considered Madame Chiang, a black-haired, stylish beauty who had been educated in the United States and held Western ideas, to be the power behind the throne. At the Cairo summit conference in 1943, Madame Chiang had taken her place with Roosevelt, Churchill, and other Anglo-American leaders. Her outspoken views angered the British, who felt she was "meddling in things that did not concern her."

Joe Stilwell was not alone among Allied military leaders in his scorn for her husband, the fifty-seven-year-old generalissimo. British Field Marshal Alan Brooke, after meeting Chiang for the first time at Cairo, penned in his diary, "The Generalissimo reminded me of cross between a pine-marten and a ferret. A shrewd, foxy sort of face. Evidently with no grasp of war in its largest aspects, but determined to get the best of all bargains."[2]

After one contentious session at Cairo, Brooke wrote acidly: "Madame Chiang was a study in herself. A queer character in which sex and politics seemed to predominate, both being used to achieve her ends." Brooke later would write, "She was the only woman amongst a very large gathering of men and was determined to bring into action all the charms nature had blessed her with."[3]

A convoluted chain of events had led to President Roosevelt's decision to fire Stilwell. Shortly after Pearl Harbor had been bombed, Roosevelt summoned Hugh Drum, the army's senior three-star general, to come to the White House from Governor's Island in New York harbor, where he was commander of First Army. Collecting a large entourage of staff officers, Drum, who thought he would be appointed commander of America's first overseas expeditionary force, was stunned after entering the Oval Office. Roosevelt had another job in mind for him: He would go to China as chief of staff to Chiang Kai-shek. It was the President's intention to boost the Chinese general as a world leader.

Drum was hardly enthusiastic about the prospect. China, with its seven hundred million people, was regarded as being in the backwaters of the war by Allied military professionals. Politics, not strategy, would dominate all discussions with Chiang, Drum knew. It would be a dead-end, no-win assignment.

After meeting with George Marshall in the Munitions Building, Drum put forth a counterproposal. Instead of being a nanny for Chiang Kai-shek, he suggested that he be put in charge of a major buildup of ground and air forces in the Southeast Asia region. Such a congregation was impossible, Marshall replied. Roosevelt and Churchill already had agreed that the major war effort would be against Hitler and Nazi Germany.

Drum persisted to argue, claiming that there were "certain inconsistencies and indignities relative to command arrangements," implying that the China post was below his stature.

"Damn it," Marshall exploded, America was at war, and he expected his generals "to submerge their personal ambitions and egos and do the needed job assigned to them."[4]

Even before the testy confrontation, Drum and Marshall had been at odds. When Roosevelt had to choose an army chief of staff in 1939, the two candidates were Hugh Drum and George Marshall. Drum lost out. Now, perhaps, he sensed that Marshall was trying to keep him from a major command out of long-standing enmity by exiling him to China as handmaiden to Chiang Kai-shek.

Due to his seniority on the army-rank totem pole, Drum could not be ordered to China. His name was withdrawn, and Marshall searched for a new candidate.

Meanwhile, Drum, who had a lofty opinion of himself not shared by most other American generals, refused to drop his demand that he be appointed commander of a large buildup of forces in Southeast Asia. Going over the head of Marshall, he wrote to Secretary of War Henry Stimson that he "would be more valuable to the country with a mission involving larger responsibilities . . . and would be lost by being involved in the heart of China in a minor effort of little decisive consequence."[5]

Stimson, who had been a colonel of artillery in the First World War, was appalled by Drum's obvious grasp for power and agreed with Marshall that someone else would have to be found for the China mission.

Marshall and Stimson now focused on Joe Stilwell, who had served for ten years in China, first as a military attaché and then as a battalion commander with the U.S. 15th Infantry Regiment. Over the years, he had developed a deep affection for the Chinese peasants but only distaste for the political leaders.

Learning through the Washington grapevine that he was being considered for the China post, Stilwell scrawled in his diary, "Me? No, thank you. [The Chinese] remember me as a small-fry colonel that they kicked around. They saw me on foot in the mud, consorting with coolies, riding soldier trains."[6]

Despite his lack of enthusiasm for the assignment, Stilwell was chosen for the China mission. Like a true soldier he told Henry Stimson, "I will go where I am sent."[7]

Joe Stilwell was a curious choice. On a confidential list, George Marshall rated him as the army's best infantry commander. Yet he was being dispatched to an assignment where diplomacy and tact would be paramount—and Vinegar Joe had neither of those traits. "Joe's a fighting man, not a political conspirator," an admiring general accurately observed.

Complicating Stilwell's assignment was the fact that he would hold down three jobs at once: Chief of staff to Chiang Kai-shek, commander of the small number of American troops in China, and administrator of lend-lease, an arrangement whereby the United States shipped the accoutrements of war to Chiang's forces with no real intention of eventual payment.

Stilwell reached Chungking, Chiang's capital, on March 6, 1942, and discovered that the veteran Japanese Fifteenth Army had conquered much of Burma, adjoining China to the southwest, and were threatening to cut the Burma Road, the chief supply route from the United States to Chiang's forces in China. Built by thousands of laborers known as coolies, the Burma Road would become a symbol of Chinese resistance.

In less than a week, Vinegar Joe, a man of action, collected a ragtag force of Chinese, Indian, and British troops and tried to block the Japanese advance northward through the Burma jungles. Wearing an old campaign hat and jungle fatigues and clutching a rifle, Stilwell trudged up and down the forward positions, urging his men to stand fast when the Japanese approached. He was shocked and angered to discover that his Chinese contingents had fled northward before the first shot had been fired. Later, the general would learn that Chiang had instructed his commanders to pull back to avoid losses—in violation of Stilwell's orders.

Disaster ensued. Outnumbered, outgunned, in disarray, the Allied force had to make its way out of Burma in tiny bands. Stilwell himself led a hodgepodge group of some 115 men over towering mountains and thick jungles to safety in India.

Never again would Vinegar Joe trust Chiang, who had withdrawn his troops at a critical moment and left Stilwell and the others to try to halt the oncoming Japanese tide and fend for themselves. Eventually reaching Delhi in India, Stilwell agreed to hold a press conference. Typically, he bluntly ticked off the reasons for the catastrophe in Burma.

"I claim we took one hell of a beating!" the general told the correspondents. "We got run out of Burma, and it's humiliating as hell!"[8]

Stilwell's unvarnished remarks hit the home front like a blockbuster bomb. Only now, in June 1942—six months after Pearl Harbor—did the American people grasp that the Japanese were not going to be pushovers, and that the war in the Pacific was going to be long and bloody.

In the months ahead, Stilwell, who did not shock easily, was stunned to learn of crass double-dealing by the Chinese Communist leader, Mao Tse-tung, whose sizable force of 150,000 men was supposed to be joining with Chiang's troops in the war with the Japanese. Based in northwest China, Mao's guerrilla army reached an unofficial truce with the invaders, which permitted the Japanese to withdraw troops and hurl them against Chiang's forces in central and southern China. Mao's scheme was to let the Japanese decimate Chiang's army so that the Communists could seize power in China after the war.[9]

Meanwhile, Vinegar Joe was locking horns with a new adversary: Major General Claire L. Chennault, lanky and leathery, who had hit it off well with Chiang and become the Chinese leader's fair-haired boy. A pioneer pilot in the fledgling Army Aviation Corps after World War I, Chennault retired in 1936 as the result of impaired hearing. After the Japanese warlords cooked up an excuse to invade China in 1937, Chennault was wooed to China (at a hefty salary) by Chiang and became a colonel in the Chinese Air Force.

In 1940, Chennault left China for the United States and recruited one hundred experienced army, navy, and marine pilots and a like number of engineers to maintain equipment. These mercenary combat fighters were melded into a group known as the Flying Tigers. Although most of the pilots were free spirits and action-ready, Chiang shelled out big bucks to lure and keep them. Each pilot was paid a whopping $750 per month (today's equivalent of $10,000), with an additional $500 bonus for each Japanese plane blasted from the sky.

In mid-1941, the Flying Tigers became operational. Soon, they were the scourge of the Imperial Air Force, credited with shooting down more than three hundred Japanese airplanes during six months of combat. After Pearl Harbor, Chennault was recalled to active duty by the U.S. Army Air Corps, promoted to major general, and put in command of the Fourteenth Air Force, whose nucleus was the gung-ho pilots of the Flying Tigers.

By mid-1942, the Fourteenth Air Force was strong and experienced enough that General Chennault, in a secret meeting with Chiang Kai-shek, claimed that he could wipe out the Japanese air force in China, demolish its widespread supply network, and knock the Japanese out of the war. All that he needed, Chiang was assured, was one hundred more fighter planes and thirty bombers.

Chiang was delighted. Under the Chennault plan, American pilots would smash the Japanese military machine in China, and Chiang would not have to expend a single soldier in the twenty-two Chinese divisions that Joe Stilwell had been training for offensive action. Chiang plotted to acquire the aircraft, fuel, and spare parts that Chennault would require to defeat Japan on the cheap.

For that purpose, the vivacious and ambitious Madame Chiang was brought into the machination. Her crucial role was to persuade the Washington power structure to accept her good friend Claire Chennault's plan for an inexpensive and virtually bloodless victory in China by utilizing American airpower alone to the exclusion of the Stilwell-trained Chinese army.

In February 1943, China's First Lady flew to Washington; her cover story was that she had come to seek medical treatment. Arriving to a fanfare of media publicity, Madame Chiang became the guest of Franklin and Eleanor Roosevelt at the White House and was feted at a series of gala cocktail parties. Washington's media fell in love with the Chinese visitor and affectionately labeled her the Dragon Lady after a sultry comic-strip heroine.

Newspaper, magazine, and newsreel stories focused not only on Madame Chiang but also on her husband's gallant and courageous fighting forces, which, as Stilwell had soon learned, were doing anything but fighting the Japanese.

Madame Chiang mesmerized Washington's leading lights. Secretary of War Henry Stimson described her in his diary as "a most attractive and beguiling lady."[10]

The Dragon Lady was both beguiling and persuasive. President Roosevelt told George Marshall that he wanted Chennault "to be given every opportunity to do what he believes he can do."

While charming Washington's elite, Madame Chiang must have gotten in her licks against Joe Stilwell, the fighting man who had been cast out of character as a diplomat. On March 8, 1943, the President sent a memo to Marshall: "Stilwell has exactly the wrong approach in dealing with Generalissimo Chiang [by] talking to him in stern tones. One cannot exact commitments from him the way we might do from the Sultan of Morocco."[11]

Perhaps Roosevelt would not have been so harshly critical of Stilwell had he known that the generalissimo was not using most of the massive lend-lease aid being sent to him in the fight against the Japanese. Rather, Chiang was hoarding it to eventually make war against a competitor for postwar power in China, Mao Tse-tung's Communist army.

A few weeks after the Dragon Lady recovered from her "illness" and returned to China, Roosevelt again went gunning for Stilwell. In a memo to Marshall, he suggested that Stilwell himself might be ill. Vinegar Joe had a pair of powerful boosters, however: Marshall and Henry Stimson. The secretary of war replied to the President that Stilwell was saddled with "the toughest task of the war," adding that "he is the only man I know who can carry that big job through."[12]

Presumably advised that he was under fire from the White House, Stilwell flew to Washington, and on May 14, 1943, he and the Combined Chiefs met with Roosevelt to thrash out the situation in China. The British had no intention of getting bogged down in a land war in China, so they favored Chennault's bomb-'em-to-hell air campaign. Marshall, on the other hand, argued that if Chennault's bombers and fighters began inflicting serious damage, the Japanese would launch a land offensive to seize his airfields. To protect those fields, the army chief declared, Stilwell would have to have adequate forces.

In the end, Roosevelt conjured up an Alice in Wonderland compromise. Since Stilwell's Chinese army required twenty-seven hundred tons of supplies a month and Chennault's air force forty-seven hundred tons a month, the President recommended that seven thousand tons be flown monthly from India to China. He breezily ignored the fact that there never had been more than a total of twenty-five hundred tons shipped in any one month.

After the conference had concluded, Roosevelt held a brief private session with his two warring China hands.

"What do you think of the generalissimo?" the President asked Stilwell.

"He's a vacillating, tricky, undependable old scoundrel who never keeps his word," Vinegar Joe snapped.[13]

Turning to Chennault, Roosevelt asked, "And you?"

"Sir, I think the generalissimo is one of the two or three greatest military and political leaders in the world today," the veteran pilot replied.

On his long flight back to China, Stilwell had time to reflect on the tangled web of politics in which he found himself caught in Chungking. His frustration boiled over. "What corruption, intrigue, obstruction, delay, double-crossing, hate, jealousy, and skullduggery we have had to wade through," he wrote in his diary. "What a cesspool. What bigotry and ignorance and black ingratitude."[14]

Joe Stilwell was fighting a losing battle against the Allied hierarchy. Chiang Kai-shek may indeed have been an undependable scoundrel who never kept his word, but to President Roosevelt he was the head of a huge country and would be needed by him after the war. In addition, the generalissimo had been played up in the American press as a Chinese George Washington of impeccable integrity, and the Dragon Lady had been almost beatified. American public opinion was on the side of the Chinese leader.

As far as the White House was concerned, Vinegar Joe was expendable.

Not long after Stilwell arrived back in Chungking, Senator Albert "Happy" Chandler demonstrated that he, too, had been smitten by the Dragon Lady's charm and guile. "General Chennault, the finest air officer in the world today, must receive the five hundred aircraft he needs to win the war [in China]," Chandler declared on the Senate floor. "If we would send them to China we might be able to save those staunch, determined, Christian, God-fearing, good Chinese, the generalissimo and his wife."[15]

A few weeks later, the Japanese in China launched a major offensive that overran almost all of Chiang's coastline, including Claire Chennault's air bases—

just as George Marshall had predicted. Even while the Japanese tide was flooding huge areas of east China, Chiang adamantly refused to give Joe Stilwell, the officer George Marshall considered to be America's best infantry leader, operational command of the Chinese army. Instead, the generalissimo took charge himself and pulled back his troops as the Japanese advanced.

On September 16, 1944, Stilwell radioed the Pentagon his blunt assessment of the situation in China. Chiang's troops were poorly led and had lost their fighting spirit—if indeed they had ever had it. Rather than battle the Japanese, Stilwell reported, the Chinese army robbed the peasants.[16]

George Marshall was infuriated by Chiang's refusal to take action against the Japanese, and he drafted a strong measure for Roosevelt to send to the Chinese leader. The President signed it. If the generalissimo refused to cooperate with Stilwell, Roosevelt warned, "he would have to accept the consequences." In order to avoid an enormous debacle, the message concluded, Chiang should place his armies under Stilwell's command.

Two days later, to his enormous delight, Vinegar Joe had the satisfaction of delivering Roosevelt's reprimand to Chiang. That night the American general gleefully told his diary, "The harpoon hit the little bastard right in the solar plexus and went right through him."[17]

Within days, the wily Chiang made a counterproposal to Roosevelt. "Your policies will be executed without delay as soon as you relieve Stilwell and replace him with an officer better equipped to discharge his duties," the generalissimo said.[18]

Stilwell was alerted by George Marshall that the executioner had his ax in hand. Two days later, Stilwell's head fell as a matter of political expediency. Roosevelt foresaw Chiang as leader of a major power in the looming United Nations organization and did not want to risk diminishing the generalissimo's global reputation.

Peanut and the Dragon Lady had triumphed.

Just before dawn on October 20, 1944, the same day that Vinegar Joe Stilwell received word that he had been sacked, General Douglas MacArthur stood on the bridge of the cruiser *Nashville* and looked out at the powerful armada of 738 ships lying off the central Philippines island of Leyte. Minutes later, a mighty roar echoed across Leyte Gulf as scores of warships sent a fusillade of shells screaming onto the landing beaches and the thick underbrush on the hills to the rear. When the thunderous bombardment lifted, hundreds of American assault troops stormed ashore.

MacArthur climbed into a tiny Higgins boat and landed on the heels of the assault waves. Japanese snipers, hidden in trees or crouched in foxholes, were steadily picking off GIs. A conspicuous figure in his gold-braided cap and khaki uniform, the general stood on a low knoll and calmly lit his pipe, then strolled inland.

Returning to the beach that afternoon, MacArthur, with the crack of Japanese rifles echoing in the background, stood before a portable radio microphone to deliver a two-minute address that would carry throughout the Philippines. A torrential rain erupted. Offshore, the big navy guns barked. Outwardly serene, the general fought off emotion as he began to speak: "People of the Philippines, *I have returned!"*

With only a toehold on Leyte, MacArthur turned his attention to officially restoring the government of the commonwealth to the Filipinos. At noon on A-day plus two, the supreme commander stood on the steps of the Commonwealth Building in Tacloban, a city a few miles from the invasion beaches, to swear in Philippine President Sergio Osmeña. A shy, reticent man, the sixty-six-year-old Osmeña was known as The Sphinx by his political foes. MacArthur considered him a lightweight and held him in low regard.

Along with former President Manuel Quezon, Osmeña had escaped by submarine from Japanese-surrounded Corregidor in March 1942. The two men eventually reached the United States, where they set up a Philippine government in exile. Quezon, a peppery, decisive individual, died on August 1, 1944, and Vice President Osmeña became President. A short time later, Franklin Roosevelt summoned Osmeña and asked him to land with the first troops to return to the Philippines. Roosevelt believed that Osmeña's presence on his home soil would win over any native groups that might tend to be hostile to the Americans.

Now Osmeña was duly installed as President of the Philippine Commonwealth, and Tacloban was designated the temporary capital pending the liberation of Manila, on Luzon island to the north.

MacArthur and Osmeña spoke over a broadcast network that carried throughout the Philippines, and troopers of the U.S. 1st Cavalry Division hoisted the American and Philippine flags simultaneously on adjoining poles.

If there had been any doubt in Sergio Osmeña's mind that his role in the overall picture was to be something other than a figurehead for American goals, it was quickly erased. Supreme Commander MacArthur and his brass climbed into jeeps after the inauguration ceremony and sped off in a swirl of dust. Left behind was a bewildered President Osmeña, who not only lacked a ride but didn't even know where he would sleep that night.

While MacArthur's men battled the Japanese on Leyte and then leaped closer to Manila with an amphibious assault on the island of Mindoro in early December 1944, Adolf Hitler was scheming to give the complacent Allies a gigantic jolt from which, he felt certain, they would never recover.

CHAPTER 33

Taken by Total Surprise

IN LATE NOVEMBER 1944, four-star German General Sepp Dietrich was back from the Western Front, where his Sixth SS Panzer Army had been battling the Americans to a standstill along the flooded Roer River west of Cologne. During a brief respite before a special operation Adolf Hitler had in mind for him, Dietrich was chatting amiably with old friends and guests at a convivial party being held at a once-plush Berlin hotel.

A burly man with a rough voice, Dietrich had been a sergeant in the Kaiser's army in World War I and a street brawler for the Nazi party after that conflict. Ever since the early 1930s, Hitler had continued to reward his loyal supporter, finally elevating him to command the Sixth SS Panzer Army. Most Wehrmacht professionals felt that Dietrich was capable of running only a division at best. Hitler knew of his friend's limitations, so he made certain that Dietrich's staff was loaded with capable military brains.

Among those present at the gala Berlin soiree was SS Lieutenant General Hermann Fegelein, who was a brother-in-law of sorts to the Führer. Fegelein, renowned in Berlin as a womanizer and a boozer, was the husband of Gretl Braun, the plump sister of Hitler's mistress, Eva.

When Gretl and Hermann had taken the vows of marriage, she was well on her way to motherhood. After the union, Fegelein skyrocketed up the Nazi pecking order.

General Fegelein was accompanied to the festivities by his latest mistress, a beautiful, bosomy Irishwoman in her midthirties whose husband, twenty-six years her senior, was a high-ranking diplomat at the Hungarian Embassy in Berlin. Vivacious and flirtatious, she was clad in an extremely low-cut evening gown that appeared to be inviting a mishap at any moment.

She was clearly well connected in Nazi power circles. Prior to her liaison with Fegelein, she had been the mistress of Josef Goebbels, Hitler's minister of propaganda. Goebbels had recently kicked her out in favor of a new conquest. If there was a bigger wolf in Berlin than Fegelein, those in Nazi social circles agreed, it had to be Goebbels.

At the Berlin party, the beautiful Irishwoman spent much of her time in the company of Sepp Dietrich, who seemed to be flattered by her attention and fulsome praise. Reinforced by champagne, he eagerly responded to her seemingly idle questions as to what he was doing in Berlin with a war going on and where he was headed after he left the capital.

Allied intelligence also should have been interested in the answers to those questions. After the bitter fighting in the mud and cold along the Roer River, Dietrich's powerful Sixth SS Panzer Army appeared to have vanished. In its complacent mood, however, SHAEF seemed little worried about the disappearance.

Twelve hours after the last guest had stumbled out of the party at the Berlin hotel, the Hungarian diplomat's wife flashed word to SHAEF that the Sixth SS Panzer Army was assembling secretly behind the Western Front opposite a Belgian region in the Ardennes Forest known as the Schnee Eifel. Leading that army would be Colonel General Sepp Dietrich.[1]

Known in British intelligence circles by the code name Mata O'Hara, the Irish beauty had been risking her life to slip information to the Allies. But her latest report, the most significant of all, was pigeonholed by an unknown SHAEF functionary who did not so much as investigate its authenticity.

Perhaps one reason SHAEF intelligence paid no heed to the alarming disclosure was the fact that the seventy-five-mile-long Ardennes sector had become known as the Ghost Front. Thickly wooded, hilly, with deep gorges and few roads capable of supporting tanks and heavy vehicles, the Ardennes was regarded by Omar Bradley as impassable. Taking a calculated risk, he thinly manned the region with a combination of newly arrived green divisions and veteran outfits decimated and exhausted from recent brutal fighting in the Huertgen Forest, just north of the Ardennes.

The Germans used the Ghost Front for the same purpose. In early December, American dogfaces and German stubblehoppers (as the infantry soldiers called themselves) were existing more or less peacefully within rifle distance of one another. An unspoken gentlemen's agreement had evolved: You don't shoot at us and we won't shoot at you. Each side sent out occasional patrols, but it was generally quiet except for the rustling of the tall fir trees in the wind.

Few, if any, of the American soldiers were aware that German armies had invaded Belgium by pounding through this same region in 1870, again in 1914, and more recently in 1940.

Forty-eight hours after the Hungarian diplomat's wife had sent her message, Sepp Dietrich was gathered along with fifty-three other field marshals and generals on the Western Front in a gloomy, chilly room in a huge concrete bunker near Ziegenberg outside Frankfurt. They had been summoned to the bunker on this day, December 12, without being told why.

While the Wehrmacht brass listened in stony silence, Hitler unveiled an audacious plan for snatching victory out of the jaws of defeat in the West.

Code-named Wacht am Rein (Watch on the Rhine), the plan had been created in the utmost secrecy in Berlin during recent weeks. It had been conceived by the Führer.

Wacht am Rein would hit where the Allies would least expect it, along the Ghost Front. Two German armies—the Sixth SS Panzer and the Fifth Panzer—would smash through thinly held American lines, then tank-tipped spearheads would race generally northwest, cross the Meuse River, seize huge Allied supply and fuel dumps at Liege, and continue to Antwerp, reaching that crucial port in a week. If successful, that drive would split the British in the north and the Americans in the south.

"The American public will never stand for the loss of several hundred thousand of its young men in one rapid, totally unexpected stroke," Hitler told his commanders. "They will scream demands for a negotiated peace."

For nearly an hour, the Führer ranted about the Allied leaders. Winston Churchill was an uncouth, unprincipled drunkard and instigator of a "holy war" against the Third Reich. His partner in crime, Franklin Roosevelt, was a dastardly schemer who, if lucky, would be thrown in jail by his countrymen after Hitler's looming counteroffensive through the Ardennes.

During the first two weeks of December, Allied intelligence continued to be lulled to sleep by its own glowing reports that the Wehrmacht was incapable of offensive action. Even the sudden cessation of V-1 buzz bombs that had been fired regularly for two months at the port of Antwerp caused no concern. This clue that the Germans had something significant brewing behind their lines was brushed off. The German railroads were simply overloaded because of heavy Allied bombings, and thus the Wehrmacht was having a difficult time bringing up the flying bombs to launching sites, went the explanation.

The most ominous signal of all—the fact that Ultra had dried up—also failed to trigger alarm in the Allied camp. Hitler had begun to suspect that his "unbreakable" Enigma code had been cracked. He directed that all orders, including his own, be sent out by land lines or couriers.[2]

Allied intelligence had become overdependent on Ultra not only as its primary source of information, but also as confirmation of other less reliable and trusted sources. But when Enigma messages suddenly vanished from the airwaves, no warning was issued.

By the night of December 15, unbeknown to either Omar Bradley or the teenage GI on outpost duty, the Germans, in a masterpiece of logistics, had moved up behind the Ghost Front some 650,000 troops, nearly fifteen hundred panzers, and more than nineteen hundred artillery pieces. The feat was equivalent to transporting the entire population of San Francisco, together with its vehicles, for many miles without anyone else in California knowing of the massive movement.

In the Allied camp, heady optimism and the Christmas spirit filled the air. On December 15, at his headquarters in Hasselt, Belgium, Bernard Montgomery signed a situation report compiled by his 21st Army Group intelligence: "The enemy is at present fighting a defensive campaign on all fronts. His situation is such that he cannot stage major offensive operations. Furthermore, at all costs, [the enemy] has to prevent the war from entering on a mobile phase. He has not the transport or the petrol that would be necessary for [offensive] operations. . . . The enemy is in a bad way."

That same day, Montgomery wrote to Eisenhower, asking permission to "hop over to England" on December 23 to spend Christmas with his son. "I have not seen him since D-day," the field marshal said.[3]

With Monty's letter was a reminder that fifteen months earlier, in North Africa, Eisenhower had bet him that the war against Germany would be over by Christmas 1944. The field marshal was good-naturedly demanding payment. "I still have nine days to go," Eisenhower replied.[4]

At Trianon Palace, Eisenhower was enjoying a shower of congratulations. Earlier that day, December 15, he had been notified that his promotion to five-star rank had been confirmed by the U.S. Senate. The elevation made the supreme commander equal in rank to his subordinate, Bernard Montgomery.[5]

For nearly two months, George Marshall had been strongly opposing efforts in Congress to create new five-star ranks for eight generals and admirals, including the army chief of staff. As far back as November 1942, Admiral Ernest King, the chief of naval operations, had been pushing for fifth stars for a handful of admirals and generals, supposedly to deal with British military leaders on an equal basis. Marshall disagreed with his argument, maintaining that the U.S. Joint Chiefs were already on an equal basis with the British Joint Chiefs, no matter how many stars men in both groups wore on their collars.

In the fall of 1944, while the five-star bill was wending its way through the congressional maze, Franklin Roosevelt, pressured by Ernest King and navy boosters in the Senate, joined in backing a proposal that would elevate his top eight military commanders. Roosevelt, in turn, converted Secretary of War Stimson, so it was now just a matter of time until the Senate acted on the bill.

Meanwhile, in the Pentagon and in the Senate, there was much discussion over the title to be bestowed on the recipients. Many favored field marshal, but that suggestion was dropped when it was realized how absurd it would sound for the army chief of staff to be known as Field Marshal Marshall. Also rejected was the proposed title arch-general: It sounded too much like arch-criminal. Marshall himself came up with the title that was finally adopted—General of the Army.

On December 16, as the inky blackness of a cold night commenced to dissolve into an overcast gray on O-day for Wacht am Rein, the quiet along the Ghost

Front was abruptly pierced by the roar of hundreds of German artillery pieces. Forty minutes later, swarms of white-sheeted Feldgrau, backed by hundreds of panzers, plunged into the thinly held and disoriented American positions and broke loose into Belgium. Total surprise had been achieved. The road to Antwerp—and a stunning German victory—seemed to be wide open.

That morning in Versailles, Dwight Eisenhower and his staff, unaware of the German offensive in the Ardennes, were attending the wedding of his orderly, Sergeant Mickey McKeogh, and WAC Sergeant Pearlie Hargreaves. The nuptials took place at the Louis XIV Chapel, the first wedding held there since the eighteenth century.

After a reception for the newlyweds that afternoon, Eisenhower returned to his office to receive a visitor, Omar Bradley, who had come to complain about the dwindling manpower situation. Minutes later, Kenneth Strong, SHAEF's intelligence chief, came into the room to inform the two generals that the Germans had launched an attack in the Ardennes.

Eisenhower and Bradley discussed the implication of the report, and they agreed that the Germans were conducting local attacks intended to slow heavy American assaults then taking place to the north and south of the Ardennes. To play it safe, Eisenhower told Bradley to shift an armored division down from the north to a locale just above the Ghost Front and to send another armored division up from the south.

Neither general was alarmed by the news from the Ardennes. That night, together with two other generals, they consumed what was left of the champagne from the wedding reception, polished off a bottle of Scotch, and played five rubbers of bridge.[6]

Two days after Adolf Hitler struck in the Ardennes, Bernard Montgomery sent a telegram to Alan Brooke: "The situation in the American area is not good. There is a definite lack of grip and control and no one has a clear picture of the situation."[7]

Now Monty seized on the German breakthrough to pound the drums again for his taking charge of the land battle. "The Americans have been cut clean in half and the Germans can reach the Meuse without opposition," he informed Brooke. With Bradley's command bisected, Montgomery contacted Major General John Whitely, the senior British officer at SHAEF. Eisenhower, Monty stated, should place all troops—American and British—north of the breakthrough under Montgomery's command.

In Belgium and Luxembourg, the roads and fields and forests of the Ardennes shook and heaved under the weight of the thrashings of thousands of tanks and vehicles and tens of thousands of soldiers on both sides. Chaos—and, in some cases, panic—prevailed in the ranks of the disorganized Americans. Surprised, outgunned, and far outnumbered, other tiny bands of GIs stood and fought and died, seldom knowing precisely where they were.

Three hundred miles from the flaming Ardennes, Eisenhower felt that he had sufficient intelligence on the German breakthrough to launch countermeasures. He ordered his top American commanders to meet him the next day, December 19, in Verdun, France.[8] The conference was held in an old French army barracks.

"The present situation will be regarded as one of opportunity for us," Eisenhower declared. "There will be only cheerful faces at this table!"

George Patton quickly picked up the theme. "Hell, the goddamned Kraut has stuck his prick in a meat-grinder," he exclaimed. "And I've got hold of the handle! Let's let the bastards go clear to Paris, then we can really chew 'em up and spit 'em out!"[9]

Confronted by the haunting specter of an Allied disaster—even the loss of the war—Eisenhower, in steady, measured tones, laid down the counteractions that would be taken to blunt, and then hurl back, the mighty German avalanche. Each shoulder of the seventy-five-mile gap torn in American lines would be firmed up with battle-tested divisions to prevent widening of the breech. Since the Germans were bent on smashing through to Antwerp, the Americans would go on the defensive along the northern portion of what the generals were now calling "the bulge." At the same time, Patton would pivot his Third Army, which had been attacking to the east, and launch an assault northward into the lower side of the deep German penetration.

As rapidly as Eisenhower had moved in countering the heavy German blow, it was not fast enough for the British. "Montgomery, Brooke, and Churchill all came at us like sharks at a shipwreck!" Omar Bradley would recall.

Back in Versailles the morning after the strategy meeting, the first shark to telephone the supreme commander was the British Prime Minister, who proceeded to give unsolicited and gratuitous advice on how to react to the surprise offensive. It seemed to Eisenhower that Churchill was parroting the views of Alan Brooke, who had telephoned the Prime Minister to remind him, in essence, "I told you so!" Brooke's inference was clear: Eisenhower was to blame for the American debacle because he had not accepted Brooke's (and Montgomery's) advice and appointed Monty commander of ground operations.

While Eisenhower had been in Verdun, Brigadier Kenneth Strong and General John Whitely, both loyal team players at SHAEF, drew up a recommendation that Montgomery be put in charge of all forces above the breakthrough, because the German penetration had cut communications between Courtney Hodges's First Army and Bradley's headquarters in Luxembourg.

Strong and Whitely took their proposal to Beetle Smith, who became infuriated. He felt that such a command shift would be interpreted as meaning that the Americans had to turn to Montgomery to pull their chestnuts out of the fire. Smith shouted at the two to "get the hell out of here!"[10]

When Smith calmed down, he became convinced of the *military* need for the change and telephoned Omar Bradley to get his viewpoint. Bradley replied that the shift would discredit the American high command.

During a conference with key aides at Trianon Palace on the morning of December 20, Eisenhower concluded that the command shift would have to be made, even though American pride would suffer.

Eisenhower put in a call to Bradley to tell him of the restructure. "By God, Ike, I cannot be responsible to the American people if you do this," Bradley bristled. "If you do it, I'll resign!"[11]

Eisenhower's face flushed with surprise and anger. Bradley had never before spoken to him in that tone. After pausing for a few moments he said, "Brad, I, not you, am responsible to the American people. So your resignation means absolutely nothing."

Bradley continued to protest. Eisenhower responded, "Well, Brad, those are my orders."[12]

After the conversation, Eisenhower called Montgomery at Hasselt. The telephone connection was faulty, the line crackled, and Eisenhower had to shout and repeat his words on occasion. Monty, however, heard all that he wanted to hear: He had been put in command of the northern sector of what newspapers had labeled the Battle of the Bulge. This change meant that Bill Simpson's Ninth Army and Courtney Hodges's First Army would be taken from Bradley and turned over to Montgomery. Consequently, the field marshal had in his command eighteen U.S. divisions in addition to the sixteen British divisions in his own 21st Army Group.[13]

No sooner had Montgomery hung up the receiver than he fired off a message to Brooke to break the good news. "[Eisenhower] was very excited," he said, "and it was difficult to understand what he was talking about. He roared into the telephone, speaking very fast." Monty said that all he wanted to know was that he had been given command of two United States armies, and added, "Ike then went on talking wildly about other things."[14]

By happenstance, George Patton had been in Omar Bradley's office when Eisenhower telephoned with word of the command shift. That night at his own headquarters, the Third Army commander took out his diary. "It is either a case of lost confidence in Brad, or having been forced to put Montgomery in through the machinations of the Prime Minister or with the hope that if he gives Monty operational control, he will get some British divisions [into the battle]," Patton wrote. "Ike is unwilling or unable to command Montgomery."[15]

Only three hours after Eisenhower's call, Montgomery strutted into Courtney Hodges's headquarters in the Palace Hotel in Chaudfontaine, Belgium, "like Christ come to cleanse the temple," in the words of a British officer who was present. Later, Monty paid a visit to Bill Simpson at Ninth Army. "American morale very low," Montgomery reported to Alan Brooke that night. "Hodges and Simpson seemed delighted to have someone to give them firm orders."[16]

CHAPTER 34

SHAEF Headquarters under Siege

AT MIDAFTERNOON ON DECEMBER 22, 1944, Field Marshal Bernard Montgomery telephoned Beetle Smith at Trianon Palace. He demanded that Courtney Hodges, the steady, sturdy leader of the U.S. First Army, be sacked. As a British officer, Monty explained, he was reluctant to relieve an American general, so he wanted Eisenhower to give the boot to Hodges, who, in the field marshal's opinion, was exhausted. Translation: Hodges had cracked under the enormous pressure of the surprise German offensive that had struck First Army.

Smith was shocked. On the basis of one short visit to Courtney Hodges a day earlier, Montgomery had decided that the fifty-seven-year-old First Army leader was incompetent.

Hodges's fighting spirit had never been questioned by the American hierarchy. In World War I as an infantry captain, he had been awarded the Distinguished Service Cross. Reserved by nature, he neither sought nor basked in the limelight. While the theatrical George Patton gained the headlines for his brilliant armored thrusts, it had been Hodges's First Army that scored the initial breakthrough in Normandy, dashed farther across France and Belgium than any other field army, was the first to enter the Third Reich, the first to capture a major German city (Aachen), and the first to crack the vaunted Siegfried line.

Smith passed Montgomery's request to Eisenhower, who promptly responded to the field marshal: "Hodges is the quiet, reticent type and does not appear to be as aggressive as he really is. Unless he becomes *truly* exhausted he will always wage a good fight."

A few days later Montgomery, apparently conceding defeat, wrote to the supreme commander, "Hodges is improving."

In the meantime, Monty wrote Alan Brooke that he was "far from impressed" by the American generals' response to the battlefield crisis, presumably meaning from Eisenhower on down. Then, in a letter to James Grigg, the British war minister, Montgomery took another potshot at American commanders: "Possibly in years to come certain people will turn in their graves when they think back on the past."[1] He no doubt was referring to the failure of

267

Eisenhower to go along with repeated British demands that Montgomery be put in charge of Allied ground battles.

Concluding his tirade to Grigg, Monty wrote gloomily, "At this moment, I do not see how this is going to turn into what Ike calls 'our greatest victory.' "[2]

Eisenhower knew that most American generals were seething over Omar Bradley's "demotion" and were galled by taking orders from Montgomery. So the supreme commander sent a pep talk to Courtney Hodges and Bill Simpson. "Now that you have been placed under the field marshal's command," he wrote, "I know that you will respond cheerfully and efficiently to every instruction he gives."[3]

While the bickering and sniping continued backstage in the Allied high command, on the frozen killing grounds of the Ardennes the German 2nd Panzer Division dashed fifty-five miles deep into Belgium and was almost in sight of the Meuse River. There the 2nd Panzer ran out of gas and was curled up in thick woods.

Aware of the enemy's predicament, the U.S. 2nd "Hell on Wheels" Armored Division, led by scrappy Major General Ernest N. "Gravel Voice" Harmon, pounced on the German force. Aided by swarms of American fighter-bombers and massed artillery, Harmon's tankers wiped out the elite 2nd Panzer Division after a vicious two-day battle.

An exuberant Ernie Harmon radioed higher headquarters: "A great slaughter."[4]

Neither Adolf Hitler nor SHAEF realized it at the time, but the blunting of the 2nd Panzer Division thrust was the beginning of the end for Wacht am Rein.

On Christmas Day, Omar Bradley, whose command now consisted only of Patton's Third Army, drove to Zondhoven, Holland, to pay a courtesy call on Bernard Montgomery. Bradley's reception at 21st Army Group was as frigid as the zero temperature outside.

Montgomery made no effort to conceal his apparent delight over the embarrassment inflicted on the Americans in the Ardennes. Nor did he attempt to soothe Bradley's anguish over losing two field armies to him. Instead, Monty ripped into the American high command, declaring that the Allies were now in a real "muddle," that the Germans had given the Americans "a bloody nose," and that it was pointless for Eisenhower and other American generals to pretend that the battle was going to be turned quickly into a great Allied victory. It had been a stunning defeat, Monty exclaimed, and "we [meaning American generals] had better admit it."[5]

An angry Bradley listened without comment to Montgomery's tirade. In the interest of Allied harmony, he did not dispute the field marshal's contentions.

Apparently sensing that Bradley's silence meant that the American agreed with his viewpoints, Monty then zeroed in on George Patton. He predicted that

Patton's counterattack into the southern flank of the German bulge (as ordered by Eisenhower at Verdun) would be halted by stiff enemy resistance. That eventuality would require Montgomery "to deal with *both* the Fifth Panzer Army and the Sixth Panzer Army."[6]

Omar Bradley, who was, in the words of an aide, "madder than a wet hen," remained in the old Dutch farmhouse for only thirty minutes. Never would he forgive Montgomery for his blunt talk and rudeness in this time of Allied crisis and Bradley's personal emotional discomfort.

Typically, Montgomery seemed to be unaware that he had brutally bruised Bradley's feelings. "[Bradley] agreed with me on everything," he wrote to Alan Brooke that night. "Poor chap, he is such a decent fellow and the whole thing is a bitter pill for him to swallow."[7]

In his fury over the mauling by Montgomery, Bradley returned to the city of Luxembourg and telephoned Eisenhower, demanding that the supreme commander return to him Hodges's First and Simpson's Ninth Armies. Harried, tugged on from all sides, still facing a battlefield disaster, Eisenhower rejected Bradley's request.[8]

Emboldened by Bradley's seeming acquiescence to his views, Montgomery again tried to gain charge of land battles. In a letter to Eisenhower, the field marshal even included the precise wording that should be used in such a directive. In the final sentence of his draft, Monty wrote:

"From now onwards full operational control and coordination of these operations is invested in Commander-in-Chief 21 Army Group [Montgomery] subject to such instructions as may be issued by the Supreme Commander from time to time."[9]

If Eisenhower were to issue this directive, it would mean that Monty would call all the shots, although the supreme commander would be allowed occasionally to inject his views on battle operations.

Montgomery then compounded the gross affront to his superior: "I put this matter up to you again only because I am so anxious not to have another failure." That is, another Eisenhower failure.

This high-handed communication thoroughly rankled the long-suffering commander, who had become almost immune to Montgomery's arrogance over the months. "You know how much I've appreciated and depended upon your frank and friendly counsel," Eisenhower responded, "but in your latest letter you disturb me by predictions of 'failure' unless your exact opinions in the matter of giving you [overall ground command] are met in detail."

Eisenhower said he hoped that this matter could be settled without involving the Combined Chiefs. "The confusion and debate that would follow," he wrote, "would certainly damage the goodwill and devotion to a common cause that have made the Allied force unique in history."[10]

Two days earlier, George Patton had received word from a contact in Washington that "some goddamned Englishmen" were lobbying the War Department and Congress to get high-level American support for Montgomery's elevation to ground commander. Patton rushed to tell Bradley of the disclosure; Bradley was so furious that he said he was going to resign. Clasping his friend by the arm, Patton replied solemnly, "If you quit, Brad, I'll quit, too!"[11]

Bradley climbed into his Packard sedan and rushed to Versailles to confront Eisenhower. "You must know that I cannot serve under Montgomery," Bradley told him. "If he is put in charge of all ground operations, you must send me home, for if Monty goes in over me, I will have lost the confidence of my command."

Silence followed. Omar and Ike had been close friends as well as comrades in arms since North Africa. His face flushed, Eisenhower looked the other man directly in the eye and said, "Well, Brad, I thought you were the one person I could count on for doing anything I asked you to."

"You can, Ike," Bradley replied. "I've enjoyed every bit of my service with you. But this is one thing I cannot take!"[12]

Then Bradley dropped another bombshell. Patton, too, would resign if Monty was put in over him.

At nightfall a day later, Bradley was on the telephone to SHAEF from his headquarters in Luxembourg. He wanted to talk to Eisenhower but was told that the supreme commander was "unavailable," an expression that irked Bradley. He settled for speaking to Beetle Smith.

"Damn it, Beetle!" Bradley exclaimed. "The Germans have reached their high-water mark. Why don't our people up north [meaning Montgomery] get off their ass and hit them with all they've got?" He reminded Smith that Patton already was attacking northward through the ice and snow and heavy German resistance.

"You're all wrong, Brad," Smith responded. "The Germans will be over the Meuse [River] in forty-eight hours."

Clearly, SHAEF was gripped by an acute case of the jitters.

At his headquarters on the night of December 26, George Patton opened his diary. "If Ike puts Bradley back in command of First and Ninth Armies, we can bag the whole German army in the Ardennes," he wrote. "I wish Ike were more of a gambler, but he is certainly a lion compared to Montgomery, and Bradley is better than Ike as far as nerve is concerned. Of course, Brad did make a bad mistake [being surprised by the Wehrmacht offensive]. Monty is a tired little fart. War requires taking risks and Monty won't take them."[13]

Across the Atlantic in Washington on the afternoon of December 27, rain and sleet were pelting the Pentagon. Inside the huge structure, Secretary of War Henry Stimson and George Marshall were discussing the unthinkable: What if Adolf Hitler was to pull off his enormous gamble? Reports from the Ardennes seemed to indicate the odds of that happening were fifty-fifty.

Marshall, always the realist, said, "If Germany beats us . . . we will have to recast the whole war. We will have to take a defensive position along the German frontier." Then he made a startling observation: "The people of the United States would have to decide whether they wanted to continue the war enough to raise large new armies."[14]

It was conceivable that should the Germans inflict staggering losses on the Americans in Belgium, a shocked and somewhat war-weary home front might say to hell with it. No more young Americans should be fed into the European meat grinder. Would then a negotiated peace have to be sought with Adolf Hitler?

The losses *were* becoming staggering. Eisenhower rushed an aide, Major General Ray Barker, to Washington to beg for replacement soldiers. Barker, as instructed, told the War Department, "Unless we are supported more strongly [with manpower], we're going to be in big trouble in Europe."

George Patton also had his manpower worries, as his Third Army had taken heavy casualties. "We can still lose this war," he confided gloomily to his diary.[15]

Early on the morning of December 27, Eisenhower left Paris by train for Belgium and a scheduled face-to-face showdown with Bernard Montgomery over the ground commander dispute and strategic plans. The rail trek to Brussels was tedious, with numerous delays due to fog and disabled tracks. When the grumpy supreme commander arrived at his destination, Montgomery was not at the station to greet him. In fact, the field marshal had left for his battle headquarters at Hasselt.

Angry and frustrated, Eisenhower boarded another train and proceeded by a long, roundabout secondary line to Hasselt. At Monty's old Dutch farmhouse, the field marshal told Eisenhower that the Germans would make one more all-out assault to break through toward Antwerp. Once that attack was blunted, Monty said, he would launch Hodges's First Army into the northern flank of the German penetration to link up with Patton's Third Army coming up from the south, thereby sawing the bulge in half and trapping large numbers of Germans in the pocket. Hodges would jump off on January 1, 1945.[16]

A day after Eisenhower returned to Versailles, Freddie de Guingand, the field marshal's chief of staff, showed up unannounced on Ike's doorstep. He brought disturbing news. Monty had decided that Hodges's attack would have to be postponed until January 3—or later.

Speaking for Montgomery, de Guingand claimed that Eisenhower had misunderstood the field marshal's intentions. Ike exploded: "Goddamn it, there was an agreement!"[17]

Eisenhower was convinced that he had been told a barefaced lie by Monty, that the field marshal had had no intention of attacking on January 1. For the furious supreme commander, this episode was the final straw. An enormous opportunity to trap large elements of the Wehrmacht in the bulge was being squandered.

Before de Guingand departed for Belgium, Eisenhower dictated a blistering letter to Montgomery. In blunt terms, he laid down an ultimatum: Either the field marshal lived up to his promises or the supreme commander would sack him. Never had the United States and Great Britain partnership come as close to disintegrating as it had at that moment.

De Guingand was shown a draft of Eisenhower's letter. He was horrified. To the British armed forces and home front, sacking Montgomery would be equivalent to banishing God Almighty. Promising to talk to Monty and report back soon, de Guingand departed for Belgium. Eisenhower, still furious, drafted a message to be sent to the Combined Chiefs. Take your pick, Montgomery or me, it said in essence. At the urging of alarmed aides, the supreme commander agreed to hold on to the potentially explosive message until word came from de Guingand.

In Hasselt, de Guingand spelled out the angry mood at SHAEF in blunt, unvarnished language. There was enormous sentiment against Montgomery, he reported.

"Who would they get to replace me?" the field marshal scoffed.

"That's already been worked out," de Guingand replied. "They want Alex."

Montgomery blanched. He had forgotten about the other British field marshal held in high esteem by SHAEF and the English home front: Harold R. L. G. Alexander, the suave, diplomatic, and capable Allied commander in Italy. "Oh, yes, Alex," Monty mumbled.

Montgomery began pacing his trailer, hands clasped behind his back. Finally he said softly, "Freddie, what shall I do?"

De Guingand pulled out the draft of a letter that he already had composed. "Sign this," the aide replied evenly. Monty glanced at the text, then wrote his signature on it. Eisenhower was confronted by many factors "beyond anything I realize," the letter said, and it assured the supreme commander that "you can rely on me . . . to go all-out one hundred percent to implement your plans."[18]

While the savage fighting was still raging in the Ardennes, London newspapers began heaping criticism on Dwight Eisenhower and Omar Bradley for allowing the surprise German onslaught. Bernard Montgomery was being hailed in the British press as the savior of the blundering Americans. Editorials were clamoring anew that Monty be named Allied ground commander.

In the Pentagon, George Marshall was angered and regarded the suggestion of a British ground commander as preposterous, since there were now fifty U.S. divisions and sixteen British divisions on the Western Front. "They may or may not have brought to your attention articles in certain London newspapers proposing [a ground commander] and implying that you have undertaken too much of a task yourself," he cabled Eisenhower. "My feeling is this: Under no circumstances make any concessions of any kind whatsoever. . . . You are doing a grand job, and go on and give them hell."[19]

On New Year's Day of 1945, Eisenhower responded. "You need have no fear as to my contemplating the establishment of a single ground commander. . . . Our present difficulties are being used by a certain group of [London] newspapers and their correspondents to advocate something that they have always wanted but which is not in fact a sound organization."[20]

From London, Field Marshal Brooke immediately advised Montgomery of Marshall's view, counseling him to remain silent for the time being. Brooke would continue the fight backstage in the highest councils of the Allied coalition.

On the evening of January 1, Eisenhower received a message from Montgomery: "Am attacking on early morning of 3 January." Beaming, Ike uttered a favorite expression. "Thank God from whom all blessings flow!"

CHAPTER 35

The Great War of Words

AT DAWN ON JANUARY 3, 1945, powerful elements of Courtney Hodges's First Army jumped off in a howling blizzard along a twenty-three-mile sector in the middle of the northern battleground. Weather conditions were horrendous—Europe's coldest winter in a century. At night, temperatures plunged to thirty degrees below zero, with icy gales producing windchill factors of minus sixty degrees. Snowdrifts, already up to a man's waist, became even deeper.

Out in the bitter cold, the GIs fought like savages, not for God or country, but for the next farmhouses in which to get warm. For their part, the Germans in the villages resisted like trapped beasts, not for the Führer or the Fatherland, but to keep from getting kicked out into the winter air. When caught out in the open overnight, GIs and Feldgrau alike often froze to death, sometimes within yards of one another.

As the death struggle raged in the thick snow forests of the Ardennes, Dwight Eisenhower continued to be burdened by colossal pressures. Kay Summersby wrote in her diary, "Not an easy job. E can never relax for a moment."[1]

On the afternoon of January 3, Eisenhower found himself embroiled in yet another showdown with an angry Charles de Gaulle. During the Ardennes battle, Adolf Hitler had launched diversionary attacks in Alsace, one hundred miles to the south, in order to keep the Americans from pulling troops from that region and rushing them to Belgium. In order to establish the strongest line of defense in Alsace, Eisenhower had ordered Jacob Devers, commander of the U.S. 6th Army Group, to pull back from the French city of Strasbourg, which was deemed to have no military value.

Strasbourg, an old city with many medieval buildings, had a wartime population of approximately 250,000. Located near the French-German border, it had been a prize of war for three centuries. After the Franco-Prussian War in 1870, France ceded Strasbourg to Germany. The city became French again after World War I, and German troops took it over again in 1940 and remained until the Allies captured it in the fall of 1944.

Eisenhower had concluded that Devers did not have enough troops to defend Strasbourg, but he failed to envision the propaganda bonanza the Germans would reap from its so-called liberation by the Wehrmacht—for Strasbourg was considered a German city by the Third Reich.

General Alphonse Pierre Juin, an old comrade of Eisenhower from North Africa and Italy and now de Gaulle's chief of staff of the French National Defense Committee, rushed to see the supreme commander. He pointed out that as soon as U.S. forces pulled back, the Germans would rush into Strasbourg and murder three thousand known Allied collaborators.

Juin's demands prompted no action, so Charles de Gaulle himself barged in on SHAEF and insisted on seeing Eisenhower immediately. Ike winced, for dealing with the Frenchman was like dealing with Montgomery.

De Gaulle wasted no time on niceties. "The French government [meaning de Gaulle] obviously cannot let Strasbourg fall into enemy hands again without first doing everything possible to prevent it," he said icily. He added that he was going to send all French forces in that direction.

Eisenhower bristled. It was a serious threat. French forces were fighting under the command of SHAEF, which had armed and supplied them. But de Gaulle was prepared to pull out all French troops and dispatch them as he saw fit.

The American general said that he, too, was concerned with the fate of French civilians in Strasbourg if the Germans returned, but added that he was grateful to de Gaulle for "indicating that you share my conclusions from a military point of view."[2]

Unimpressed, de Gaulle fired back, "Nothing of what you have been told from me . . . can make you think that from the military point of view I approve of your views. I should tell you that the truth is just the opposite."[3]

Struggling to control his temper—a split with the French could be damaging to the Allied cause at this time—Eisenhower strolled to a large wall map and with a pointer began explaining to the other general why it was necessary to pull back in Alsace. De Gaulle cut in, snapping, "If we were at Kriegspiel [simulated war games], I should say you are right . . . but retreat in Alsace would be a national disaster!"

Now the confrontation grew acrimonious. Both men threatened each other. De Gaulle exclaimed that he would have to remove French forces from SHAEF. Eisenhower shot back that if he did so, he would cut off supplies to the French army.

Undaunted, de Gaulle barked that if Eisenhower was to go to that extreme, SHAEF's line of communications, which ran from the ports of Marseille and Toulon, and others in Brittany and Normandy all the way across France, would be in dire peril. This threat implied that French gangsters, hijackers, and other criminals—of which there was no shortage—might be encouraged to wreak havoc on Allied supply trucks and trains.

Galling as it no doubt was to him, Eisenhower was forced to capitulate. While de Gaulle sat nearby, looking pleased, Ike telephoned Jacob Devers and canceled the order to pull back from Strasbourg. After de Gaulle left his office, Eisenhower's aides entered in time to hear the general unloose a volley of profanity.

Then he fired off a cable to George Marshall about his just-completed shoot-out: "I must say that next to the weather I think they [the French] have caused me more trouble in this war than any other single factor."[4]

Four days later, on January 7, the harried Eisenhower met with trouble again—this time in the form of Bernard Montgomery. For whatever reason, Montgomery chose to hold a press conference at his headquarters to discuss the Ardennes battle. No remarks made by any Allied general during the war came as close to rupturing Anglo-American solidarity than did those by the British field marshal.

"As soon as I saw what was happening on the very first day," Monty told the press, "I took certain steps myself to ensure that if the Germans got to the Meuse they would certainly not get over the river.

"Then the situation began to deteriorate. But the whole Allied team rallied to meet the disaster. . . . General Eisenhower placed me in command of the whole northern front. You thus have the picture of British troops fighting on both sides of American forces who have suffered a hard blow."[5]

Montgomery then explained that after taking command he had carried out "certain movements" so as to provide balanced dispositions to meet the threatened danger. Condescendingly, he added: "I was thinking ahead."

American correspondents took that remark to mean that Eisenhower and Bradley had *not* been thinking ahead.

The field marshal continued in this vein for thirty minutes and summed up his views by declaring, "It has been an interesting battle; I think possibly one of the most interesting and tricky battles I have ever handled." Then he uttered the most damaging remark of the war as far as Anglo-American unity was concerned: "American GIs [make] great fighting men when given the proper leadership."[6]

Nearly every American senior officer on the Western Front was furious at Montgomery. As they saw events, the German steamroller nearly had been brought to a halt before the British field marshal entered the picture. Montgomery, too, had been taken by surprise. Only a day before the big German attack, Monty had asked permission from Eisenhower to spend Christmas in England with his son.

What the American generals found especially irritating about the press conference remarks was that Montgomery seemed to be pleased that the Americans had been caught with their battle flags down and suffered much loss of face. As the American commanders saw it, Montgomery, far from pulling Eisenhower and Bradley out of the fire, had injected himself in everyone's way and, indeed, had botched the counterattack that was to link up American forces heading southward with those driving to the north.[7]

George Patton was nearly apoplectic. "Had it not been for Montgomery," he wrote in his diary, "we could have bagged the whole German army [in the Ardennes]."

The volatile Third Army commander didn't limit his observations to the privacy of his diary. He made identical remarks about the British field marshal to any American reporter who would listen—and all of them did so.

At the urging of his staff, Omar Bradley held his own press conference, ostensibly to review the Ardennes battle. Actually, he aimed to refute the charges and claims made by Montgomery. Although no doubt seething within, Bradley was composed and failed to leap for the bait tossed by reporters who sought his views on Monty's remark about GIs and proper leadership. However, the 12th Army Group commander did assert that the German offensive had run out of steam before Montgomery took over the northern sector of the bulge.

Now the war of angry words between the American and British commanders spilled over into the United States and England. A furious debate erupted in the press of both nations over which general or generals should get credit for halting the Hitler offensive. So acrimonious did the London media become that Winston Churchill felt compelled to address the House of Commons on the highly controversial topic. He paid tribute to the fighting tenacity of the American GIs, who, he declared, were carrying the burden of the fight. What's more, Churchill explained that British troops, by and large, were playing a backup role in the battle.

In the meantime, the intensity of the inter-Allied squabbling increased when Bradley's 12th Army Group intelligence monitored a radio newscast that was mistakenly thought to be the BBC in London. Actually, it was a secret ploy of Josef Goebbels, whose propaganda agency was operating a radio station broadcasting in English from Arnhem in the Netherlands.

When German intelligence learned of dispatches in London newspapers concerning Field Marshal Montgomery's inflammatory press conference remarks, Goebbels's minions, quite cleverly, rewrote the statements, inserting violently anti-American comments and placing them in Montgomery's mouth. When word of the phony Arnhem broadcast reached Bradley and his commanders, the roof, in the words of one angry colonel, was "blown right off the headquarters building."

Even the congenial Bill Simpson, leader of the U.S. Ninth Army, which had been under Montgomery's command for many weeks, was angry, although his troops were not directly involved in the Ardennes fighting. Bradley, who was steaming, told Simpson privately that he could hardly wait for the chance to tell Montgomery to his face what he thought of him.

While the Great War of Words was raging in the Anglo-American high command and in the American and British press, the average American soldier in the Ardennes was unconcerned with—and usually unaware of—the acrimonious clashes in the stratosphere. For the GI dogface, the battle was merely an hour-by-hour matter of survival.

Finally, on January 16—precisely one month after Hitler launched his surprise offensive—spearheads of Lightning Joe Collins's VII Corps, slugging their way southward, and leading elements of Troy Middleton's VIII Corps, driving northward from the Bastogne region, linked up in "heavily liberated" Houffalize, as George Patton described the pulverized town. A gigantic trap had been snapped shut. However, most SS formations and much of the surviving German armor already had escaped to the east.

With the nose of the bulge flattened, Eisenhower returned Hodges's First Army to Bradley's 12th Army Group. Aware that his friend had been forced to undergo a humiliating ordeal, the supreme commander awarded Bradley the Bronze Star, a modest decoration. Cracked a cynic on Bradley's staff, "Omar received the medal for continuing to breathe throughout the battle."

Despite the devastating pounding the Feldgrau had received during the previous three weeks—especially from powerful Allied air and massed artillery—the Germans began conducting a carefully orchestrated fighting retreat back to the jumpoff positions of Wacht am Rein. On January 19, Kay Summersby wrote in her diary, "German morale is very high right now."

In Washington, bafflement was the order of the day in the upper councils of the government and in the Pentagon. A confidant mentioned to Franklin Roosevelt that American newspapers were saturated with articles wondering how SHAEF could have been so totally surprised by Hitler's masterstroke. "I've been wondering that myself," the President responded dryly.

Tempers were still short in the American high command as the result of Bernard Montgomery's explosive press conference. On January 24, Omar Bradley was visiting George Patton's headquarters when Jock Whitely, the senior British officer at SHAEF, telephoned for Bradley just as the two Americans had completed arrangements for a coordinated attack by the First and Third Armies. Whitely, who was well liked by most American generals, said that Eisenhower wanted Bradley to give up several divisions "to help Jakie Devers clean up the Colmar pocket." Devers's Sixth Army Group to the south had been running into heavy resistance from German formations that had crossed the Rhine and established a large bridgehead near Colmar while the Battle of the Bulge had been raging.

Patton wanted these same divisions for his looming attack in the direction of the Siegfried line on the heels of the withdrawing Wehrmacht. He had never seen Bradley so angry. "We would be giving up a sure thing for a sideshow!" the normally placid general shouted into the telephone at Whitely.

"Go ahead and take all my corps and divisions!" Bradley bellowed. "As far as I am concerned, you can take every goddamned division and corps in the 12th Army Group. Do with them as you see fit, and those of us that you leave back will sit on our asses until hell freezes!" He paused for a moment, then concluded, "I trust you do not think I am angry. But I want to impress upon you that I am goddamned well incensed!"

Jock Whitely had no doubt already reached that conclusion.

In the meantime, a frowning George Patton rose from his chair and moved behind Bradley. Knowing that his voice would easily carry over the telephone, Patton rasped, "Tell them all to go to hell and all three of us will resign! I will lead the procession!" Presumably, the third potential resignee would be Courtney Hodges of First Army.

Uncharacteristically, Bradley slammed the receiver down in Whitely's ear. Every officer on Patton's staff leaped to his feet and applauded.[8]

A few hours later, Whitely called back. Eisenhower, he told Bradley, had changed his mind about taking Patton's divisions. Jakie Devers would have to make do with what troops he had.

By February 1, the whipped Wehrmacht had limped back behind the Siegfried line after six weeks of savage warfare. Kenneth Strong, SHAEF's G-2, estimated that the Germans had lost eighty thousand men. And the Americans had absorbed what Montgomery had called a bloody nose—seventy thousand casualties.

CHAPTER 36

A Shouting Match
at Malta

On the bitterly cold day of January 27, 1945, George Marshall lifted off from Washington in a C-54 transport plane and headed across the Atlantic for a secret rendezvous with Dwight Eisenhower. Neither man wanted the British to know about it. A few days later, Marshall would take part in a meeting of the Combined Chiefs in Malta, a fortress island in the Mediterranean sixty miles south of Sicily. He wanted to discuss privately and in advance Eisenhower's strategy for crossing the Rhine River and knifing on into the heart of the Third Reich.

Marshall knew that he would lock horns with Alan Brooke at Malta and wanted to have ammunition to fire back at the field marshal, who could be counted on to be well versed in arguments backing his own Rhine-crossing strategy. Furthermore, Marshall wanted the face-to-face session with his protégé to assess how shaken Eisenhower might have been by the surprise German Ardennes offensive that had come within a whisker of succeeding.

On January 29, the U.S. Army chief and the supreme commander met in the Château Valmonte, a luxurious villa forty-five miles outside Marseille in southern France. The two generals spent the dreary Sunday reviewing Eisenhower's end-the-war strategy. Marshall gave his approval to the plan and departed for his confrontation with the British chiefs.

Tension hung heavy as the Combined Chiefs convened at Montgomery House at Malta on the morning of February 3. Both sides were aware that a full-fledged dispute would break out when Eisenhower's strategy plan was unveiled. George Marshall already knew from confidential sources that Alan Brooke and the British chiefs were bitterly opposed to Eisenhower's conception and wanted to substitute Montgomery's scheme.

Beetle Smith, widely known for his sharp tongue and lack of tact, had been dispatched to Malta to brief the Combined Chiefs on SHAEF's plan. Smith, in the view of some, was a curious choice for a task in which fireworks were bound to erupt. His mere presence in a room antagonized the British brass.

Smith launched his briefing by pointing out that time was now crucial, implying that there should be no prolonged squabbling over Rhine-crossing strategy. During the past three weeks, the Soviet army had plunged ahead for an astonishing two hundred miles to the Polish-German border, Smith observed. If the Anglo-Americans dawdled, the Russians might conquer all of the Third Reich while the Western Allies were still west of the Rhine, leaving the Anglo-Americans at a critical disadvantage at the postwar peace table.

Alan Brooke frowned. He needed no lecture on the military and political picture by an upstart from the colonies.

SHAEF's grand design for victory in the West called for all Allied armies to push forward and eliminate German forces west of the Rhine, Smith said. Then Montgomery's 21st Army Group, beefed up to thirty-six divisions, would cross the Rhine above the Ruhr and charge on toward Berlin.

Churchill and the British chiefs nodded in silent agreement. This was precisely what they had in mind all along. Then Beetle Smith delivered the kick. Despite the gigantic massing of troops and firepower, there was always the chance that Monty might get bogged down across the Rhine, he said. Therefore, Omar Bradley's 12th Army Group would make a secondary crossing south of the Ruhr *after* Monty was over the river.[1]

When Smith concluded his briefing, the most heated dispute of the war erupted. Alan Brooke leaped to his feet and angrily ripped apart SHAEF's plan. There was not enough manpower or supplies for two thrusts across the Rhine, he exclaimed, so only Montgomery should make a maximum effort.

When Brooke took his seat, George Marshall spoke out forcefully in defense of SHAEF's plan and Eisenhower. Brooke had implied that the supreme commander had no real grasp of grand strategy and was not competent to command large armies.[2]

Brooke's unspoken concern was that an American secondary crossing of the Rhine, which had not been breached by a hostile army since Napoleon Bonaparte in 1806, might develop into as significant an operation as Monty's main assault. Any attack involving George Patton, Brooke no doubt felt, was bound to become a full-blooded offensive—whether or not it had been planned that way.

Soon a shouting match punctuated by ham-fisted table banging broke out. So intense was the argument that Marshall demanded that a closed session be held, with only the principals remaining in the room. Shorthand stenographers, who had furiously been trying to jot down who was yelling at whom about what, were dismissed.

Parliamentary niceties had long since flown out the window. The debate over a plan to deliver a knockout blow to Adolf Hitler was cast aside, and a scathing denunciation of personalities raged. Brooke hollered that the British chiefs were appalled by the fact that Eisenhower was "overly influenced" by Omar Bradley.

"Well, Brooke," a red-faced Marshall shot back, "they are not nearly as much worried as we are about the pressures Mr. Churchill puts on General Eisenhower!"[3]

Marshall exclaimed that President Roosevelt almost never saw or was in contact with the supreme commander "because Eisenhower is not just an American but an Allied leader." While Roosevelt restrained from poking his nose into SHAEF's doings, Marshall bellowed, Churchill and the British chiefs were constantly exerting pressure on Eisenhower.

Marshall had by now built up a full head of steam, declaring that Brooke was "overly influenced" by Bernard Montgomery and that much of Brooke's distrust of Eisenhower and his plan for crossing the Rhine resulted from Monty's conniving. Brooke and the other British chiefs gripped the arms of their chairs in white-knuckled fury as Marshall bluntly asserted, "I want to express my full dislike and antipathy for Field Marshal Montgomery."[4]

Perhaps suffering from combat fatigue, the Combined Chiefs agreed to a truce until the next morning. When the session began, the British wasted no time in launching an assault on Eisenhower's lack of judgment and strategic know-how. Brooke insisted that a deputy supreme commander was crucial. Since the Americans refused to accept Bernard Montgomery in that role, Brooke put forward another candidate: British Field Marshal Harold Alexander.

Beetle Smith exploded. *He* was, in essence if not in title, SHAEF's deputy commander.

Smith demanded to know just what Brooke meant by his suggestion. "Goddamn it," he barked, "let's have it out here and now!"[5]

Taken aback, the field marshal replied that Eisenhower was too easily swayed, particularly by Patton and Bradley, and added that the supreme commander responded to the views of the last general he saw—including George Marshall.

If Brooke felt that Eisenhower was incompetent, Smith shot back, then why did he not officially recommend that the supreme commander be sacked?

That brutally frank suggestion stunned Brooke into silence. Neither George Marshall, Franklin Roosevelt, nor the American home front would condone such a drastic move on the brink of victory in Europe. Besides, three-fourths of the manpower for the offensive into the Third Reich would be American.

An astute old warrior, Brooke knew when it was time to conduct a tactical retreat. If Eisenhower would give him assurances in writing that "every single German soldier" would not have to be cleared from the west bank of the Rhine before Montgomery crossed the water barrier, and that Omar Bradley's *secondary* crossing would not evolve into a major drive into Germany, then Brooke would approve SHAEF's plan.[6]

George Marshall had scored a resounding victory, thwarting British demands that Montgomery be allowed to dash for Berlin while Bradley's powerful First and Third Armies languished in the backwaters and out of the spotlight.

A few hours later, Brooke administered final burial rites to Churchill's scheme to get the Anglo-Americans involved in the Balkans in order to keep that mountainous region out of Stalin's Communist empire. Now that the acrimony on both sides had vanished, Brooke proposed that three British and two Canadian divisions be shifted from the Italian front to reinforce Montgomery for his Rhine crossing.

Meanwhile, Franklin Roosevelt, ensconced regally on the quarterdeck of the cruiser *Quincy*, sailed into Valetta harbor at Malta. A mere shadow of his former robust, exuberant self, the President was a dying man, his face etched with pain, his once-silver hair now white. At nearly the same time, Winston Churchill, also weary after five years of war, arrived on the HMS *Sirius*. The two heads of state were en route to Yalta, in the Crimea of the Soviet Union, where they would meet with Josef Stalin to carve up much of the world.

Before leaving the White House for the Mediterranean, Roosevelt had been warned by Bernard Baruch, a confidant in whom the President had great faith, to "keep your guard up" when dealing with the shrewd Soviet leader. "Don't worry, Bernie," Roosevelt had replied airily. "I can handle Uncle Joe!"[7]

Churchill and Roosevelt were briefed by the Combined Chiefs on SHAEF's end-the-war strategy, and both political leaders gave it their approval. Then, just past midnight on February 3, Churchill, Roosevelt, the Combined Chiefs, and their entourages climbed into twenty-five transport planes at Malta's airport. One by one, at ten-minute intervals, the lumbering, unarmed craft lifted off and set a course for Yalta on the shores of the Black Sea.

As soon as the British and Americans arrived, the deft hand of Josef Stalin was visible in a series of Soviet machinations. Roosevelt and the other Americans were assigned billets in the palace of Livadia, a huge limestone and marble structure where Russian nobility had once frolicked before the 1917 Communist revolution that overthrew the czar. Five miles away, Churchill and the British were put up by the Russian hosts in the Vorontzo villa. Stalin and his delegation took over the Yusupov Palace, halfway between the British and the Americans. This arrangement by the Russians apparently was calculated to prevent any private contact between Roosevelt and Churchill without the knowledge of the Soviet secret police.

Shortly before 5:00 P.M., Roosevelt and Churchill were seated at a large circular table in the conference room at Livadia. Moments later, Stalin, clad in a nifty field marshal's uniform, walked in surrounded by a phalanx of bodyguards armed with submachine guns. It was as if Stalin expected the Americans and British to try to assassinate him on the spot. Standing every few feet along the balcony surrounding the room were other Soviet soldiers, clutching weapons and watching every move.

Kicking off the conference, Stalin cagily proposed that there should be no rotation of the chairmanship, as had been standard practice at earlier Big Three summits, and that Roosevelt should preside at all of the sessions. No doubt it was clear to the Soviet leader that the President had deteriorated badly, which could be useful to Stalin.[8]

That night, Anthony Eden, the British foreign secretary, recorded his impressions in his diary. "[Roosevelt] was vague and loose and ineffective, letting the discussion drift on," he wrote. "Key points on the agenda were discussed unmethodically, by fits and jerks. Several times Harry Hopkins, Roosevelt's closest aide, had to bring the talks back on track by slipping notes under the table to the President.

"Stalin as a negotiator is the toughest proposition of all," Eden added. "The man is ruthless and knows his purpose. Never wastes a word."[9]

Cunning and mentally tough, Stalin proved to be more than a match for the fading Roosevelt. He mesmerized the President and a curiously pliable Churchill into giving him Austria, Hungary, Poland, Czechoslovakia, Bulgaria, Romania, and the Baltic countries of Latvia, Lithuania, and Estonia. In one masterstroke, 130 million people had been swept into the Communist empire.

Far from the connivance and manipulation at Yalta on February 4, Dwight Eisenhower and Omar Bradley talked far into the night at 12th Army Group headquarters in Namur, Belgium. Eisenhower had driven up from his advance base at Rheims and had summoned Bernard Montgomery to meet him in Namur the next day. Bradley was still furious over Monty's explosive January 7 press conference. Intensifying Bradley's anger was the fact that Monty now had fifteen divisions of Bill Simpson's U.S. Ninth Army under his command for the assault over the Rhine. Ninth Army had been taken from Bradley and assigned to Montgomery by the happenstance of being on the field marshal's right flank. Once Monty was over the Rhine, Bradley complained, London newspapers would ballyhoo that the field marshal once again had rushed to the rescue of the blundering, stumbling American generals.

Early the next morning, Montgomery strolled jauntily into Bradley's headquarters and was greeted icily. If the field marshal noticed the affront, he gave no indication. During lunch, he joked, gesticulated, and talked almost constantly—and too loudly, the stone-faced Americans thought.

The luncheon ended quickly. Bradley abruptly got to his feet, excused himself without looking at Monty, and left the field marshal sitting at the table. An embarrassed Eisenhower, who could do nothing about Bradley's rudeness, soon prepared to depart for Bastogne to meet with George Patton.

Forty-eight hours later, Patton, frustrated and gloomy, returned to his headquarters after visiting his combat units in the Eifel, a hilly, thickly wooded region cut by deep ravines and gorges. It was footslogger terrain—tanks were largely road-bound—so advances were costly and measured in yards. The general had just lighted a cigar when Omar Bradley telephoned.

"Well, Monty did it again, George!" Bradley said bitterly. "You and Hodges [First Army] are to conduct aggressive defenses while most of the fuel and supplies will go to Monty so he can push up to the Rhine for his crossing."

Patton, stunned and furious, loosed a string of curses largely aimed at Eisenhower for allowing Montgomery to have his way.

"It wasn't Ike this time," Bradley explained. "Orders from the Combined Chiefs. Even Marshall went along. Probably he's anxious to get Monty's fourteen divisions sitting on their asses in Belgium back into action."[10]

"What in the goddamned hell are they hoping to accomplish?" Patton exploded.

"Monty wants to secure a wide stretch of the Rhine in case Germany would suddenly collapse."

"Horse shit!" Patton barked. "We've got a much better chance of getting to the Rhine first with our present attack."

After a moment of silence, the Third Army commander snapped, "And what in the hell are we supposed to do in the meantime?"

"You can continue your attack until February 10th, and maybe even after that," Bradley replied, "provided your casualties are not excessive and you have enough ammo."[11]

That night, George Patton vented his anger in his diary. In nearly illegible handwriting, he scrawled, "Hell and damn! This is another case of giving up a going attack in order to start one that has no promise except to exalt Monty, who has never won a battle since he left Africa—and I won the Mareth Line for him there."

Within two days, Omar Bradley received another jolt. Montgomery already had Simpson's Ninth Army for the Rhine crossing. Now, SHAEF informed Bradley, the 95th Infantry Division and five artillery battalions were being taken from Patton and given to Simpson. None of the American generals faulted Simpson for accepting the "stolen" outfits from Third Army.

A bitter Patton predicted in his diary, "I will be the first to the Rhine yet!"

In the meantime, Eisenhower was furious with Montgomery—again. While on a short leave in England in recent days, the field marshal had met with the press and implied that he should be in charge of the overall land battles. It was the same old tune.

Eisenhower called in Jock Whitely, his British aide, and ordered him to telephone Monty in England. "Tell him if he or one member of the 21st Army Group talks to the press [again], I'll turn over command [of the Rhine crossing] to Bradley!"

Whitely blanched. It was common knowledge that Monty would succeed Alan Brooke as chief of the Imperial General Staff after the war, and thus would control Whitely's destiny. Now he was put in the unenviable position of having to telephone the field marshal and tell him, in essence, to keep his big mouth shut. Whitely made the call.[12]

That night U.S. Army Lieutenant Kay Summersby (she had been commissioned despite regulations against foreigners becoming officers) moaned in her diary, "Of all of E's commanders, Monty is the one who has given him the greatest number of headaches."[13]

All along the 450-mile front, Eisenhower's armies were struggling ahead against two tenacious foes: The steadfast German soldier and the nasty winter weather. In late February, George Patton was trying to capture Trier, one of Germany's oldest cities, which lies on the swiftly flowing Moselle River. Time was running out on February 27; Patton had promised Omar Bradley that he would halt his attack at dark if he had failed to seize Trier by then.

Just before dusk, the Third Army commander telephoned Bradley, who authorized him to keep going until SHAEF intervened to halt him. SHAEF would have to issue a stop order through 12th Army Group. Bradley slyly told Patton, "I don't expect to be listening for my telephone."

Trier was captured two days later. "A hell of a way to run a war!" Patton groused to his coconspirator.

All the while, Bernard Montgomery, a master of the set-piece battle, was feverishly preparing for Operation Plunder, the Rhine crossing, which would rival Normandy D-day in terms of intricate planning and coordination of ground, air, and amphibious forces. One million men would be involved—eighty thousand in the assault, including the U.S. 17th Airborne and British 6th Airborne Divisions. Thousands of field guns were lined up along the west bank. Swarms of tanks crept up to the river. To conceal this mighty force from German eyes, a smoke screen—history's longest—would be laid along the Rhine for seventy-five miles three days before the crossing.

On the afternoon of March 4, Major General Raymond S. McLain, leader of XIX Corps of Simpson's Ninth Army, was perched on the west bank of the Rhine a short distance north of Düsseldorf, a major industrial city on the east bank. Peering through binoculars across the wide river, McLain, an Oklahoma City investment banker in peacetime, could see no sign of German activity. The road into the heart of the Third Reich appeared to be wide open.

McLain, excited and eager to push across the Rhine, hurried to telephone Bill Simpson and inform him of the beckoning opportunity. In turn, Simpson rushed to see Bernard Montgomery to tell him of McLain's revelation. He unfolded a map to explain the situation, but Montgomery refused to even look at it, rejecting Simpson's plea. The field marshal would make the Rhine crossing farther north as planned.

Monty's rejection of Simpson's proposal for McLain to leap the Rhine more or less unopposed rekindled the acrimony between top American and British commanders. Montgomery's staff was convinced that the U.S. generals were conspiring to antagonize the field marshal by making it appear that Monty lacked boldness.

Bradley, Hodges, and Patton, as well as other American generals, were furious. Patton ranted that his longtime antagonist wanted to "hog the spotlight."[14]

For nearly a month, the eyes of American commanders had been on the many Rhine bridges. But Wehrmacht engineers had feverishly blown up the huge spans, often in the face of onrushing American spearheads. No U.S. leader counted on a bridge being left intact.

On the evening of March 7, Courtney Hodges of First Army telephoned his boss, Omar Bradley, at Namur. "Brad," Hodges observed in his customarily casual way, "we've gotten a bridge."

"A bridge!" Bradley replied. "You mean you've got a bridge intact on the *Rhine?*"

"We nabbed the Ludendorff Bridge at Remagan."

"Hot dog, Courtney! This will bust the German wide open! Are you getting the stuff across?"

Hodges replied that he was sending Major General John W. Leonard's 9th Armored Division, which had seized Ludendorff Bridge, and two infantry divisions across.

"Shove everything you can over there!" Bradley ordered.

Bradley, still smarting from Montgomery's press conference remarks after the Battle of the Bulge, was euphoric. No matter how highly touted Monty would be when he launched Plunder, Bradley had beaten him over the Rhine.

CHAPTER 37

A Hoax Impacts Allied Strategy

OMAR BRADLEY KNEW THAT if Dwight Eisenhower was to change strategy to take full advantage of the unexpected seizure of Ludendorff Bridge, abuse would be poured on him by Winston Churchill, Bernard Montgomery, and Alan Brooke. They would accuse the supreme commander of a breach of faith for altering the plan adopted by the Combined Chiefs at Malta in which Montgomery would swing the main blow into the heart of the Third Reich.

Bradley and Courtney Hodges agreed that the Ludendorff bonanza was a golden opportunity for the Americans to gain par with Montgomery in the final offensive of the war. Therefore, they conspired to get First Army so deeply committed on the far side of the Rhine that neither heaven nor hell nor even Winston Churchill could pull the Americans back.

At his headquarters in the Château de Namur, Bradley conveniently forgot to inform Eisenhower of the seizure of the Ludendorff Bridge. Each minute that elapsed meant that Hodges was pouring more troops, guns, and tanks over the Rhine.

Major General Harold "Pink" Bull, Eisenhower's G-3 (operations officer), happened to arrive at the château two hours after Bradley had learned about Ludendorff Bridge. Bull, rather small and reddish-haired, and Bradley had long been good friends. The 12th Army Group leader was convinced that, in Bull, he would have a backer at SHAEF.

When Bradley took Bull to his war room and told him the news about Ludendorff Bridge, however, the SHAEF general was bitterly opposed to its exploitation. Grabbing the bridge was a heroic feat, Bull declared, but there was little that could be done with it because of the rugged, hostile terrain.

"You're not going anywhere down there," Bull told his friend. "Besides, it doesn't fit into the overall plan."

Bradley was thoroughly angry. Bull had become so totally inflexible, so pro-British, or both, that he was blinded to the strategic opportunities at Remagen, Bradley felt.

"Then what in the hell do you want me to do?" he shouted at Bull. "Pull back and blow up the goddamned bridge?"[1]

A half hour later, Bradley telephoned Eisenhower at Rheims and blurted out the news. No doubt to Bradley's enormous surprise, Ike replied enthusiastically, "Brad, that's wonderful! Get four divisions across. It's the best break we've had!"

A jubilant Eisenhower hung up and returned to the table where he had been hosting a dinner for four of his American airborne generals. Here was just what he needed, he said with a broad smile, a Rhine bridgehead that would draw off German forces from Bernard Montgomery's maximum effort in the north.[2]

A few days after the capture of the Ludendorff Bridge, Beetle Smith tried to convince Eisenhower that he should take a brief vacation. The heavily burdened supreme commander had shown signs of wearing down from the barrage of demands and criticisms being hurled at him by both American and British commanders. "Sometimes when I get tired of trying to arrange the blankets smoothly over the several prima donnas in the same bed," Ike wrote to George Marshall in frustration, "I think no one person in the world can have so many illogical problems."[3]

Those closest to Eisenhower were worried about his physical condition. Smith told him bluntly that if he didn't let up and take some time off, he would surely have a breakdown. The general started to become angry, then relented—under the condition that Omar Bradley would come, too. Bradley also had been in a pressure cooker ever since North Africa.

Smith, perhaps without Eisenhower's knowledge, decided to turn the four-day holiday into a gala affair by inviting twelve of the commander's friends and acquaintances—mostly generals—to participate in the interlude on the French Riviera. It would be held in a magnificent mansion, owned by an American businessman, that overlooked the blue Mediterranean at Cannes, the peacetime playground of Europe's rich and idle.

Most of the brass traveled there in style. J. C. H. Lee pried himself away from his luxury digs in Paris and flew to the Riviera, followed by his special twelve-car train carrying his Packard limousine. On board the train was Robert M. "Big John" Littlejohn, a SHAEF general of whom Eisenhower was fond. Before leaving Paris, Littlejohn had arranged for current newspapers to be delivered to him at each stop en route. Other generals flew to Cannes, including Toohey Spaatz and his lady, Sally. On March 19, Eisenhower, Beetle Smith, and four WACs, including Kay Summersby, boarded a train and left for the Riviera.

Eisenhower had indeed been exhausted. While most of the other generals played high-stakes poker, drank Scotch, gossiped, and hobnobbed with the ladies, the supreme commander slept. On occasion, he got up to eat; then he went back to bed. Invited to play a round of bridge, a favorite pastime, he declined, saying, "I don't want to do any damned *thinking!*"

Early on the morning of March 23—D-day minus one for Montgomery's massive Rhine crossing—Omar Bradley was back from the Riviera and eating breakfast at his Namur château when he received a telephone call from George Patton.

"Brad, don't tell anyone," Patton said excitedly in his high-pitched voice. "But I'm across!"

Bradley was silent for a few moments. "Well, I'll be damned," he blurted finally. "You mean across the *Rhine*?"

"Sure as hell am! I sneaked a division over last night. But there are so goddamned few Krauts around they don't know it yet. So don't make any announcement. We'll keep it a secret until we find out how things go."

Bradley authorized Patton to rush troops and tanks over pontoon bridges at Oppenheim, where the sneak crossing had been made under the cover of darkness.

Shortly after dinner that night, Patton was again on the telephone to Bradley. His foothold was firm on the far bank.

"Brad, for God's sake tell the world we're across!" shouted the triumphant Patton. "I want the world to know Third Army made it *before* Monty starts across!"

Earlier that day, Bradley had been contacted by Eisenhower, who apparently anticipated that Montgomery soon would be in the world spotlight and wanted to cast some of the glow on American accomplishments. Bradley was only too happy to comply and held a press conference after receiving Patton's second call. Needling the field marshal's monumental buildup for Plunder, Bradley claimed that with Hodges and Patton already on the far bank, the Americans had crossed the Rhine "without air-bombing, airborne troops, smoke screens, or artillery bombardment."

Bradley's sniping before the press hardly cemented Anglo-American harmony—but he no doubt felt he had paid Monty back for the field marshal's Battle of the Bulge press conference remarks about having to tidy up Bradley's mess.

In the meantime, a jeep adorned with a red metal pendant bearing the three stars of a lieutenant general edged onto the pontoon bridge at Oppenheim, heading for the east bank of the Rhine. George Patton was crossing Germany's historic river for the first time. Nearing the middle of the Rhine, Patton called out: "Hold up! Time for a short halt."

Without a word, Patton got out of the jeep and walked to the edge of the bridge, peering down briefly into the swiftly flowing current. Then he unbuttoned his trousers and urinated into the Rhine. Back in the jeep, Patton exclaimed joyfully to an aide, "I've been waiting a long time to do that!"

On March 24, thousands of large field guns began pounding the east bank of the Rhine in the vicinity of Wesel. Swarms of bombers and fighter planes struck at German positions. Bernard Montgomery's Plunder had been launched. Elements of the British Second Army and the U.S. Ninth Army, in tiny assault craft, reached the far shore against sporadic resistance. A short time later, Allied parachute and glider forces pounced on the bewildered Feldgrau ahead of the waterborne troops. Pockets of Germans resisted stubbornly near Wesel, but by nightfall the Plunder forces had carved out a sizable enclave on the east bank of the Rhine. Soldiers, tanks, and artillery were pouring over the river on pontoon bridges and by amphibious vehicles.

Basking in the glow of his successful river crossing, Montgomery fired off a message to Alan Brooke in London: "My main goal is to drive hard for the line of the Elbe [River] . . . thence via the autobahn to Berlin, I hope."

In his deep bunker under the garden of the Reich Chancellery in bomb-battered Berlin, Adolf Hitler flew into a rage over news that the Allies were over the Rhine in strength at Wesel. The Führer promptly ordered that poison gas be unleashed against Montgomery's bridgehead and all other Allied enclaves east of the Rhine and that thousands of American and British airmen who were POWs in the Third Reich be shot. Cooler heads, pointing out that the Allies would retaliate on a far more massive scale, prevailed.[4]

Eisenhower now had three powerful armies over the Rhine. He was preparing for an all-out offensive that would smash the remaining remnants of the once-vaunted Wehrmacht. When plans for Overlord had been drawn up in England prior to D-day, the ultimate objective was Berlin. At that time, no Allied general could have foreseen that the Soviet army would have advanced within forty miles of Adolf Hitler's bunker in downtown Berlin and that the Western Allies would still be two hundred miles from the German capital.

In light of unexpected developments, Eisenhower now had doubts about taking Berlin and sought the views of Omar Bradley, still his closest confidant despite their periodic fusses.

"I think it will cost us one hundred thousand casualties to capture Berlin— a pretty stiff price for a prestige objective, especially when [President Roosevelt] has already conceded the eastern region of Germany to the Soviets," Bradley said.

In Washington, George Marshall held the identical view. In a message to Eisenhower, he recommended that the Allied attack be altered from due east toward Berlin to the southeast "to prevent the enemy from organizing resistance in southern Germany."[5]

Eisenhower's viewpoint also was influenced by a haunting report. Early in March, Kenneth Strong, SHAEF's G-2, had received information from a mysterious source in Germany that Adolf Hitler and other Nazi bigwigs would abandon Berlin in the next two weeks and flee to a National Redoubt in the towering Bavarian Alps of southern Germany, where a quarter of a million die-hard German troops would barricade themselves and prolong the war indefinitely.

Strong's weekly intelligence report stated that the National Redoubt was "by rugged terrain, practically impenetrable. Defended by the most efficient secret weapons yet invented, the powers in Germany will survive to reorganize her resurrection." Armaments would be manufactured in bombproof factories, and food had been stored in underground caverns, Strong reported. An entire underground army would fight until the Americans and British grew weary and went home.

Some Allied generals scoffed, doubting that such a place even existed. Others took the intelligence report quite seriously—including Eisenhower and George Marshall.

As the Allies would learn later, the National Redoubt was an ingenious Nazi hoax intended to misdirect Allied strategy. The monumental canard had its origin in November 1944, when Eisenhower's armies were pushing up toward the German border. At that time, Franz Hofer, a Nazi functionary in Bavaria, sent a letter to Hitler, detailing a plan for conducting a last-ditch stand in the Alps of southern Germany. However, the memorandum was put on ice by moon-faced forty-three-year-old Martin Bormann, who had clawed his way up the Nazi pecking order to become the Führer's confidential secretary and thereby one of the Reich's most powerful figures.

Bormann regarded Hofer's idea for a National Redoubt as defeatist, so he kept it from Hitler. However, German intelligence advised the Führer that radio intercepts disclosed that the Western Allies were worried that the Germans might make a last stand in the Bavarian Alps. So Bormann dug out Hofer's plan and showed it to Hitler, who ordered Hofer brought in to give a detailed briefing.[6]

The Führer liked what he heard but realized that it was far too late to build a National Redoubt. After conferring with Josef Goebbels, he decided that the Alpine fortress concept could be developed into a scheme to confuse and confound the Allies. He directed Hofer to launch a crash project that might cause the Anglo-Americans to alter their strategy and head for the National Redoubt instead of Berlin.

Hofer rushed back to Bavaria and rapidly began a series of elaborate machinations to coerce the Allies into believing that Hitler was building a superfortress in the Alps. Partial fortifications—just enough for Allied air reconnaissance to photograph—were erected. Agents in civilian clothes were dispatched into surrounding villages and cities to pass whispered revelations about the doings in the National Redoubt, information that undercover Allied agents could pick up and send to SHAEF.

Explosions rocked the region—presumably the work of engineers blasting for concrete bunkers, underground warehouses, and factories for building secret weapons. Teams of geologists and faculty members from the SS Mountaineering School were sent to the region, and Goebbels made certain that Allied intelligence knew of their presence. Fake orders transferring phantom SS units to the

National Redoubt were picked up by Allied radio monitors, as intended. In official newscasts over Radio Berlin, subtle clues were dropped to convince Allied electronic eavesdroppers that something big was going on in the Bavarian Alps.

Based on the heavy evidence that a National Redoubt could drag on the bloody war for years, and unwilling to pay one hundred thousand casualties to capture Berlin, Eisenhower issued one of his most fateful strategy directives of the war. It would create a colossal uproar in the British hierarchy.

Montgomery's Berlin Express was sidetracked before it could pull out of the Wesel bridgehead station. Instead, his 21st Army Group would drive northeastward and capture Hamburg, Bremen, Lübeck, and other Baltic ports to keep Stalin's armies from gobbling up Denmark and Norway. At the same time, Hodges's First Army would break out of the Remagan bridgehead and charge generally to the east, linking up with the oncoming Russians at the Elbe River, ninety miles west of Berlin. Patton's Third Army would barrel out of the Oppenheim enclave and head southeastward to the Bavarian Alps and beyond, while Jake Devers's 6th Army Group farther to the south would push ahead toward Munich and the National Redoubt.

After issuing the directive, Eisenhower—without consulting the Combined Chiefs, Roosevelt, or Churchill—radioed Stalin directly that the Western Allies were leaving it up to the Red Army to capture Berlin.

Stalin was delighted, promptly assuring Eisenhower that the SHAEF plan for concluding the war "entirely coincides with the plan of the Soviet high command." He then added, "Berlin has lost its former strategic importance. The Soviet high command therefore plans to allot secondary forces in the direction of Berlin."

If the cunning Stalin's response was intended to lull SHAEF about his strategic and political intentions, it succeeded. At the precise time he had dispatched his message to Eisenhower about the "secondary importance" of Berlin, five Soviet tank armies of 1.5 million men and twenty-five thousand guns along the Oder River were massed for an all-out assault on the German capital.

Eisenhower's revised end-the-war directive and his personal contact with Stalin, a head of state, enraged British leaders. "To start with, [Eisenhower] has no business to address Stalin directly," an irate Alan Brooke scrawled in his diary. "Secondly, he produced a telegram which was unintelligible. And finally, what was implied in it appeared to be entirely adrift and a change from all that had been agreed to."

At the same time, the angry British chiefs fired off a cable to the American chiefs, complaining bitterly that leaving Berlin to the Soviets was "a grievous political and military blunder." Furthermore, the British stressed that their intelligence agencies doubted whether the National Redoubt even existed.[7]

Winston Churchill was stupefied and told confidants that Eisenhower had committed a gigantic blunder in handing over Berlin to the Russians. "Berlin is the prime and true objective of the Anglo-American armies," the Prime Minister said. Russia had become "a mortal danger to the free world," he added, and its "sweep to the west should be halted as far east as possible."[8]

Eisenhower, aware that he had stirred up a major controversy, took pains to explain his decision. In a letter to a fretful Bernard Montgomery, the supreme commander exclaimed angrily, "That place [Berlin] has become, as far as I am concerned, nothing but a geographical location."

As distraught as were Monty and other British bigwigs, Omar Bradley and George Patton were elated by the dramatic turn of events. Monty's Berlin Express had been derailed, and Bill Simpson's Ninth Army, which had taken its orders from the 21st Army Group, was returned to Bradley.[9]

Meanwhile, the various thrusts into the Third Reich by several powerful Allied armies were making steady progress. With the outcome of the war no longer in doubt, Eisenhower issued a proclamation on March 31, calling on German troops to surrender and the German people to "begin planting crops." Their situation was hopeless, he declared, and further resistance would only add to their miseries. So tight was Adolf Hitler's hold and so fearful were German soldiers and the home front of the unconditional surrender terms of the Allies, however, that Eisenhower's plea was ignored.[10]

By April 3, elements of the U.S. First, Ninth, and Fifteenth Armies had forged a ring of steel around the vast expanse of the Ruhr, the heart of Hitler's industrial might. A day later, the American forces started putting the squeeze on what became known as the Ruhr Pocket. It was flattened on April 18, and some 325,000 dispirited and haggard Feldgrau, along with twenty-nine generals, straggled into captivity.

Their commander was not among the POWs. Field Marshal Walther Model, who had thwarted Montgomery's Operation Market-Garden in Holland the previous September, felt that he had failed his Führer. Two days before the Ruhr Pocket collapsed, Model entered a woods, pulled out his Luger, and put a bullet through his head. Aides buried him in a secret grave near Wuppertal.[11]

Meanwhile, Eisenhower's spearheads continued to plunge deeper into Germany. At 7:56 P.M. on April 11, elements of Simpson's Ninth Army reached the Elbe River, just south of Magdeburg, where it had been ordered to halt to await the arrival of the Russians from the east. Simpson established a bridgehead on the far bank, then sent reconnaissance patrols forward. They reported back that there were few German troops to Ninth Army's front. Berlin was only ninety miles away.

CHAPTER 38

A Scheme to Prove Patton "Crazy"

SINCE THE RUSSIAN ARMIES along the Oder River forty miles east of Berlin had not yet launched their assault to seize the German capital, Bill Simpson felt that he could dash ninety miles to the prestigious objective with minimal casualties. Simpson asked Omar Bradley for permission to push on; Bradley asked Eisenhower, who said no.

American generals were irate. Here was a golden opportunity to take the global spotlight from the Soviets.

"I don't see how in the goddamned hell you figure this one," George Patton told Eisenhower. "We better grab Berlin—and quick!"[1]

The supreme commander testily replied that it was far more important to take Lübeck in the north and occupy the National Redoubt in the south. There was no way that Simpson could reach Berlin ahead of the Russians, Eisenhower declared, so it would be militarily foolish to try.[2] It was April 13.

Only hours after Eisenhower dampened Simpson's hopes for a spectacular feat, Adolf Hitler and some forty members of his entourage were ensconced in his bunker listening to a news bulletin over BBC in London at about 11:00 P.M. (middle European time). A solemn broadcaster announced that Franklin Roosevelt had died suddenly earlier in the day at his retreat in Warm Springs, Georgia. Strangely, there were no shouts of joy in the bunker, only a subdued mumble by those conjecturing what the American President's death would mean to the war.

An hour later, Josef Goebbels drove up to his residence, five blocks from the bunker, after a visit to the Oder River front. Aides told him the news. Goebbels and a few of his officers went into his study, and the propaganda minister telephoned Hitler.

"Mein Führer, this is the miracle we have been waiting for!" he excitedly exclaimed. "This is the turning point predicted in your horoscope!"[3]

Goebbels was referring to the lifetime horoscope that Hitler had drawn up for himself by an astrologer on January 10, 1933, the day he was sworn in as chancellor of Germany. It had predicted, quite accurately, the outbreak of "a big war" in 1939, amazing German victories until 1941, a chain of setbacks in the early months of 1945, to be followed by an overwhelming German victory in the second half of April 1945.

To boost the German people, Goebbels had Hitler's horoscope broadcast over Radio Berlin the next day.

Late in April, two paratroop regiments of Major General Eldridge G. Chapman's U.S. 13th Airborne Division were at airfields in the Paris region, eagerly awaiting word to launch Operation Effective, a mass parachute jump onto the National Redoubt. Morale was never higher among Chapman's men, who had arrived in Europe only a few weeks earlier. This would be their first combat mission.

Ther operation had cloak-and-dagger overtones. Each man had been given a list of Nazi bigwigs—including the name of Adolf Hitler—thought to be holed up in the lofty Alps of southern Germany. Just as the several hundred paratroopers were preparing to board C-47s, Operation Effective was canceled. Alexander Patch's U.S. Seventh Army and de Lattre de Tassigny's First French Armies were already converging on the National Redoubt.[4]

Meanwhile, the Wehrmacht as a cohesive formation had collapsed. Tens of thousands of exhausted Feldgrau were surrendering to the Americans and British. Bernard Montgomery's Canadian First Army reached the Netherlands, and his British Second Army was charging northward into Schlesweig-Holstein and Denmark. Elements of Courtney Hodges's First Army rendezvoused with the Russians on the Elbe River at Torgau, near Leipzig, slicing the Third Reich in half. Jakie Devers's 6th Army Group overran Bavaria and exposed the National Redoubt as nothing more than a hoax. George Patton's swift-moving Third Army barreled across the German border into Czechoslovakia.

Patton was almost within sight of Prague, the historic Czech capital, while the Soviet army was a hundred miles away. Eisenhower forbade him to capture Prague, however, saying that the city would be left to the Russians. Patton was infuriated. In the days ahead, he talked loudly and indiscreetly about the need for the American and British armies to join with the Wehrmacht in "kicking the Mongols' asses all the way back to Moscow." Patton always referred to the Soviets as Mongols, a nomadic race that wandered over the broad grasslands of outer Mongolia for centuries.

Writing to wife Beatrice in Boston, Patton called the Soviets "a scurvy race and simply savages. We could beat the hell out of them."

In these waning days of the conflagration in Europe, Patton and Montgomery finally agreed on something: War could break out between the Western Allies and the Soviet Union, and the threat should be confronted right now while the Americans and British had air superiority and powerful armies on the scene. Possibly at the instigation of Winston Churchill, Monty had the tens of thousands of weapons taken from surrendering German troops stacked in such a way that they could be rapidly handed back to the Feldgrau, who would then fight the Russians side by side with the Western Allies.

Meanwhile, Soviet armies had launched a massive offensive over the Oder River. By the night of April 30, Russian soldiers were within a quarter mile of the Berlin bunker in which Adolf Hitler was holed up. A day earlier, the Führer had married his longtime mistress, Eva Braun, and had instructed his personal surgeon, Professor Wernher Haase, to come to the bunker and administer a lethal injection to Hitler's favorite Alsatian dog, Blondi.

At about 2:30 A.M., Hitler and his wife shook hands with about forty people, then retired to their suite. Moments later, a single shot was heard. After a while a few aides entered the room. Hitler was lying on a sofa, having shot himself through the temple. Mrs. Hitler was also on the sofa, quite dead. She had swallowed capsules of cyanide.

SS officers, following instructions, carried the two corpses outside the bunker, poured gasoline over them, and set the bodies ablaze. Early on the morning of the following day, Soviet troops overran the Reich Chancellery.

Three days later, on May 5, the Russians had the two charred bodies taken to Poletzensee. Two of the Führer's dentists were located and brought in the next day. Through dental charts, Hitler's corpse was positively identified.

On May 6, the same day that Hitler's corpse was forensically identified, Colonel General Alfred Jodl, who had been the Führer's most trusted military confidant since 1939, walked briskly into the red-brick schoolhouse that served as Eisenhower's advance headquarters in Reims. Jodl had come to discuss surrender terms with Eisenhower, who refused to see him. Beetle Smith conducted the discussion. After two hours of talk, Smith became convinced that Jodl was stalling, hoping to give some one million German soldiers still facing the Soviet armies time to head westward and surrender to the Western Allies, where they would receive more humane treatment.

Jodl's argument was the same as that put forth by George Patton, Bernard Montgomery, and presumably Winston Churchill. The Anglo-Americans would soon be fighting the Russians, Jodl said, so "if Germany were given time to evacuate as many troops as possible to the west" they could help the Western Allies in their struggle against Russia and the spread of communism.[5]

Smith snapped that unless Jodl signed the surrender document, Anglo-American lines would be closed and no more German civilians could flee from the Soviets. Jodl signed.

An hour later, Eisenhower sent a dispatch to the Combined Chiefs in Washington: "The mission of this Allied Force was fulfilled at 0241 [2:41 A.M.], local time, May 7, 1945."

After sixty-eight months of relentless bloodshed and destruction, a shaky peace hovered over Europe.

On May 23, two weeks after Victory in Europe Day, George Patton established his headquarters in a huge complex of buildings known as the Junkerschule, a facility that had trained officer cadets of the Waffen-SS, overlooking the pictur-esque Bavarian town of Bad Toelz. Since Douglas MacArthur had made it clear that he did not want Patton for the invasion of Japan, Patton remained in command of Third Army and was appointed military governor of the eastern half of the U.S. occupation zone (roughly southern Germany).

Patton's appointment was a major blunder. He was ordered to denazify (a new word), demilitarize, and deindustrialize Bavaria and rid the region of the last shred of Nazism. In this role, the two-fisted fighting general would have to be transformed into a politician, judge, administrator, and diplomat.

Privately, the realistic Patton doubted whether denazification would work. All members of the Nazi party were to be "removed from public and semi-pub-lic office and from positions of important private undertakings."

"How in the hell am I supposed to govern Bavaria when three-fourths of the Germans are members of the Nazi party?" Patton growled.

On August 11, a frustrated Patton wrote to Dwight Eisenhower: "A great many inexperienced and inefficient [Germans] are now holding positions in local government as a result of this program. It is no more possible for a man to be a civil servant in Germany and not have paid at least lip service to nazism than it is possible for a man to be a postmaster in America and not have paid at least lip service to the Democrat or Republican party, when one was in power."

Patton tried to convince Eisenhower that the defeated Germans were no longer the real threat, but rather that the danger lay with the "Mongols." In the interest of putting Germany back on its feet as a bulwark against the Soviets, he continued to use many local officials who had had Nazi party connections.

Alarmed, Eisenhower traveled to Bad Toelz to preach the need for Patton to repent. His sermon, however, fell on deaf ears. On his return to Frankfurt, the supreme commander wrote to George Marshall: "The fact is that [Patton's] own convictions are not entirely in sympathy with the 'hard peace' concept. Being Patton, he cannot keep his mouth shut."[6]

A few days later, Lieutenant General Joseph McNarney, who had spent the war in Washington and recently arrived to become Eisenhower's deputy, tele-phoned Patton. The two men were old friends. McNarney, no doubt at the instigation of an exasperated Eisenhower, admonished the Third Army leader to speed up the release of captured SS troops, explaining that the Russians were upset because he was too slow in disbanding those units.

"Hell and goddamn!" Patton exploded. "Why do we care what those son-of-a-bitching Mongols think? We are going to have to fight those bastards sooner or later. Why not do it now while our army is intact and we can kick their asses back to Moscow in three months? We can do it easily with the help of the Germans troops we have. We can arm them. They hate the Mongol bastards!"

McNarney was horrified. "Shut up, George, you damned fool!" he ex-claimed. "This line might be tapped, and you'll start a war with your big mouth!"[7]

Indeed, the line was tapped—but not by the Soviets. Listening in were U.S. Army sleuths who had been handed the spying task by Major General Clarence L. Adcock, the civil affairs officer at SHAEF, and a mysterious figure, Walter L. Dorn, who apparently had been sent to Europe to "straighten out" the denazification situation. A fifty-one-year-old historian on leave from Ohio State University, Dorn was outgoing, jovial, and talkative.

Robert Murphy, Eisenhower's longtime political advisor (who had the code name Lieutenant Colonel McGowan when he was the underground chief in French Northwest Africa prior to the Allied invasion in late 1942), was supposed to be one of Professor Dorn's bosses, but the smooth diplomat never referred to him by name. Dorn, Murphy did say, was a "wild-eyed intellectual" who had been snooping around Patton's domain for several weeks.

Patton had never been advised that Dorn was an official in the U.S. military government. When the two men finally met, the general distrusted Dorn at first sight. He reminded Patton of "one of those smooth, smart-ass academic types." Patton scribbled in his diary, "[Dorn] very probably is a Communist in disguise."[8]

Dorn issued his report to SHAEF, and it was damning to George Patton. His "preferential treatment" of the German people amounted to gross discrimination against victims of Nazism, the professor declared. Even more explosive was Dorn's charge that Patton had sequestered a secret army of German troops and planned to use them against the Russians after he had provoked an incident to justify the Allies' going to war against them.

General Adcock, a West Pointer, apparently was persuaded by Dorn that Patton had taken leave of his senses and agreed to go along with a bizarre scheme hatched by the professor. In utmost secrecy, the Signal Corps was instructed to tap all telephones in Patton's headquarters at Bad Toelz and to slip a few "bugs" into his residence in nearby St. Querin.

Reinforcing the taps and bugs in the effort to prove that Patton was crazy, Adcock (or an emissary) obtained the services of a psychiatrist from the Medical Corps and sent him to Bad Toelz masquerading as a supply officer. The psychiatrist's orders were to insinuate himself as closely as possible to Patton and observe his every move and gesture.

Patton's days as commander of Third Army and military governor of Bavaria were numbered. He was convinced that Beetle Smith, General Adcock, and Professor Dorn had joined in an "evil conspiracy" to get him booted out.[9]

When an aide suggested that Robert Murphy might have been the ringleader, Patton replied, "No, not him. Murphy I trust. It's that son of a bitch Beetle Smith I suspect!"

Later that day, Patton read an article in the *Stars and Stripes* that convinced him that Smith was the chief stiletto wielder. Under a United Press dateline, Smith was quoted as saying, "George's mouth doesn't carry out the instructions of his brain!"[10]

The handwriting was on the wall. George Patton, a war hero to millions of Americans, was transferred to command the new U.S. Fifteenth Army—a hollow post. Wags quipped that the Fifteenth designation came from the fact that the total number of persons in the army was fifteen. Its mission was to write about the U.S. Army's role during the war in Europe.

"They've turned me into a paper-shuffler," a crestfallen Patton wrote to his wife. "We're supposed to write a lot of stuff that nobody will ever read."[11]

In the summer of 1945, the victorious Allies were drawing up charges of war crimes against leaders of the vanquished Third Reich. These crimes included the massacre of eleven thousand Polish military officers, government leaders, clergymen, and intellectuals. Piled up twelve deep in seven mass graves near Katyn, six miles west of the Russian city of Smolensk, the victims had been felled by pistol shots to the back of the neck. Although the grisly discovery had been made known to the world by the Germans in April 1943, Soviet dictator Josef Stalin promptly blamed the Nazis for the "frightful butchery."

At that time, news of the mass murder of the Polish leaders touched off widespread indignation in the free world, which, in turn, led to the Third Reich inviting twelve prominent forensic experts to visit the Katyn slaughterhouse and conduct postmortems freely on whichever bodies they chose. With the exception of Professor Andre Naville of the University of Geneva, the experts belonged to occupied or German satellite countries.

After examining the mummified bodies, their clothing, and the documents found on them, the forensic specialists concluded unanimously that the mass slaughter at Katyn could not have occurred any later than early 1940—when the Soviet army controlled the area.

The Soviets, however, claimed that the massacre had been perpetrated during August 1941, just after the Wehrmacht overran the entire Smolensk region. Allied government leaders and the media chose to believe Stalin's version and trumpeted it throughout the world.

Perhaps President Roosevelt's views were shaped by a report sent to him by his ambassador to Russia, W. Averell Harriman, on January 25, 1944, after the Red Army had retaken the Smolensk region. Oddly, Harriman did not go to the site but instead sent his daughter, Kathleen.

Harriman wrote Roosevelt, in part: "The proofs and evidence are not very conclusive but Kathleen . . . believes that the massacre was probably committed by the Germans."

Shortly after the Katyn discovery in 1943, U.S. Army Colonel John van Vliet and a number of other prisoners of war were taken to the massacre site by the Germans. At that time, the colonel secretly recorded his observations, but kept them to himself until his release from German captivity in early May 1945.

"The bodies wore winter uniforms," he wrote. "If the Germans had been responsible for the murders, they would have taken place at the time the Germans invaded the Smolensk region [in the hot months of July and August 1941]. . . . I was convinced without any doubt of Soviet guilt."

Major General Clayton Bissell, who headed the United States Information Services, stifled van Vliet's revealing report and allegedly ordered the colonel to make no mention to anyone about his conclusions at the Katyn slaughterhouse.

Had General Bissell, a middle-level official in the Allied totem pole of power, taken it upon himself to gag Colonel van Vliet, presumably basing his action on reasons of major national interests? Or had Bissell been acting under direct orders handed down from the White House?

Clearly, an American cover-up had been launched to conceal the Soviets' perpetration of the Katyn massacre. At the war crimes trials held by an international military tribunal at Nuremberg in succeeding months, all mention of German guilt for the Katyn butchery was dropped.

CHAPTER 39

"Today the Guns
Are Silent"

No SOONER HAD THE INK DRIED on the unconditional surrender document at Reims in May 1945 than thirty American divisions, along with air corps and naval units, began rushing from Europe to join in Operation Downfall, the looming invasion of Japan. Douglas MacArthur planned a two-step assault, the largest amphibious and airborne invasion that history had known. Downfall would begin with Operation Olympic—a frontal assault on Kyushu, the southernmost island, by nearly eight hundred thousand men—on November 1, 1945. The second phase, Operation Coronet—the landing by two million more troops on the largest island, Honshu—would follow on March 1, 1946.

America—and the world—stood on the brink of the most horrendous massacre of the human race since the Mongol warlord Ghengis Khan and his armies swept across northern Asia and eastern Europe in the early 1200s. MacArthur held no illusions about the savagery that lay ahead: He told the Pentagon that Downfall would "cost over one million casualties to American forces alone."[1] Perhaps as many as five million Japanese military men and civilians would die.

As welcome as would be the massive reinforcements from the European theater, MacArthur was not enchanted by the prospect of Eisenhower's generals joining his command. In an interview with Bert Andrews of the *New York Herald Tribune* at MacArthur's headquarters in Manila, the general soundly criticized the SHAEF commanders, who he claimed "made every mistake that supposedly intelligent men could make." The "North African operation was absolutely useless," MacArthur said, and the "European strategy was to hammer stupidly against the enemy's strongest points."[2]

As a result of what MacArthur called "the Bulge fiasco," he was especially leery about the prospect of having Omar Bradley and Courtney Hodges assigned to him for Downfall. And George Patton was out of the question, presumably because the Pacific was not vast enough to hold two flamboyant generals at the same time.

On evenings when he was relaxing with a closely knit coterie of aides, MacArthur exercised his flawless rhetoric by holding forth on the strategic

302

faults of Admiral Chester Nimitz and his marine commanders in the series of bloody island assaults across the Central Pacific. His principal criticism was that they spent their men's lives needlessly.

In the savage fighting on the island of Okinawa in April, May, and June 1945, seven thousand of Nimitz's marines and soldiers were killed and nearly thirty-seven thousand were wounded. MacArthur said these heavy casualties occurred because the commanders insisted on killing all Japanese on Okinawa (ninety-one thousand of them did die). In four days, the general continued, Nimitz and his field leaders had all the area they needed to establish air bases.

"They should have had the troops go into a defensive position and just let the Japs come to them, . . . which would have been much easier to do and would have cost less men," MacArthur exclaimed.[3]

In the meantime, the Pentagon, acting on the instructions of President Roosevelt, had reorganized the Pacific commands. MacArthur was to be in charge of all ground forces, and Nimitz was to head all naval units. They were to cooperate closely with General Curtis LeMay (Iron Pants, to his subordinates), the commander of the B-29 Superfortresses that had been and were pounding the Japanese homeland.

Soon after Roosevelt had been laid to rest at his Hyde Park estate in April, high-level skirmishing erupted to change the command arrangements once again. A formal conference was held on Guam involving delegates sent by MacArthur and Nimitz. It was conducted "almost on the level of international diplomacy," Secretary of the Navy James Forrestal would write. "MacArthur's people sought to secure command over all land and air forces in the Pacific, relegating the navy the minor role of purely naval support."[4]

George Kenney, MacArthur's air chief, and a representative of Nimitz got into a dispute over who would bomb what and where during the invasion of Japan. Nimitz refused to have Kenney's pilots bomb ships or to operate closer than ten miles offshore. Nimitz sent word to his delegate at Guam not to "surrender" to MacArthur's representative. The heated sessions broke up with no real meeting of minds.

Meanwhile, Emperor Hirohito's warlords in Tokyo were grimly preparing Ketsu-Go (Operation Decision), the last-ditch defense of every foot of the home islands that all Japanese held sacred, believing them to have fallen as drops from the sword of an ancient god. Although several strategic islands had been lost in the Pacific, the Japanese warlords told one another, most of their vast conquests were still held by Imperial forces, and the bulk of their huge army had not yet been defeated. Even with U.S. forces only 750 miles below Tokyo on the tiny island of Iwo Jima, Japanese leaders felt that the Americans would not be so stupid as to invade the homeland itself. If the "white devils" were foolish enough to try, the warlords knew, the invaders would have to shed blood for every foot of sacred soil.

Ten thousand kamikaze planes were ready to crash into invading ships. Hundreds of Shinyo suicide boats, each armed with a 4,406-pound warhead fused to detonate on impact, were concealed in coves, ready to spring. Scores of one-man suicide torpedoes were scattered along the coastlines. Under arms on the home islands were 2,350,000 soldiers, 250,000 garrison troops, and 32 million men and women of the militia—each pledged, even eager, to die for the emperor. Males between the ages of fourteen and seventy-five and females between sixteen and forty-five had been drafted and, together with children, instructed on how to tie explosives to their bodies, scramble under American tank treads, and blow up the vehicles—and themselves.

In Washington, Pentagon officials were haunted by General MacArthur's prediction of one million American casualties to conquer the Japanese homeland. Secretary of the Navy James Forrestal, who was privy to Magic (the secret interception and decoding of Japanese messages), wrote in his diary that the Japanese had concluded that "the war must be fought with all the vigor and bitterness of which the nation is capable."[5]

The Magic intercepts told of a fight-to-the-death resistance. "Even if the war drags on and it becomes clear that it will entail much more bloodshed," Foreign Minister Shinegori Togo declared, "the whole country . . . will pit itself against [the American invaders] in accordance with the royal will." War Minister Korechika Anami boasted that the Imperial Army would "fight to the end" and "find life in death."

Yet another grim factor alarmed General MacArthur and the Pentagon— the fate of 410,000 Western POWs, mainly American, British, Australian, New Zealand, and Dutch soldiers and sailors captured in the early black months of the war when the Philippines, Guam, Wake Island, Hong Kong, Malaya, Singapore, Indonesia, and Burma fell to the Japanese. Some 180,000 Asian soldiers were captured as well, but nearly all were released in a few months. Now, only the whites remained in the brutal POW camps. After the Americans seized Okinawa, Magic disclosed, Field Marshal Hisaichi Terauchi had ordered POW camp commandants to kill all their captives the moment the Allies invaded Japan.

Confronted by the specter of a frightful American bloodbath, General George Marshall proposed the use of "disabling gases" to drive Japanese foot soldiers from their bunkers and spider holes (as the Japanese called foxholes), after which they could be wiped out by standard infantry weapons and artillery. Use of noxious gases was in violation of the Geneva Convention, to which the United States was a signatory.

Marshall argued that gas was no more inhumane than were phosphorus shells and flamethrowers. In the face of vigorous British opposition, however, his proposal succumbed.[6]

In July, President Harry Truman traveled to Potsdam, a virtually unscathed suburb of Berlin, to meet and size up Josef Stalin for the first time. Winston Churchill, war weary and lacking the pep and decisiveness that had been his hallmarks, was also present, as was Chiang Kai-shek. At noon on July 17, Truman received a sensational piece of news: U.S. scientists had perfected an explosive device known as an atomic bomb. Truman and his Joint Chiefs agreed to keep the colossal secret from Stalin, but they shared it with the British. General MacArthur was kept in the dark.

Before the Potsdam conference adjourned, the Allies issued a final ultimatum to the Japanese warlords: Surrender unconditionally or suffer "prompt and utter destruction." Prime Minister Kantoro Suzuki responded in a cabinet meeting with one word: *Molusatsu*, meaning "kill with silence" or "no comment."

In Manila, Douglas MacArthur was appalled. The Potsdam unconditional surrender ultimatum—signed by Harry Truman, Winston Churchill, and Chiang Kai-shek—was a monumental mistake, MacArthur complained to aides. The general knew that the Japanese people, most of whom regarded Hirohito as a god, would never renounce their emperor and that each Japanese soldier would fight until killed to defend him. So would most civilians. Without Hirohito, the Japanese people would never agree to an orderly transition to peace. No one at Potsdam had asked for MacArthur's advice, however.

The ghost of Adolf Hitler hovered over the conference room. Stalin, for whatever devious reason, insisted to President Truman and U.S. Secretary of State James Byrnes that the Führer was alive and residing comfortably in Spain or perhaps Argentina. Earlier, Marshal Grigori K. Zhukov, the Soviet commander in Berlin, had been convinced by overwhelming forensic evidence that the charred corpse found outside the Führer's bunker was indeed that of Hitler. When Stalin decided he would float rumors that the German leader was alive, however, Zhukov changed his mind.

Zhukov held a Berlin press conference and referred to Hitler's "death or disappearance." A few days later, the Soviet marshal called on Dwight Eisenhower at the supreme commander's headquarters at Frankfurt on the Main River. He told the general that there was "no solid evidence" of Hitler's death. Curiously, Eisenhower echoed Soviet doubts at a press conference four days later in the Hotel Raphael in Paris.

After the Potsdam conference, *Isvestia*, the newspaper mouthpiece of the Soviet leadership, splashed a story across the front page declaring that the Führer and Eva Braun were "alive and well and living in a moated castle in Westphalia."

In London, British leaders were irate; Westphalia was in the British occupation zone of Germany. Stalin, in essence, was publicly accusing his "ally" of knowingly harboring and nurturing Adolf Hitler.[7]

Back in Washington, President Truman listened to views from his military advisors about whether the A-bomb should be used. Among the options considered was dropping a demonstration bomb to show the Japanese the enormous destructive force of the new weapon. A committee headed by Dr. J. Robert Oppenheimer—research director of the program code-named Manhattan Project, which developed the atomic bomb—concluded, "We can propose no technical demonstration likely to bring an end to the war."

While the Tokyo warlords were engaged in final preparations to massacre invading GIs, Professor Yoshitaka Mimura, an eloquent and popular instructor at Hiroshima Bunri University, was lecturing a group of five hundred Japanese army officers posted in and around Hiroshima. A city founded by a feudal lord of the Mori family in 1589, quaint Hiroshima (population 350,000) was a manufacturing and distribution center for military weapons and equipment. It was August 5, 1945.

Mimura, a theoretical physicist, was speaking to the officers about the possibility of revolutionary new weapons that could result in a dramatic change in fortune for the Japanese in the war.

A lieutenant colonel asked, "Sir, can you tell us what an atomic bomb is?"

Researchers at Tokyo University had theoretically penetrated the secrets of nuclear fission, the professor explained. "If they could apply their theories practically, an atomic bomb, if exploded above a populated city, could possibly destroy two hundred thousand lives," he added.

A hush fell over the room. Then the army men realized that the atomic bomb was only a "scientific theory."[8]

Less than twenty-four hours later, thirty-year-old Colonel Paul W. Tibbets piloted an American B-29 Superfortress named *Enola Gay* high above Hiroshima. Suddenly, a brilliant flash split the sky. A vast portion of the city virtually disintegrated; perhaps fifty thousand Japanese died. Among them, no doubt, were the army officers who, hours earlier, had been so eager to learn about a theoretical atomic bomb.[9]

In the Pentagon, Major General Leslie R. Groves, military director of the Manhattan Project, was a bundle of nerves. Every twenty minutes after the scheduled time for the Hiroshima explosion, he telephoned the communications room. Always the reply was the same: No word yet.

In nearby Fort Myer, the customarily serene George Marshall also was anxious. Just past 11:15 P.M., he telephoned Colonel Frank McCarthy, secretary of the general staff. No, nothing had been heard from the Pacific.

Fifteen minutes later, General Groves received a terse bulletin from Tinian, the flyspeck Pacific island from where the B-29 had lifted off for Hiroshima: "Successful in all respects." Colonel McCarthy immediately telephoned Marshall, who had been asleep, and gave him the news. The low-key army chief merely replied evenly, "Thank you for calling."

Soon after dawn, Marshall met with Groves in the Pentagon. Groves was jubilant. Marshall cautioned against excessive celebration, because so many Japanese had died. "I was not thinking so much about those casualties," Groves replied, "as I was about our men who had made the Bataan death march."[10]

Hap Arnold, the air corps chief, was present and followed Groves out into the corridor. Slapping the A-bomb shepherd on the shoulder, Arnold exulted, "I'm glad you said that. It's just the way I feel." So did everyone in the Pentagon—George Marshall included, no doubt. So did most Americans.

Less than twenty-four hours after the Hiroshima blast, Soviet dictator Josef Stalin repudiated his friendship treaty with Japan and sent two powerful armies, totaling 1.5 million men, into Japanese-held Manchuria, a huge area of northern China that Japan had seized in the early 1930s. At about the same time that powerful Soviet tank spearheads were invading the mountainous province, the Japanese ambassador in Moscow, Naotake Sato, was handed Stalin's declaration of war.

Again, President Harry Truman called on the Japanese warlords to surrender. When they stonewalled the ultimatum, a second A-bomb exploded over Nagasaki two days later. Another fifty thousand people were killed.

Now the forty-four-year-old, myopic Emperor Hirohito, a figure so sacred to the Japanese that they had never even heard his voice, defied his generals and admirals. On the night of August 14 (Tokyo time), he recorded a message to be broadcast over radio the next day. "The enemy has begun to employ a new and most cruel bomb, the power of which to do damage is incalculable," Hirohito said. He ordered an end to hostilities at 4:00 P.M. that day.[11]

Chaos erupted in Tokyo. Young military officers were convinced that the emperor's recorded capitulation message was a devious American hoax, and they intended to continue the war despite the obliteration of Hiroshima and Nagasaki. Shouting and brandishing weapons, the hotheads crashed into the Imperial Palace and engaged in a shoot-out with Hirohito's guards, who killed thirty-two of the intruders. A warrior's death, even from the guns of his own countrymen, seemed preferable to the disgrace of surrender.

At Atsugi Airport outside Tokyo, the commanding officer gathered his pilots and declared that capitulation would be treason. "Join me in destroying the enemy!" he shouted. Scores of voices screamed, "Banzai! Banzai! Banzai!"[12]

In Washington, President Truman acted quickly. Consulting with no one except his inner circle in the White House, he appointed Douglas MacArthur Supreme Commander for the Allied Powers (SCAP). For his part, MacArthur was jubilant over the abrupt end of hostilities, no doubt reflecting on his haunting estimate (and that of Chief of Staff George Marshall) that one million American casualties would have been the price for achieving the same goal.

Perhaps referring to his old antagonists in Washington, MacArthur slapped General Robert Eichelberger on the shoulder and remarked buoyantly, "Well, Bob, they haven't got my scalp yet!"[13]

Hirohito's surrender broadcast was still echoing across the Japanese homeland when Soviet Commissar for Foreign Affairs Vyacheslav Molotov summoned U.S. Ambassador Averell Harriman to his office in Moscow. Based on the few days that the Red Army had been in the war in the Pacific, Josef Stalin demanded that a Soviet marshal be a full partner to MacArthur in presiding over the surrender ceremony in Tokyo and, later, in ruling over Japan. Harriman was stunned, replying that it was "unthinkable" that the supreme commander would be anyone other than an American.

Stalin's impudent demand was relayed to President Truman, who, in a reported burst of profanity, soundly rejected the proposal. MacArthur would remain in complete command and control during and after the surrender. Truman told aides that he did not intend to be "disturbed by Russian tactics in the Pacific."[14]

In Washington, meanwhile, Admiral Ernest King learned that a State Department planning committee was preparing to propose that Douglas MacArthur be the sole American officer authorized to sign the document of surrender. King was irate and sent an aide bustling to the planning committee to demand that the surrender ceremony be altered. After protracted wrangling, the committee decided that MacArthur as SCAP would be joined by Admiral Chester Nimitz as the delegate from the United States.

In Manila, MacArthur informed his staff that he was going to land at Atsugi Airport just after the arrival of a tiny contingent of paratroopers from the U.S. 11th Airborne Division. Nearly every officer on MacArthur's staff was nervous about the prospect, except for the supreme commander himself. Within two hours' marching time of Tokyo were three hundred thousand armed and zealously loyal Japanese soldiers, all of whom had pledged to defend their sacred soil to the last drop of blood.

Shortly after dawn on August 28, Colonel Charles Tench, a member of MacArthur's staff, climbed down the ladder of a C-47 on Atsugi's bomb-pocked runway. Tench became the first hostile soldier in history to set foot on the Japanese homeland. With Tench were 150 paratroopers, uncertain of their fate.

In the meantime, MacArthur was winging toward Atsugi in his C-54, the *Bataan*. As the craft drew closer to the airport, aides became increasingly jittery. MacArthur would land unarmed in a recently hostile country, his only weapon a fingernail clipper. "All of us paratroopers at Atsugi were excited, to say the least, when word spread that General MacArthur was arriving," recalled George Doherty, who had been a corporal with the 11th Airborne Division. "When the

Bataan landed, all of the American brass in the Pacific advanced to the aircraft ramp. After what seemed an interminable time, the door of the *Bataan* opened and there stood the great general. Wow! I thought—this is the hour, the minute, of one of history's most momentous occasions. I also thought that if Japan was ever going to pull a second Pearl Harbor, this was the time and place to do it. Had they been so inclined, the Japs could have wiped out General MacArthur, all of the Pacific brass, and us paratroopers in one blow."[15]

Just before MacArthur started down the ramp, an excited aide rushed up with an alarming report. A group of kamikaze pilots, who already had received the last rites for the dead customarily given before the final takeoff, was in the neighborhood. Japanese police had tried to capture them, but they had fought back and both sides had suffered casualties. These fanatical suicide pilots might be lurking nearby. MacArthur shrugged, climbed down the steps, and strolled about shaking hands with almost everybody who had a convenient hand to shake.

Later, Winston Churchill said, "Of all the amazing deeds in the war, I regard General MacArthur's personal landing at Atsugi as the bravest of the lot."

In the meantime, Admiral Bull Halsey began moving his powerful fleet into Sagami Bay, southwest of Tokyo. The huge guns of his warships pointed toward the Kanto Plain, where MacArthur had expected to lose one hundred thousand soldiers in savage fighting. At dawn the next morning, the 4th Marine Regiment poured ashore and began blowing up the muzzles of guns protecting the harbor. A marine officer chuckled and told General Eichelberger, "The first wave was made up entirely of admirals trying to get ashore before MacArthur."[16]

To many of MacArthur's aides, it appeared that the navy was plotting to steal the spotlight from the supreme commander during the surrender ceremonies to be held on the deck of the 45,000-ton battleship *Missouri*, anchored in Tokyo Bay. Only twenty-four hours before the big event, a press release widely distributed by the navy described how the *Missouri* had been prepared for the historic event, with a specially built platform for photographers and cameramen. The release concluded, "Everything has been arranged by the Navy for stylish [media] coverage." No mention was made of Douglas MacArthur.

At 8:55 A.M. on September 2, a sixteen-member Japanese delegation started up the gangway of the *Missouri* and took its assigned place before a battered mess table covered with green felt cloth. Moments later, Douglas MacArthur, flanked by Admirals Halsey and Nimitz, strode onto the deck.

Two copies of the surrender document lay on the table. A stern MacArthur beckoned for the designated Japanese delegates to sign. Foreign Secretary Mamoru Shigemitsu, who had lost a leg to an assassin's bomb years earlier, hobbled forward, sat down, and began fumbling with his cane, eyeglasses, and formal top hat. Bull Halsey, thinking that the diplomat was stalling, felt like rushing forward, slapping his face, and shouting, "Sign, damn you, sign!"[17]

After the Japanese, representatives of nine victorious Allied nations paraded, one at a time, to the table to sign the instrument of capitulation. Then MacArthur affixed his signature, using five pens. At 9:25 A.M., he rose and solemnly said, "These proceedings are now closed."

Three years, eight months, and twenty-four days after the Japanese warlords launched a sneak attack against the U.S. fleet at Pearl Harbor, World War II had ended.

Only a few days after Douglas MacArthur established his headquarters in one of the few structures in the Hibiya business district left undamaged by B-29 Superfortress raids, a six-story insurance building to be known as the Dai Ichi (Number One), he was confronted by more Soviet chicanery. Josef Stalin demanded that a four-power council be designated to supervise SCAP, a procedure that would, in essence, give the Soviet dictator a veto over MacArthur's authority in the occupation of Japan. Much to his consternation, MacArthur learned that certain influential officials in the U.S. State Department were backing Stalin's grasp for power in the Far East.

MacArthur countered Stalin's machination by leaking word of the scheme to the Tokyo bureau of Reuters, a respected British news agency. As SCAP had anticipated, Reuters' story hit Washington and the rest of the United States hard: "General MacArthur will resign supreme command in Japan should a four-power commission be appointed, a high officer stated here tonight, adding MacArthur will 'drop a few sticks of dynamite when he goes.' "[18] So strident were the outcries on the home front and in Congress that Stalin's boosters in the State Department scurried for cover and the scheme to impose Soviet control on MacArthur drifted away.

Tokyo, MacArthur knew, was an eye in the hurricane of the "cold war" that had erupted between the Soviet Union and the United States, the world's two superpowers. He was aware that Josef Stalin had once declared, "With Japan, we are invincible." And MacArthur made no effort to conceal his total distrust of Stalin, describing him to reporters as "the Muscovite bulging his muscles and lusting for power."[19]

On occasion, Lieutenant General Kuzma N. Derevyanko (Stalin's liaison officer in Tokyo) or another Soviet leader would accuse MacArthur of "antidemocratic measures" that threatened a "revival of the old fascist order in Japan." Nothing could have been farther from the truth. MacArthur had introduced to the ancient nation a new concept, a new word: *Demokrashi*.

N O T E S

The following abbreviations are used below: NA, National Archives, Washington, DC; DDE, Dwight D. Eisenhower; LC, Library of Congress, Washington, DC; EL, Eisenhower Library, Abilene, Kansas; MM, MacArthur Memorial, Norfolk, Virginia; EP, Eisenhower Papers.

CHAPTER 1   Washington: Hotbed of Rivalries

1. Viscount Alanbrooke, *Diaries*, vol. 1 (London: Collins, 1957–59), pp. 292–93.

2. Winston S. Churchill, *The Second World War*, vol. 3 (Boston: Houghton Mifflin, 1948–54), p. 540.

3. Elliott Roosevelt and James Brough, *A Rendezvous with Destiny* (New York: Putnam's, 1975), p. 306.

4. Stilwell's Personal File (Wilmington, Del.: Scholarly Resources, 1976), p. 16.

5. Dwight D. Eisenhower (hereafter DDE) Diary, January 5, 1942, Eisenhower Library (hereafter EL), Abilene, Kansas.

6. Ibid., January 10, 1942.

7. Robert E. Sherwood, *Roosevelt and Hopkins* (New York: Harper, 1948), p. 455.

8. Forrest C. Pogue, *George C. Marshall* (New York: Viking, 1969), p. 280.

9. In the 1940 Hollywood movie *The Fighting 69th*, George Brent played the role of the regiment's commander, William Donovan.

10. Charles A. Lindbergh, *Wartime Journals* (New York: Harcourt Brace Jovanovich, 1970), p. 573.

11. Henry H. Arnold, *Global Mission* (New York: Harper, 1979), p. 206.

12. Fred Israel, *The War Diary of Breckenridge Long* (Lincoln: University of Nebraska Press, 1966), p. 234.

13. Dwight D. Eisenhower, *Crusade in Europe* (Garden City, N.Y.: Doubleday, 1948), p. 106.

14. In his memoirs, Admiral Ernest King admitted that he had been deliberately rude to Andrew Cunningham because of the British admiral's remarks at the press conference.

15. Thomas B. Buell, *Master of Seapower* (Boston: Little, Brown, 1980), p. 427.

16. DDE Diary, February 10, 1942.

17. Ibid.

18. Dwight D. Eisenhower, *At Ease* (Garden City, N.Y.: Doubleday, 1967), p. 252.

CHAPTER 2   Howls along Constitution Avenue

1. When Franklin D. Roosevelt accepted the Democratic nomination for President in 1932, he closed his speech with the declaration that the country "awaits with confidence the promise of a new deal." The liberal measures he proposed for combating the Great Depression came to be known as the New Deal, and those who supported his new laws were called New Dealers.

2. Clark Lee and Richard Henschel, *Douglas MacArthur* (New York: Putnam's, 1953), p. 99.

3. Stephen E. Ambrose, *Eisenhower* (New York: Simon & Schuster, 1983), p. 138.

4. DDE Diary, January 19, 1942.

5. Ibid., January 23, 1942.

6. Ibid., January 29, 1942.

7. USAFFE-War Department messages, December 27–28, 1941, MacArthur Memorial (hereafter MM), Norfolk, Virginia.

8. Ibid., January 3–5, 1942.

9. *Washington Times-Herald*, January 9, 1942.

10. Francis B. Sayre, *Glad Adventure* (New York: Random House, 1957), p. 222.

11. Frazier Hunt, *The Untold Story of General MacArthur* (New York: Simon & Schuster, 1944), p. 70.

12. Eisenhower, *At Ease*, p. 67.

13. Dorris Clayton James, *The Years of MacArthur* (Boston: Houghton Mifflin, 1970), pp. 491–92.

14. Pogue, *Marshall*, p. 374.

15. After rescuing Douglas MacArthur, John D. Bulkeley fought as a guerrilla on Mindanao, escaped to Australia, returned to the United States, and was decorated with the Congressional Medal of Honor by President Roosevelt.

16. James M. Burns, *Roosevelt* (New York: Random House, 1970), p. 204.

17. James, *MacArthur*, p. 112.

18. George Marshall to Franklin Roosevelt, May 4, 1942, Eisenhower Papers (hereafter EP), EL.

19. Stephen Ambrose, *The Supreme Commander* (Garden City, N.Y.: Doubleday, 1970), pp. 41–42.

20. DDE Diary, May 5, 1942.

21. Ibid., May 6, 1942.

22. Ed Cray, *General of the Army* (New York: Norton, 1989), p. 301.

CHAPTER 3 A "Sales Force" Goes to London

1. Thomas M. Coffey, *Hap* (New York: Viking, 1982), p. 264.

2. Henry L. Stimson Diaries, April 1, 1942, Yale University.

3. Arthur Bryant, *Turn of the Tide* (Garden City, N.Y.: Doubleday, 1957), p. 354.

4. Ibid., p. 28.

5. Ibid., p. 359.

6. Alanbrooke, *Diaries*, p. 358.

7. Hastings Ismay, *Memoirs* (New York: Viking, 1960), pp. 249–50.

8. Cray, *General*, pp. 311–12.

9. DDE Diary, May 27, 1942.

10. Bryant, *Turn*, p. 341.

CHAPTER 4 A Showdown over Strategy

1. DDE memorandum, July 19, 1942, EP.

2. Harry Butcher Diary, July 20, 1942, Yale University.

3. Mark W. Clark, *Calculated Risk* (New York: Harper, 1950), p. 106.

4. Butcher Diary, July 23, 1942.

5. Pogue, *Marshall*, p. 348.

6. Clark, *Calculated*, p. 37.

7. George Patton reportedly gave his army salary to charity.

8. "Hun" was a derogatory term for the Germans used by Allied troops in World War I.

CHAPTER 5   Skirmishes among the Admirals

1. William F. Halsey, *Admiral Halsey's Story* (New York: McGraw-Hill, 1947), p. 69.

2. Buell, *Master*, p. 236.

3. Ibid., p. 227.

4. Sherwood, *Roosevelt*, p. 509.

5. Lee and Henschel, *MacArthur*, p. 163.

6. Henry L. Stimson, *On Active Service in Peace and War* (New York: Harper, 1948), pp. 506–7.

7. In mid-1943, American fighter planes ambushed and shot down a Japanese aircraft carrying Admiral Isoroku Yamamoto on an inspection trip in the South Pacific.

8. Buell, *Master*, p. 219.

9. Ibid.

10. Stimson Diaries, September 3, 1942.

11. John Slessor, *The Central Blue* (New York: Praeger, 1957), p. 494.

12. Hanson W. Baldwin, *Great Mistakes of the War* (New York: Harper, 1949), p. 178.

13. George C. Kenney, *General Kenney Reports* (New York: Duell, Sloan & Pearce, 1949), pp. 116–17.

14. Ibid.

15. Douglas MacArthur had been a baseball star at West Point, so he often used baseball expressions. When a major league player, Wee Willie Keeler, had once been asked about his success as a batter, he replied, "I hit 'em where they ain't."

CHAPTER 6   A Visit with Uncle Joe

1. Many persons have considered the Mediterranean strategy one of the Allies' major blunders. It required far more troops, planes, and resources to clear North Africa, Sicily, and Italy than it did the Axis powers to defend those regions.

2. DDE Diary, August 25, 1942.

3. George Marshall cable to DDE, August 25, 1942, EP.

4. Butcher Diary, August 26, 1942.

5. Clark, *Calculated*, p. 138.

6. Ibid., p. 140.

7. Ibid.

8. Winston S. Churchill, *Hinge of Fate* (Boston: Houghton Mifflin, 1948), pp. 542–43.

9. Pogue, *Marshall*, p. 402.

10. Butcher Diary, August 28, 1942.

11. Ladislas Farago, *Patton* (New York: Ivan Obolensky, 1963), p. 183.

12. Ismay, *Memoirs*, p. 213.

CHAPTER 7   "Like a Bulldog Meeting A Cat"

1. Ambrose, *Eisenhower*, p. 186.

2. Eisenhower, *Crusade*, p. 55.

3. Butcher Diary, September 17, 1942; Kay Summersby Diary, September 17, 1942, EL.

4. Lucian K. Truscott, Jr., *Command Missions* (New York: Dutton, 1960), pp. 17–18.

CHAPTER 8   The French Political Mess

1. As far as is known, the missing page 117 was never found.

2. George S. Patton Diary, October 5, 1942. In *The Patton Papers*, edited by Martin Blumenson (Boston: Houghton Mifflin, 1974).

3. Ibid., October 7, 1942.

4. After the war, Alfred M. Gruenther rose to four-star rank and was commander of the North Atlantic Treaty Organization (NATO).

5. Lyman L. Lemnitzer was elevated to full general after the war and became army chief of staff.

6. Before he departed for England on the secret mission, Mark Clark was spotted by a few junior officers. Unaware of his disguise, they thought the lieutenant colonel insignia he was wearing meant that he had been demoted several ranks.

7. Clark, *Calculated*, p. 78.

8. Ibid., p. 84.

9. Much later, it was learned that Tessier's Arab servants had tipped off the Vichy French police.

10. While rowing over rough waters back to the offshore submarine, Mark Clark lost his trousers—an episode that would much later be highly publicized in the U.S. media.

11. Clark, *Calculated*, p. 90.

12. Major Paul Tibbets would become a historical figure later in the war when he piloted the B-29 Superfortress that dropped the atomic bomb on Hiroshima.

13. After the war, Jerauld Wright rose to three-star rank and commanded NATO's Atlantic Fleet.

14. Butcher Diary, November 6, 1942.

CHAPTER 9   Dealing with "Selfish, Conceited Worms"

1. In 1983, General Mark Clark told the author that he was so furious with General Giraud that he uncharacteristically used the term "ass." Clark only rarely used risqué words and never swore.

2. Butcher Diary, November 8, 1942.

3. Some historians would later say that Admiral Darlan was not in Algiers to see his critically ill son, but because he had secretly learned of the Torch invasion and wanted to join the Allies. This viewpoint fails to take into account the fact that a casket had already been purchased for his son's funeral.

4. General Alphonse Pierre Juin would prove to be one of the ablest commanders in Mark Clark's Fifth Army in Italy.

5. Later, General Louis-Marie Koeltz would distinguish himself fighting under Allied command against the Germans.

6. Five-star General Auguste Paul Noguès continued as resident general of Morocco under the Allies.

7. Butcher Diary, November 9, 1942.

8. Ibid.

9. DDE to Bedell Smith, November 9, 1942, EP.

10. Ibid.

11. Clark, *Calculated*, p. 87.

12. Ibid., p. 94.

13. In 1983, Mark Clark told the author that it was all he could do to keep from punching the obstinate Admiral Darlan.

14. Robert Murphy, *Diplomat among Warriors* (New York: Doubleday, 1964), p. 138.

CHAPTER 10 Uproar over the Little Fella

1. Ambrose, *Supreme Commander*, p. 130.

2. Harold Macmillan, *The Blast of War* (New York: Harper & Row, 1968), p. 174.

3. DDE to John Eisenhower, April 8, 1943, EP.

4. DDE to George Marshall, November 14, 1942, EP.

5. DDE to Winston Churchill, November 14, 1942, EP.

6. Milton Viorst, *Hostile Allies: FDR and DeGaulle* (New York: Macmillan, 1965), p. 137.

7. *New York Times*, November 18, 1942.

8. Butcher Diary, December 9, 1942.

9. Bryant, *Turn*, p. 430.

10. Murphy, *Diplomat*, p. 143.

11. Clark, *Calculated*, pp. 130–31.

12. John Bulloch, *M.I.5* (London: Barker, 1963), p. 689.

13. Anthony Cave Brown, *Bodyguard of Lies* (New York: Harper & Row, 1975), p. 145.

CHAPTER 11 High Strategy and Low Tactics

1. Foreign Relations of the United States, *The Conferences at Washington and Casablanca*, II (Washington, D.C.: Government Printing Office, 1968), p. 506.

2. Ibid., p. 508.

3. Buell, *Master*, p. 269.

4. Considerable criticism erupted in the United States about the Allied leaders' sons being brought to Casablanca.

5. "United States Joint Chiefs of Staff: The War Against Germany" (Washington, D.C.: Government Printing Office, 1947), p. 180.

6. Foreign Relations of the United States, *The Conferences at Washington and Casablanca*, II, p. 537.

7. Ibid., p. 583.

8. Macmillan, *Blast*, pp. 193–94.

9. Bryant, *Turn*, p. 550.

10. Ibid., p. 453.

11. DDE to George Marshall, February 8, 1943, EP.

12. General Ulysses S. Grant was given the nickname "Unconditional Surrender" when he and his men attacked the Confederate stronghold of Fort Donelson. When the Confederate general asked for terms, Grant replied, "Only unconditional surrender can be accepted."

13. Sherwood, *Roosevelt*, p. 696.

14. Farago, *Patton*, p. 157.

15. Ernest Dupuy, *Men of West Point* (New York: Sloan, 1952), p. 324.

16. Several years after the war, Alger Hiss was convicted for lying to Congress and sent to prison. In 1995, long after serving his term, he maintained his innocence.

CHAPTER 12 Ike's "Neck Is in the Noose"

1. DDE Diary, February 19, 1943.

2. Dwight D. Eisenhower, *Letters to Mamie* (Garden City, N.Y.: Doubleday, 1978), p. 98.

3. Butcher Diary, January 23, 1943.

4. After the war, Eisenhower admitted that his decision to keep the French

happy and to coordinate tactics in Tunisia himself was a major mistake.

5. Cray, *Marshall*, p. 380.

6. Ibid., p. 381.

7. Eisenhower, *Crusade*, p. 149.

8. *Outline History of II Corps* (Washington, D.C.: Government Printing Office, 1947), p. 2.

9. Pogue, *Marshall*, pp. 188–89.

10. Arthur Tedder, *With Prejudice* (London: Cassell, 1966), p. 410.

11. Ibid., p. 411.

12. Ibid., p. 412.

13. Ibid., p. 413.

14. Farago, *Patton*, p. 163.

15. W. G. F. Jackson, *North African Campaign* (London: Cassell, 1966), p. 410.

16. Patton Diary, April 11, 1943.

CHAPTER 13 Dueling with Joan of Arc

1. Author interview with John H. "Beaver" Thompson, who, as a correspondent for the *Chicago Tribune*, parachuted into Sicily with the 82nd Airborne Division—after twenty minutes of "training." He was the first American reporter in history to jump into combat.

2. R. Harris Smith, *OSS* (Berkeley: University of California Press, 1972), p. 68.

3. OSS Report Number 2553, "The Organization of the French Intelligence Services," January 11, 1945, National Archives (hereafter NA), Washington, D.C.

4. M. R. D. Foot, *SOE in France* (London: Her Majesty's Stationery Office, 1966), p. 231.

5. Ibid., p. 232.

6. *Foreign Relations of the United States*, vol. II, 1943, pp. 152–55, NA.

7. Ambrose, *Eisenhower*, p. 239.

8. DDE to George Marshall, June 19, 1943, EP.

9. Ibid.

10. DDE to George Marshall, July 22, 1943, EP.

11. Winston S. Churchill, *Closing the Ring* (Boston: Houghton Mifflin, 1951), pp. 182–83.

12. Farago, *Patton*, p. 271.

13. Ibid., p. 272.

14. Ibid.

15. The British government has never made known the true identity of "Captain Martin," who saved perhaps thousands of British and American lives.

CHAPTER 14 Plot and Counterplot

1. Omar N. Bradley, *A Soldier's Story* (New York: Holt, 1951), p. 149.

2. Author interview with General Matthew Ridgway (Ret.) (1989).

3. Author interview with Lieutenant General William P. Yarborough (Ret.) (1994).

4. Eisenhower, *Crusade*, p. 174.

5. Churchill, *Closing*, pp. 55–65.

6. DDE to Combined Chiefs of Staff, July 26, 1943, EP.

7. Ibid., August 4, 1943, EP.

8. Author interview with Colonel Carlos C. Alden, Jr. (Ret.) (1991). American paratrooper Alden, along with a companion,

sneaked into German-held Messina the night before Patton's spearheads barged into the city. He and his companion greeted the Americans on their arrival.

9. John Grigg, *The Victory That Never Was* (New York: Hill & Wang, 1980), p. 95.

10. Ambrose, *Supreme Commander*, pp. 228–29.

11. Eisenhower, *Crusade*, p. 182.

CHAPTER 15   Stormy Weather over Château Frontenac

1. Brown, *Bodyguard*, p. 323.

2. Arthur H. Vandenberg, *The Private Papers of Arthur H. Vandenberg* (Boston: Houghton Mifflin, 1952), pp. 48–49.

3. William D. Leahy, *I Was There* (New York: McGraw-Hill, 1950), p. 175.

4. Ibid.

5. Maurice Matloff and Edwin M. Snell, *Strategic Planning for Coalition Warfare* (Washington, D.C.: Chief of Military History, 1953), p. 221.

6. Alanbrooke, *Diaries*, pp. 705–7.

7. Ibid., p. 708.

8. George W. Ball, *The Past Has Another Pattern* (New York: Norton, 1982), p. 29.

9. Author interview with General Maxwell D. Taylor (Ret.) (1989).

10. Eisenhower, *Crusade*, p. 187.

11. Author interview with Lieutenant General James M. Gavin (Ret.) (1987). Gavin said the parachute assault on Rome was conceived by non-airborne officers and, had it not been canceled, the 82nd Airborne Division would have been destroyed.

12. Charles B. McDonald, *American Armed Forces in European Theater* (New York: Oxford University Press, 1969), p. 178.

CHAPTER 16   Rejection of an Anti-Hitler Conspiracy

1. Alan W. Dulles, *Germany's Underground* (New York: Macmillan, 1947), p. 142.

2. Ibid., based on Alan Dulles's memo from Jacob Wallenberg.

3. Sherwood, *Roosevelt*, p. 791.

4. DDE to George Marshall, September 23, 1943, EP.

5. Butcher Diary, September 23, 1943.

6. Allied leaders called Kesselring "Smiling Al" because he was always beaming widely when his photo appeared in German newspapers. He was a master of parlor magic and a gifted piano player.

7. Kay Summersby, *Eisenhower Was My Boss* (New York: Prentice-Hall, 1948), p. 114.

8. Long after the war, John Daly became familiar to Americans as the suave host of a popular television program, "What's My Line?"

9. DDE to George Marshall, December 17, 1943, EP.

10. DDE to George Patton, December 24, 1943, EP.

11. Butcher Diary, September 16, 1943, EP.

12. DDE to George Marshall, October 7, 1943, EP.

CHAPTER 17   Brawls in Cairo and Teheran

1. Matloff and Snell, *Strategic*, p. 335.

2. Pogue, *Marshall*, vol. 3, p. 297.

3. U.S. Joint Chiefs of Staff, Report 533, Meeting with Roosevelt, November 15, 1943, NA.

4. Matloff and Snell, *Strategic*, p. 330.

5. Buell, *Master*, p. 404.

6. Alanbrooke, *Diaries*, vol. 2, p. 74.

7. Lord Moran, *Diaries* (Boston: Houghton Mifflin, 1966), p. 14.

8. Pogue, *Marshall*, p. 305.

9. Moran, *Diaries*, p. 142.

10. Alanbrooke, *Diaries*, p. 249.

11. Moran, *Diaries*, p. 141.

12. Ibid., p. 144.

13. Leahy, *I Was There*, p. 206.

14. Ibid., p. 207.

15. Jael was the original code name of the Bodyguard plan.

16. Leahy, *I Was There*, p. 202.

17. Winston Churchill, *Their Finest Hour* (Boston: Houghton Mifflin, 1949), p. 338.

18. Ibid., p. 345.

19. Eisenhower, *Crusade*, p. 206.

20. Ibid., p. 207.

21. Alanbrooke, *Diaries*, vol. 2, p. 106.

CHAPTER 18   The Pacific "Political Front"

1. Clark, *Calculated*, p. 132.

2. Ibid., p. 133.

3. Churchill, *Closing*, p. 103.

4. Stimson Diaries, November 22, 1943.

5. Jay Luvaas, ed., *Dear Miss Em* (Westport, Conn.: Praeger, 1972), pp. 99–101.

6. Pogue, *Marshall*, p. 374.

7. Frazier Hunt, *The Untold Story of Douglas MacArthur* (New York: Devin-Adair, 1954), p. 314.

8. Douglas MacArthur, *Reminiscences* (New York: McGraw-Hill, 1964), p. 183.

9. Ibid.

10. Pogue, *Marshall*, p. 375.

11. William F. Halsey, *Admiral Halsey's Story* (New York: McGraw-Hill, 1947), p. 186.

12. MacArthur, *Reminiscences*, p. 117.

13. James, *MacArthur*, vol. II, p. 413.

14. *American Mercury*, November 1944.

15. Luvaas, *Dear*, p. 90.

16. Burns, *Roosevelt*, p. 501.

17. Joseph P. Lash, *Eleanor and Franklin* (New York: Doubleday, 1971), p. 689.

18. James, *MacArthur*, vol. II, p. 387.

19. Halsey, *Story*, p. 189.

20. Ibid., p. 190.

21. Ibid.

CHAPTER 19   A Stranded Whale at Anzio

1. Stimson Diaries, January 3, 1944.

2. Ambrose, *Eisenhower*, p. 279.

3. Butcher Diary, December 31, 1944.

4. Eisenhower, *Crusade*, p. 218.

5. Clark, *Calculated*, p. 179.

6. Ibid., p. 185.

7. Martin Blumenson, *Anzio* (New York: Lippincott, 1963), p. 93.

8. Clark, *Calculated*, p. 206.

9. George Marshall to Jacob Devers, February 18, 1944, NA.

10. After the war, General George Marshall endorsed General John Lucas's tactics on Anzio. For each mile Lucas advanced, Marshall said, an additional division would have been required to fill in the line—and there were no extra divisions to throw into the battle.

11. More than fifty years after the battle of Anzio, U.S. military men still debate the wisdom or lack of boldness on the part of General Lucas.

CHAPTER 20   An Ultimatum to Ireland

1. OSS Report A22884A, "Ireland as a Source of Information to the Germans," March 16, 1944, Record Group 226, NA. "The United States Government to the Irish Prime Minister," February-March 1944, pp. 623–27, NA.

2. Gordon A. Harrison, *Cross-Channel Attack* (Washington, D.C.: Government Printing Office, 1951), p. 68.

3. Butcher Diary, January 25, 1944.

4. Bryant, *Turn*, pp. 146–47.

5. Pogue, *Marshall*, vol. III, p. 379.

6. Ibid., p. 380.

7. "The Reminiscences of Harvey H. Bundy," Oral History Research Office, Columbia University, 1961, pp. 201–5.

8. Ibid.

9. Field Marshal Sir John Dill died in Washington in November 1944. His good friend General George Marshall circumvented army regulations that forbade the burial of foreign soldiers at Arlington National Cemetery. Dill was interred there, fulfilling the field marshal's often expressed wish.

10. Ambrose, *Eisenhower*, p. 287.

11. Ibid.

CHAPTER 21   Patton: Frame-up Target?

1. Farago, *Patton*, p. 364.

2. Ibid., p. 372.

3. DDE letter to General Brehon Somervell, May 3, 1944, EL.

4. Bradley, *Story*, p. 184.

5. Ibid., p. 186.

6. Francis de Guingand, *Operation Victory* (New York: Scribner's, 1947), p. 317.

7. Bryant, *Turn*, pp. 189–91.

8. Ibid., p. 139.

CHAPTER 22   The Unconditional Surrender Brouhaha

1. U.S. Joint Chiefs of Staff, "Effect of Unconditional Surrender Policy on German Morale," February-March 1944, NA.

2. Ibid.

3. Brown, *Bodyguard*, p. 660.

4. David Dilks, ed., *The Diaries of Alexander Cadagan* (New York: Putnam, 1973), p. 620.

5. Butcher Diary, April 16, 1944.

6. U.S. Joint Chiefs of Staff, "Unconditional Surrender," February-March 1944, NA.

7. Winston Churchill letter to Dwight Eisenhower, in SHAEF files, "Security for Operations," NA.

8. Author interview with Vice Admiral John D. Bulkeley (Ret.) (1993).

9. Samuel Eliot Morison, *The Invasion of France and Germany* (Boston: Little, Brown, 1954), p. 71.

10. Eisenhower, *Crusade*, pp. 246–47.

11. Until his death, General Eisenhower maintained that the Normandy airborne decision was his most difficult of the war.

12. Brown, *Bodyguard*, p. 650.

13. After the war, when the Allies examined German intelligence files, it was found that the only accurate report on Overlord had been received from a French colonel on de Gaulle's staff in Algiers. It was dated June 4, 1944—less than forty-eight hours prior to D-day.

CHAPTER 23   De Gaulle Threatens to Arrest Churchill

1. Charles de Gaulle, *The War Memoirs of Charles de Gaulle*, vol. II (New York: Simon & Schuster, 1959), p. 244.

2. Ibid., pp. 246–47.

3. Arthur Funk, *Charles de Gaulle* (Norman: University of Oklahoma Press, 1959), pp. 257–59.

4. Charles de Gaulle served as president of France for many years. He would never forget nor forgive his humiliation at the hands of the Americans and Brits prior to D-day.

5. No notes were taken of this crucial conference. Eisenhower's comments are the consensus recollections of the Allied commanders present.

6. Ambrose, *Eisenhower*, p. 304.

7. de Gaulle, *Memoirs*, p. 256.

8. Bradley, *Story*, p. 184.

9. Ibid., p. 186.

10. Author interview with Major General Francis Sampson (Ret.) (1993). Sampson had been a chaplain with the 101st Airborne Division and was present.

11. Butcher Diary, June 6, 1944.

12. Charles Bohlen, *Witness to History* (New York: Norton, 1973), p. 259.

CHAPTER 24   Strategy Gridlock

1. John Stagg, *Forecast for Overlord* (New York: Norton, 1972), p. 125.

2. Eisenhower, *Crusade*, p. 247.

3. Ibid., p. 281.

4. Leahy, *I Was There*, p. 241.

5. Forrest Pogue, *The Supreme Command* (Washington, D.C.: Department of the Army, 1954), pp. 219–20.

6. Eisenhower, *Crusade*, p. 254.

7. Arthur Bryant, *Triumph in the West* (Garden City, N.Y.: Doubleday, 1959), p. 218.

8. Pogue, *Marshall*, p. 404.

9. Stimson Diaries, June 15, 1944.

10. Ibid., June 23, 1944.

11. Carl Spaatz Diary, June 15, 1944, Manuscript Division, Library of Congress (hereafter LC), Washington, D.C.

12. Ibid., June 17, 1944.

13. Stimson Diaries, June 15, 1944.

CHAPTER 25   Bogged Down in Normandy

1. Ambrose, *Eisenhower*, p. 316.

2. Bryant, *Triumph*, p. 178.

3. Tedder, *Prejudice*, p. 557.

4. Farago, *Patton*, p. 238.

5. Bernard Montgomery to DDE, July 17, 1944, EP.

6. Martin Blumenson, *Breakout and Pursuit* (Washington, D.C.: U.S. Army Chief of Military History, 1961), pp. 193–94.

7. Butcher Diary, July 21, 1944.

8. P. J. Grigg Papers, Churchill College, Cambridge, England.

9. Ibid.

10. Ibid.

11. Omar Bradley, *Story*, p. 267.

12. Brown, *Bodyguard*, pp. 801–2.

13. Field Marshal Erwin Rommel's role in the underground Schwarze Kapelle was unmasked by the Gestapo in the fall of 1944. Summoned to Berlin from his home in southern Germany, Rommel took poison and died within minutes.

CHAPTER 26   The "Friendly Bombs" Fiasco

1. Within hours of the assassination attempt against Adolf Hitler, Lieutenant Colonel von Stauffenberg was arrested and executed.

2. Tedder, *Prejudice*, pp. 565–66.

3. After the war, Omar Bradley vigorously denied that he had stolen George Patton's scheme for Cobra.

4. DDE to Omar Bradley, July 24, 1944, EP.

5. Bryant, *Triumph*, p. 181.

6. Never again would General Leland Hobbs permit heavy bombers to strike in front of his troops in an attack.

7. After the war, General Elwood "Pete" Quesada named General Doolittle as the bomber baron who had altered the approach direction.

8. The author was among the American soldiers deluged by friendly bombs for more than an hour. He emerged unscathed.

9. Summersby Diary, June 25, 1944.

10. Butcher Diary, June 26, 1944.

11. Field Marshal von Kluge killed himself with poison a short time after the Cobra breakthrough when the Gestapo linked him to the Schwarze Kapelle.

CHAPTER 27   A Meeting with "Mr. Big"

1. Luuvas, *Miss Em*, p. 75.

2. William Manchester, *American Caesar* (Boston: Little, Brown, 1978), p. 364.

3. Ibid.

4. Buell, *Master*, p. 467.

5. Manchester, *Caesar*, p. 365.

6. Earl D. Blaik, *The Red Blaik Story* (New York: Norton, 1974), p. 500.

7. Daniel E. Barbey, *MacArthur's Amphibious Navy* (Annapolis: Naval Institute, 1969), p. 219.

8. James, *MacArthur*, vol. II, p. 530.

9. Leahy, *I Was There*, p. 263.

10. Ibid., p. 264.

11. Ibid.

12. Manchester, *Caesar*, p. 256.

13. Leahy, *I Was There*, p. 267.

14. Burns, *Roosevelt*, p. 489.

15. Lee and Henschel, *MacArthur*, p. 172.

CHAPTER 28   A Gut-Wrenching Discussion

1. Butcher Diary, August 4, 1944.

2. A few Brittany ports held out until the end of the war in Europe.

3. DDE to George Marshall, August 5, 1944, EP.

4. A short time later, Admiral Bertram Ramsay was killed in an airplane crash.

5. DDE to George Marshall, August 5, 1944, EP.

6. Butcher Diary, August 5, 1944.

7. Moran, *Diaries*, p. 173.

8. DDE to George Marshall, August 11, 1944, EP.

9. Ismay, *Memoirs*, p. 248.

10. Brest was besieged by Troy Middleton's U.S. VIII Corps and French underground detachments organized into battalions. However, the thirty-two thousand German defenders held out stubbornly and inflicted heavy casualties before surrendering in early September 1944.

11. The Jedburghs took their name from their training base in a royal burgh on the Jed River in Scotland.

12. Brown, *Bodyguard*, p. 876.

13. OSS memorandum, L Document, August 11, 1944, NA.

14. Bradley, *Story*, p. 323.

15. Ibid., p. 341.

CHAPTER 29   High-Level Bungling

1. HQ, U.S. Forces, European Theater, Intelligence Section, "Transcript of Fragments of Hitler's Conference at Wolfsschanze, August 31, 1944," NA.

2. The figures for the number of Germans escaping from the Falaise pocket are SHAEF intelligence estimates.

3. Brehon Somervell Diary, August 15, 1944, LC.

4. DDE to George Marshall, August 24, 1944, EP.

5. Several years after the war, Senator Albert "Happy" Chandler became commissioner of organized baseball.

6. Bernard Law Montgomery, *Memoirs* (Cleveland: World, 1958), p. 240.

7. Ibid., p. 243.

CHAPTER 30   "The War in Europe Is Won!"

1. Courtney Hodges Diary, August 25, 1944, LC.

2. Bradley, *Story*, p. 276.

3. Eisenhower, *Letters*, pp. 209–11.

4. SHAEF G-2 Report, August 23, 1944, in SHAEF Record Group, NA.

5. Ambrose, *Supreme Commander*, p. 510.

6. German losses since Normandy D-day were estimates of SHAEF intelligence.

7. Pogue, *Supreme Command*, pp. 263–64.

8. DDE to George Marshall, August 27, 1944, EP.

9. Lewis H. Brereton was a U.S. Naval Academy graduate who switched to the fledgling army air service just prior to World War I.

CHAPTER 31   Frigid Reception for a Pentagon Inspector

1. *New York Times*, September 25, 1944.

2. Richard N. Smith, *Thomas E. Dewey and His Times* (New York: Simon & Schuster, 1982), p. 426.

3. Ibid., p. 427.

4. "Statement for Record of Participation of Brigadier General Carter W. Clarke in the Transmittal of Letters from General George C. Marshall to Governor

Thomas E. Dewey, in September 1944," p. 3, Record Group 547, NA.

5. Ibid., p. 4.

6. Smith, *Dewey*, p. 429.

7. Pogue, *Supreme Command*, pp. 293–94. Patton Diary, September 22, 1944.

8. George S. Patton, *War As I Knew It* (Boston: Houghton Mifflin, 1947), p. 125, 133.

9. Montgomery, *Memoirs*, p. 254.

10. "George C. Marshall Interviews and Reminiscences," transcripts and notes. George C. Marshall Research Library, Lexington, Virginia.

11. DDE to Bernard Montgomery, October 9, 1944, EP.

12. Ambrose, *Eisenhower*, p. 354.

13. Henry S. Aurand papers, EL.

14. DDE to Bernard Montgomery, October 9, 1944, EP.

15. Pogue, *Supreme Command*, p. 298.

CHAPTER 32 Vinegar Joe, Peanut, and Dragon Lady

1. Theodore H. White, *In Search of History* (New York: Warner Books, 1979), p. 134.

2. Eddy Bauer, *Illustrated History of World War II*, vol. 11 (New York: Marshall Cavendish, 1972), p. 1433.

3. Ibid., p. 1431.

4. Stimson Diaries, January 14, 1942.

5. Ibid

6. Joseph Stilwell and Theodore H. White, eds., *The Stilwell Papers* (New York: Sloane, 1948), p. 274.

7. Stimson Diaries, January 13, 1942.

8. Barbara Tuchman, *Stilwell and the American Experience* (New York: Bantam Books, 1972), p. 385.

9. Mao Tse-tung's Communist army drove Chiang Kai-shek's Nationalist army from the Chinese mainland in 1949 after a bloody civil war.

10. Stimson Diaries, February 23, 1943.

11. Franklin Roosevelt to George Marshall, March 8, 1943, George C. Marshall Research Library, Lexington, Virginia.

12. Stimson Diaries, May 3, 1943.

13. Claire L. Chennault, *Way of a Fighter* (New York: Putnam's, 1949), p. 226.

14. Eddy Bauer, *Illustrated*, vol. 20, pp. 2713–14.

15. *Congressional Record*, April 16, 1943, p. 3454, LC.

16. Cray, *General*, pp. 475–76.

17. Tuchman, *Stilwell*, p. 631.

18. Leahy, *I Was There*, p. 271.

CHAPTER 33 Taken by Total Surprise

1. After the war, General Sepp Dietrich was sentenced to twenty-five years in prison for "war crimes" by his troops in the Battle of the Bulge. He served five years and was released.

2. Incredibly, after the Battle of the Bulge the Germans resumed using Enigma until the final collapse in May 1945.

3. Bernard Montgomery to DDE, November 16, 1944, EP.

4. Ibid.

5. Those promoted to five-star rank at the time were Admirals Nimitz, King, Halsey, and Leahy, and Generals Marshall, Eisenhower, MacArthur, and Arnold.

6. Pogue, *Supreme Command*, pp. 372–74.

7. Viscount Alanbrooke Diary, December 18, 1944.

8. Twenty-eight years earlier at Verdun, a young corporal in the kaiser's army, Adolf Hitler, had been badly wounded and received the Knights Cross for gallantry.

9. Farago, *Patton*, p. 680.

10. Beetle Smith later apologized to Kenneth Strong and John Whitely for his outburst.

11. SHAEF Office Diary, December 20, 1944, NA

12. Ibid.

13. Bryant, *Triumph*, p. 272.

14. Ibid., p. 373.

15. Patton Diary, December 20, 1944.

16. Montgomery, *Memoirs*, p. 296.

CHAPTER 34   SHAEF Headquarters under Siege

1. P. J. Grigg Papers, Cambridge, England.

2. Ibid.

3. DDE to William Simpson and Courtney Hodges, December 22, 1944, EP.

4. Much to the astonishment of his wartime fellow generals, rough-and-ready Ernest Harmon became a college president after the war.

5. Bryant, *Triumph*, p. 278.

6. Bernard Montgomery message to Alan Brooke, December 25, 1944.

7. Ibid.

8. Bryant, *Triumph*, 278.

9. SHAEF Office Diary, December 26, 1944, NA.

10. Ibid., December 28, 1944.

11. Farago, *Patton*, p. 302.

12. Bradley, *Story*, p. 306.

13. Patton Diary, December 26, 1944.

14. Stimson Diaries, December 28, 1944.

15. Patton, *War*, p. 247.

16. Montgomery, *Memoirs*, p. 284.

17. Ambrose, *Eisenhower*, p. 375.

18. Montgomery, *Memoirs*, p. 289.

19. Message W-84337, George Marshall to DDE, December 30, 1944, NA.

20. Message S-73275, DDE to George Marshall, January 1, 1945, NA.

CHAPTER 35   The Great War of Words

1. Summersby Diary, January 2, 1945.

2. DDE memorandum for record with regard to the Charles de Gaulle discussion, January 3, 1945, EP.

3. Ibid.

4. DDE to George Marshall, January 3, 1945, EP.

5. Montgomery, *Memoirs*, p. 279.

6. Bradley, *Story*, p. 484. Pogue, *Supreme Command*, pp. 387–88.

7. After the war, Bernard Montgomery replaced Alan Brooke as chief of the Imperial General Staff. He admitted that his Battle of the Bulge press conference was ill-timed and that his choice of words had been poor.

8. Russell Weigley, *Eisenhower's Lieutenants* (Bloomington: University of Indiana Press, 1981), pp. 580–81.

CHAPTER 36   A Shouting Match at Malta

1. SHAEF Office Diary, Book XV, pp. 2033–34, NA.

2. Ibid., pp. 2035–36.

3. John Toland, *The Last 100 Days* (New York: Random House, 1966), p. 72.

4. SHAEF Office Diary, Book XV, pp. 2038–39, NA.

5. Ambrose, *Supreme Commander*, p. 586.

6. SHAEF Office Diary, Book XV, pp. 2041–43, NA.

7. Toland, *100 Days*, p. 65.

8. Bauer, *Illustrated*, vol. 17, p. 2036.

9. Anthony Eden, *The Reckoning* (Boston: Houghton Mifflin, 1965), p. 326.

10. Bradley, *Story*, p. 307.

11. Ibid., p. 312.

12. John Whitely's qualms over telephoning Field Marshal Montgomery proved to have considerable merit. After the war, when Monty became chief of the Imperial General Staff, neither Whitely nor other British generals associated with Eisenhower at SHAEF fared well.

13. Summersby Diary, February 9, 1945.

14. Farago, *Patton*, p. 287.

CHAPTER 37 A Hoax Impacts Allied Strategy

1. Bradley, *Story*, p. 291.

2. Author interview with Lieutenant General James M. Gavin (Ret.) (1988). Gavin was one of the airborne generals present at the dinner hosted by Eisenhower.

3. Ambrose, *Supreme Commander*, p. 620.

4. Chester Wilmot, *The Struggle for Europe* (London: Fontana, 1959), p. 690.

5. George Marshall to DDE, April 15, 1945, EP.

6. Martin Bormann escaped from the Führer's bunker after Hitler's death. He has never been seen again, nor has his corpse been located.

7. George Marshall to DDE, message FWD-18331, March 27, 1945, NA.

8. Churchill's views outlined in George Marshall to DDE, message W-60507, March 29, 1945, NA.

9. DDE to army group commanders, message FWD-18475, April 2, 1945, NA .

10. Eisenhower, *Crusade*, p. 405.

11. It would be four months before Allied intelligence learned about the fate of Field Marshal Model and located his grave.

CHAPTER 38 A Scheme to Prove Patton "Crazy"

1. Weigley, *Lieutenants*, p. 698.

2. DDE to George Marshall, April 29, 1945, EP.

3. James P. O'Donnell, *The Bunker* (Boston: Houghton Mifflin, 1978), pp. 91–92.

4. Author interview with Jack W. Bauer (1992). Bauer was a wartime paratrooper in the U.S. 13th Airborne Division.

5. Kenneth Botting, *From the Ruins of the Reich* (New York: Crown, 1985), p. 87.

6. DDE to George Marshall, September 29, 1945, EP.

7. Account of Patton-McNarney telephone conversation told in diary of Colonel (later General) Paul D. Harkins, EL.

8. Patton Diary, September 5, 1945.

9. Ladislas Farago, *Patton's Last Days* (New York: McGraw-Hill, 1981), p. 279.

10. *Stars and Stripes*, European edition, October 3, 1945.

11. In December 1945, George Patton died of a broken neck sustained in an automobile accident. Strangely, Beatrice Patton also died of a broken neck suffered in a fall from a horse in 1954.

CHAPTER 39   "Today the Guns Are Silent"

1. Leahy, *I Was There*, p. 375. Mac-Arthur, *Reminiscences*, p. 261.

2. Manchester, *Caesar*, pp. 431–32.

3. Ibid., p. 433.

4. James Forrestal, *The Forrestal Diaries* (New York: Viking, 1951), p. 293.

5. Ibid., p. 306.

6. David E. Lilienthal, *Journals of David E. Lilienthal* (New York: Harper & Row, 964), p. 199.

7. O'Donnell, *The Bunker*, pp. 369–70.

8. Stanley Weintraub, *Long Day's Journey into War* (New York: Dutton, 1990), p. 387.

9. Only God knows how many Japanese were killed in the Hiroshima blast. The approximate figure of fifty thousand came from a lengthy study released in 1950 by General Douglas MacArthur's headquarters.

10. Leslie M. Groves, *Now It Can Be Told* (New York: Da Capo, 1962), p. 324.

11. *St. Louis Post-Dispatch*, August 15, 1945.

12. Gavin M. Long, *MacArthur as Military Commander* (London: Collins, 1969), p. 178.

13. Robert Eichelberger, *Our Jungle Road to Tokyo* (New York: Viking, 1950), pp. 285–86. MacArthur, *Reminiscences*, p. 264.

14. C. L. Sulzberger, *A Long Row of Candles* (New York: Dutton, 1969), p. 777. Harry S. Truman, *Memoirs*, vol. 1 (New York: Harper, 1956), p. 412.

15. Author interview with George Doherty (1991).

16. Eichelberger, *Jungle*, p. 294.

17. Halsey, *Story*, p. 282.

18. James, *MacArthur*, p. 28–29.

19. William J. Sebald and Russell Brines, *With MacArthur in Japan* (New York: Dutton, 1965), p. 102.

SELECTED BIBLIOGRAPHY

Books

Adams, Henry H. *Harry Hopkins.* New York: Putnam's, 1977.

Alanbrooke, Viscount. *Diaries.* London: Collins, 1957-59.

Ambrose, Stephen E. *Eisenhower.* New York: Simon & Schuster, 1983.

————. *Supreme Commander.* Garden City, N.Y.: Doubleday, 1969.

Arnold, Henry A. *Global Mission.* New York: Harper, 1949.

Baldwin, Hanson. *Great Mistakes of the War.* New York: Harper & Row, 1950.

Ball, George W. *The Past Has Another Pattern.* New York: Norton, 1982.

Barbey, Daniel E. *MacArthur's Amphibious Navy.* Annapolis: Naval Institute, 1969.

Baruch, Bernard. *The Public Years.* New York: Holt, Rinehart & Winston, 1960.

Bauer, Eddy. *Illustrated History of World War II.* New York: Marshall Cavendish, 1972.

Blaik, Earl D. *The Red Blaik Story.* New York: Norton, 1974.

Blumensen, Martin. *Anzio.* New York: Lippincott, 1963.

————. *Breakout and Pursuit.* Washington, D.C.: Chief of Military History, 1961.

Bohlen, Charles. *Witness to History.* New York: Norton, 1973.

Botting, Kenneth. *From the Ruins of the Reich.* New York: Crown, 1985.

Bradley, Omar N. *A Soldier's Story.* Chicago: Rand McNally, 1951.

Brereton, Lewis H. *The Brereton Diaries.* New York: Morrow, 1946,

Brown, Anthony Cave. *Bodyguard of Lies.* New York: Harper & Row, 1975.

Bryant, Arthur. *Triumph in the West.* Garden City, N.Y.: Doubleday, 1959.

————. *The Turn of the Tide.* Garden City, N.Y.: Doubleday, 1957.

Buell, Thomas B. *Master of Seapower.* Boston: Little, Brown, 1980.

Bullock, Alan. *Hitler.* New York: Harper & Row, 1962.

Burns, James M. *Roosevelt.* New York: Harcourt Brace Jovanovich, 1970.

Butcher, Harry C. *My Three Years with Eisenhower.* New York: Simon & Schuster, 1946.

Chandler, Alfred D., Jr., ed. *The Papers of Dwight Eisenhower.* Baltimore: Johns Hopkins, 1970.

Chennault, Claire. *Way of a Fighter.* New York: Putnam's, 1949.

Churchill, Winston S. *Closing the Ring.* Boston: Houghton Mifflin, 1951.

————. *The Grand Alliance.* Boston: Houghton Mifflin, 1950.

————. *The Hinge of Fate.* Boston: Houghton Mifflin, 1960.

————. *Their Finest Hour.* Boston: Houghton Mifflin, 1949.

————. *Triumph and Tragedy.* Boston: Houghton Mifflin, 1953.

Clark, Mark W. *Calculated Risk.* New York: Harper, 1950.

Codman, Charles R. *Drive.* Boston: Little, Brown, 1950.

Coffey, Thomas M. *Hap.* New York: Viking, 1982.

Cole, Hugh M. *The Ardennes.* Washington, D.C.: Chief of Military History, 1964.

Colville, John. *Winston Churchill and His Inner Circle.* New York: Wyndham, 1981.

Cray, Ed. *General of the Army.* New York: Norton, 1989.

Cunningham, Andrew B. *A Sailor's Odyssey.* London: Hutchinson, 1950.

de Gaulle, Charles. *War Memoirs.* London: Weidenfeld & Nicolson, 1959.

de Guingand, Francis. *Operation Victory.* London: Hodder & Stoughton, 1947.

Dilks, David. *The Diaries of Alexander Cadagan.* New York: Putnam's, 1973.

Dulles, Allen. *Germany's Underground.* New York: Macmillan, 1947.

Dupuy, Ernest. *Men of West Point.* New York: Sloan, 1952.

Eden, Anthony. *The Reckoning.* Boston: Houghton Mifflin, 1965.

Eichelberger, Robert. *Our Jungle Road to Tokyo.* New York: Viking, 1950.

Eisenhower, Dwight D. *At Ease.* Garden City, N.Y.: Doubleday, 1967.

———. *Crusade in Europe.* Garden City, N.Y.: Doubleday, 1948.

———. *Letters to Mamie.* Garden City, N.Y.: Doubleday, 1978.

Farago, Ladislas. *The Game of the Foxes.* New York: McKay, 1970.

———. *The Last Days of Patton.* New York: McGraw-Hill, 1980.

———. *Patton.* New York: Ivan Obolensky, 1964.

Foot, M. R. D. *SOE in France.* London: HMSO, 1965.

Forrestal, James. *The Forrestal Diaries.* Walter Millis, ed. New York: Viking, 1951.

Funk, Arthur. *Charles de Gaulle.* Norman: University of Oklahoma Press, 1959.

Grigg, John. *The Victory That Never Was.* New York: Hill & Wang, 1980.

Groves, Leslie M. *Now It Can Be Told.* New York: Da Capo, 1962.

Halsey, William F. *Admiral Halsey's Story.* New York: McGraw-Hill, 1947.

Harrison, Gordon A. *Cross-Channel Attack.* Washington, D.C.: Government Printing Office, 1951.

Hemingway, Ernest. *The Way It Was.* New York: Scribner's, 1974.

Hohne, Henry. *The General Was a Spy.* New York: Coward, McCann & Geoghegan, 1971.

Hull, Cordell. *The Memoirs of Cordell Hull.* New York: Macmillan, 1948.

Hunt, Frazier. *The Untold Story of Douglas MacArthur.* New York: Devin-Adair, 1954.

Ismay, Hastings. *The Memoirs of General Lord Ismay.* New York: Viking, 1960.

Israel, Fred. *The War Diary of Breckenridge Long.* Lincoln: University of Nebraska Press, 1966.

Jackson, W. G. F. *North African Campaign.* London: Cassell, 1966.

James, Dorris Clayton. *The Years of MacArthur.* Boston: Houghton Mifflin, 1970.

Kenney, George. *General Kenney Reports.* New York: Duell, Sloan & Pearce, 1949.

King, Ernest J., and Whitehead, Walter Muir. *Fleet Admiral King.* New York: Norton, 1972.

Lash, Joseph P. *Eleanor and Franklin.* New York: Doubleday, 1971.

Leahy, William D. *I Was There.* New York: McGraw-Hill, 1950.

Lee, Clark, and Henschel, Richard. *Douglas MacArthur.* New York: Holt, 1950.

Lilienthal, David E. *Journals of David E. Lilienthal.* New York: Harper & Row, 1964.

Lindbergh, Charles A. *Wartime Journals.* New York: Harcourt Brace Jovanovich, 1970.

Long, Gavin M. *MacArthur as Military Commander.* London: Collins, 1969.

Luvaas, Jay, ed. *Dear Miss Em.* Westport, Conn.: Praeger, 1970.

MacArthur, Douglas. *Reminiscences.* New York: McGraw-Hill, 1964.

Macmillan, Harold, *The Blast of War.* New York: Harper & Row, 1967.

Manchester, William. *American Caesar.* Boston: Little, Brown, 1978.

Marshall, Katherine Tupper. *Together.* New York: Love, 1946.

Matloff, Maurice, and Snell, Edwin M. *Strategic Planning for Coalition Warfare.* Washington, D.C.: Chief of Military History, 1953.

McDonald, Charles B. *American Armed Forces in European Theater.* New York: Oxford University Press, 1969.

Merriam, Robert. *Dark December.* Chicago: Ziff-Davis, 1947.

Montgomery, Bernard Law. *Memoirs.* Cleveland: World, 1958.

Moran, Lord. *Churchill: The Struggle for Survival.* Boston: Houghton Mifflin, 1946.

———. *The Diaries of Lord Moran.* Boston: Houghton Mifflin, 1966.

Morgan, Frederick. *Overture to Overlord.* Garden City, N.Y.: Doubleday, 1950.

Morison, Samuel Eliot. *The Invasion of France and Germany.* Boston: Little, Brown, 1954.

Murphy, Robert. *Diplomat among Warriors.* Garden City, N.Y.: Doubleday, 1964.

O'Donnell, James P. *The Bunker.* Boston: Houghton Mifflin, 1978.

Patton, George S. *War As I Knew It.* Boston: Houghton Mifflin, 1947.

Pogue, Forrest C. *George C. Marshall.* New York: Viking, 1969.

———. *The Supreme Command.* Washington, D.C.: Chief of Military History, 1954.

Roosevelt, Elliott. *As He Saw It.* New York: Duell, Sloan & Pearce, 1946.

———, and Brough, James. *A Rendezvous with Destiny.* New York: Putnam's, 1975.

Sayre, Francis B. *Glad Adventure.* New York: Random House, 1957.

Sherwood, Robert E. *Roosevelt and Hopkins.* New York: Harper, 1948.

Slessor, John. *The Central Blue.* New York: Praeger, 1957.

Smith, R. Harris. *OSS.* Berkeley: University of California Press, 1972.

Smith, Richard N. *Thomas E. Dewey and His Times.* New York: Simon & Schuster, 1982.

Stagg, John. *Forecast for Overlord.* New York: Norton, 1972.

Stillwell, Joseph, and White, Theodore H., eds. *The Stilwell Papers.* New York: Sloan, 1948.

Stimson, Henry L. *On Active Service in Peace and War.* New York: Harper, 1948.

Sulzberger, C. L. *A Long Row of Candles.* New York: Dutton, 1969.

Summersby, Kay. *Eisenhower Was My Boss.* New York: Prentice-Hall, 1948.

Tedder, Arthur. *With Prejudice.* Boston: Little, Brown, 1967.

Toland, John. *The Last 100 Days.* New York: Random House, 1966.

Truman, Harry S. *Memoirs.* New York: New American Library, 1965.

Truscott, Lucian R. *Command Missions.* New York: Dutton, 1954.

Tuchman, Barbara. *Stilwell and the American Experience.* New York: Bantam Books, 1972.

Tully, Grace. *F.D.R.: My Boss.* New York: Scribners, 1949.

Vandenberg, Arthur H. *The Private Papers of Senator Vandenberg.* Boston: Houghton Mifflin, 1952.

Viorst, Milton. *Hostile Allies.* New York: Macmillan, 1965.

Weigley, Russell. F. *Eisenhower's Lieutenants.* Bloomington: Indiana University Press, 1981.

Weintraub, Stanley. *Long Day's Journey into War.* New York: Dutton, 1990.

White, Theodore H. *In Search of History.* New York: Warner Books, 1979.

Whitehall, Walter M. *Fleet Admiral King.* New York: Norton, 1951.

Whitney, Courtney. *MacArthur: His Rendezvous with History.* New York: Knopf, 1956.

Wilmot, Chester. *The Struggle for Europe.* London: Fontana, 1959.

Wilson, Theodore. *The First Summit.* Boston: Houghton Mifflin, 1969.

Winant, John G. *Letter from Grosvenor Square.* Boston: Houghton Mifflin, 1947.

Winterbothan, F. W. *The Ultra Secret.* New York: Harper & Row, 1973.

Zacharias, Ellis M. *Secret Missions.* New York: Putnam's, 1946.

Principal Archival Records

Headquarters, U.S. Army Forces in the Far East (USAFFE), 1941–42, MacArthur Memorial, Norfolk, Virginia.

Headquarters, Southwest Pacific Area (SWPA), 1942–45, MacArthur Memorial.

Headquarters, U.S. Army Forces, Pacific (USAFPAC), 1942, 45, MacArthur Memorial.

American Historical Association, Committee for the Study of War Documents, Washington, D.C.

VII Corps in Operation Cobra, Chief of Military History, Washington, D.C.

VIII Corps, Operation Cobra, Chief of Military History, Washington, D.C.

Chester B. Hansen Diaries, U.S. Army Military History Institute, Carlisle Barracks, Pennsylvania.

German Military Intelligence, National Archives, Washington, D.C.

Foreign Relations of the United States (FRUS): The Conferences at Cairo and Teheran, 1943, National Archives, Washington, D.C.

Foreign Relations of the United States: The Conference at Quebec, 1944, National Archives, Washington, D.C.

United States Joint Chiefs of Staff: The War Against Germany, National Archives, Washington, D.C.

Author's Archives

Transcripts and tapes of past interviews by author: Colonel Carlos C. Alden (Ret.), Jack W. Bauer, Vice Admiral John D. Bulkeley (Ret.), Colonel Henry A. Burgess (Ret.), General Mark W. Clark (Ret.), Colonel Thomas R. Cross (Ret.), Lieutenant Colonel Jack Darden (Ret.), Lieutenant General Edward M. Flanagan (Ret.), Lieutenant General James M. Gavin (Ret.), General Alfred M. Gruenther (Ret.), Rear Admiral John Harllee (Ret.), Brigadier General George M. Jones (Ret.), Colonel Edward H. Lahti (Ret.), Colonel Barney Oldfield (Ret.), Major General George Pearson (Ret.), General Matthew B. Ridgway (Ret.), Major General Francis L. Sampson (Ret.), Lieutenant General Richard J. Seitz (Ret.), Ernest T. Seigel, William S. Story, General Maxwell Taylor (Ret.), Lieutenant General John J. Tolson III (Ret.), Lieutenant General William P. Yarborough (Ret.).

INDEX